The Scent of Yellow Roses

The Scent of Yellow Roses

A MEMOIR OF HOPE & HEALING

by

SUSAN HARRIMAN SMELSER

The Scent of Yellow Roses
A Memoir of Hope & Healing

Copyright © 2021 by Susan Harriman Smelser
All rights reserved.
HOPE HOUSE COUNSELING, PLLC

Cover Image by Jeremy Bishop at Unsplash
Interior Layout and Cover Design by Philip Alera

No portion of this book may be reproduced in any form whatsoever, except for brief quotations used for review, without the written permission of the author.

Some names and identifying details have been changed to protect the privacy of individuals.

Library of Congress Control Number: 2021913821

ISBN: 978-0-578-95065-5 (Hardcover)
ISBN: 978-0-578-94879-9 (Paperback)

The cover photo by Jeremy Bishop is symbolic of grief. You can view it at its darkest depths, the hope emerging, and finally the gift that comes from traveling through the darkness into a different but livable life.

Dedications

To Jennifer Marie Smith, who has transitioned into a new life and a beautiful spirit.

To Jamin, who lost his only sibling along with her support and counsel and still managed to become a son of whom anyone would be proud. I love you both to the depths of my soul.

To James, Jennifer's father, who shared and understood the same loss. You have her in your arms again.

To Jesse, who was the love of her life and held her in her last moments. You are our forever Hero.

To Jackie, her cousin and best friend, who shares my pain and remembers birthdays and anniversaries. You are a daughter to me.

And finally, to all Jennifer's family and friends who loved her throughout her short life. I am sure she is still giving you advice in her own way.

On a cool dry evening in March 1994, twenty-year-old Jennifer went out to a birthday party. She never returned home. In the middle of the night, policemen were calling and knocking at the door. They had to deliver the worst news a parent can hear. Jenny was never coming home again.

After the shock comes survival. How does a family go on? Some survive better than others. This is a true story of one woman's attempt at enduring the pain that comes with the loss of a child and the slow but steady loss of a marriage.

This is a story that spans more than twenty years. It is a case study in grief and the impact it has on a family over time. Just one moment, one decision, the timing of a traffic light, a missed exit, or even a couple's wedding date, can change a family's life forever. May this book of letters let you know that you are not alone in grief, and that sometimes faith, hope and purpose are all you need to survive.

Contents

Dedications	v
Acknowledgments	xi
Prologue	xiii
1995	xv
A Letter to Jenny	1
Early Journaling and Jenny's Beginning	3
Some of Jenny	11
The Morning After	14
One Month Before	16
Dreams	18
Other Letters	21
Letters to Jennifer	29
Jackie's Best Memories of Jenny	57
My First Time Alone (except for my dog)	60
A Diary of Prozac Days	66
Voice Recordings	114
Journaling	144
Voice Recordings	147
Letters on a Laptop	280
Jamin's Letter	339
My Letter	341
Epilogue	351

Last photo of Jenny January 1994

Acknowledgments

A special thank you to author Ron Herron who motivated me to begin putting my journals and letters into a book.

Another special thank you to Shani Kedrowski at USAType for transcribing my voice recordings. It was not an easy task.

A special thank you to all who wrote letters and poems about Jenny and let me share them here. I would have loved to have shared them all.

Prologue

As I work on this book, I wonder how I will begin to tell a story that spans more than twenty years. In fiction, time can stand still or fast forward to another era just because authors can do as they please. As we read, we fill in the blanks in between. In writing non-fiction, how does one weave together twenty years of research, handwritten journals, recordings, computer journals, letters, books, clippings, cards, memories, and living?

As in life, you spread it all out on the table, organize, prioritize, and choose what you believe will tell the story best. I did all of this in an attempt to release the demon of grief that resides within me. Now, for a little while, I must invite that demon back in as I share what I have learned by living all these years.

Just like any human being that has lived through the unthinkable, I have learned to hope and to survive. It is my hope that my words and experiences will help others as well. This story is the truth I have carried in my heart all these years.

1995

I am just a normal mother. I have no credentials that would allow me to give advice or promise hope that in time the pain of grief would lessen, or that with spirituality there is healing. At this writing, I am a high school graduate with one year of college who was married at the young age of nineteen. This is not being written with the hope that it will one day be a book. It is being written as a therapeutic tool. I'm not sure how that will work, but I do believe that writing helps heal heartache.

I cannot promise hope to anyone, as it is something that comes from within. I've learned that some carry more hope than others.

Magic answers do not exist; I have not found even one in all the books I have read since the death of my daughter, Jennifer. Believe me when I say that I have searched. Reading was my personal savior. I read every secular, religious and fictional book I could find on the loss of a loved one. I camped out in the grief and self-help section of every bookstore I came across, often sitting cross-legged on the floor with books all around me. I decided there were no answers to the question *why*. There is no easy way out of this pain. God is not going to come down from Heaven, sip tea with me, and explain why my girl had to leave. No therapist or man of the cloth will say magic words that bring relief. I have asked them all.

Grieving parents continue to search. It's part of our therapy. We look for just one sentence that will become our epiphany or shed some light on our situation. We want to tie it all together in a neat little box that we can store in our hearts to put away or take out as needed. We need our grief to be neatly organized instead of scattered all over our lives. If we have some control over it, maybe we can make it through another day.

We search in vain. What is out there? We find stories written by people who understand and let us know we are not alone. We find in Scripture the idea that there is a plan for all of us that remains a mystery.

Some days I feel betrayed by God, I feel guilt, I feel I've lost faith in hope, prayer, angels, and anything spiritual. But that doesn't mean I give up. It is not my nature to give in to my pain; it is my nature to fight, to survive, to try to recapture just a part of the person I used to be.

One day when I mentioned to my aunt that I felt anger toward another family member for something they had said, she remarked, "Don't be mad at us; we love you. Be mad at God." I cannot be. I tried. How can I turn my back on the only One who can help me?

One day I was blaming myself and felt like I was being punished. Jenny's father said, "Maybe it's me that is being punished. Did you ever think of that?" He also told me I wouldn't find what I was looking for in all the grief books. He simply said, "Why don't you read just one book, the Bible?"

All I can do for now is let time pass and see how life progresses. I must ride the wave and let it take me safely to shore. Answers will be found only within my own soul. Everyone grieves differently and every story ends uniquely.

I have decided to write to my daughter as if I were sending letters to Heaven. That is my therapy. I have hope that there will be a happy ending. Hope is my new favorite word. To those who may someday read these words, please understand that I don't consider myself to be a writer. I am a mother who is writing.

Hope

Hope has vision.
Hope sees dreams within our souls.
Hope reaches into the future.
Hope guides us gently to where we want to be.

—S. Harriman-Smelser

> *"Believe, when you are most unhappy,*
> *that there is something for you to do in the world.*
> *So long as you can sweeten another's pain,*
> *life is not in vain."*
>
> –Helen Keller

A Letter to Jenny

2015

July 20

Dear Jenny,

Today is your forty-second birthday. I get shivers when I think of your next birthday, as you will be the same age I was when you left us. I cannot even comprehend that because, to me, you are twenty. I try to imagine how you would look at forty-two, whether you would be married with children or single in New York (just one of the options you discussed), and how maturity may have changed you, your personality, or your perception of life.

Would you have a political affiliation, would you be positive or negative, happy or unhappy? Would we be close like you said we would be? Would we talk often, or would you be too busy with a family of your own? These things will forever remain a mystery because Heaven removes all decisions, all problems, and sadly, all relationships.

Today I have a cloud over my head. I've carried it on and off for many years. It's always there, though sometimes I can't see it if I allow the sun to chase it away. It waits patiently for me to ponder the past, and then I carry it again. I wake up with it often and remind myself that currently I have no reason to feel that way.

I usually shake myself out of the fog as I focus on the positive. I relax in the fact that it usually doesn't last more than a day or two. But I still must deal with it right now.

So today, instead of heading out of the house with a friend or celebrating your birthday in some way, I decided to start on the book that has already been written.

I am fortunate that I am a healthy 64 year old and realize there is a time for everything, and this time I have to complete the process instead of starting and stopping when it gets to be too much to handle. Now is the time for me to share how your death changed my life and the lives around me. Before I can start, I must go and plant flowers on your grave.

I love you,

Mom

Early Journaling and Jenny's Beginning

1971

JULY 12

Today I found out I am not pregnant. When Jim and I decided to have a baby, I suppose I thought I would conceive right away. I recently read in *Cosmopolitan* about a woman who kept a diary of her pregnancy. I thought how exciting it would be to read about what it was like for your mother while she was carrying you.

People keep diaries of their romances when they are young, but the most exciting and memorable time seems to be after you are married and have children. I wish my mother had written about her pregnancies or her children. Just when I became interested in those types of questions, my mother wasn't here anymore. Well I'm certainly not pregnant, so I can't write about that; but maybe someday if we are lucky enough to have a baby, he or she will have something to read.

I quit my stressful job, and we decided to have a baby instead of my going back to work right away. I've been home four months, and I'm starting to feel guilty about not contributing. If I don't conceive before the end of summer, I'll go back to work. I wonder if anyone ever kept a diary about trying to have a baby? I know I am rather young to want a child. I have a love that already exists for a child that isn't even here. I love a hope and a dream. I love the way my nephew Davy looks at me and puts his arms out for me to pick him up. I love how he gets excited when he hears my voice. My sister says it's not always as wonderful as I think. My mother used to say that kids are well worth it.

July 14

I found a job. My father asked if I wanted to do inventory control for his business at my home. He is paying me two dollars an hour. The job requires a great deal of typing. He will bring over the inventory sheets and receipts, and I will subtract or add and retype them. It will be never ending, as they have to be done every month.

1973

April 1

I really can't believe it's for real. I am finally pregnant. Six months have passed, and I feel little J kicking regularly. Most of the time I feel wonderful. I enjoy being pregnant, but as each day passes, I want to hold little J in my arms. It's so much fun fixing up the nursery. I cannot wait to rock my little J in the nursery chair.

After one and a half years of trying to conceive, I think the baby must be Heaven sent. The doctor suggested Jim try boxers instead of briefs…and bingo. I consider myself so fortunate because I have heard of couples waiting ten years. I would wait that long if I had to because I'd never give up.

After a year, I started to think pregnancy was something that happened to other couples. I think I've said this before, but I wonder how I can love someone so much when I've never met him or her. I love my baby so much it hurts.

I worry sometimes, as every mother does, about the health of my unborn child, yet I have dreams of how beautiful my baby will be. This baby will be so lucky to be loved so much. We are two parents who are going to put everything we have into making him or her the most contented child.

I hope the next three and a half months pass by quickly, and I hope they last forever.

1974

MARCH 18

I don't know why I feel like writing things down, but I want to. I had diaries when I was a teenager, but they were full of silly facts, not feelings. I have very little left of my past other than letters from my husband when he was in the Air Force Reserves, a black scrapbook made by my mother with shower cards and birthday cards, and a little snippet of my hair. When I was sixteen, Dad remarried and we moved, taking only what was necessary.

My mother passed away when I was fifteen. I never got to have an adult relationship with her. I long to ask her so much since Jenny was born. When I see other young women with their mothers and their children, I am so envious. If something happens to me, perhaps Jennifer's questions will be answered by my writings.

While I'm writing, Jenny is supposed to be sleeping, but I hear her playing. That little monkey hardly sleeps anymore. She's so energetic, and at eight months old, she's crawling around and standing up while holding on to things. I bet she'll be walking very soon. I hope I don't spoil her.

I can't say I love staying home every day, but I sure don't hate it. It tends to make me less organized and lazy. Being the person I long to be is just a matter of willpower. So I must quit writing and get Jenny's bottles washed before she wakes up.

MARCH 19

Jennifer is sleeping so I thought I'd write, though I should clean my stove. She's been fussing a lot lately and waking up in the middle of the night. It could be her teeth. She has two on the bottom, and the cuteness tugs at my heart when she smiles. Maybe she wakes up at night because she wants me. She cries when I put her to bed at night and doesn't want us to leave her.

My flowers are coming up but winter is holding on. Jenny will be walking by the time they bloom. It seems she was born yesterday, and it's hard to believe that little eight-month-old girl is the same infant that kicked so fiercely inside of me for so long, as if she was anxious to begin her life.

April 9

Jenny is taking her afternoon nap. I believe she's trying to say "mama." I let her crawl around the house now. Her favorite pastime is fumbling through the magazine rack. She pulls them out, rips them up, and then I put them back so she can do the same thing tomorrow. Today she pulled the thing right over on top of her.

I continue to think I will keep journaling, but one day I'll forget, and then a month will go by. I'll put the journal away when I'm cleaning, and a year will pass. I want Jenny to really know her mother and what she herself was like as a baby. I wish I knew my mother now. I need her. One day I saw her burning her diaries in the back yard. I think she knew she was dying and didn't want us to discover them later. I can't blame her, but I wish I had them. Perhaps I will burn mine someday.

I hope to be a friend to Jenny, as well as her mother. But mother comes first. I want her to come to me with every problem and know she can talk to me. I hope I live long enough to watch her grow up and hopefully get married. That is, if people still get married twenty years from now. I pray I can watch her children grow up. I know how much she'll need me then even if she doesn't show it. I'm only twenty-three, and I've needed my mother so badly the last eight years since breast cancer took her life at age forty-five. I want to live to enjoy Jenny and have her enjoy me. A girl needs her mother, and when she doesn't have one, no one can fill the void left in her life.

So, I love you Jennifer. Every time I go in your room, you get so excited that you can hardly control yourself, and you are a daddy's girl. You cling to me and you need me, and that feels so good. At other times you seem so independent and need to be off doing your own thing. Someday when you grow up, I know you'll think you don't need me anymore, but you will.

November 6

Jennifer is sleeping. She is down to one nap a day after lunch. She seems to have developed the habit of carrying her blanket around with her. She comes up stairs to get it and then comes back down to suck her thumb. She is the most wonderful thing in my life. She is so pretty and really starting to take to people. I wonder what she will be like when she's twenty-four. I hope I'm around to enjoy her children. My mother has three she has never met. We have her sister, Aunt Jackie. She is a mother and grandmother to us all.

February 5

It's been so long since I've written. Christmas was great this year with Jenny being older. She is now 18 months old, and boy can she ever wear you out. She is using quite a few words and will probably start with sentences soon. I'm attempting to potty train, and she loves her little toilet. Her hair is so blonde. I wonder if it will change. Jim and I are closer than ever. He said he would send me roses if he had the money, and he calls me "cutie pie" all the time.

Last night I saw the movie *Death Be Not Proud*. I get so emotional when I see a movie in which a young person dies. I was awake half the night thinking about death. Jenny was awake too. Are we that connected that she feels my anguish? I really don't understand that very well.

February 5

I can't believe the date. I put this book up in my closet and forgot about it. I knew I would do that. It wasn't meant to be a diary, but something for Jenny to read when she grows up. It's been exactly two years since I wrote in this journal. Jenny is three and a half, intelligent, beautiful, bubbly, and fantastic. I am twenty-six and pregnant for the second time.

So much has happened in the past two years. I worked at a gift shop for a year and a half to pay for a piano. I continued to work for my father doing inventory control for his business, and Jenny really grew up. As I write this, Jenny just came up to get her blankie (yes, still).

She's sporting a little blonde ponytail and jeans. I'll write later, as she needs me now. I let her color in this journal with a red crayon. She drew an apple, her daddy, a person, a doggie and me. I'll always have this.

1994

August 16

I guess I didn't do a very good job keeping up this journal. My last entry was in 1977. I never was good at keeping things going. I do regret being lazy about this one. I guess I kept enough. Seventeen years have passed, and I must close this one now because there is no more to add.

Over the last seventeen years, I gave birth to Jamin, my wonderful son. He and Jenny grew up adoring each other, at least most of the time. We moved to a new home in 1978 when Jamin was one. We lived in a friendly neighborhood and made great friends.

We joined a church and became baptized Lutherans. We were very involved. In many ways, I still am. Like most families, we bought a dog in 1984 whom we call Pokey. She's still with us, though she has epilepsy and coughs a lot. We bought a pop-up camper and camped often in many different places, our favorite being near the Mackinaw Bridge and the Island in Lake Huron. Later we bought a cabin near Houghton Lake where Jenny was completely and utterly bored. She often stayed with her best friend or her cousins, Jackie and David, instead of going there with us.

She dated, had two different boyfriends (not at the same time!) and numerous close friends. I have worked for several doctors over the years, owned a business with a friend, and for short periods of time I stayed home to enjoy just being a mom. However, my children liked it better when I worked. When I stayed home, their rooms were too neat for their liking, and I was overly concerned about cleanliness. Jim has done very well in his career, and though we are not rich, we are comfortable.

Jenny graduated high school in 1991. She worked many different jobs. If she was at one place and a better offer popped up, she would take it. She even worked with me for a short time at a local shopping village but left after a while. Jenny has driven across the country with her chorus group, taken trips with friends to Myrtle Beach, North Carolina, and took her senior trip to Cancun, Mexico. I'm glad she had these experiences.

Jamin has completed eleventh grade and will graduate in 1995. He loves motorcycles, snowmobiles, four wheelers, and now a Sea-Doo. He plays guitar and often gets together with his cousin, Dave, and his friend, Mike. His life is really just beginning. Jamin loves home.

Jenny loved freedom, her independence being very important to her. She did indeed grow up to be a beautiful blonde with her blue eyes and perfect, glowing skin. She was also argumentative and difficult at times, in addition to being softhearted and forgiving. She was just coming into adulthood and enjoying it immensely. She almost made it to twenty-one.

Earlier in this journal I wrote about young death in *Death Be Not Proud*. I wonder now if I had a premonition. Jenny put so much life into her twenty years. Perhaps she somehow knew that would be all she had, so she had better make it count. A drunk driver ended her life on March 26, 1994, around 2:15 a.m., a few miles from a birthday party she had attended.

I've been writing to her since she passed from this world to the next. The pain and emptiness are the hardest one can imagine. We will love her and miss her forever.

Jenny had the most beautiful service I have ever seen. Friends commented on its uniqueness. The lines of attendees were out the door. The music was heartbreaking and beautiful. With the help of friends, it all came together.

I pray for Jamin often. I pray he will have a long, healthy life with a wonderful woman and family to love him. I pray for him differently than I did his sister. I am careful with my words.

I always prayed for Jenny's safety because she had no fear. I asked God to watch over her and protect her from harm and hold her hand wherever she went, because she was too old for me to hold on to her. Now He has her.

We will move to another city and build a home in the woods. We must start over and learn to be a different family than we were before. I wonder how long I will reach for four dinner plates or how long I will notice the empty chair? We will survive and make the best of what God has left us. We don't have any other choice.

Some of Jenny

1986

MAY

What Jesus Means to Me

By Jenny Smith

Jesus, to me, means love, peace, eternal life, and sharing all of this with the people around you like friends and family. He also means Faith. You have to have faith in Him – true faith, not just a faith you see but a faith you feel truly in your heart.

I know Jesus cares for you and me because He suffered on the cross for us so our sins could be forgiven. This shows us that Jesus truly loves you and me.

I feel each time I go to church or pray, that I'm closer to Jesus. When I pray, I pray to give thanks for everything Jesus has given me. I pray for the forgiveness of sin, and also for the ill to be healed. I pray for God to be closer to them and help them because they need Him most then. I hope that someday I can help others to feel closer to Jesus and spread His word.

Age 13: Confirmation Speech

1989

DECEMBER

Mom,

I did the laundry, vacuumed, and the dishes. If there was anything else, I'm sorry. I'll do it tomorrow. I'm so sorry for always acting like such a snot. It's just really hard not to be when I always have been. I'd like to talk to you about that later if I can. I tried today but you weren't exactly in a good mood when you got home. I hate my mouth because it always gets me in trouble. I will try harder because I know that you don't deserve to be talked to that way. It is improving though because now every time I say something mean to you, I feel guilty. I know that I want us all to get along. I hate the fighting, so can we try to get along?

I love ya,

Jen (age 16)

P.S. Maybe we'll talk in the morning if we can both be nice and not argue. I think we can if I don't get snotty, and you don't start yelling right off the bat.

(Sometimes Jenny chose housework as her punishment. She couldn't handle grounding or being confined to her room.)

Summer

By Jenny Smith

The seashells
Washing
Upon the shore
As I lay
Basking
In the sun
Not a cloud
In the sky
Just the warm breeze
Birds flying
Seagulls
Skimming the waves
The dry sand
Blowing
On my blanket
Here I will lie
Until the sun
Goes down
Because here is where I come
To be alone
And collect my thoughts

1991 (Myrtle Beach)

The Morning After

1994

MARCH 27

    The morning after Jenny's death, I woke up very early. I had slept on the couch in our family room, and Jim was upstairs. The floor was covered in blankets and pillows. I was careful not to awaken her brother, cousins and friends sleeping among them. We needed to be together. I was so grateful. I had to take medication to sleep at all. I awoke once in the middle of the night, and I wanted to scream, but covered my mouth with my hand. My niece Jackie must have heard me, and we cried quietly together. When I awoke once more, I decided I needed to write a letter to put into Jenny's casket. I had done that for my mother, grandparents, and father. I tiptoed into the kitchen to get paper and pen, and then into the dining room where I sat down and stared out at the sun coming up in the east. I needed to let her know what she meant to me, how much I would miss her, and how I longed to be with her. What started as a letter ended up as a song. I don't remember who was kind enough to do this, but her poem *Summer* and my *Song for Jennifer* were printed and left on a table at her funeral for others to take as a memory.

Song for Jennifer

Life is too short for some,
Taken away before it is begun.
I will never accept you've been taken from me.
This is why this song must be sung.

My joy has been taken away,
Though I still must keep facing each day.
There are those who need me, so I must remain
On this earth and so I must pray.

(Chorus)
That you are in the arms of the One who's so great,
Who loved you so much that He just couldn't wait.
So I'll let time pass by until I see you again
In the light that's as bright as the sun.

Your dreams have been taken away,
And your loved ones, they always will say,
That your hair was so golden, your eyes were so blue,
Your many friends loved you, so it must be true.
(Chorus)

Your spirit and love will live on
In the hearts of the ones left behind.
I will talk to you daily and not say goodbye.
I will see you in dreams and the light of the sky.
I'll be brave just like you, and I'll try not to cry.
I know I will see you again when it's time.
(Chorus)

One Month Before

February 26

Jenny and her cousin Jackie were late. They were supposed to meet my two sisters, my young niece, my stepmother, and me at a restaurant to celebrate my stepmother's birthday. We were getting together to do two of our favorite things, eat and talk. We sat in the car waiting together for the two girls. Jenny was to drive her cousin to work afterwards, so we drove separately. I began to get anxious, as I usually do. Why do I constantly worry when she is on the road?

I couldn't enjoy the conversation and watched every car going by, searching for her little white truck. It seemed like forever before I spotted them coming, and they drove right past us. Eventually, Jenny turned around and found the small restaurant, and I suddenly became joyous.

"They found it. They found it. Those smart girls," I said excitedly.

"Oh, Susie," my stepmother replied, "You are just too much." Maybe I was, but only I was aware of my fears.

The cousins were more like sisters than best friends. We sat down together at a long table, Jenny to my left. As we waited for our food to arrive, my stepmother commented on Jenny's appearance.

"My God, Jenny, you have beautiful skin," she remarked. Everyone agreed. More than once, as she prepared to go out with her boyfriend and came up to her father and me to say goodbye, we would look at each other and ask, "How did we make her?"

Jackie proceeded to tell us how Jenny threw herself together in a few minutes after helping her get ready, doing her college laundry, and ironing her work clothes before they left to meet us. They had tried in vain to put Jackie's thick dark hair into a French twist like Jenny's, but it kept falling out because of the heaviness.

"We should all have that problem," I said. Jenny's light blonde hair was very long, and she could always make it look gorgeous in just minutes. The conversation continued, but I tuned out momentarily. I looked at my daughter. She was luminous. She always wore just the right amount of makeup. She had on blue jeans, a white turtleneck, black boots, and a new short black leather jacket her boyfriend Jesse had given her for Christmas. Her hair was done up in a twist with wisps of blonde hair hanging down around her face. Her bangs were perfectly placed. She looked like a movie star. She often did, but today she glowed from inside like an angel. She was happy. Her cousin Jackie was home for the weekend, and Jenny was in love with Jesse.

We soon said our goodbyes, and Jenny took Jackie to work. She then went home to finish Jackie's laundry so they could spend more time together when Jackie finished her shift. Jenny had to work at the same restaurant the very next day, and Jackie had to go back to Michigan State. It was the last time my sisters, my young nieces, and my stepmother ever saw Jenny. It was Jackie's last weekend with her cousin and best friend. I wonder if Jenny glowed because she was so close to being in Heaven. One month later, Jenny was gone.

Dreams

I am not sure how I feel about dreams. Are they fears being woven into a story while we sleep so they are somehow organized or even released? Are some dreams premonitions? My mother used to tell us of a reoccurring dream she had. My brother, two sisters, and I were with my mother in an elevator. She would push the button for the destination floor, and when the elevator doors opened, one of us would be missing. She expressed how awful she felt.

Though Mom never lost one of us, we lost her instead. She received a cancer diagnosis at age forty when I was ten years old. She passed away five years later. I remember dreaming that she came back to us, and I saw her walking up to the back door. I think it's strange that I don't dream of Jenny very often. I don't remember dreaming at all for at least a year after she passed away. It could have been the sleep medication I took or perhaps my mind knew I wouldn't be able to go there just yet. I finally did start to dream again and told Jenny all about them in the following letters.

I didn't realize how fearful I was of Jenny's birth until I came down with a horrible case of hives a few weeks before her due date. I had never had hives before, but I was covered in huge, ugly, itching welts from stomach to ankles. I was miserable. The doctor prescribed antihistamines to ease the itch, so no matter where I was, I wanted to sleep. The large purple marks started to fade just before her birth, which was two weeks later than predicted. However, just days after we brought Jenny home from the hospital, my hives surfaced once more. This time they were even more aggressive and took even longer to subside. I had purple marks on my legs most of the summer, but I never had hives again.

Once while I was expecting Jenny, I dreamt that she was in bed with me. I didn't even know I was going to have a girl. She somehow rolled off of the bed and was lying on the baseboard heater. I remember my horror but do not remember the outcome. Like most nightmares, I woke up in a sweat. However, after she was born, I had a few more of those horrifying dreams. These are the dreams I wrote down shortly after her death. I never forgot them and can recall every detail.

Jenny-Bug (a pet name), her daddy, her Grandpa Harriman and I pulled into the driveway of our first home on a dark, clear evening. Jenny-Bug was about two or three. We got out of the car, and Jenny-Bug stood on the driveway with her blankie.

Suddenly, a large bird swooped down from the sky and grabbed her with its large talons, then quickly darted back into the sky, wings flapping, and disappeared from sight. I just screamed and screamed before yelling, "I'll never see her again, I'll never see her again," over and over. When we realized the bird was not going to bring her back, my father took me inside and walked me up the stairs, saying, "You'll get over it." I woke up from the dream saying, "I'll never get over it, I'll never get over it."

In another dream Jenny was around five or six. She got into a very small, round vehicle that she thought she could drive and started down the road. I chased her over lawns and down streets, but the car was just out of reach. Finally, she turned and drove slowly between two houses on a canal. I ran behind her screaming as I noticed water and docks in the backyards. The car got closer and closer to the water. She drove the little car on to one of the docks and dropped off into the deep, dark water. I ran to the dock and could see the car sinking down deeper and deeper until it was out of sight. We never even lived close to a canal, but I can still remember the feeling I had after that dream. Thank God, I woke up.

Having dreams or nightmares does not mean you will lose your child. I think it is normal to have anxiety dreams about our children. Once they are born, we wear our hearts outside of our bodies. We react to every boo-boo, and every tear breaks our hearts. We love so deeply that we become vulnerable to every little mishap and sometimes these become exaggerated in our dreams. Watching television shows and listening to the news can leave a vision that comes alive in a dream.

Just a few years ago, I had a dream about my son Jamin. He was about ten, and Jamin's father and I were riding bikes with him in the mountains. He suddenly made a wrong turn and went right off a cliff. We knew that was it. We both said, "There goes our boy." I awoke in a sweat, breathing heavily. We hadn't even been to the mountains with Jamin since he was about five, and we never rode bikes. Jamin was well into his thirties when I had this dream, but I sent him a text immediately just to say hello. I was depressed the rest of the day.

I do not have the same fears about him as I used to have about his sister. What is ironic is that Jenny always thought he was our favorite. It wasn't that at all, as I tried in vain to explain to her. He just needed us differently. Jenny was independent and fearless. She resisted all the coddling and affection, while Jamin loved it.

Other Letters

MARCH 26

The Day of Jenny's Death

Tracy Smith (Cousin)

What are we? Why are we here? These are questions humankind has asked throughout the years. These questions never die and are never answered to our satisfaction, though it is not because we haven't tried. And when death touches our lives, the questions seem all the more elusive and that much more important.

What was Jennifer? A daughter. A sister. A granddaughter. A niece. A cousin. A friend. She was a beautiful 20-year-old woman who left us behind. But Jennifer has not just left us. She has moved on. She is not the first, and she is not alone. She is with her grandmother Mary, and her Uncle Steve. She is safe, and we can take comfort in that.

Why was Jennifer here?

That is the more difficult question. It is a question that we each must answer individually. Her life, her presence meant something different to each of us. Personally, Jennifer taught me something very important about life that I will never again forget. Jennifer brought something to each of us in her lifetime, and that is what we should remember.

What are we? As Tolstoy once said, we are "a part of the infinite." And, as part of the infinite, we are each "an enduring entity that the hand of death cannot touch." Jennifer will live on in our memories and beyond, though her presence here will be missed. Good-bye, Jenny Bug. We love you.

March 30

Lynn Smith (Aunt)

>Don't weep for me, for I have not gone.
>I will be there in the words of a song,
>In the warmth of the sun,
>In the sound of the wind,
>Listen for me in the voice of a friend.
>In the warm summer sun,
>Or on a cold winters' day,
>I'll be with you always – I won't go away.
>When the flowers bloom and winter's chill leaves the ground,
>Just look for me – I can be found.
>No need to look far, we are never apart,
>For I will live on – I am there in your heart.

March 1994

A School Paper

Bill V – My Memories of Jenny "Bug" Smith

I was awakened at about 6:30 a.m. on Saturday morning to learn that a really good friend of mine, Jenny Smith or "Bug," had been killed in a car accident. I couldn't believe it.

When I was little, Jenny and I fought like brother and sister. I can't remember not knowing her. As for her brother, I've been a friend of his, off and on, all of my life. Jamin is a junior, as I am. His mom and dad have been like second parents to me. They've helped me through so much. It doesn't seem fair for a family such as this one to be torn apart.

Jamin and Jenny were completely different from anyone else you've ever met. Jamin wasn't your average eleventh grader. He doesn't listen to the same music as everyone else or dress the same way as everyone else. He's unique. She was the same way. She would have been twenty-one on July 20. She lived every day to the fullest. She was as beautiful as a yellow rose. She was very outgoing and said what was on her mind. Because of that, Jenny and her mom had their fair share of disagreements. If you knew Jenny, then she touched you. She was always there to give advice or just listen.

I can remember hearing Mrs. Smith, her mom, say that she died young, but was happy she lived life how she wanted. I never really understood why Mrs. Smith worried so much. With the death of her daughter, I now understand. As a teenager or adult, you can't live life like you're indestructible because you're not, and Jenny proved that to us all. "Don't ever take life for granted because it can end at any time," said Mrs. Smith on Tuesday after a prayer at the site of the accident.

Jenny and her family have touched me in so many ways I will never forget. The family and friends of Jenny don't deserve the hell they are going through. It's just not fair!

Jenny's boyfriend, Jesse, unfortunately went through the same thing last year with the death of his best friend. Jesse has been through a lot and still has a lot to overcome. He's strong and in time will overcome this tragedy. Jenny was his first true love, and I know he will never forget her.

Jenny will never be forgotten in the eyes of the people who loved her. My heart goes out to her family and friends. She will be deeply missed by all of us.

May 31

Dear Mr. Fabiano,

After looking over materials given to me by MADD, I discovered that family members are entitled to write a victim impact letter or speak for an allotted amount of time before a judge. There is no judge, jury, or defendant, but I feel compelled to write something about the impact of my daughter Jennifer's death on her father, brother, relatives, friends, and myself. I must say that these are my thoughts and no one else's. My husband and son know I am writing this letter, and my husband encourages it. This letter or statement is to be read by you and other lawyers involved in the case. This letter is not to be viewed by, or sent to, anyone to whom it would cause pain.

I hope this is legal and above board. If not, please just mail it back to me, and I will understand. I have so many thoughts and feelings that go on in my head every moment of every day, and I suppose I always will. These are only words, and words cannot fully communicate my true feelings. The shock of the accident has worn off, and I find myself no longer protected by the brain's naturally occurring chemicals that allow us to withstand the horror of such a horrendous loss. The letter is enclosed.

Regards,

Susan Marie Smith

May 26

Victim Impact Letter

My Only Daughter

When I was a young girl, I dreamed of having a little girl and I knew, even then, that her name would be Jennifer. I thought it was the most beautiful name I had ever heard. It took my husband and me over a year to conceive our first child, and we were naturally elated. I don't have to convey to you the magical love a parent feels. We were in awe of this little girl.

I knew the kind of heart Jennifer would have by the time she was two years old. She often did sweet things, like give you a toy that she loved or a flower she picked. On the day she turned three, she stood in her little wading pool in our front yard holding a toy camera she had received for her birthday. The little boy next door came over, grabbed it from her, and tossed it in the pool. She never got angry. She just picked it up.

Since the day she was old enough to have friends, she was devoted, kind, giving, and forgiving. She had so many friends who are struggling, just as we are, to endure this tragedy.

Jenny had one younger brother to whom she was devoted. They rarely fought and had a wonderful and trusting relationship. He is very quiet and shy, and Jenny being very bold and outgoing helped him in many ways. He is lost without her and wonders how he will get through the rest of his teen years without her counsel. She helped him get his first job, even after her death. She had just finished helping him fill out an application for a local store in which she once worked. He finished this application started in his sister's handwriting, took it to the store, and is now working at the same place.

I pray that her strength will live on in him.

I can't describe the love I have for my daughter. I knew I loved her before, but now my love has surpassed anything I have felt before. Being in my home is painful, and yet the thought of leaving twenty years of her memories behind and moving on is just as painful. My family is caught in a web of pain and sorrow that will take years to get used to.

At this time, I feel I will never escape this feeling. Everyday a new thought of what will never be comes to haunt me. Without my faith, I don't think I would be sitting here writing this letter.

My family is unable to sleep in our upstairs bedrooms even after two months. The emptiness of her room is unbearable. Knowing that someday I will have to go through twenty years of her life collected in her room and in storage is unthinkable, but still ahead of me. Her collection of birthday cards ends now.

Jenny was dating a young man who treated her with love and respect. She was happier than I had ever seen her. Their one-year dating anniversary would have been one week after her death. It was written in her date book, along with her approaching twenty-first birthday. This young man who loved her had to watch her life come to a tragic end, and I cannot even imagine how he will overcome that nightmare. He tried so desperately to save her, and he is our hero.

Our grandchildren died with her that night. It didn't occur to me at first. One day my husband and I drove past the location of her death, and I said suddenly, "We lost our grandchildren. They are gone. They died with her." Jenny always wanted two boys.

We will never have that twenty-first birthday party, become excited over an engagement, pick out a wedding dress, plan a wedding, shop, see a movie, go out to a restaurant, or talk on the phone. I will remember to buy her favorite yellow rose on the twenty-sixth of each month, even if she never sees it.

I lost all the things a mother and daughter share. I'll even miss our squabbles, her five pairs of shoes by the front door, the messy bathroom, and the smell of fresh nail polish. I will miss her beauty because it filled our home along with her spunk, her never-ending energy, and seeming control over most situations. I lost my own mother when I was fifteen years old, and I am once more deprived of a mother/daughter relationship.

Though I know she is with the Lord, I mourn for the earthly things she will miss out on.

Why her? Why now? She did nothing wrong. She rarely missed curfew, she always called, she was responsible for the most part, she was reliable and a "good kid," as her father always described her. We have a car phone for emergencies, a beeper, AT&T home link, and she knew she could call us anytime with no questions asked. None of that could stop another car from crossing the line.

I look at her photos and feel I could touch her. I hear her voice in my dreams. The last time I saw her, she was heading to a birthday party with the hope of returning and living out the rest of her life. Ironically, my husband and I bought a video camera that same night so we could start filming our children before they were old enough to leave home. I yelled a quick goodbye before she left, along with my usual, "Be careful." I didn't see her leave, and I never saw her again. Unless one has gone through this, no one will ever understand what was taken from us that night. I read somewhere that when you lose your parents, you lose your past; but when you lose a child, you lose your future. Thank you for allowing me to express my thoughts in this letter. I appreciate your counsel and your understanding.

Regards,
Susan

April 8

On a sweltering hot summer day in August 1993, Bradley, the son of my good friends Ross and Joanne, was injured in a swimming accident. The neighbors met the family at the hospital. The news was not favorable. Brad, sixteen, was paralyzed; his life and the life of his family were forever changed. We all helped as much as we could, and there were fundraisers to help this wonderful family. Jenny helped along with the others.

Brad was a handsome young man with great athletic ability. Our hearts were broken for him and his family. When Jenny passed away, Brad was unable to come to the funeral. A couple of weeks later, Joanne mentioned to me that he had questions about Jenny's death that she could not answer. I don't remember what those questions were, but I felt compelled to write him a letter.

Dear Brad,

I have been doing so much thinking since I lost Jenny. I will never understand why until the day I pass on and see her again. Your mother told me you had some questions.

I always prayed there was something I could do for you. It frustrated me that I could only pray. I know your parents would have given their lives to make you walk again, and I would give my life to have Jenny back to live hers. We can't bargain with God. I pray that there will be a medical breakthrough in your lifetime.

What happened to Jenny did not take away the beautiful person she once was, as what happened to you did not take away your handsome face, your kind spirit, and your continuing presence. Brad, you are here because your spirit lives on in you. You are still our Brad with the same personality and intelligence. You can give and receive love. I was blessed with a precious daughter, but I think had she lived, she would never be the Jenny we knew. Her injuries were severe, though at the time of this writing, I don't know exactly what they were. I don't think she would have ever regained consciousness and would have been locked inside of herself where she couldn't share her spirit with others. I am sure her spirit soared to Heaven because her spirit soared on earth.

Jenny lived more in her twenty years than I have in my forty-three years on this earth. She had more courage, more nerve, and more confidence than I ever had. Someone at Canterbury described her as the only person "not intimidated by the powers that be." That was her personality, and she never changed. She left so much with so many. Knowing her changed her boyfriend, who witnessed the accident and held her in his arms. He had a stormy and troubled past, and friends say he changed completely when he met her. He described her as his soul mate. Another friend of Jenny's, who was once an enemy, said Jenny saved her life more than once.

Brad you have a special purpose in your life. God saved you for a reason. It is not our bodies that really serve others, but our hearts, our spirits, our love, and our compassion. If we are lucky enough to touch one life, or hopefully many, we have served a blessed purpose and honor on this earth. You have many lives left to touch. This is a different beginning for you. You will bring courage to others who lack it, you will bring strength to those that are weak, and hope to those who have no hope. You have already touched at least one life and given courage and strength – mine, and I am sure there are many others of whom you are unaware. Jenny completed her reason for being here, and I believe she now has another. God bless you, Brad.

Love,

Sue

Letters to Jennifer

April 26

Dearest Jenny,

Today marks one-month since your trip to Heaven. A woman at church gave me a journal to write down my feelings. I'll write to you instead. I have so many emotions I want to explain that, if you were here, we would be talking for days.

First, I love you and miss you more than a million philosophers could possibly imagine. I cleaned your room just the way you would do it. It's ready for you, but you are not coming home. You are with Jesus, and my mother has held her first grandchild in her arms. I am happy for her and all others who have gone before you. I wouldn't want to take that joy away from you or mom, but I would give my life in a second if you could be here to live yours.

You can't label pain, so I won't try. Your dad, Jamin and I all sleep in the family room because that is where we are the most comfortable. Sleeping upstairs without you seems impossible. We are going to get a car with airbags so we will feel safer. I wonder if an airbag would have saved you. We'll keep your truck because it was part of you. It was your first new car.

You are a hero to me, Bug. You were wise to drive your friend's car under the circumstances. God just chose that moment to take you. I didn't see you right before you left all dressed up, but you were happy that night. I hope you had a wonderful time, and I am glad you had pizza.

Your Aunt Carol bought a yellow rose bush for you. We will plant it in the front yard, though I bet the ones where you live are too numerous to count and the scent more lovely than one could imagine. I can almost smell the heavenly scent of yellow roses.

I guess you know by now how many people love you and miss you. You are special, Bug. You always were, even when we had our stormy moments, because I wanted to hold on and you wanted me to let go. I always wanted you to be happy, but I also wanted you to be safe. I cannot describe the emptiness I feel. We all feel it. Jamin still needs you, Jen, so please watch over him always. Watch over your daddy, Jen. You are his special girl. He would die for you.

As for me, I was always concerned with keeping myself healthy for you and your brother, hoping that I wouldn't leave you too soon, as my mother left me. I no longer fear death. I will welcome it, because then we will hold each other in Heaven and there will be no more misunderstandings. We will feel only peace and joy together. You are in our hearts and thoughts every second of every day. I love you. Mom

April 29

Bug,

Were you with us? You would have been happy. Your dad, Jamin, and I went to the Knights of Columbus hall with some of our friends, and some of your friends, to say goodbye to neighbors that were moving to Atlanta. Do you already know that? I'll probably ask you that often.

I don't know what it's like for you. I wish I did. I can hardly stand life without you. I feel like I am watching life go on for others from inside a giant bubble. I can see them, and they can see me, but it's difficult to focus and hard to hear.

I don't want to go on, but I have no choice if I want to be with you again. Why you, Bug? You never hurt anyone. Sometimes I would give anything to go back to that point in time when you were safe and sound inside of me. It comforts me to think you are whole and perfect in Heaven. I may be young when I meet you again, or I may be old. Right now, tonight, I don't care if it's tomorrow.

I love you so much. I wonder how many times I will write that sentence to you. I fear you don't know how much you meant to me. I don't like our house without you in it. Everything looks the same, but I have no understanding of why it's here and what I'm supposed to do with it. It has become a stranger's house and strangers live all around it.

We love Jesse, too. I miss him. Do we have to lose him too? I hear songs and think that I would have loved to sing one at your wedding. You know, the wedding with the huge bowl of chilled shrimp?

> *The most beautiful spirit ever to be,*
> *Was welcomed by Heaven but left you and me.*
> *She soars with the angels, but visits us all,*
> *She dries all our tears that continue to fall.*
> *She adds peace to our hearts until we can see,*
> *That making it through tomorrow will be.*
> *Love, Mom*

May 10

Bug,

Jamin gave me a beautiful pen for Mother's Day so I'm using it to write to you. I thought of you all day. We were at our cabin (where you were so bored), and the sun shone all day long. I looked for you in the sky, as I always do.

It is becoming spring on earth Jenny. We didn't know in March that you would never see another spring blooming, did we? Soon the tree by your bedroom window will blossom, and I will remember how you looked as you stood in front of it before your prom. Your dress almost matched the colors of the coral blossoms, and the sun was in your eyes. Most likely you were anxious for me to take the picture so you and your date could be on your way.

Your dad is going to have a necklace made for me that says, "BUG." It will be in the shape of a heart with a gold rose on the edge. The heart will be gold, but your name will be silver. I always loved gold, and you always wore silver. He said it would be my Mother's Day gift from you.

Your friend, Heather, gave me a sterling silver bracelet just like the one you used to wear. It was so kind of her to think of me. Jackie liked it so much that she is buying one too.

Did you see Jackie's graduation from Michigan State? She carried a yellow rose for you. She loves you and misses you so much, Jenny. You were cousins, best friends, and sisters. I sat next to your Grandma Ginny, Grandpa Harriman's wife. I whispered to her my hope of seeing Jamin walk across a stage after completing college. She made a face and laughed at me, and her reaction hurt me deeply. She seems to have the ability to add pain on top of pain with no regard for a person's feelings. I left the auditorium and sat alone, crying at her cruelty. Jamin is unmotivated right now, but not hopeless. After the ceremony, she came out and sat next to me; she must have seen the pain on my face, yet she said nothing to comfort me. I forgave her.

Once again, I ask you Jenny, if you are able, please help me watch over Jamin. He is so tired and struggles with school. I can only watch and feel his broken heart continue to suffer. Jamin and your dad are my reasons for living. One day, with God's help, I will be strong again. I ache for missing you.

P.S. I found your class ring. Thank you.

May 13, 1994

Dearest Jenny,

I've been very confused about life after death and if there is ever some sort of communication between loved ones. Pastor came to visit me. I was hoping that you had the freedom to come to us when you desired. I need you near.

Some books say that is possible, but according to Pastor, the Bible says it is not. I had hoped that you were the one who made my flowers bloom unexpectedly and helped me find missing objects. I never saw a Christmas cactus bloom profusely in the spring. Maybe God's presence is the answer, and not yours. Pastor explained that you are in Heaven to stay. He explained that if you were around us, you would see our pain and grief. Therefore, you would not have perfect peace as the Bible describes. He said you know us and feel our love but are protected from our pain.

I guess I can accept the fact that you are not here. Maybe you won't be around me as I wished, but you will live on in my heart every moment throughout eternity. My love for you is endless and fills me so that I could burst, and that has to reach all the way to Heaven. I will talk to you and write to you through God. He has let me know you are happy.

Love, Mom

May 20

Jenny,

Two months from today you will be twenty-one years of age. I'm not sure what we should do on that day. Maybe God will let me know. I asked God to let you read these words, but I'm not sure that is possible. Every day I change my thinking about the afterlife. I know you are in Heaven, because I see beauty where I didn't before, though some of what I thought was beautiful no longer seems so.

At two o'clock today, we are planting a beautiful flowering crab apple tree in your honor. Your Aunt Laurie and I picked it out. Your friend Tara helped us at the nursery. It will be planted at the Township Park. I pray that God will let you watch. Don't forget us, Bug.

Love,

Mom

May 24

I have decided that some days I will just write. Sometimes writing to Jenny just hurts. It will get easier. I will call this entry, "My Daughter."

She was born on Friday July 20, 1973. I remember going out for dinner and then coming home to watch Johnny Carson. Her dad, Jim, and I made popcorn and settled in. Around 2:00 a.m. on Thursday the 19th we went to William Beaumont Hospital in Royal Oak, Michigan. I guess I walked in looking pretty spry because they put me in an exam room and said that someone would come in and check to see if I was in labor. They sent her father to a waiting room. I told them my water broke. No one came. My water continued to leak with every contraction. I stuck my head out and called for a nurse. Again, no one came. I thought I might give birth on the floor in that tiny exam room.

Finally, someone heard my call. By then, my clothes and shoes were soaked. The shocked nurse quickly took care of me, and Jenny was born at 11:56 a.m. She was healthy and beautiful.

I read so much then about how to mother…now I am reading about how to grieve and cope with the death of a child. Twenty years was not nearly enough for Jenny or for me. Fifteen years was not nearly enough time with my own mother. I do not understand why God chose to shorten both of these wonderful female experiences for me. When I get to Heaven, the answers will become known to me and until that time, I must let God be God and as Job says in the Bible, "Though he slay me, yet will I trust in him." But I sure plan on asking.

Jenny slept so much during the day as an infant, and then stayed awake until midnight. We would sit on the couch together while she just looked at me smiling, and I struggled to keep my eyes open. She never made a fuss about eating. Everything I put in front of her went into her mouth. I often wondered why she wasn't chubby.

Her baby hair stuck straight up so she wore cute little hats often. We walked her around and around in the family room while music played on our record player, hoping to calm her or help her sleep. That's probably why she always loved the Steve Miller Band. We took car rides to get her to sleep at night. She carried her blankie with her all the time. She took her first steps on Mackinaw Island. She was two when she saw me crying because my grandfather had just died. She climbed the stairs to her room, grabbed her blankie, and then came down and handed it to me. To Jenny the blanket was comfort. I cried even harder at her sweetness.

June 20

Footsteps

By Lynn Smith (Aunt)

You walk into the empty room and hear the footsteps of years gone by.

The creak of the rocking chair as you soothed her to sleep.

Your footsteps as you walked the floor on one of her fussier nights.

You hear the pitter patter of pajama feet as she creeps out of her room to come and fling herself onto your bed for just "one more story" or maybe only a reassuring hug.

You hear the footsteps of a young girl running to her room, stomping around loud enough for you to hear so you will know she is not pleased with you at this moment.

You hear the footsteps of a young lady preparing for her first date, full of herself but still a little unsure, looking to you for approval.

You hear the footsteps of a first attempt at wearing high heels and the peals of laughter as she watches her first awkward steps in the mirror.

You hear the footsteps of a confident young woman ready for the world and you wonder where have the years gone?

Then one day the only footsteps you hear are in your mind. And you treasure your memories for they are all that is left of a beautiful young lady who walked with you through her short, sweet life.

June 21

Tracy (Jennifer's cousin)

Dear Aunt Sue,

It was so good to see you in Mackinaw last weekend. I was so glad you came. I really enjoy spending time with all of you, and it was great to see you have a good time. When you, Mom, and I took a walk out on the pier, I was so impressed with how you handled yourself. It's still hard for me to talk about Jennifer, so I can only imagine how difficult it is for you. But you were calm and understanding, and you made me feel better.

There was one thing in particular that you said that really hit me, and that was the uselessness of Jennifer's death. It hit me because I believe there is a reason for everything, even though we may not be able to see it as clearly as we would like. And maybe Jennifer's death, as her life, means something different to each person. Do you remember what I wrote about Jennifer teaching me something very important about life that I will never again forget? That something was the will to live…the strength to carry on through everything around you seems to be a waste.

I've never told anyone else in my family (not even my mother) how depressed I used to get. The joy I had in my life did not overshadow the pain, as it should. I didn't see any purpose in life, and I often wished for death. I don't believe I ever would have committed suicide, and thank God now I will never know, but I just had lost the will to live.

When Jennifer died, I finally realized how selfish I was being. It was like the dark cloud that had been hovering over me for so long was finally blown away. I see things more clearly now, and I love more deeply. I've always known that my family means a lot to me, but now I realize exactly how much. I know that I have to be there for my family because they need me as much as I need them.

After Jennifer's death, I felt so guilty about the way I had felt, about wishing for my own death. No one should have to go through that kind of pain. But if we have enough faith and enough love, we can get through anything. I learned a hard lesson, a lesson I will never have to repeat. I wanted to tell you this because I don't want you to think that Jennifer lived and died for no reason. I believe she left something with each of us, something that we as individuals have to work out. It may take some time to find, but it is there. We just have to find it. I wrote a poem on March 31st to help me work out my feelings on what Jennifer left for me. I hope you don't mind if I share it with you. I love you, Aunt Sue.

Love,

Tracy

Take Me Now

Take me now, I once prayed.
Take me before the light of day.
There is nothing more I wish to see,
There is nothing more that I can be.
My life was simple, no strings attached,
No meaning to bring, no symbols to match.
I asked for death as I lived each day;
I prayed for release from this endless stay.
But I was wrong, as I so often am.
The answers were there in the palm of my hand,
In a caring touch, in a warm embrace,
In the feeling of love, my saving grace.
It's not yet my time, I know that now.
I don't want to go – it would be wrong somehow
To leave behind those that I love
In my selfish longing for peace up above.
For the peace is here, it shines all around.
It just needs acceptance before it can be found.
I accept it in mind, I accept it in soul.
I accept that I am here, and that I am whole.
Now I pray for forgiveness in the black of night,
In the face of death, I pray for life.

JUNE 27

Dear Jenny,

I wrote another song. I continue to sing at church, and one Sunday I sang this for you.

Love, Mom

My Promise

I don't think it could happen, and I don't expect it can,
but I would do most anything to see you once again.
And oh, how I would love to have things like they used to be,
For each day that I had you was a gift from God to me.

Refrain: I promise this to God, I wouldn't keep you very long,
I'm not asking for a day, maybe an hour is too long.
But only for a moment to say I love you so,
And maybe He'd allow a hug before I let you go.

I didn't know that this would happen, I didn't know this was the end.
I never got to see your face or hear your voice again.
So, I don't think what I'm asking is so very hard to do.
If it can't be real, God, then in my dreams will do.
(Refrain)

It wouldn't take too long to ask you what I want to know.
How happy you are in the arms of One who loves you so.
Can you hear me when I talk to you, or feel my love so strong?
Can you come to me and comfort me when nights are much too long?
(Refrain)

I always wished that time could stand still, never liked this growing old.
I wanted to be with my children so that I could watch them grow.
But things they seem so different now, those feelings aren't so true.
Each day that passes by me now is a day closer to you.
(Refrain)

JULY 8

There are some things I must learn for my daughter, Jenny. Some of these things must be in her death as they were in her life.

I must learn to keep her without holding on.
I must learn to love her without being loved in return.
I must learn to remember her without longing for her.
I must learn to live without her but remember her laughter, her voice, and her ways.

I must learn to go on though my heart tells me I cannot.

I must learn to remember how it felt to hug her, touch her hair and skin, and admire her.

I must learn to remember what she was and not dwell on what she will never be.

I must learn to keep her alive in my heart though her heart no longer beats.

I must remember she is in Paradise and, God willing, I will see her, touch her, hear her, and feel her love again.

July 22

Her special day came and went. She turned twenty-one on July 20. Maybe she knew, maybe not. Her relatives, friends, and family remembered her in a special way. Her party occurred all by itself with little planning. There was a special movie to watch called "Angels in the Outfield." Flowers were spread around her tree in the park, and balloons were tied to it that reached into the sky. Friends sat in her room to reminisce. Many brought yellow roses, and friends sent flowers. Her last meal of pizza was served to everyone. Her hand-written poem Summer was immortalized by Stephanie. She received a beautiful picture of Jesus holding a soul in Heaven from her Aunt Carol. Her boyfriend Jesse, her cousin Jackie, and her family went to her favorite restaurant to have dinner.

I hope she was with us. Did you see it all, Jenny? Did you hear your friends missing you? Did you have a party in Heaven? It would have been your best party yet. It happened without you, Jenny, and I only pray you were with us in spirit. You almost made it to twenty-one. It was a goal you seemed to be striving for. You almost had your independence. You almost came of age. You almost became a legal adult. I'm so sorry you didn't get that chance. We will never have that margarita together. You will never tell me all the secrets you agreed to share on your twenty-first birthday. I try to write about you but end up writing to you. You are my angel, Jenny. You are sparkling and full of light. True love always,

Mom

> *"The pain now is part of the happiness, that's the deal."*
> –C. S. Lewis

August 15

You filled me today, Jenny. You gave me your peace. You hugged me. Someday I will write about it, but now I cannot. I miss you so. After the shock comes the missing. That is where we are. MISSING. You gave me hope. I am not afraid. Let me feel you again. Thank you for helping me locate your missing necklace.

August 18

Always with You

I knew you in my womb. You were eager to be born and full of energy.

I knew your name. You knew my voice.

I knew you at the moment of your birth when you would be trying something new – life.

I knew you when I would be trying something new – motherhood.

I knew you when you were an infant, small, defenseless, needing me as I needed you.

I knew there was love, and I would always be with you.

I knew you when you were one. We made it through, the two of us, in one piece. You took your first steps and giggled with laughter when I came into your room. I didn't do everything right, but I was always with you.

I knew you when you were two and played with everything but your toys.

I knew you when you discovered what freedom was. I didn't know how important it would become, but I was always with you.

I knew you when you were three and we played, and you talked and talked, and you were your father's pride and joy. You had us all to yourself, and we were always with you.

I knew you when you were four and saw your brother growing inside me. You patiently waited with us and enjoyed your school time. You came to visit at the hospital and saw your little brother for the first time. Your mommy couldn't come home with you for a few days, but I was always with you.

I knew you when you were five. You waited for the school bus so patiently while your brother and I waved goodbye, your little pigtails bouncing as you climbed the steps to take your seat. I hope you didn't think I was sending you away. You would be back soon, but I was always with you.

I knew you as you grew and became each Jenny you would ever be. You were the sweet preteen with the loving and giving heart, and the smart-mouthed teen whose parents could do no right. I knew you through your first love and happiness and heartache. You cried in my arms when life was unkind.

You blossomed from braces and perms to grace and loveliness. You grew into independence and promised to tell me everything I never knew when you were twenty-one. I wanted to hear all about your life without me by your side. Perhaps you thought you were full of secrets, but I was always with you. Perhaps you think you are gone now, but I am always with you. I always was.

Mom

August 22

Jen, I spent time with your friend, JoJo, and she said something about you I will never forget. She remarked, "Sometimes I'll stop and think, and I'll smile just for having known her."

We said goodbye to neighbors that were moving to Georgia. We went to the restaurant where you were working when you passed away. This ends another phase of your life. Your friends are leaving.

> *"Treasure each other in the recognition that we do not know how long we shall have each other."*
> –Joshua Loth Liebman

August 29

Dear Jesse,

I appreciate your visit last night and all visits before. I appreciate you picking up the old chair because, believe it or not, that chair will always be special to me. I remember it sitting in my aunt's bedroom when I was a child. It was gold then, with a huge button in the middle of the back. My grandfather later reupholstered it for her in its current bright blue floral print. I remember telling Jenny that I should get it reupholstered where you work. I will always remember you and Jenny lugging in all those heavy books for me to look at and dropping them in the middle of the floor. You were both so adorable and out of breath. I will always remember going through them and trying to decide, and when I did, how long it took for me to get the two of you to take the books back.

Getting the chair reupholstered will be something I can always remember you by. Seeing you is like seeing a valuable part of my daughter.

I ask you to always remember that we are here for you. We care about you and your future. We will never forget you or your kind voice. We will always wonder what would have been. I will always see, in my mind's eye, two tiny little boys running around, but never really seeing their faces because they exist only in my heart. But exist they will, because they were her dream; and now, they will be mine.

I could continue because my mind never stops, but I will not. I will only say we love you. Please keep this poem as a remembrance of us while you are away. You will be an honorable Marine. We wish you the best in the world, for your life will go on. I know you will never forget, but new joys will come, and your dreams will continue. We know, through faith, and feeling her presence, that we will see her again.

Love,

Sue

For Jesse

You loved her...
Not as long as we,
Not the same as we,
But in the way only a man could.
You knew a part of her we never would,
A starry-eyed passion new, a heart filled,
And we love her still.

She loved you...
Not as long as she loved us,
Not the same as she loved us,
But in the way only a woman could.
She gave a part of her only you could have.
"I'm so in love," she said, a love fulfilled,
And she loves us still.

We were here when she came in.
You were there when she went out.
We knew her coming home.
You knew her going home.
We held her many years,
And we held her fast.
You held her but one year,
But you held her last.

OCTOBER 13

My Jenny Bug,

One perfect and beautiful yellow rose sits on the table next to me. My rosebush had one last bud. It bloomed on my birthday, which was yesterday, and I cut it. It is so perfect that it seems as if it was created by an artist and made of silk. It's too perfect to be considered earthly. I would describe it as a Heavenly or celestial rose.

I know it's from you. No artist could paint it. No other rose could match it. Even the color and shape of the leaves are exquisite. They frame the rose as if they are framing a portrait. You couldn't be with me on my first birthday without you, but you sent me a gift. Perhaps I have you with me in the form of a yellow rose. Thank you.

Love,

Mom

October 29

Dear Self,

You are reading book after book looking for one paragraph, one sentence, or one word to help you live the rest of your life. You don't have to write a story, a book, or publish a song. You don't have to accomplish some great feat in Jenny's name. All you have to do is get through each day and do the best you can. And, compared to how you thought you might end up if something like this heart-wrenching thing ever occurred, that in and of itself is a miracle and a blessing. She would be happy knowing you are doing your best and being there for her brother. Just try and stay sane. That's all. Trust God with the rest.

Love,

Your Heart

> "Life must go on. No it mustn't, but it surely does."
> –C. S. Lewis

November 19

Mother's spend so much precious time arguing with their daughters. I wanted my daughter to listen to my views and perceptions. She had her own ideas of what her life should be. Suddenly I notice mothers and daughters arguing in stores. I never used to notice. I feel such anguish inside. It's just a dress, it's just a pair of shoes. I want to walk up to them and tell them to hug and go get ice cream. I wish I could tell every mother with a daughter just how beautiful and fragile that relationship is. Treasure it always.

November 29

Dear Jenny,

I can't talk to you in person, but I remember asking God to please let you know what I write to you. Only God and you know. It seems when I get down on my knees, He does help me. I listened to a Christmas tape today. I had to for Jamin, and for you. You loved Christmas. I must pull myself together, so I don't spoil it for others. I am having a positive mood after many days of deep depression and negativity. I will write this now before I go down again. Then when I am down, this may help me.

I will tell myself that I cannot dwell on the fact that if my life had been different, maybe yours would have been as well and you would still be here. I cannot change anything now, so why do I go there? I cannot. If I could have done something to save you, I would have. I will tell myself that your passing was written the day you were born, and God called this girl home to him because He needed her spirit in Heaven.

Why was your purpose fulfilled so soon? Perhaps He thinks you touched many lives and will always leave your mark on the world. I will tell myself that God isn't punishing us. You are in the only place where there is no pain or grief.

God never promises happiness all the time. He only promises happiness and peace in Heaven. We will have our trials and suffering here on earth. All people do at some time or another. We are not exempt.

I will tell myself that I mustn't keep regretting the years we won't have together, but cherish the years we did. We had twenty plus glorious, stormy, spirited, heartwarming, and heartbreaking years together. Thank God I had you that long.

What if I never knew you at all? Would I trade away those years to avoid this unbearable pain? Never. I was chosen to be your mother, and I am honored to have brought you into this world, no matter how cruel or how short.

I will tell myself that, God willing, we will be alright someday, because you have a brother you love, and I have a son I love, and even though you are not here to guide him and give him advice, that he will always remember things you taught him, and that he will be as strong as if you were still alive. I will tell myself that you still are and will never leave us and may even help us to live without you until we meet again. Only God knows when that will be, just as He knew when you would be coming back to Him.

Thank you, God, for my beautiful, spirited daughter. Thank you for her craziness, her kindness, and the forgiving, accepting heart, which is what brought her home to you. Bless you, Bug, and amen to God. I re-read the last few paragraphs. I think I am going crazy.

Mom

November 29

MADD

I attended MADD meetings shortly after our loss. I attended only a few as I found them depressing, and I would be down for days after going. What else would they be? Watching and listening to families in pain years after their loved one's death scared me. Was I going to feel that way five years from now? If so, how could I go on? What about hope, what about healing? Didn't people eventually feel better?

I have the utmost respect for the organization and what it has accomplished. Perhaps I just wasn't ready. I did attend the first few Christmas Vigils for those killed by drunk drivers along with family and some friends. Again...heart-wrenching. My first Christmas without Jenny, I donated her gift to MADD. I received the check back with this note:

Susan,

Even though donations are greatly appreciated, this check was not necessary. So, I am respectfully returning it. We had so many ample donations in Jennifer's name, plus getting her photo as part of the Vigil is something of an honor for us. Please let us do this small thing for you.

Sincerely,

Debbie

December 1

Jenny,

I heard something last night at the Advent service. Pastor said, "Jesus loves you and would never hurt you." I must remember that. It made me cry. I can't go to church without crying. I have to realize how much He loves us. He would never hurt you. He loves us more than anyone. This morning on television a woman said, "Only Jesus knows what is best for each soul." I must remember that as an answer to my constant question "why?" I will tell myself daily. I love you.

Mom

December 18

I was invited to The Compassionate Friends Holiday Candlelight Memorial Service. I did not feel up to attending, but this poem was written on the back of the invitation. It was also written that the first Christmas is the most difficult as it seems like everyone goes on with the festivities as usual. The author wished someone had said something similar to her.

Because I really care about you, I'm not going to pretend and wish you a Merry Christmas as if nothing's happened. Instead, I'm going to reach out to you and tell you that I realize this must be a very difficult time for you. It probably doesn't seem fair that everyone else is smiling and laughing and enjoying the holidays as usual, while your heart is aching. There may be times a favorite carol that used to bring a smile to your face now brings tears to your eyes. You may feel confused, cheated, and even angry...and I wouldn't blame you. But rather than force yourself to fake the holiday spirit, please be honest with your emotions.

Cry, be angry, do whatever it takes to get through this...always remembering that you will get through this. Remember, too, that in time you'll be ready to celebrate Christmas again. And until then, know that there are many people whose hearts are with you, especially now...people who care about you very much and always, always will. –Renee Duvall

December 21

Jenny, it's almost Christmas. Really, it doesn't much matter. The tree is just a tree. It's looks nice but I feel nothing. This is the first Christmas in my lifetime that I have not felt the joy that the holidays bring. Christmas was a big deal when I was growing up, and you know that stayed with me. The tree is for Jamin. I wrote you a song called *Christmas in Heaven*.

That seems to me to be where the true Christmas is. Here, it is shopping, wrapping, baking, and sometimes stress. There have been a few fleeting moments when I have felt the true meaning. That lies in giving and love. I try to remember Jesus and what he did for us as the ultimate gift.

I long for you, and the ache is so deep. Your stocking is hung as always. The only thing in it is your song. I wrote it out and put it in an envelope for you. I cannot leave your stocking empty.

I continue here for Jamin. He is what keeps me earth bound. That and the fact that God chose to leave me here for some unknown reason. I guess I have not yet finished what He needs me to do. I am surely no stranger to death or grief. The other deaths were more kind, if there is such a thing, though they started when I was seven. God gave me a lifetime to grieve and learn to live without my mother. I did find joy again. Grandparents are usually older, and though sorely missed, their death is timely and expected. You miss them and long for those years when they were such a glorious part of life, but once again time is on your side, and you get used to missing them. My father was very difficult because I knew him for forty-one years. He may have lived longer if he had lived differently, but maybe not. Was it his time? This drives me crazy.

Do we have a time? I mourned him deeply, but I had my little family and knew I would find joy again. I knew that time would heal because I was experienced at grief. I just had to cross over that bridge of pain. I didn't know I should rush my grief because an even more difficult one was coming. One that would last a lifetime with no reprieve.

Jennifer, you, this one, I cannot do. I don't know how God thought I could. I hate the phrase God doesn't give you more than you can handle. I cannot handle this. Who could? Maybe He knows I can't. Maybe, maybe,

maybe! I am so sick of maybe. I love Jamin and will stay here to try and make his life as normal as I can. I love you both the same. How cruel to have your love divided between two different planes of existence.

I know I have to be patient. Right now, my only joys are Jamin and your father, and the knowledge that when God chooses to take me, I will die with a smile on my face for I will lay my eyes on you once again. What is hard about being here is that I feel as if I'm already dead. This body merely lives on.

There is one thing I can tell Jamin if he ever reads these words. He is fortunate in that he can see and feel my love for him in these words to you. My love is not different. He can understand what a mother's love is and feel its depth and fullness when he is still alive. How does a mother choose between her only son on earth and her only daughter in Heaven? She doesn't. She has no choice. I do believe there are still miracles on earth because I felt you even after you were gone. I know part of you is alive. A part of you swims through my soul. Thank you for the gift of your presence. I will endure this pain because I did have you.

Always,

Mom

Being called "Bug"

Christmas 1994

Jenny's Grandfather Smith gave her the nickname "Bug." He had a nickname for everyone. I was "Little Toot" due to the fact that I had a t-shirt in the late 60s that had little flags and horns on it. I wore that shirt often. One day, at her grandparent's home, Jenny, age two, was following a fly on the window. She kept saying, "Buggie, Buggie." That was enough for grandpa. She was Bug or Jen-bug the rest of her life. After Jenny's death, or the first Christmas without her, he sent money to his daughter Cathie and asked her to give it to the grandkids at Christmas. Bug was one of eleven. He had already lost a son of his own and later his wife.

Dear Cathie:

Since my gifts are all in one envelope, before passing them out will you all take a minute of silence to remember your mom, Stevie, and my "little Bug."

Happy Holiday,

Dad

December 31

Hi, Jenny,

I am starting the first year that you won't be with me. Right now, I can say you were with me this year. This is the last day of my life I can ever say those words. Therefore, I do not want this year to end. People say, and I say, that your spirit lives and will always be with me. That isn't enough, and that doesn't help me now. I want to feel the warmth of your body. I want to hug my baby, my little girl, my teenager, and my young woman. I want to hear your voice and your laughter.

I want to hear you come through the door, knowing you are now safe at home and I can sleep. I want to see your smile. I want to look at you and say to myself, *how did I make her?* I want to see your cute face, your soft skin, your blonde hair, and your healthy body. When I ask how I could possibly have made you, I must remember that I really didn't. God gave you to me. He had you before and He has you now. You are forever His. I love you. I wish you a Happy New Year in Heaven, Jennifer.

Mom

January 1

Dear Mrs. Smith,

I'm sorry I've not written sooner. Things are so stressful around here. Time is everything. I try to write Jackie as much as possible. She is the only thing that keeps me going. Being here, I've had so much time to think about things. I hate to say it, but things are getting harder for me! I think about Jenny so much; sometimes I find myself daydreaming of all the things we ever did. I'm sure you do also.

I wanted so bad to talk to you on Christmas, but I didn't get to. I thought the sound of my voice would help make you feel closer to Jenny. If I had only one phone call, I would have called you because I feel by talking to you it also makes me closer to Jenny. Talking to Jackie does that also. Does this sound strange?

I've got twenty-seven days until I'm home. I'll be making my first stop at your house. Well I'm out of time. Sorry this is so short. I've got so much to say, but I can't put it on paper. I need to be face to face. I'll see you soon. Tell Mr. Smith and Jamin I said hi. I'll talk at ya later.

Love,

Jesse

January 5

Dear Susan,

I have been going to write to you for a long time, but I tend to put off hard things to do. I hope and pray that the deep hurt from the loss of your daughter will slowly diminish. I know how it hurts, a different hurt like something taken out of my body, when our son Jack was taken so suddenly away, December 14, 1969. I still have a good cry once in a while and can't understand why, but God knows and maybe we will too, one day.

Maybe his work was done on earth; maybe he would have had to go through many troubles or sickness here. When God closes one door he opens windows, perhaps you can look through the opened window and see something new ahead that will help fill the void. You are so talented in music, and after you move and get settled in your new home, you'll feel refreshed. Pray to the Lord to guide and lead you into new interests.

We really have to fight this depression. I know I felt better when I got out and worked again and was among people. May the love of the Lord help you to look to the future and not dwell on the past. Jenny is probably saying, "Mother I love you and miss you but get on with your future, I am just fine."

With the Love of Jesus and My Love and Best Wishes for the Future,

Marion (My Pastor's Mother)

February 6

Dear Marion,

I have been meaning to write you for some time now. It was so kind and thoughtful of you to write me and open up your heart. I cannot tell you how many books I have read on getting through loss. They seem to help for a day or two and then all the misunderstanding and guilt come flooding back, and I must once again pray it away. Every parent feels some amount of guilt in not being able to prevent the death of their child. I seem to travel back and forth between acceptance and asking why, why, why?

Sometimes I feel this pain will never leave me, and I only look forward to Heaven to see Jenny. I know she is happy, and she walks with the Lord. I also know that she knows why she had to go home and that one day we will also. I long for that moment. Until then I trust God allowed what was best for her. It is hard to remember this beautiful, happy girl and think that there would be something in her life that God wanted so much to spare her from. I pray that God will put acceptance in my heart someday, and I will no longer beg Him for answers. If He provided me with a reason, He would have to provide one for every mother who has lost a child before me, and every mother after me.

I think the hardest part is the physical feeling of emptiness and hopelessness. I believe that He did open a door for my family, but we must find out what He has in mind for us. I pray about that often. We will take one step at a time. One book I read said that we must not ask why, but instead ask what now? When I first learned of your loss many years ago, I remember thinking how hard it must have been and wondered how a family makes it through a loss like that. I never thought I would know.

I do know one thing in my heart. My healing lies in helping others. That is where I will find my joy again. God will guide me when the time comes. For the moment, He is keeping me quiet and letting me get used to Jenny's absence. Thank you for letting me vent some of my feelings. One thing that can never be taken from us is our memories. They were our children and always will be. With surviving children we have every reason to be on this earth, but we also have every reason to long for Heaven, for in either place a child we love will be with us. The fact that you have the courage to face the loss of Jack and still have raised such wonderful, kind, and beautiful children is an inspiration to me. Thank you again for your beautiful letter and may God bless you and keep you and yours.

With God's love,

Susie

FEBRUARY 24

Dearest Jenny Bug,

Yesterday we moved. Did I tell you we were moving? I call it my Jennifer Juniper House. I prayed for God to bless our new home. You are in your new home, and your dad, Jamin and I are in ours. I hope you will be able to find us. I know that is quite silly, but I can't shake the feeling. You would love this house, Jenny. It backs up to the woods, and it's a soft yellow. It's not any bigger, just different. Please come and visit anytime you want. I'll know you are here. I promise to plant yellow rose bushes and try to be more proficient at caring for them.

Missing you, Mom

MARCH 18

Dear Mrs. Smith,

It's been a long time since I've talked to you. I tried to call today, but I couldn't get through with your new number. In a few short hours, I will be twenty-one, except the birthday will not be a good one. I can't explain how much I've been hurting these past few weeks. I try not to show it. I am finally realizing that I will never see, hear, or feel Jenny again. The shock is over, and reality is hitting me.

In a couple of weeks, it will be one year. I've got so many things going through my head, and I keep on messing up. Don't mind all my scribbles. I sit and think the dream girl that I always wanted was taken away right in front of my eyes, and there wasn't a damn thing I could do except watch. I've never been so close to a woman in my life. She could make me feel so wanted. God, I miss her! I was walking down the sidewalk today, and I felt lost. My life is no longer complete. I could just sit and stare at your daughter's eyes for hours. I felt that she gave me 100% love, and it was all in those eyes. How can I go on knowing that I will never find a woman like her?

March 26

(Continued)

When Jenny died, there was a hurt right in my heart that I've never felt before. The pain will never go away. Mrs. Smith, I will never forget you or Jenny. It goes through my mind every day; sometimes it's every hour and minute the times we shared. I know I was only with her for a year, but it felt like five.

I think day after day about the last night we were together. There is a part missing from me I will never get back. It's hard trying to study and do everyday things when the last night keeps running through my head. A while back, I thought that everything was getting better, but it's not. Everybody else is going on except for you, Jackie, and me just to name a few. I try to write but it's hard. I don't know what to say. I'm afraid that I might say the wrong thing. Maybe it's all in my mind, but I felt I needed to write you. I got your card you sent me. I know I've been through some hard stuff, but being through it makes me the best. Every day I try to better myself. Jenny always wanted me to do something with my life, and I won't let her down ever. I love all you guys.

Love,

Jesse

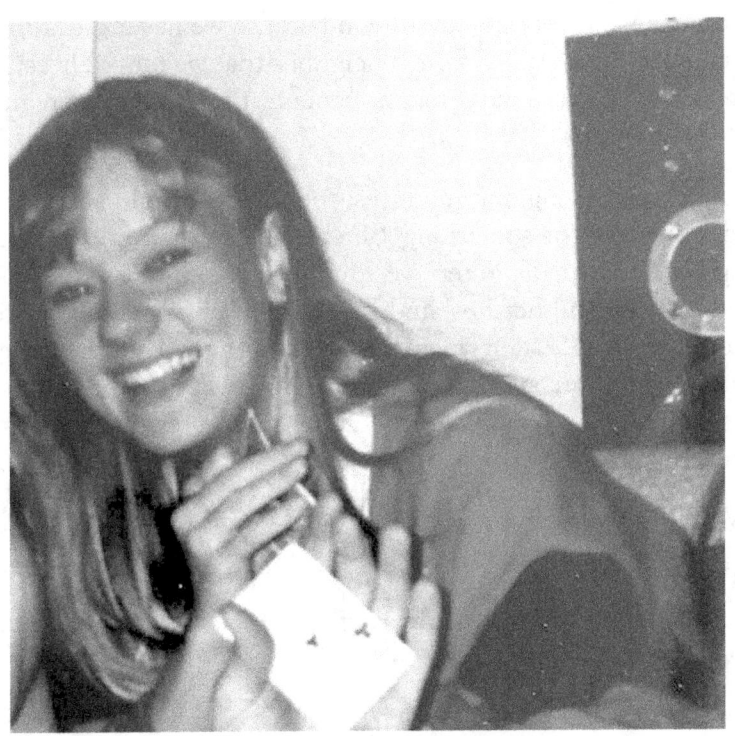

Jenny 1993 - A friend holding the ace

May 26

Dear Jenny,

The strangest thing, at least in this world, happened today. The woman who bought our Regency house called me and told me she had a package that had been delivered for us. When I arrived to pick it up, she came and met me on the porch. I'm glad, as I didn't really want to go inside. She handed me the large envelope and told me how much they liked the house and the neighbors. There was a sadness in her voice. I knew someone had told her about you because we never did. I told her that I was sorry if she heard from a neighbor that we moved because our daughter died. She told me someone came by the day they were moving in [and mentioned it].

[As]we were saying our goodbyes, she turned around and asked If I minded if she told me something. She began to explain that one night, not long ago, her twin daughters were in their room. Their room was your room, Jenny. She and her husband heard them talking and kept telling them to go to sleep. Later when the adults went to bed, the little girls continued to talk and laugh. Again, from their own bed, the parents told them to stop talking. Finally, after scolding them a few more times, they went into the girls' room.

"Why are you talking when you should be sleeping?"

"We have been talking to the angel," the girls replied. "She is all white and glowing and making us laugh," one of the twins replied. "She went away now."

She said she understood now why I had asked them to leave the heart inside the closet that said *Jenny was here.* They left it when they painted. She told me she hesitated to share the story but changed her mind when I stopped by. I like to think it was you Jenny. Once you glowed for me.

Jackie's Best Memories of Jenny

MAY 29

Our last weekend together:

My friend and roommate, Sue, dropped me off at your house. I ran up to your room where you were still in bed. You told me how good I looked because I had been exercising and tanning for Spring Break. You got ready quick, of course, with your perfect complexion and natural beauty. You put your hair in a twisty bun and mine into a French twist with a zillion bobby pins that you said I could keep. It was the first and only time that my hair was that way. Of course, it fell out before we left because my hair is too heavy. Then, I realized that I still had to iron my work shirt. You got everything out for me to do and I started. You realized that I was taking too long and did it for me.

We loaded my stuff into your truck and took off to meet the family for Grandma Ginny's birthday lunch. You had on a white shirt, your black leather jacket, blue jeans, your big black shoes and your black purse with the silver handle. We jammed tunes on your CD player – Janet Jackson, Mariah Carey, and Radiohead – "Creep" and "Paperboy" and "Ditty" – and tried to find the restaurant we were supposed to go to using Grandma's funky (wrong road name) directions. Of course, we had to turn around on Rochester Road after we passed Big Beaver, and after I hopped out and asked for directions. We finally found the place (which was in a shopping center) and then followed the family to a different Thai food place because the other one was too full. My mom, Erin, your mom, G'ma Ginny, you and I were there. We had those funky puffed rice Styrofoam appetizer pastel things and then food that I was kind of allergic to. I gave Erin her "Beauty and the Beast" music box for her birthday. G'ma commented on how your skin was flawless and how utterly beautiful you were (are).

We had to get out of there quick because I had to get to work. You took me to work (more Jams) and waited for me while I changed in the bathroom. Then you took my stuff out to the car and left. While I was at work, you left me a message to call you. When I did, you told me that you were going to pick me up after work and that you, Tara and I were all going to go out after work and then I was going to stay over at your house. You had already called and asked my mom. I was happy and asked Bridgette if she wanted to go. You picked me up, brought in my stuff so I could change, and waited around for me for about a half hour.

Finally, Bridgette and I went in her car, and you and Tara in your truck. We stopped at Amy's (from work) to get her and then went to that girl's (from work) party in Pontiac. We really didn't know anyone but sat down and started playing pyramids and getting goofy. We had fun.

Bridgette started sharing her secrets with us in the bathroom. Amy left with one of the cars early, so when it was time to go, all four of us had to squeeze into your truck. I offered to drive. The three of you laid on each other and I (with the seat all the way back so you guys could have room) sat up on the edge of the seat so I could reach the pedals. We went to Amy's so Bridgette could get her car, but she locked her keys in Amy's apartment. So, we took her to the 7 Eleven to call someone and tell them to pick her up where we work. We drove there and let her out but wanted to stay with her for a little while. So, you, Tara, and I turned on "Ditty" as loud as we could and sang/screamed it and bounced around in the truck.

Finally, we left, and I dropped off Tara, then you told me to go to the Shell station to get some cherry chew. I stopped there while you ran in and grabbed it, and we drove back to your house. We ran up to your room and chatted. We talked about Bill and Jesse and you told me that since I had decided not to get back together with my former guy, I was being my old fun self again and you loved it. You loved the crazy, carefree side of me that he stomped on, and I never realized it.

It got late so you put the chew away and said we'd do it next time. Then we slept together in your double bed, as we had millions of times before. Your alarm went off early because you had to work that afternoon. Of course, you groaned and hit snooze quite a few times before you got up. I slept a little while longer and got up too. You brought up my basket of laundry that I had brought home and didn't have time to do, so you did it for me. I sat on the edge of your bed and folded it and talked to you in your white oxford and tie, khaki pants and low ponytail (our work outfit). You said bye, but then came back up and talked a little more because you were early. Then you said, "Bye, I'll call ya," and ran downstairs.

I watched you get in your truck and back out of the driveway from where I was sitting, and when you pulled away, I got up and looked out your window until I couldn't see you anymore. I stared out and thought about all you had done for me that weekend, with me during my life, and how lucky I was to have you.

Love,

Jackie

Jackie's Best Memories of Jenny

My First Time Alone

(except for my dog)

SEPTEMBER 2

I sit on the porch of our cabin in Harrison near Houghton Lake. It's eleven in the morning, and I am still in my robe, which is nothing new, having my cup of coffee. I listen to the wind blowing through the tall trees in the yard and watch them sway back and forth as if they are made out of rubber. First it starts softly and then escalates to such a force that one would think a storm was brewing. But it quiets down again as the gust of wind settles. I watch this over and over. I love it. It is hypnotic. Jim often sits out here while Jamin and I are inside. I always wondered why. Now I understand that he has the ability to feel completely alone even when others are near. With the rise and fall of the wind, he listens to the trees.

Jim comes up alone often since Jenny died. I could never understand the attraction. It would be lonely, boring, and desolate. But still I have been talking for years about going on a vacation alone, to one of my favorite northern Michigan towns, and staying at a quaint B & B. I imagined I would sip tea on the porch in a white wicker rocker; walk through cute shops and read a beach novel alone in my room curled up on the bed.

My older sister would say, "I don't think you can be alone." I thought she was probably right. But, packing up my car yesterday, along with my dog, I felt like a teenager being allowed to go away without their parents for the first time. But I am alone, driving, stopping for gas at a popular restaurant, and browsing in their gift shop as long as I wished (keeping in mind Pokey was in the car). How strange that this small act would make me feel free.

When I finally arrive at the cabin, I call home to let them know I made it without incident then ride the long dirt road through the woods into town. Funny thing is, I don't know what to do when I get there. I have no desire to browse the shops like I do when someone accompanies me.

I drive back to the cabin but then question what I should do next. I can read one of the six books I brought, hand sew clothes for a teddy I was making, or get the sewing machine out of my trunk for tomorrow. I opt for reading a romance novel and eating pistachio nuts. I find the romance novel next to Jenny's bed. She read it, so I will read the words she read and go where she went. I call Jim back after realizing he left a message, but I call him again later in the evening when the cabin goes totally dark for about thirty seconds and I sit frozen in the chair. He reassures me, and I try to forget about it, though he does say it never happened to him. Therefore, I'm spooked.

I ready myself for bed and decide to sleep in my daughter's rarely used, "dumb up north room." It's a sunny yellow color, a color I thought might add some joy to her time at the cabin. It's also the size of a closet.

Sleep is strange. I dream all night long. I have adventure after adventure as if I have left my body and actually experience these things. I haven't dreamt in so long, most likely due to depression or medication. I am catching up on lost dreaming.

When I wake up, for good, I think it is nine in the morning. Not too bad, I figure. After looking at the old windup clock a few more times, I realize it's ten. I immediately try to justify my oversleeping. I tell myself that I'll jump in the shower and then clean the entire cabin top to bottom. Instead, I choose to drink coffee and eat an English muffin on the porch. Maybe I'll squeeze in the craft show in town, along with my cleaning, sewing, and reading. Maybe I will sit here.

SEPTEMBER 3

I'm so proud of myself. I only feel the pain of loneliness for a few seconds. Also, to my surprise, I don't even go into town. Instead I read, write, and stare. I try in vain to convince Pokey that she doesn't have to be petted or taken outside constantly. It's as if she knows I am zoned out, and she is trying to make sure I'm okay. The craft show is not appealing at all. Being alone makes me feel like I need less. Less food, less stuff, less people.

I don't need much in town my first evening here. I buy very little food. Nothing looks appetizing, but I add cookies because I do need a treat.

One purchase I have to make, and God knows I don't need them, is a set of crocheted and embroidered pillowcases. They are so girly and beautiful. I need to put them on Jenny's bed. I need to dream on them, so I spray them with a little perfume before I sleep. It's okay as it is the only crazy thing I have done yet. At least, I think so.

I do have a one-sided conversation with a rather large spider. Since Jenny passed, I have a hard time ending the life of an ant. I have begun the practice of capturing insects in my house and tossing them outdoors where they belong. The silly spider sits as big as life on my sparkling clean floor as if it's waiting for a fight. I picture one of the legs paused over a gun in a holster. Who will make the first move? I say out loud, "You've been discovered. We have two choices here. You can let me capture you in a cup, and I'll take you outside into the woods and you can have a second chance at life, food, new babies, or whatever. But, me being who I am, we cannot reside in this cabin together. You understand that, right?" The spider does not budge. He is taunting me, testing me. I wait patiently. "Okay," I continue, "hold still because if you try to run for it, I'll only have one choice." I approach him slowly, talking to him softly as if my voice has some sort of hypnotic quality to it. "Boy, you sure are one homely creature," I say. As soon as I get the cup one inch from him, he runs like the wind. He stops again, but I can still see him near the cupboard from which he came. "Listen, Buddy, it's your freedom or your life, your choice," I explain. Buddy takes off again.

I spray half of a can of Raid, or so it seems, under the cupboard and grab Pokey and go out on the porch to avoid the fumes. I try to tell myself that Buddy escaped anyway. After all I tried to save him, right? After talking to a spider, I wonder if one day alone is all it will take to make me crazy. But then I remind myself that I've always talked aloud to myself. Jenny would yell from upstairs jokingly asking, "Who are you talking to, Mom?" "The dog," I would answer. My therapist told me that talking to oneself is therapeutic. It helps one organize their thoughts and put things into proper perspective. It's a sign of intelligence. I was glad to hear that. But I still hope no one hears me.

September 4

This is the first Labor Day I spend alone. Today I sit once again on the porch with Pokey curled up beside me. She is my companion, my sleeping partner, my warmth, and my dinner date. Her contentment feeds my own. I sit and play remembering.

I begin to feel guilt for the times I dragged my daughter up here regardless of her protests. Yes, she did enjoy it a few times when we had company, or she brought a friend. But she was fifteen, and you don't drag a girl that age up to a place in the woods with nothing but her annoying family and a twelve-inch television with three channels. "All I do is sit because there is nothing to do," she would complain. I attempted to provide crafts and go into town often. These things made it bearable for her. Once she brought a close friend and, out of boredom, they ate so many snacks in her room that they actually did get sick. They did laugh about it the next day.

Up north was not Jenny's thing. We started allowing her to stay the weekend with her cousins Jackie and Dave, or her friend Kimmy. We put in a phone so we could stay in constant contact. She was happier but I missed my shopping buddy and up north was not the same for me. One of her many crafts was a sign for her bedroom door. It is decorated with flowers and multitudes of different colors, but it says clearly, *Jenny's Dumb Up-North Room*.

Jenny did come with us when we took a week vacation, but it always seemed to rain and make matters worse. Jamin, who will be eighteen this month, loved it here and still does. However, he had the companionship of his two male cousins right down the road. They had minibikes, then snowmobiles, and now Jet Skis. Jenny had her moment when she finally fell in love with up north, two months before her death. Jesse bought a snowmobile, and they came up that January in 1994. She had finally found her comfort zone.

Jenny had a blast and it was all she talked about. She even came up with the guys while I stayed home. She drove my snowmobile. The excitement in her voice and the joy on her face were exhilarating. She was a city girl turned country. I'm sure this summer she would have enjoyed Jamin's jet ski.

Jesse, the love of her life, was no city boy. One day at home, she was pacing waiting for him to call. "Where is Jesse," I asked. "Oh, probably up a dumb tree," she said sarcastically. He took her hunting with him once, carefully clothing her in the correct camouflage outfit. Oh, I wish I could have seen that. He shot a rabbit and put it in his pocket, but later lost it. I remember her recalling the experience of combing the woods searching for the poor deceased bunny rabbit. If only she had such patience with her family. Young love is amazing.

I snap out of my memories. I will stay one more night to avoid the holiday traffic heading south. Pokey and I are getting much too close. As I write this, she sleeps on the cushioned chair soaking up the sun while I sit in the hard rocker. I don't think a morning will pass that I will be able to get away without giving her exactly six dog biscuits. She stares at me constantly. I guess she knows she's my little girl now.

Tonight, as I go to bed, I do something very good for myself. It's something I don't get to do often at home. I lie down and have a good cleansing cry for as long as I want. There is no one to ask if I'm alright, no one to try to distract me, no one coming over soon or home soon that I have to explain red, swollen eyes to. It is a relief.

SEPTEMBER 5

I wake up and decide I need to go home. I make my coffee and take it out to the porch with Pokey. This time we share the comfortable chair. I sit and stare at the trees again, watching and listening to them sway back and forth. I think about what I have learned about being alone. What can I take with me? First, I did make it and could stay even longer. I read, sewed, cleaned, shopped, and wrote in my journal. I realize I did a little bit of everything I had planned. The only two items I finish are a pillow and a small doll I purchased that looked so much like Jenny. Not the twenty year old, but the six year old. The doll has long blonde braids. I purchased it naked, but I dress it and make a necklace out of small beads and add a small brass angel. I also put a small teddy bear in the doll's hand and give them matching red ribbons. As I am not usually into dressing dolls,

I think of it as part of the grieving process. I realize that I tried to create a tiny Jenny. As long as I realize this, I have not gone mad.

The morning I leave, I wake up, open my eyes, and notice Pokey's head on the other pillow and the covers over her as if I had tucked her into bed with me. How did she do that? She is great company, but how do I get her back into doggie world? She is eleven years old, and I decide she should just enjoy herself. Would I do this again, this experiment of being alone? I do want to go back to the cabin and finish some projects. But should I decide to go to one of those quaint B & B's, I'd have to explain to Pokey, *No Dogs Allowed*.

A Diary of Prozac Days

SEPTEMBER 18

This diary starts at a crossroad in my life. I am attempting to grieve the loss of my daughter without writing her letters. I find it helpful to write letters, but I fear it may not be the healthiest thing for me to do. If the diary doesn't work, I will return to letters. I fear this will sound like a diary. It will be short and to the point. I'm not sure I can write this way. My therapist thinks writing to Jenny may not be helping me.

Never before have I faced such sadness in almost every aspect of my life. Jamin's eighteenth birthday was on the sixteenth. One of his gifts was a framed poem written by his sister. He hugged me when he received it. We also took his cousin Jeff and him to the Rock and Roll Hall of Fame in Ohio. They both loved it.

Today is my mother's seventy-fifth birthday. She passed away thirty years ago. Next month, I will be the age she was when she died. At my current age, she was already dying. I am so lucky to be healthy and alive.

I never did go back to work after Jenny passed, so when I saw my church needed someone to clean, I jumped at the chance. It's hard work but pays well. It's not that I don't want to work; I just don't want to be around people. I also started cleaning for my sister-in-law Cathie and one of her friends. I don't enjoy it, but I'm good at it, and I can be alone. When Aunt Jackie is in Michigan, I clean for her as well. She takes me to lunch and we have a cocktail.

SEPTEMBER 19

My beautiful daughter has been with God for a year and a half. I settled things at home and came up north again by myself. I think I learned to enjoy it, and I need it. The last time it was beautiful. This time it's raining. I don't think I care. Pokey is with me. When I arrived, I went into town to get groceries. This time I watched television, as there are new season shows. Now I will read until sleep comes.

Joanne and her daughter Kristin may come Thursday. Joanne and I struggle together. Since her son Brad's accident and the loss of my daughter, we are partners in pain. Our losses are different, but we react to them similarly. I don't know what I would do without Joanne and her family. I hope all is well at home.

SEPTEMBER 20

It's not a good day. It's cold, cloudy, and lonely. I didn't go into town. I talked too much on the phone to Joanne and my stepmother Ginny. After a shower, I went back to sleep for three hours. I'm reading a book on Prozac because I started taking it for depression. Therefore, I can feel too much or not feel much at all. I notice the difference. It's 12:30 a.m., and I'm still reading. Why does someone who gets so lonely want to be totally alone? Will I ever be the least bit normal again?

SEPTEMBER 21

I went into town to wash all the bedding. I met Joanne and Kristin at US10 and I-75. I bought another Boyd's Bear in the gift shop called *A Mother's Love*. I have a couple now. Why is a grown woman buying teddies? It continues to rain with no end in sight. The dirt roads are a quagmire of mud. On the other hand, it's so nice to have company. Joanne is on the same energy level as me.

SEPTEMBER 24

We came home from up north. It's back to our lives as usual. No more escaping or pretending. I ache for missing Jenny.

The owner of the shopping village where I worked when she died wants me to come back. I wanted to say I would come back, but I left without any commitment at all. He said to name my job and my price.

He was so kind, and I was so indifferent. I had no desire to do anything but survive.

September 25

What a bum day. I couldn't wake up. I wonder what [this Prozac] is doing to my brain. I have too many bad dreams. The newspaper and television report car accidents involving drunk drivers. A pregnant woman is hit on her way to a hospital to deliver her baby. Another is in a coma. My niece, on Jim's side, loses twins at three months. Jim's sister, Cathie, has a friend who has brain cancer at age forty-two.

I managed to get myself over to a friend's house to clean. I am telling myself that I do this for Jim, so I won't ask him for pocket money. I still don't want to get a job where I'm around people and have to act normal and pretend to be cheerful. This pain only gets worse, and I do wonder if it will continue to worsen until I die.

September 26

I have a yellow rose for Jenny. It's the twenty-sixth of the month, and exactly a year and a half now. I went to lunch with my sisters, Carol and Laurie. Some days it's an effort just to get through the hour, let alone the day. I bought some pumpkins and mums and tried to put a little fall cheer on the porch. Jamin came home tired and went right to his room. I'm worried about him. What can I do? He needs a very understanding girlfriend. Please God, he's so lonely.

September 27

I cleaned Aunt Jackie's house today. She irons while I clean. I hear her listening to the radio. I feel good while I'm there as we talk a lot and have a nice lunch. However as soon as I leave, depression pours down on me like a hard rain with no protection. I had an appointment with my psychiatrist on the way home. My therapist sent me to him for medication. We had an interesting talk, and he doubled my medication. It helped so much at first, but it doesn't help now. He said I might feel guilty about the medication making me feel better. Also, he made the comment that

I want to be like my mother and Jenny, not living, but alive. I told him I was afraid of becoming incapacitated with grief.

I volunteered to help with MOPS (Mothers of Preschoolers) at church. I am hoping that, by volunteering, I will feel like I am contributing and getting out of my head and into the hearts of others. Mainly children.

September 28

MOPS went very well. I did my best. I helped watch the babies. I saw my therapist afterwards. Once again, she said I feel guilt for having outlived my daughter and soon I will outlive my mother. She said I must start living because I am alive. It's not that easy.

September 30

It's another low day. How should I describe a day: low, sad, miserable, or depressing? I could say unbearable, but it isn't, because I'm bearing it. I am here, so I guess I am fortunate. I only took one Prozac again. I forget to take two. I can't burn scented candles anymore. I love fall candles, but I seem to be allergic. Maybe soon I will be allergic to life.

October 1

Jim's sister, Cathie, and I walked around the mall today. I came home around 5:00, and no one was hungry. That happens often. Jim went to bed and fell asleep. It was not a good day for us. I don't think we can make it. He's only slept up in our bedroom a couple of times in eight months. I wonder if he stays downstairs to drink.

October 3

I am beginning to feel better on the 40 mg of Prozac. I took Jim to MacDonald's, stopped at the food market, and came home and napped. When I clean a house, I have the overpowering desire to nap when I am done. When I woke up, I rummaged in the basement to find items for the MOPS sale at church. I'm not sure if forcing myself to volunteer so I keep my mind off of my personal issues is helpful or not. I could be avoiding. I had to stay up to do laundry before I could go to bed. I miss not having time to do my own chores and cleaning. It is a dark and dreary day.

October 4

My sister Carol came over early, and we went out to breakfast and then to see some property and a house that she is interested in. It was a pleasant morning. When I returned home, I read (my saving grace) for a while and attacked a box of Famous Amos cookies. Jamin and I love them and, though they are on hand, I try to avoid them. Sometimes I am weak, and I don't care. I think the Prozac takes that willpower away from me. I eat, knowing that I shouldn't, but don't care. I took my items up to the church for MOPS. Again, I am so tired. I fall asleep on the couch very early in the evening. I never used to nap.

October 5

I am trying to keep my head above water. I move too slowly in the morning. I barely made it to my therapy session on time. The weather is horrid, as least in my eyes. I stopped at Taco Bell, which I often frequent these days, and then over to church to help with the MOPS sale. By the time I got there, I just ended up doing dishes in the church kitchen and running the vacuum. It seems I am always cleaning somewhere. I came home, read, and napped again. I spent the evening on the couch. I hate that. I should be sewing. Where is my motivation? Fall, the time of year that brought me joy and hope, just brings pain.

October 6

I cleaned my stepmom Ginny's house today. I want to keep busy, but I end up forcing myself to move my body. I don't get home until 6:00 p.m. I am exhausted. Again, I fall on to the couch for a bit. Then I realize Jamin is home and I perk up. I end up making some dinner for the three of us. As I look at him, I realize that we are such lonely souls. I believe Jim enjoys his aloneness. He, unlike Jamin and me, has his routine and seems to find comfort in the television and falling asleep in his chair, leaving the two of us alone. He sleeps the sleep of a man without a care, but I know that is his perfect escape.

I am so unhappy and hopeless that, coupled with my grief over Jenny, it is almost unbearable. I must learn to look to myself for happiness and joy. Somehow, please God, somehow.

OCTOBER 7

I pray this will be a blessing. I brought home 12-week-old *Uma* today. Jamin named her. She is his. She is a tiny Chihuahua puppy. I don't really know how this happened. Joanne and I always look at puppies. This is the first time in eleven years that I've come home with one.

Uma and I ended up in the "bonding" room at the pet store, and I reviewed my current life. Jamin's birthday was in September, my birthday is coming up, Pokey is lonely, Joanne's son Adam loves her, and I can get her for Jamin. I called home.

"Jamin, I'm bringing you a birthday present."

OCTOBER 8

The Chihuahua's name is no longer Uma. At the moment, it's Lady Bug. I like Copper or Penny. I decided to let Jamin name her. It's amazing how much company arrives when there is a new puppy. My sister Carol, husband Jerry, my niece Erin, Joanne, Adam, Kristin, Cathie, and my niece Nicki. I baked oatmeal cookies for the occasion. She is more popular than a newborn. However, even though she goes out often, the Chihuahua keeps doing her business in the house. She kept us so occupied it didn't seem as sad today. She may be a little terror right now, but will soon be a savior and a blessing. Pokey is so tired. She cannot handle this toddler puppy.

OCTOBER 9

Well the name for the puppy stands at Hannah. All agreed. Hannah stayed with Joanne while I shopped for food with Kristin. Joanne sent her with me so I wouldn't cry.

I cannot shop without tears running down my cheeks as I pass Jenny's favorite foods. Once when I came home to unload groceries, I broke down in front of Jim and Jamin. I cried uncontrollably when I put cucumbers [a favorite of Jenny's] in the refrigerator. I was embarrassed, and they hadn't a clue as to what to do for me. Kristin was a blessing.

OCTOBER 10

I have found that pets are so helpful for depression, and having a puppy that needs your constant attention and loves to fall asleep on your lap is the best medicine. My spirits are lifted, at least for now. I made a nice dinner, and Jamin was home. I talked to one of Jenny's friends that I call *Jenny C* and Jackie. They may go up north with us and bring some videos of my Jenny. I am so scared. Will I be able to watch it? Will it help or drop me back into the depths of grief?

OCTOBER 11

Tomorrow, I will be forty-five. My mother died at that age. My sister Carol came over, and we picked up my sister Laurie and went to lunch. Adam and Kristin gave me a VCR re-winder for my birthday last Sunday. It was so sweet.

I actually talked to some neighbors today before getting ready for MOPS tomorrow. I don't talk to neighbors often, but taking a puppy outdoors draws people to you. I've been doing pretty well since Hannah, and the weather is great. I pray I can keep up this positive outlook. Please outlook, don't leave me.

OCTOBER 12

Today is my second birthday without my girl. I did go to MOPS and all went well. The children sang to me and brought over a cupcake with a candle. Later Joanne and I dropped Brad off for his therapy and went to lunch and to a pet shop. Joanne gave me a pillow decorated with yellow roses and an angel. Jim brought home a dozen yellow roses and a card. Jamin gave me a card and a beautiful basket. Lisa, from across the street, brought me a cake. Jim, Jamin, and I went out to dinner. It was a blessed day from God, and once more Jenny sent me a single yellow rose on a bush. It's my October rose. How does she do that?

October 13

Jim went up north early in the morning and took Pokey with him. After cleaning the church, I followed with Jackie, Jenny C, and Hannah. We left Jamin at home for the first time. He is eighteen, so I shouldn't be worried; but I am. I am still thinking about my time vacuuming the Sanctuary. I was on the last row of pews when suddenly I smelled something beautiful. I looked all around me. No one was there. There were no flowers or candles in sight. The sweet smell seemed to follow me as I looked around for the source. I decided to just enjoy it. I started to vacuum again and realized the lovely smell was completely gone. Of course, I always think of Angels.

October 14

The girls "lazed out" until 1:30 p.m., then Jim and I took them into town for a late breakfast and shopping. We came back and just hung around all evening. It was relaxing. I love this female energy around me. I miss it. We did watch the video with Bug in it. She was so cute and serious. I watched her lips move and her expressions. She came alive. It was so good to watch, but I didn't cry. I felt numb. How could she be so alive there and not be here with us? Jim and the girls went to bed, and I watched it alone. I didn't notice it much when she was alive, but sometimes she looked so much like me.

October 15

Jim woke up early, as usual, and went for a ride into town. The girls and I slept in until he returned. We did a repeat of yesterday with breakfast out and shopping. We visited Tara, a friend of Jenny's, at her mother's resort on the lake. Later, back at the cabin, we took the girls to a local bar for a burger and came back to clean the cabin. We started home, and I felt an emptiness growing inside me. The small part of Jenny I had with me for a few days would soon be gone. However, I was going home to my son.

October 16

I cleaned a house today but had a hard time getting there. I'm tired. I need a day at home alone. I used to have too much time after Jenny died, and now it seems as if I have none. I feel like a failure as a wife and mother. I am so caught up in my own web of grief. How are my guys doing? They won't talk. It's a beautiful day outdoors but dark in here.

> *"Sorrow and the scarlet leaf,*
> *Sad thoughts and sunny weather; Ah me! this glory and*
> *this grief Agree not well together!"*
> –Thomas William Parsons, *A Song for September*

OCTOBER 18

I fell back to sleep after Jamin left for work. I didn't take my sleep medication last night. I'm trying not to take it as often. I'm so fearful of becoming addicted to something. I must not ever depend on anything other than my own strength, or I will never heal. I would only be masking my feelings. There is no escape, and I cannot even try to take that route.

I finally made it to Cathie's to clean around noon. When I finished, I took Hannah to the veterinarian. She may have kennel cough and they put her in steam for 30 minutes. She must have been terrified without me. But we went shopping after and no one knew she was with me. Tiny dogs are awesome.

I made dinner for my guys, and then I sat on the couch the rest of the night. I feel as if I'm wasting precious time.

I still don't feel well. I harbor a fear that I will become ill from the stress and pain of the last year and a half. I've read that can happen to parents after the loss of a child. The chances of illness and divorce are increased. Part of me doesn't care, however, I cannot let it happen. I must be here for Jamin.

> *"The more we anticipate escaping –*
> *the less strength we have to endure."*
> –Ron Dunn

October 19

I sat around all morning until shower time, then went to see my therapist. We talked about my friendship with Joanne. I told her that I felt I was beginning to separate myself from everyone I depend on for emotional support. Actually, I think I'm beginning to look only to myself for answers, or else I want to separate myself from others to avoid any more pain. I stopped on the way home to buy Jamin new pillows. I have to do something to make me feel like a mother.

October 21

I stayed home yesterday. It felt good not to leave the house. I wasted the day and the night. Jim fell asleep at 8:00 p.m. again and never woke up. I envy his sleep. I wonder if he takes something I don't know about. I never see him take or drink anything. I waited up for Jamin until 12:30. I sat on the couch in the living room and watched for his headlights to illuminate the road. As soon as he pulled into the driveway, I ran up to bed. I always wait for him. He never knows.

October 22

I'm getting tired of writing this journal. Nothing changes. It's hard to describe how I feel some days. I could say out of sorts, but that is too simplistic. Nothing satisfies, nothing comforts, and I am jumpy. I really don't know what to do next sometimes. I miss Jenny, and I miss writing to her. I'm trying to do what is best, but maybe this is not best for me.

I did a few minor chores, read, sewed, and watched a movie. I need some energy and motivation. I feel like this Prozac just takes everything from me. I eat for comfort, or maybe I just don't care what I eat. How long can I do this? God please help us all. Jim comes home, eats, and goes to sleep.

October 23

I find that writing is a chore. I am trying to keep this up, so I won't be a quitter. Again, I have very trite information. Again, I wasted my morning. I didn't get to the house I was cleaning until 11:30 a.m. I left at 3:00 and followed my usual habit of stopping at Taco Bell. It's pretty sad that it may be the highlight of my day.

My allergist said I should never be cleaning houses, especially with animals. I had a chest x-ray at the hospital, and I'm very nervous for some reason.

October 24

I don't believe my anti-depressant is working. I cannot even move when I wake up. I don't want to. It takes such effort to even get to a house to clean. I attempt to get all errands done on my way home so I don't have to go out again. I want to hide. I want to disappear so I am not asked to even talk.

I called about my chest x-ray. It was negative, and I was so relieved that I made a nice dinner for a change. The three of us sit at the table, but we don't talk. We are silent because we are all in our own heads and caught up in our shared but separate grief.

October 25

I usually have some positives and negatives in each day. I seem to improve as the day goes on. Jamin and Jim work. I wake up and sit for hours with coffee. I look forward to their coming home, but nothing changes when they do. I talk to Jamin more than Jim. Jim is in his own private world. I'm not sure what is going on there. He sleeps in his chair. I don't wake him. I go to bed without him. It is 12:00 a.m., and I am waiting for Jamin to get home. He went to a concert. I try hard not to worry about him.

October 28

I skipped the last few days. I know I went to visit my stepmom Ginny, and she gave me some birthday gifts, but other than that, it's a blur. Today I cleaned the church for four and a half hours. I like that no one is there. When I am alone in the sanctuary, I feel as if I am alone with God. When I finished cleaning, I sat in the front pew and talked to God about anger. I asked Him to help me get rid of it or to take it from me.

While cleaning I saw a scrapbook about our church. In it was an article about how it's okay to be mad at God and it's supposed to be healing to let it out. God understands. How do I let it out? Do I scream at God?

October 29

Boy, did we get up early. Erin spent the night. Pokey had to go outside. She woke Erin, Jim, Hannah, and me with barking and crying. I felt a burst of energy and did some laundry and gardening. I'm so grateful for any amount of energy, no matter how short lived. Jamin is with a friend tonight. I hope he gets home soon. I asked Jim if we are ever going to have a normal marriage. As usual, he went on the defensive, but later on, he softened. What a stupid question. How does he know?

October 30

I cleaned a house from eleven to three today. That is too long to clean. I stopped at a drugstore to get Neutrogena on sale. I want to help my skin that must be reacting to stress. Though I'm certainly not old, I'm too old for breakouts. I stopped and brought home dinner, but Jamin didn't come home. He went to the movies with his cousin Dave and then spent the night. I wonder if he doesn't like being home with a depressed mother and a sleeping father. While Jim slept, I cut coupons and went grocery shopping. He never woke up.

October 31

October, my favorite month, is done for another year. Now I must think about another Christmas. Halloween was quiet this year. I made my usual Halloween chili because we don't really have a dinnertime on this night. I watched television and Jim slept. We were both angry tonight. I believe we are feeling tension about the lawsuit. We received so many calls from lawyers after Jenny's death. We ignored them all. Finally, we found one on our own to see if we had any rights. I don't think people get much for losing a child. They are not breadwinners, nor do they have others dependent on them. A child's true value exists only in the hearts of the parents.

November 1

I didn't even shower today. I didn't get to Cathie's to clean until noon. I think I did a great job in two and a half hours. I left her two of my pink roses. I stopped at McDonalds on the way home. I have to stop eating this fast food. I used to be so careful about eating healthy. I was proud that I passed that on to my daughter. Like me, she did cheat sometimes.

I did my first walk-in to get a haircut. Jenny's friend cut it. It looks great, and it feels good. I came home and actually cleaned my own house. How can I clean two houses in one day and still not lose weight? Jamin spent the night at Dave's again. I miss him.

November 2

I sat all morning until it was time to get ready for my therapy session. I think it went well. I am learning to speak up for myself. I've never been good at it. Jim calls me a doormat. I tell him that he wipes his feet on me more than anyone. This evening, I took Hannah and went to visit Joanne and Kristin. Her three guys were gone for the evening. My guys were gone too.

November 3

I wasted the morning. I'm getting tired of writing it and tired of doing it. It is becoming a bad habit that I'm not sure I will ever have the ability to overcome. I ran a few errands and then took Hannah over to Joanne's so Adam could play with her. He has a special connection with her as he was with us the night we brought her home. I feel bad leaving Pokey but she, like Jim, is content to sleep. She continues to have seizures even though she has been on medication most of her life. When I am home, she is by my side. She has always been by my side.

Jim and I went to dinner with his sister Cathie and her husband Chuck. On the way to the pub, Jim and I argued about the settlement. I will not touch Jenny's friends or the family of the man who hit her. The lawyer suggested suing the people who hosted the birthday party because people under twenty-one were drinking. Our argument escalated to other issues. We ate dinner, left, and didn't speak the rest of the night.

November 4

Jim got up early and left for up north. I was going to stay home to rest and finish a few projects. Instead, Joanne took me to a craft show. We ran into Cathie and her friend. I had Hannah in a puppy bag. When they asked to see her, I took her out. She urinated down my jeans and all over my boots. Social anxiety? While we were chatting, Joanne snuck away and bought me a small cradle and a doll dress I liked. I promised to pay her back. My interest in dolls, teddy bears, and little girl items concerns me.

November 5

Jamin and I had pancakes for breakfast. It was so nice spending some time with him. I showered, and then Jim came home early. He brought home Joanne's birthday present I had ordered up north. Jim, Hannah, and I went to the pet store to get a larger kennel. We act as if nothing negative ever happens between us.

When I returned home, I cut out six Jenny bears to sew. I made one for a sample and loved it so decided to make them for people I love. Jim's father Ed called this morning. He wants the three of us to come down to Florida after Christmas.

November 7

I try to be normal through the pain. I smile, laugh, and work hard. The mornings continue to be the worst time. I can't seem to pray. I don't know what to say. I start, but then I just stop. It's as if I have writer's block. I am afraid to pray for Jamin because I prayed so much for Jenny.

I cleaned Cathie's house and then baked cookies. Jamin loves it when I bake. I love how it calms me and makes the house smell like home. I'm getting addicted to a television comedy that takes place on Nantucket Island. It makes me want to run away and live in a tiny half cape on the ocean. I dream of it often.

I gave Hannah her first bath. The dogs seem to be getting used to each other. I miss my Jen so much. I feel such a deep longing for her. The hole in my heart burns. I miss Jamin too. He's never around. My niece Jackie turned twenty-three today.

November 8

I met my sister Laurie at her church to listened to a guest speaker and bought her book on prayer. I used to think that prayer really worked until Jen died. Maybe I didn't pray correctly. Maybe God didn't listen because I wasn't worthy. Perhaps I prayed too much. I speculate. I must read her book soon and try to pray.

November 9

Today we had a Teddy Bear Picnic for the children at MOPS. It was total chaos but the children had a wonderful time. Planning events like this gives me a sense of purpose and takes me out of my own thoughts. Helping others is very therapeutic. I do believe God knew that might be my path to healing.

November 10

Joanne and I decided to go to Ohio to visit a friend of ours. We took Hannah with us. It was a long drive and we shared the driving. It was so good to finally get there and the three of us stayed up talking until the early hours of the morning. It was so healing for both of us. We needed that break from our routines and our heartache. I had never been to this house before and actually got lost in the dark upstairs in the middle of the night. I had turned on the light in the bathroom and turned it off before opening the door. It was one of the most frightening experiences as it was pitch dark. I just sat down and prayed until I found my way back to my room. Hannah made a noise which led me to her. Our friend was a wonderful hostess and it was a pleasant escape. We ran into a horrible snowstorm on the way back to Michigan. I got lost in Detroit. I vowed I would stay home and avoid the stress. Grief, all by itself, is hard enough.

November 13

I stayed home all day and slept for half of it. I cannot stop thinking of Jenny even for one minute. Perhaps spending time with my friend's daughter triggered me. Sometimes I feel as if I am living in a dream because it's the only way I can survive. I pretend life is one big movie or a novel, and I'm only watching or reading. I think I will always be this way. Jamin is at Dave's again. Jim and I had a quiet evening. We all survive in our own way.

November 14

I cleaned Cathie's and then rushed home to change, take out the dogs, and get over to the shopping village where I used to work to meet Aunt Jackie. She and I walked around, talked, and then met my sisters and their children at a restaurant in the village. I actually saw Jamin there. We all had a great time. I came home and found out that Jesse is engaged. It was a shock. I so want him to be happy. He deserves that so much. Someone please explain that to my aching heart. It aches for Jenny's loss of love. I start getting to the top of the deep hole I live in, and then something kicks me back in. She is truly gone. The love of her life has moved on. Tonight I had no block when it came to prayer.

November 15

I couldn't sleep last night. I had anxiety attacks over and over. I went over to clean Aunt Jackie's house but was very late. I did cheer up on the way. I talked to God. I am happy for Jesse. Jenny would want him to be happy. It only makes the reality of it all hit a little harder. I tell myself it's not a big deal. It's to be expected. I have no daughter, no marriage, and my son rarely talks. I will fight this. I will survive with God's help. I do have fleeting moments of hope. I hold on to those with all my heart and soul.

November 16

I am getting tired of this journal. I want to stop. It doesn't help. As I have written a zillion times, it was not a good day. I don't know if there will ever be one. I fear the future. Jenny is gone, and Jim and Jamin will not open up to me. I have bought them grief books, one for a father and one for a sibling. They haven't touched them. I am worried about Jamin. I can tell he is lonely. My little family needs help badly. What can I do?

Tomorrow I am taking Jackie out to lunch for her birthday. We are taking Jenny's picture and a poem to MADD for the candlelight vigil in December. Now prayer is my only hope.

November 17

Jackie and I took Jen's picture and poem to MADD. Then we had a nice lunch. We went to the same place Jenny took her friends on the last day of her life. We walked around the mall all day. Jim and I went to dinner later and had a huge fight. I'm pretty sure he is drinking. I wanted to leave for the night, but Joanne wasn't home and the snow was coming down hard. Our life is coming down hard.

November 18

I stayed on the couch until 4:30. I then took a shower and rented two movies. I will not feel sorry for myself. I will not have a pity party. I'm just resting. It's Saturday.

November 19

Joanne, Kristin, and I went to the movies and saw *Home for the Holidays*. It was refreshing. On the way home, we stopped at Kmart and shopped too much as usual. It seems to be cheering us up, but it is dangerous. Jim and I made up. I completely backed down.

November 20

I cleaned a house, and then my sister Carol and I went to visitation for our friend Tracey at the funeral home. He had lived in our neighborhood. We both babysat his daughter when she was young. He would drop her off and then have me fasten a man's ID bracelet on his wrist. He always smelled good. He was friendly and kind. Jenny and his daughter looked so much alike, and they had a good time together.

Tracey died of a brain tumor at forty-six. We saw his wife and daughter at the funeral home. When I hugged his daughter, she smelled like Jenny, and the tears started. I also saw the friend Jenny was driving the car for on the night she died. It was a shock. I haven't seen her in a while.

November 21

Joanne and I went to Kristin's school to watch her do line dancing. She was adorable. I brought Adam home with me to play with Hannah while I did some cleaning in my own house. I took him home after dinner and cried for Jen all the way home. Like the shower, the car is a safe place to cry. I wish I had windshield wipers on my eyes.

November 22

I spent time with Carol and Erin today. We had a good time shopping and eating. I went to see my psychiatrist, and he increased my meds once more. How much medicine must one take to lessen the horror of grief? There is something to get me through the day and something to help me sleep at night. My depression has not gone away. I'm just numb about everything else. Jim and I ran errands together tonight. Tomorrow is Thanksgiving. I keep forgetting.

November 23

I did some more cleaning for myself today. I then cooked and decided to color my hair. I found a few greys. It felt good to do that. Laurie hosted Thanksgiving, and we had a nice dinner. Jamin brought his cousin Jeff home with him. I love when my nieces and nephews come over. It cheers me up, and I feel more like I have a family.

We decided to let the guys have fun so Jim, Hannah, and I went to see Joanne and Ross. I'm always asked to bring Hannah. I felt close to normal for a little while. Thanksgiving. Thanks be to God.

November 26

I went to church today. I got brave and sat in the front row. I never sit in the front. I'm not sure why I did that. Was I telling God that I'm not going to be timid about my grief and my faith? I'm sure I just had a burst of courage. I try to help Joanne by spending time with her younger children. Brad needs her. I picked up Adam and Kristin, and we went to see *Toy Story* and out to eat. Then we bought candy. Kids are the best therapy.

November 27

I was supposed to clean a house today, but I didn't make it. I couldn't get out of bed. I'm getting exhausted fighting depression. I had a few good days, and I feel like I used up whatever burst of courage and energy I had. Perhaps it's a letdown from the holiday. I must keep fighting until I beat this. I can let the light go out of my eyes from the agony I feel, or I can choose to let my eyes shine even brighter. It's my decision. I just won't make it today. I finally got moving by giving myself a pep talk and called Joanne. She, Brad, and I went out to eat.

December 4

Again, how many times will I write this? It has to stop. I couldn't get up again. I did finally move because I had to take my guitar to a friend's house so she could borrow it. She sang at Jenny's funeral. I then went and cleaned a house for three and a half hours.

I got ready for Jenny's night at MADD's Candlelight Vigil. It is excruciatingly sad, but something I must do. So many young, vibrant people have their lives snuffed out or put on hold due to drunk drivers. Many of my family members came. There were too many sad souls in one place.

December 7

I got to stay home again today. My Christmas shopping is done. Yesterday I bought a book called *We Don't Die* by George Anderson. I saw it on my niece's bedside table while I cleaned. Perhaps it helps her deal with her cousin's death. I am excited to stay in and read. I read every day. I realized I have another George Anderson book called *Our Children Forever*. I am fascinated. Is it possible? His stories seem to help grieving parents.

December 8

I am home again. I can't believe it. I did take Joanne to pick up their new van for Brad. Jamin has his ACT test in the morning, and I must clean the church. Jackie and I will take a Christmas wreath we made to Jenny's tree in the park.

December 9

It is highly unusual, but Jamin and I were up at 6:00 a.m. I made him a good breakfast and took him to his ACT testing. I left from there to clean the church. I've never arrived there so early. I cleaned for four and a half hours. I drove home, picked up Jenny's wreath and met Jackie for lunch. We had a nice talk, and then went to the park and attempted to tie the wreath to the tree. I hope it stayed on. I will have to keep checking. Jackie stayed until late in the evening, and we made popcorn. She helped me put lights on the tree. I don't want to decorate. My house is a total mess. I love my niece/daughter. We comfort each other.

December 10

I have absolutely no idea who I will be when I wake up. I was going to go to church but felt like I was having a nervous breakdown. I was shaking and overwhelmed. I looked and thought about all I should do, and I couldn't do anything. Jim came home and helped clean the kitchen while I did the floors. Pokey urinated on my bed for the second time since we have had Hannah. She is jealous and trying to get my attention. I needed a puppy, but Pokey didn't. I'm going crazy. My brother Nick is coming in from North Carolina soon.

December 18

My brother arrived on the sixteenth. We've been visiting with family members and talking a lot. I wish he could be happy. I don't think he enjoys being happy for long. As soon as he gets his life settled, he finds a way to unsettle it. If I weren't struggling so hard in my own life, it would be easier to empathize with him. I cleaned two houses today. Jim, Nick, and Jamin had dinner ready when I got home. I love them.

December 24

I practiced my music for the Christmas Eve services. I've sung at most Christmas Eve services since Pastor first asked me to sing *Oh Holy Night* almost twenty years ago. I took Jenny's memory candle to Carol's and tried hard to focus on the present rather than drift back into sadness. I went to church and sang *Christmas in Heaven*. My family was with me. Later

I went back to the candlelight service alone. I prayed that I wouldn't cry. God answered. The evening ended singing *Silent Night* with my favorite singing pal Joel. God blesses me through music. I hope it blesses others.

December 25

It was the second Christmas without our Bug, and the first Christmas in our new home. I thought it would be slightly less painful. When the three of us sat together to open gifts, there was an obvious presence missing in the room. There was a voice that was aching to be heard and a form that was longing to be seen. For secretly, in each of our hearts, we felt her there with us.

We enjoyed our gifts and we were thankful for each other. We ate breakfast, we smiled, and we talked. You would think we were normal. We went through the motions, but I knew it would never be less painful with the passing of time.

December 31

It's New Year's Eve again. Jim said if I got up early, he would go grocery shopping with me. I actually did. We shopped and had breakfast out. We came home around noon, and I got a lecture on spending. I know I do. I don't want to, and I don't buy things I don't use. I buy things that remind me of Jenny. I finally feel like fixing up this house and trying to make it cozy. I don't buy big-ticket items. I buy small things. A friend called me $3.50 Sue. Joanne and I find it pleasurable to shop even if we don't buy anything. One more pleasure gone. I gave Jim my credit cards. I feel like a child being punished.

I made a steak dinner for Jim, and Jamin stayed at Brian's. Cathie and her husband Chuck stopped by, and we watched *Harold and Maude*. I hadn't seen it in a long time and had forgotten how much I loved it. I notice every movie about love. I try to remember what it felt like and how it usually changes one for the better. I must start 1996 on a positive note. I must exercise, clean, read, sew, eat healthy, and forgive all. Even as I write this, I am afraid of the New Year.

1996

January 1

I feel like I must catch up on the days I didn't write in December. I can't remember any of it. I just remember being tired and depressed. I guess that's it in a nutshell. Today, New Year's Day, Jim tried to help me set up a Franklin Planner he gave me for Christmas. He uses one and explained the benefits. I didn't grasp it, or perhaps I didn't want to. I write something down that needs to be done, I don't feel like doing it, so I move it to the next day, week, or month. I'll try it.

Carol and Erin came over to visit, and my brother called. Jamin was home, and his friend John came over to eat. We watched G*host*. It was a gift from Jim. It was one of Jenny's favorite movies. I enjoyed it so much. Of course, I cried. The idea that your loved one can stay with you even if you don't see them is so bittersweet. They try to get your attention, but all you feel is grief and pain. I loved and hated the ending. I wanted the ghost to stay.

Today we found out the Jim's father has three to six months to live. God bless him.

January 2

Jamin is hanging around with his friend John more often. They actually stayed and ate with us. I exercised for twenty minutes, did dishes, and went to bed to read and write. I'm thinking of writing a book called *My Only Daughter* or *Longing for Jenny*. I doubt all this writing will ever come to that. I also wrote a letter to Jim's dad. It was a good-bye letter for me, though I didn't imply that. I'll see him again, but I would never say the same things. I'm better at writing than talking.

January 3

Jamin and I hung out today. We went to Penney's to use a gift certificate from Jim's dad. I got a Cherished Teddy called Ed and Mary (Jim's parents), and Jamin bought a couple of shirts. We had lunch at Ruby Tuesday's. I like to go to the last place Jenny ate. We talked about so many things including relationships. He respects women. He really opened up, and I felt very proud of my teenage son and his mature beliefs. He is usually so quiet that I'm never sure how he feels about anything. It made me feel happy.

January 5

I'm not fond of diaries. I feel it's just an obligation. I'm staying up too late reading and waking up much later than I would like. Jamin and I took down Christmas decorations and then had tea. All of a sudden, he is here. We took newspapers up to the church as they get money for paper. He is being so kind and attentive, and I am not going to question why. I'm just going to enjoy it for now. Later Jim, Jamin, and John went up north. It is too cold for me. Joanne and I hung out tonight. We did just a *little* shopping and had a good time. I adore her. I thank God for such a special friend.

January 7

I woke up very depressed and laid on the couch with the dogs. I prayed for energy but didn't move until two o'clock. God answered my prayers because Carol came over and helped me for two hours. We cleaned and then watched a movie. God bless her. Jim and Jamin came home from the cabin.

January 8

I cleaned a house for four hours. I stopped and got Taco Bell for Jamin and me. It was lunch and dinner. I busied myself with my own household chores until midnight. As usual, I stayed up to read. I'm reading *The Hiding Place* by Corrie Ten Boom. I am drawn to books about suffering and hope. Also, I don't seem to be happy unless I have two or three books going at once.

January 10

I stayed in bed until eleven. I hate that. What can I do? I then sat and drank coffee for another hour just to get myself moving. My couch faces the woods. I stare at the trees. I am so grateful for those moments of time when I have energy and a positive outlook however few and far between these gifts may be.

I showered and started laundry. I know I am grieving, but I also know I hate my marriage. I've always been slender, so I hate my weight. When I'm eating, I don't care. Why can't I fight for these things? I hate this dullness and emptiness. I went and bought some things for MOPS and decided to get some Ginseng. I'm desperate.

January 11

Days can start out well but not end well. In getting ready to leave for the late MOPS Christmas party I dropped all the cupcakes I made on the floor. I had to remove most of the frosting but made them presentable. Then I locked my car keys in the house and had to wake up Jamin. I've read that these types of things happen to people who are grieving. We aren't careful or cautious and are more prone to accidents. On the first anniversary of Jenny's death I fell down the stairs and tore a ligament in my knee. I must stay alert.

January 12

Carol and Erin invited me out to lunch. Afterwards we went back to her house for tea, which is always pleasant. Erin and I left to get some movies and she spent the night. Carol has always shared her girls. My mother shared her children with her sister, Aunt Jackie, as she had no children of her own. Having Erin here gave me the push I needed. I put the last of Christmas away. Jim went up north after work.

January 13

It's Saturday. I got up early and made Erin breakfast. Having her here brings a sense of normalcy to my life. Carol came over to get her, and we had coffee together. I must remember Isaac Newton's theory, *What goes up must come down.* I know it won't always be this way, but it is for now. After they left I watched *Mad Love* and then crashed on the couch until three o'clock.

Jamin got me going again. He invited me to go with him and his friend John to trade in his old guitar. We then went and got tuna melts. When we arrived home, we watched *The Babysitter*. Books and movies get me by. John spent the night. I had *two* kids in the house. I had such a nice time with Jamin, my boy. Jim is staying up north and going to work from there on Monday.

January 16

I had another house to clean. Today was Cathie's. I picked up a movie and take out for Jamin and me on the way home. Movies seem to be something I look forward to. I live in someone else's world for a few hours. Sometimes I get so caught up in them and become very emotional. Jamin had an interview where Jim works and starts his new job tomorrow. I'm so happy for him. A new start.

January 17

I made pasta shaped like angels for dinner. Jim stopped for a beer with a friend. My psychiatrist said I should start doing things for Jenny in her memory. I want to so badly, but I just can't get moving; and I don't even know what to do. I already do so much volunteer work at church. When Jim got home, he and Jamin went shopping for work clothes. Some much needed father/son time.

January 18

I'm starting to realize I am addicted to books and movies. I stayed up to read much too late and couldn't get up. I did talk to my stepmom Ginny and we decided to meet at the theater to see *Sense and Sensibility*. Before I met her, I did a few chores and watched *The Man Who Climbed a Hill and Came Down A Mountain*. I can't think of a less destructive way to escape from grief and loneliness. I rented another movie for tomorrow. Whatever gets me through?

January 19

Somehow, I managed to squeeze in *First Knight* in the morning before packing and picking up the house. I headed over to the Troy Marriott for an overnight prayer seminar called *Abiding in the Vine*. I met Laurie, we checked in, and had a nice dinner. Later we went down to the pool and met Carol, my pastor's wife, Judy, and her daughter-in-law Penny. Judy led us in prayer, and we headed to our rooms for rest and reading.

JANUARY 20

Carol, Laurie, and I got up at 6:45. All three of us had to shower and be down to the seminar by 8:15. We had a small meal and started listening to music and speakers. Prayer is the key to Jesus, peace, and joy. I've always prayed but I have never devoted myself to prayer. I feel if I can pray effectively that things can change for the better. As Corrie Ten Boom said, "Jesus can turn loss into glory." When I arrived home, Jim and I went out to dinner and had a pleasant time.

JANUARY 21

I got up and prayed the first thing this morning. Jim left to go shopping, and I finished *The Hiding Place*. I fell in love with Corrie and Betsie ten Boom who helped many Jewish people escape during the Holocaust. God bless their beautiful souls. They were such Godly people. I loved when Betsie said, "There is no place on earth safer than another place. It all depends on God's will." I realize it was time for God to call Jenny home. I trust Him. I also trust Him to lead me in the direction to turn my loss into glory for Him and Jenny. Corrie wrote, "Never be afraid to trust an unknown future to a known God." Both Jim and Jamin were so sweet today.

JANUARY 23

Today wasn't as successful as yesterday. I have to remember that sometimes I will take four steps forward and two steps back. I can live with that as long as I move forward slowly. I didn't do my Bible study, but I did pray. After Jamin left for work and Jim for Ohio, I went back to bed. I slept in late and then put on a baseball cap and went to clean Cathie's house. I sat all evening watching television and talking on the phone, which resulted in going to bed late. Jim's father is having out-patient surgery tomorrow to help with his jaundice. Jim needs to come home.

There is a winter storm watch. Please God, I'm trying. Don't let me slip back into my hole.

January 24

I was supposed to go to Ginny's to clean today but the weather was doubtful. As usual, I sat around all morning. I put on my baseball cap and comfort clothes and hung curtains in the dining room. I then made dinner and spent the rest of the evening getting ready for MOPS tomorrow. Now I'm not even bothering to shower in the morning. I need to get back to my Bible study. Why can't I stay on track?

January 26

I woke up at eight this morning, which I consider great. I was sitting and enjoying coffee on this peaceful Friday and thinking about what to do around *my* house for a change. I was feeling quite relaxed. Then I received a call from the church. I must clean today instead of Saturday. I cleaned from two until eight o'clock. I'm so very tired right now. My body is aching all over. Thank you, Lord, for getting me through. Jim was sleeping when I got home and never woke up to say hello or have something to eat.

January 28

I woke up early again. Jim was fixing breakfast when I went downstairs (bless him). I started to help and almost fainted for the second time this week. I was still resting when Jackie came over. She is getting into religion once more, and I'm so happy for her. She thinks I should send *Christmas in Heaven* to Mariah Carey. Jenny loved her. I used to hear her singing along with Mariah up in her room.

February 1

Today I attended a MOPS meeting about an upcoming Focus on the Family convention in Denver. I would be able to meet Dr. James Dobson. I didn't mention it previously because the entire idea seemed much to overwhelming. Too much interaction.

February 5

Maybe I'll take a clue from my mother and burn this before I die. Perhaps she had something good in hers. If I don't write about the day I just talk constantly about Jenny. I am lovesick for her. I hurt inside as if something is eating at my insides. Sometimes it feels like I've been shot in my stomach. I cleaned a house today and then ran errands. I got the car washed and made a good dinner. I actually ironed, which I hate, and kept busy all evening. I'm learning.

February 6

I cleaned another house today. Why do I continue to do this? I'm tired of writing that I cleaned a house. I'm good at it and I don't have to be around people. I also have flexibility. I came home tired but was committed to attend a hair treatment talk at a local salon…The woman who spoke was 50 plus and she seemed amazing and looked so healthy. Although I'm forty-five, she seemed so much younger than me.

Afterwards, I told her my hair was thinning due to stress and grief. I told her about Jenny and how I don't take care of myself anymore. She took me to a quiet spot and prayed for me, and it felt like a miracle. Many things seem like miracles for a short time. Perhaps I don't embrace them, so they don't hold. Every time something feels like a blessing, I have hope that the worst is over. I know better.

"The only way I thought I would feel better was to do something worthwhile that I might not have done if she didn't die."

February 7

I watched Erin today. Tomorrow is her sixth birthday. Jenny adored her and used to let Erin brush her long blonde hair.

I saw my psychiatrist in the evening. He said that I don't want to be happy because I think Jenny can't, but that my being so miserable makes her sad in Heaven. I sometimes wonder if they really think before saying something. I don't think Jenny is unhappy where she is.

I try so hard. but I just can't feel well. I have my moments. One day is decent and the next day is horrible. I shopped for MOPS supplies and stayed up until 1:00 in the morning getting ready for the Valentine party.

FEBRUARY 8

I got up early and was at the church by 8:50 a.m. The MOPS party was great because I only had eleven children. I left for home and ran out of gas before I got out of the parking lot. Thank God I was still at church. Again, I am being careless. Carol had just arrived, so I took her van to see my therapist. She said, "You are not going to wake up one day and be okay. You have to make yourself live." What does she think I'm doing? I'd like to make myself do a lot of things.

FEBRUARY 10

It's Saturday so I did some afternoon cleaning in my own house. In the morning I sat in a catatonic stupor. I didn't get motivated until I talked to Joanne. Jamin went to Purdue University with his cousins. He's 18 now and I'm glad he's having some fun. Jim and I met Cathie and her husband Chuck for dinner. Jim and I loved each other for the first time in ages. It makes one feel human again. However, I still went to bed alone.

FEBRUARY 11

Jim and I went to the mall today. We had a great time, and I bought him lunch. Jim bought me a pin and a trinket box with yellow roses on them. They are beautiful. I love these friendly, peaceful days. Jamin is still in Indiana. Cathie and her family went to Florida to help her dad. Jim and I leave for Florida on the seventeenth. Ed needs us.

FEBRUARY 12

Jamin just phoned, and he is on his way home. Jim and I met at the lawyer's office and closed Jenny's case. Thank God it is over. During questioning, the drunk driver's friends stated that he left the bar at closing time. During legal depositions, they changed their story and said he left around 10:00 p.m. Though disheartening that they would lie when a young girl died, it doesn't really matter. All they did was keep us from getting money from the bar, which was the lawyer's suggestion. I don't care, as it wouldn't change a thing. The magic of living is gone anyway. It's death money.

FEBRUARY 14

Happy Valentine's Day. It used to be a special day in our house. I'm trying to keep it up. I must feel guilty when I sit and do nothing because today, I got moving. I ran five errands before cleaning a friend's house. I bought a card, a fresh yellow rose, and a Cherished Teddy for Jenny. I bought candy and cards for Jim and Jamin. Two years ago, today, I bought Jenny her first Cherished Teddy. We went to dinner with her and Jesse. After dinner, they went to the theater to see *The Getaway*. I will never forget. Even though, I still cleaned until 8:30 p.m.

FEBRUARY 26

Time has passed because Jim and I left for Florida on the seventeenth. My memory for days past is so poor. I think it may be that my thoughts are focused on Jenny to the point that making my way through the day is automatic. I don't think my actions register in my brain when I am thinking of her.

Jim's father Ed is very weak and doesn't eat much. It was so hot in Florida, but we didn't dare put the air conditioning on, as it would be too cold for Ed. I cleaned, made food he might eat, and did laundry. One day Jim went out and came home with a yellow rose. What a sweet thing to do. We got along very well in our shared quest to take care of his father. Aunt Jackie came up from Estero, and she took me to the Tarpon Springs Sponge Docks. Our time together was quite special. I can't believe she drove all that way to spend four hours with me. She is so kind that surely God sees her heart.

Every day, Jim got his father up early and they went to see his doctor at the hospital. Ed was supposed to have out- patient surgery and four times they sent him back home. He was so sad and disappointed. Bless his heart. He asks for so little. I wish I could have gone up to him, held his hand and talked of Heaven. He seems so afraid. I often think that dying is like being born. A baby leaves a tight, warm, dark cocoon for a cold, spacious, bright room. Fortunately, we don't remember our fear or shock. When we pass on it seems as if again, we are thrust into a different realm after being used to our comfortable surroundings. I often say that I look forward to death and being with Jenny; however, I know I would still be afraid of the transition.

We left Florida at 5:45 a.m. We woke Jim's father to say goodbye. I hugged him and said, "I love you." He said it back, which is unlike him. He then said, "Goodbye, Haas," to Jim. That was his chosen nickname. Ed would be alone only for the morning. Jim's brother Bill and his family were set to arrive in the afternoon.

FEBRUARY 27

I cleaned a house today then rented a movie called *Joni* about Joni Eareckson Tada and how God helped rebuild her life after she was paralyzed in a diving accident at seventeen. I seem to be drawn to these types of movies and books. I zone right in on them. It is my guess that I find comfort in the courage of others. I am drawn to the many ways they fight and attempt to overcome adversity. It's as if I am doing research. These stories lead me to believe that it is possible to survive the devastation life can throw at you. Perhaps they tell me I may be normal one day.

FEBRUARY 29

Today I packed for Colorado and the MOPS Convention. I'm getting nervous about going. I knew I would. I, who loved being around people before 1994, now become lost in a crowd. My body reacts as if everyone I meet is happy and lives a normal life. My mind tells me that's ridiculous, but I fear the feeling, nonetheless. I am more comfortable in small groups and with people who already know me. I know that part of it centers around one question. *How many children do you have?* I stopped to take a break and turned on Ricki Lake. The show was about communicating with loved ones who have passed on. Even when I'm not seeking them out, these programs find me.

March 1

Today I left for Colorado. I am not used to traveling by myself. Especially places that require getting on a plane. I had to get up at 2:30 a.m. I didn't sleep long or well. I picked up a few ladies for the trip. The flight was pleasant and the mountains snowcapped and breathtaking. In the beauty and vastness of the earth, why would one unimportant person and her grief matter to God? There are things much worse than grief in this world. Though I need Him, I guess I would rather He deal with those who have no hope.

Our group went to *Focus on the Family* in Colorado Springs. It's founder, Dr. James Dobson, has created such an amazing place with so many resources to discover. Of course, I bought more books. At the hotel, 1,700 women gathered for the General Session with inspiring speakers and talented musicians, but I could not shake the feeling of being so alone.

March 2

I was up early and had a small breakfast with my pastor's wife, Judy. Judy and Pastor have been blessed with six children. Jenny and their son Michael wanted to go to a dance together when they were thirteen years old. Pastor and I discussed it and decided they were too young. I wonder what would have been different if we had given them our blessing.

My most memorable session was *Personal Growth*. I actually spoke out loud during question time. The leader's topic was *Loving Yourself*, and I was pulled into her thoughts. I asked about feeling blame for Jen's passing. She stated, "We have to talk," and we did. I didn't have much time, but I left her feeling a sense of peace. I know it won't last long, as it never does; but I'll hold onto it for now, and as long as I can, before the black cloud descends on me once more. She'll be one of the many people who come into my life and my searching: authors, speakers, singers, and friends. They will all touch me, and in some way linger inside. It's all part of healing.

Some of us shopped the convention store. There were books, books, and more books. You never know which one will bring comfort and healing. Which book will hold the magic words that will end all the misery? Though being here is slightly painful, it is a distraction. I see so many young mothers who are enjoying their time away from home and the female connection. I want to scream out and tell them to cherish every moment with their children, no matter how stressful or frustrating. Never take them for granted, as they are the most precious blessings in your life.

March 3

God is here. The General Session started at 8:30, and our group attended together. The session was mesmerizing. I was so moved and affected beyond belief. I spoke with some of the speakers on a personal level, and Judy was by my side. I know what I must do now. God made it very clear to me. When?

March 4

We all got up early and readied ourselves to leave this beautiful place. Everyone appeared to be carrying some sadness, though they spoke of the excitement of heading home. The plane came down in a severe snowstorm at the Detroit airport. We had a long drive home and we arrived very late. Funny, but I wasn't the least bit nervous.

March 5

It was quite late when I woke up. I didn't see Jim or Jamin when I got home. During my morning coffee time I called them and so many others to tell them I was home safe. After dinner I went over to my sister Carol's to help with her basket open house. When I got home, I heard the news that Ed was quite sick. Jim and I will try to go to Florida this weekend.

March 10

I left for Florida this morning. I traveled alone as Jim had a work class in Reno, Nevada. I arrived around five, and Cathie, Lynn, and I stayed with Ed. Lynn is a nurse, which helped Cathie and me feel more comfortable. His son and daughter-in-law are in a hotel nearby. He is still conscious but dying. He said, "Little Toot," his nickname for me. I cried. We didn't get much sleep.

March 11

Ed left this world at 10:45 p.m. Bless his gentle heart. Cathie, Lynn, and I were just getting to bed. We had a baby monitor in our room even though he was close by. We heard a loud breath, his last, and Lynn went in and confirmed that he was gone. We comforted each other as best we could and then made some calls.

Earlier in the day, as he lay dying, I kneeled next to his bed and prayed. I knew it was all I could really do for him. When Cathie's brother and his wife arrived, we went in to sit with him and say our goodbyes. We held his hands until they were no longer warm. Hospice didn't come until 2:00 a.m. Watching them take him out of his own house, never to return, caused such anguish for all. What comfort I could gather came from knowing that he was now with his son Steve, his wife Mary, and his Little Jenny Bug in heaven. I wasn't sure exactly what the others were thinking. I hope they all had their own peaceful thoughts.

March 15

We picked up Ed's ashes for the long drive home. It was difficult for all of us. I felt faint, as it triggered my memories of driving home from the funeral home with my daughter's ashes in my lap.

March 25

I cleaned a house today and stopped at the flower shop on the way home. I purchased one dozen yellow sweetheart roses for Jenny's two-year anniversary. Anniversary is the common word to mark the passing of another year. I don't like the way it sounds. An anniversary should be a celebration, a commemoration, a holiday, a ceremony, or a festival. I will call it an observance.

Tomorrow I will observe Jenny's passing. Today was for remembering her last day on earth. First, I relive the last week, then I relive the last day. For example, at this time Jen had only eight hours left to live, or she was doing this or that, or we were talking to her right about now. Or, my last memory; she was getting ready for the party and we would never see her again.

March 26

I love you, Jennifer. Today is my observance. Today I will write to you. You were gone by 2:15 a.m. I woke up alone between two and three in the morning. Loneliness set in, and I relived your life over and over. Am I better yet? I would say I am not. Perhaps I am feeling numb. There are so many yellow roses from so many loving people who love and remember you. All I could smell were yellow roses. I do believe they smell sweeter than any other color. Once again, my violets are blooming profusely. There are soft pinks, vibrant purples, and variegated combinations of colors sitting on the windowsill. I don't even remember watering them.

Your thoughtful aunts kept me busy all day. When we returned home, Jackie called and came over for a surprise visit. Your dad, Jamin, and I all enjoyed seeing her. Love, Mom

March 30

Ed's service was beautiful. Pastor did a great job speaking, and that was no easy task being that most of the relatives attending were not religious. The family went to the cemetery so we could bury Ed's ashes next to his wife Mary and his son Steven.

It was two years ago today that we had Jenny's funeral. A week or so ago, I asked the family if they would mind if we put Jenny's ashes in with her grandpa. I didn't want her name on the stone. I didn't need her name mentioned. I just wanted her to be with family. All agreed except for Jim's oldest brother. He was highly offended and angry and told me that we already buried her two years ago and it was over. There is no description for the pain that shot through me when I heard those words. It will never be over.

I can't expect people who have their families intact to understand what it is like to experience the loss of a child. How could they? My parents were gone before I lost Jenny. For Jim's brother, this is his deepest loss. However, it will never be over for Jim, Jamin, and me. I guess I just wanted her at rest with someone who cared about her. After I thought about it, it was just my grief talking. I'm glad I still have her. For now, she stays in her memory box in our home.

March 31

We left for Florida again to start settling Ed's estate and clean up his condo. Our own packing and cleaning finished, a nervous Jamin took us to the airport at 4:00 p.m. Our flight was delayed, and we got lost in our rental car. We finally arrived in the middle of the night. All looked well except the guest room ceiling, which hadn't looked safe for a long time. It had been leaking, and one of the twin beds was damp. We corrected that problem and moved the large garbage can, which had been placed in the room, closer to the bed. We fell into the beds and though the drip, drip, drip was annoying, we went right to sleep. Pure exhaustion.

Around 3:00 a.m., Jim sat bolt upright and yelled, "It's gonna blow." We got up and ran into the hallway just in time to see the ceiling cave in and his bed covered with debris. There was nothing to be done until morning, and we needed sleep. Neither of us had the desire to sleep in the bed where Ed had passed away. We ended up on a cot and the couch and discussed the irony of the situation. Just like Ed had waited for his family to arrive before letting go, the ceiling had waited for us.

April 1

What a mess to wake up to. We must get the guest room cleaned up and find someone to repair it. The weather is beautiful, but we remain indoors sorting and packing for the Salvation Army. Jim is busy finding a lawyer to handle the estate. I must find a place to get boxes for dishes. Dismantling a home is physically and emotionally draining. This home doesn't just need to be packed up but repaired as well. We can't stay here so we must find someone we can trust. I am worried about the pressure on Jim. I am trying to distance myself emotionally by taking one moment at a time. Tomorrow we will take some time off to relax and get out of the condo.

April 3

Jim doesn't talk about how he feels. I observe it more than hear it. I am depressed and having a hard time even putting one foot in front of the other. We bagged and bagged all morning. Jim suggested a ride, and we drove quite a distance. We ended up at one of my favorite stores, and

Jim let me walk around and dream without complaining or rushing me. We soon came back to the condo and started sorting again.

Later in the evening we took a walk to see the eclipse. That walk was a gift. No matter how gloomy life seems, God always throws a few roses in among the weeds. Sleep eludes us. What we need the most to finish our task has gone AWOL. Jim watches television, and I read. We agree that our life seems like one big roller coaster. However, sometimes I don't feel we are on the same ride.

APRIL 4

Jim found a lawyer to help him settle his father's estate. We decided that a break might help us sleep better. We drove to Estero to see Aunt Jackie and Uncle George. We took turns driving and talked. I believe this helped us both. We took Aunt Jackie a birthday gift and had dinner at their clubhouse. It was so good to be with them and relax. We then drove the three hours back and arrived at the condo at 10:30. Sleep.

APRIL 7

Our flight left very early in the morning. Jamin and his friend picked us up from the airport. We dropped our things at home and went straight to Carol's for Easter dinner. It was so good to be home and with family. Afterwards, sleep, dishes, sleep, bed. I read something in *Six Hours One Friday* by Max Lucado. "How can you be satisfied with existence once you've lived with purpose?" I love when I find even one sentence that describes how I feel.

APRIL 8

We are back from working so hard, and then we return to work. Tomorrow I go back to cleaning houses. I dread it. I picked on Jim at dinner. I teased him. He came home so cheerful, and I believed it was because he got to go back to what he loves and the people he loves to be with. Work is his first love, and his employees respect him. I told him that I would like to be treated the way he treats them. I put up a wall of resentment. I fear I am losing more in my life. Not only am I losing myself, I fear I am losing Jim.

April 9

I cleaned a house today and crashed when I got home. I did my necessary chores and made dinner. I am in bed reading. I am so deep into this book I mentioned a couple of days ago. Max Lucado describes perfectly how I feel about my music. I try to sing, but there is no life in my voice. He writes, "Death steals our reason to sing. Death takes the songs from our lips and leaves in their places stilled tongues and tear-flooded cheeks."

April 10

The couch and coffee are my friends. I sat until 12:30 staring out the window and trying to get up enough courage to do something I have been thinking about for months. I got out the phone book and looked up a number. The address was correct, so I dialed as my heart was pounding out of my chest. How can a heart pound so hard without exploding? I called the wife of the man who hit Jenny two years ago. I felt I needed to talk to her and see how she was doing. I wanted her to know that I cared about her and her children. They lost a husband and a stepfather. There was no answer. I left a message on a machine. If it was hers, I don't think she will call back. I probably wouldn't.

April 11

I agreed to sing a song for Pastor at his 25th year anniversary party as a Minister. God help me. I cleaned Cathie's house, showered, and read my book. That's about it for today. The books I read are not always helpful. Sometimes they hurt. Sometimes God lets truth and reality in for a few minutes. I think of Jenny in a different way than others. I think of her as gone, really gone, and I can hardly stand it. If I ever feel like dying or losing my mind, it's in those moments. At least until I snap out of it and back into my fantasy world.

April 16

We watched a documentary on concentration camps in Germany during World War II. Watching the inhumanity and suffering causes such an ache in the heart. I think of death. Every life is so precious and yet so easily taken away. I cannot begin to comprehend the physical and emotional pain of these poor souls. My thoughts turn to God. Why? I'm sure everyone has the same question. These people were just as precious to Him as anyone else. I try to remind myself that God takes tragedy and uses it for good. He does not make it happen. If God did not intervene in that, why would he have prevented Jenny's accident? I cry myself to sleep.

APRIL 18

I ended up writing a special song for Pastor's anniversary party this Sunday. The songs I researched didn't say what was in my heart. I also shopped for a new dress. Jenny would be so surprised to see her previously slim mother overweight. I am twenty pounds heavier than when she passed. I use food as a pacifier. I don't feel right, move slow, and have little energy. Jenny would tell me to "get a life." I will, Bugs. I will someday.

APRIL 22

As if it fell from the sky or was granted by God, I had so much energy today. I have no idea how this works. What happens in my brain or body, or the combination of both that provides this? What is the precursor for such a phenomenon? I wish I knew because I would do the same thing every day. I cleaned a house well and quickly. I wasn't tired when I finished. I drove home, did chores, made dinner, and then cut Jamin's long hair. He looks so handsome. I showered before bed and then watched a movie called *Voice from the Grave*. Everyday something tells me that Jen is more alive than I thought.

APRIL 25

MOPS started at 9:00 a.m. Our theme for the day was *Heaven*. It went very well but by the time I returned home depression was weighing heavy on me. I ran out of Prozac, but I don't think that's the reason. It's what I was thinking about yesterday and most of the night. Jim had slept upstairs, which is rare, so that is another reason I didn't sleep well. I'm so used to sleeping alone.

I went to see my therapist after MOPS. I have been dealing with such guilt. This monster comes and goes. Sometimes I feel that if I had lived my life differently, if I had made one decision that altered the outcome, she would be here. She said my thinking was "self-centered." Why would I be so important to God that he would take the life of a young girl to change or punish me? Perhaps she's right, but I think I would have handled a hurting, confused person a bit gentler. I discussed it with Jim at dinner. Of course, we ended up arguing. It was my fault.

April 26

Today was brighter. I spent the morning with Cathie. Jim went up north after dinner, and Jamin left for his cousin Brian's. Jenny received a yellow rose for two years, and one month. I bought her a new Cherished Teddy with a bug on it. Why does it help to buy gifts for someone who isn't here? It just does.

April 28

I didn't go to church again. I miss often. I want to but taking my medication has caused me to gain so much weight, and I feel horrible and fat. I only have a few items of clothing that fit. I refuse to buy myself bigger clothes. I will become more comfortable in them and forget to watch what I eat. That is my philosophy. Joanne and I went to the mall. We stayed quite a while and I bought a small fluffy Boyd's Bear. I like them way too much. I put it next to Jen's picture.

May 5

Jim and I went out to lunch. Once more I enjoy our "normal" time together. Later Jamin and I recorded *Pastor's Song*, which I wrote earlier, on his four track. I harmonized with myself. I've never done that before. I believe Jenny inspires my song writing. I couldn't really write until she made me. I feel I could write anything now.

Later, I went to see my sister Laurie's pastor. I've seen him a few times. He lost a two-year-old child and is trying to help me cope. He revealed that his wife told him that her loss could have been much worse…she could have lost him instead. I was surprised to hear that. They must have had a blessed marriage. I feel bad, but my marriage is lonely. I would rather have my child.

May 6

It bothers me that I'm getting so good at cleaning houses. I need more in my life. I'm not sleeping again. Aunt Jackie called; she's home. I'm so happy. She always comes home from Florida right before Mother's Day. I will see her Friday when I clean her house.

Later, Joanne and I went to the mall again. It's our escape. We talked about being so different now and never being normal again. I'm not sure what normal is, but I know we miss our *before* lives…*before* Brad's accident and *before* Jenny's accident. We wonder why some people have to do this.

May 9

I saw a new psychiatrist. I couldn't understand the other one very well as he spoke broken English. The new doctor told me I was suffering from Post-Traumatic Stress Syndrome and depression. I guess that makes sense. He put me back on the higher dose of Prozac. When can I stop all this?

May 11

I woke up again at the same time I do every night. It's always around 3:33. I see the numbers 333 so often that I try not to look at a clock. If I awaken in the middle of the night, I know if I look, the clock will say 3:33. So I wait before I look. It doesn't work. It happens so often that it scares me. I try to go back to sleep but it just doesn't happen. The numbers are everywhere and not just on my clock. Jamin sees them as well.

I decided to look up 333 in numerology. I reviewed many thoughts and ideas. From what knowledge I could find, it could be related to angels and masters. Spirit guides could be involved. I don't know anything about spirit guides. It's meant to bring comfort and remind you of inner strength. It suggests you are being protected on your journey. I like that. I will try not to be fearful and just smile.

The only reason I was able to get moving this morning is because Joanne called. We went out shopping again. Why is it that everything that takes my mind off of my pain is detrimental to me? We stayed out much too late and didn't get home until 11:15 p.m. One of the stores we enjoy is open 24 hours a day.

May 12

It was Mother's Day today. Jackie was home and suggested our families meet at a local restaurant for dinner. Jackie gave me a garden set and Jim and Jamin gave me cards. It was a pleasant day. I can't help but wonder if Jenny knows, or if she comes to visit and I'm just not aware. On our last Mother's Day together, she took me to brunch at one of my favorite places. I remember thinking how grown up she was. She took *me* out. I knew she would be an attentive daughter.

June 1

Jackie graduated from Oakland University with her master's degree in counseling today. I'm so proud of her. Jenny would be too. I cleaned the church until 10:30 tonight. I hurt everywhere from sleeping so poorly. My brain is alive; however, it feels as if my body is dying.

July 21

I made the decision to write only when I have something important to say. It is too draining to live a day and live it again before I go to bed. It makes me think too much before sleep. In June, Jim and I went to Mackinaw City with Cathie, her family, and Lynn and her children. While we were there, we also went to the Island. When everyone left, I met Joanne and her kids and stayed a while longer. I bought some great books, my favorite being *God on a Harley* by Joan Brady. Reading it really helped me realize how little one needs to live and be happy. I did a lot of thinking while I was gone. Some things will have to change.

I will go off of all medications, stop eleven years of allergy shots, discontinue therapy, and try for more energy. So far, I am doing better. I take one Prozac every other day. However, I think I am done with those as well. When given the choice to sink or swim, the Lord said to me, "Swim, and I will keep you afloat." I am tired of being weak and dependent. I continue to be hooked on books, but I'm doing much better at leaving them on the store shelves.

Jim called me while we were still in Mackinaw City and asked me to stop by a log cabin in Prudenville on our way home. We were ready to sell our other cabin with so many memories. Joanne, her kids, and I stopped on our way home and though I only saw the outside I fell in love with it. It ended up being something both Jim and I liked. It is very old and has a lot of character. I have a knack for looking at something and seeing the possibilities instead of the problems. That is what I saw, what it could become. It would be a place we could go together or alone. Perhaps it could be a place to heal. The lake is just a block away. Either way, we decided to buy it.

One day in June I got a call from one of Jim's co-workers. She had taken Jim to the hospital with chest pain and dizziness. I rushed over to see him, and I'll never forget the look of fear in his eyes when he looked at me. I had never seen that look before. It was as if he was trying to say so many different things to me in a single glance. I had been worried about him for a long time. I knew that men handled grief differently from women. I've been living it while he has been trying to bury it. I believe that denying our emotions can make us ill. However, projecting your negative feelings on to another in order to relieve your own agony is harmful as well. If the person is empathic, they will carry your burdens for you. I feel we must all heal our own pain.

The hospital kept him for a few days and ran some tests. The tests results were negative, however, they put him on blood pressure and heart medications. I still worry. I will always worry.

On the way home from cleaning last week it was raining and sunny at the same time. I looked at the sky and was overcome by the beauty of it. I felt sudden joy. I felt true happiness. I felt hope for the future. I started to cry. God had given me a gift, a remembrance of what it was like before Jenny died. Even if it was just for a moment, it was magical. I won't forget that feeling. I don't know when it will come again.

Jenny's twenty-third birthday was yesterday. It's a twenty-four-hour period we have to endure. We have no choice. It was also the same day as Jim's work picnic and the weather couldn't have been more perfect. Jim and I took dried yellow roses I'd been saving along with a fresh yellow rose and laid them at the base of Jenny's tree in the park.

I opened up a little angel I had bought for Jenny a while ago. I put it on her memory chest with a birthday card. I always write a message to her just as I did when she was with us. I seal it. I'm not sure if or when anyone will ever open it. I also put a small bunch of imitation yellow roses on her chest. They will not wither and die.

I wrote a letter to the parents of a woman who was killed in TWA flight 800 on the seventeenth of July. I wish I could help them, but I respect their privacy. I will also send them a yellow rose and just wait. If they are like me, they will read it and feel nothing. The rose will die and be tossed away. Like Jenny, she was their only daughter. I sometimes think of all the cards and notes I received. If I could, I would go back in time and answer every letter. People put their heart and soul into the words that were intended to bring comfort. I was not willing to be comforted.

July 28

Unfortunately, I have something to write about. I don't want to, but it's part of this story. It's part of Jenny's story. It's part of her youth when she was having her first crush and dreaming about a boy. I remember writing earlier about a boy she wanted to go to a dance with. My pastor and I talked about how young they were and decided against it. My daughter and his son had a crush on each other. I wish we had let them go.

Pastor and Judy's beautiful son Michael died in a car crash yesterday around 6:00 p.m. He was twenty-two years old. The pain in my heart is not just my own, but their pain as well. I ask myself how will they cope? Then I remember, I already know.

When Jenny died, my pastor came right over in the middle of the night. He sat with me and held my hand for a long time. He prayed with me. He made funeral arrangements. My sister Carol had called him. She feared Jim and I would not be able to comfort each other.

Who will go to him? Where is his pastor? He will attempt to comfort his wife. Will anyone sit by him and hold his hand? He will probably continue to minister through this, his own son's death. I believe, like Jim, everyone rushes to the mother. The father is expected to be strong. I find comfort in the thought that Jesus will be his pastor. His children will comfort their parents while they need comfort themselves. How does anyone get help in this circle of pain? I hope he and Judy will let go for now and let others hold their hands.

I went over to see them and took a single yellow rose. Judy knew what it meant. She looked at me and said, "Now I know." I saw it in her eyes. The look that only a grieving person could recognize and understand. It's the look that contains a thousand different feelings and questions at once. The look that says all hope is gone. The look that asks why.

Judy asked me to sing the song I wrote for Jenny at Mike's funeral. It's called *My Promise*. In it, I promise God that if He would just let me see her one more time, and let me say how much I love her, I would promise to let her go. I will be strong. I will do this. I must be there for them. They have more than just grief and loss to contend with. In the accident, Mike hit a car with two young men inside. They both died as well. Please God; send the parents of these young men the peace that passes all understanding.

"I think of grief as having a wound on your heart.
You put a bandage on it. Some wounds heal and leave a scar.
Others you have to keep bandaged because
they continue to bleed."

August 5

I didn't feel like writing until now. I still don't. Mike's funeral is over. I did sing that song, but I also wrote another and sang that as well. Judy asked me to keep it a surprise for Pastor. I called it, *Who Will Hold Your Hand?* Though you always give love away, who will hold your hand today? I wanted to help make the day more bearable for them, and God granted me that privilege. I will pray for them.

Jim upset me last night when we arrived home from up north. I cried so hard. I was in so much internal pain. His anger eats away at me. I see it all, I hear it all, and I get it all. He has nowhere else to dump it. Even though it crushes me, I understand its source. I forgave him and went to bed with a broken heart. In the middle of the night, I awoke and started to cry again. I felt a sudden spiritual presence. It's not the first time. I recognize these many magical moments I've had since Jenny died. I felt a tingling all over my body. I experienced a euphoric peace inside. My ears rang. Then I fell into a deep sleep.

SEPTEMBER 1

I must reassess my goals. I can't keep cleaning. I'm starting to resent it. I think it hurts my body more than helps it. I hurt all the time. I think controlled exercise may be more beneficial. Plus, it has not helped me lose my anti-depressant weight. MOPS is starting up again. There is so much to do. A woman at church approached me and asked if I would be interested in becoming a Stephen Minister. They are laypeople that provide one-to-one care to people who are having difficulty in their lives. It would involve a great deal of training. I told her I would consider it.

I am getting nervous and depressed again. I wish I could write about happy days. But instead I have bad dreams, bad mornings, and I miss my daughter so much. I won't write until I'm feeling better.

SEPTEMBER 9

We spent another weekend at the log cabin. It's getting to look quite cozy. Joanne may go back with me this coming weekend. I bought us both a copy of *Simple Abundance: A Daybook of Comfort and Joy* by Sarah Ban Breathnach. I hope to read that and my Bible every morning. I hope it changes things in my life. Joanne and I started Weight Watchers tonight.

SEPTEMBER 19

I haven't lost any weight. I did so well too. I wonder if there is something wrong. It's hard to tell if how I feel is emotional or physical. My nerves seem to be on fire. I don't really feel nervous, but my skin does. It's driving me crazy. Jim says that I'm depressed. I deny the accusation even though he is right. I won't be, I can't be. I won't go backwards or on medication. He tells me that he sees it in my eyes and that they droop with sadness. I admit I think of Jenny all day long.

I played Jen's favorite songs today. It hurts to hear them, but it's as if I dare myself to listen. Once in a while I just have to torture myself in order to feel just a touch closer to her.

I can't seem to stop buying and reading books on grief and loss. Why? When will I stop? Maybe I should write one of my own. I am trying so hard to, as Jenny would say, "Get a life." I have dreams, I have plans, I read self-help books, and I try.

Perhaps it's autumn. I always loved my favorite time of year. Maybe I can't and I miss that. Maybe I feel the earth dying slowly and life fading away. I'll just have to wait for it to come back to life. Perhaps it's the approaching holidays? Recovery is truly four steps forward and two steps back. No wonder grief takes so long. God, I am so lonely and I'm not even sure what it is I miss other than Jenny. Maybe I miss the old me.

I am looking at her prom picture next to my bed. The sun is reflecting off of her face and her milky shoulders in the photo. It's the same sun that shined today. That exact same sun. It's just not shining on her anymore.

September 24

This is my last entry in this diary. I'm tired of writing in it. I'm tired of writing sad things. I'm just tired. If it weren't for Joanne, I wouldn't have a single friend. It is strange how I'm so lonely and at the same time I avoid people. Jim came home very late tonight, and Jamin went to Dave's, which he often does. I don't blame him. I waited for Jim to get home before I ate dinner. We sat down at the table, and I had hardly begun to eat before he was finished. He got right up and went into the other room. I was not in a mood to be left. All of a sudden, I was alone again.

I have been feeling that my marriage is over, but I fear giving up. I feel scared and anxious. I made a comment to Jim in the other room. "I hope that when Jamin is married, he will sit with his wife and eat. I think it's rude to leave someone alone at the table unless you're in a hurry," I spouted. I said something else that I can't remember, and Jim came flying into the kitchen. We were both yelling, and I said in a pathetic voice, "I don't have anyone to talk to all day." He sat down miserably at the table. He just stared at me. I eventually told him to leave because I couldn't eat with him sitting like a prisoner. He left.

I ate the rest of my dinner alone and then continued to clean up and finish some chores. I went to bed without saying goodnight. Later he came up. He approached me cautiously and then hugged me. Perhaps he thought I would punch him. He explained calmly, "I didn't mean to blow up at you like that. I got up at 5:00 this morning and had meetings all day. I'm tired." Then he shared, "You're the second most important person in my life. Hannah is the first." Later I cried from relief. Jim doesn't say he's sorry.

"You learn to merge loss into your life.
The pain hides, but it never leaves because you can be called
back into it at any moment. It really never disappears,
but it does become manageable."

Voice Recordings

It's November 2, 1996. Jim and I are at the cabin, and we raked leaves today. The first snow of the year fell on top of the leaves making them twice as hard to rake up and twice as heavy. Jim bought me this little tape recorder so that I could talk to Jenny when I want to talk to Jenny, and so I could have memories, thoughts, and stories. I hope that someday all my thoughts about her life will be on these tapes. I also wonder if I will listen to them. If I transcribe these tapes, it will sound more like talking. It will read differently than well thought out sentences.

Good morning Jennifer. It's Monday, November 4, 1996. I don't like Monday mornings. It seems to be the hardest morning to start. Remember when you used to say to me "Who you talking to, Mom?" One thing we both knew was that I was very good at talking to myself. Since I'm so good at doing that, that is how I'll write to you. Because I talk to you all the time…for two and a half years since you've been gone. Actually, it's two years and eight months on the 26th of this month.

I had a very unusual weekend. Your dad and I went up north Friday night to rake leaves. I went to a bookstore called The Lamb Shop to buy a couple of books for a woman whose son had committed suicide a couple of weeks ago. He was fourteen. She knows Aunt Cathie, and I guess she would like to talk to me.

I ended up buying her a little booklet called *When Grief Breaks Your Heart* and a book called *The Lessons of Love*, by Melody Beattie, which I read last summer. I hope they will work out for her. While I was checking out, the lady asked me what I was looking for, and we started talking. I told her just a little bit about you and learned that she'd lost a daughter who was the same age. Her daughter died after a long illness. I said, "Well, you look like you have made it." She replied, "I have made it, and I am better. I am even better." That was encouraging.

I am always looking to learn something because I am constantly reading. It started the day MADD brought a packet with several books to the funeral home where you were – *Bereaved Parent, No Time for Goodbyes* and a few others. I tried to give Jamin one for teens, but Jamin does not like to read, not yet. But I learned something from those books. They gave me comfort and the assurance that I was not alone; I certainly wasn't the only person to whom this horrible tragedy ever happened.

The week after your funeral, your father, Jamin, Brian and I decided to take that trip to Florida that we had been planning. We had planned to leave you and Jamin home together since you were almost twenty-one. I read all the way down and the entire time I was there and all the way back and I just haven't stopped.

At this moment I am sitting in my bedroom looking at your picture because I like to look at you when I talk to you. I guess if you are going to get into any kind of addiction after a tragedy, books are not a bad one. I have them piled and lined up by the TV. Some are fiction, but even some of the fiction books have something to do with losing someone. I have a few mysteries. I have a book about sisters. I have a book about angry marriage, but then that is another whole story. One book is about men and grief; maybe it can tell me something about your father and your brother, because they really don't tell me much. They don't talk about it, especially Jamin.

A lot of the books are Christian, and every one that I read helps me just a little bit in some way. If I retain one or two thoughts from each book that can comfort me, it's worth it.

The pile by my bed includes books on mourning and recovery as well as the loss of a child. One I truly identify with is *In the Wake of Death* by Mark Cosman. This one has been a little more difficult to read. I am almost done with it. This man's thoughts are so deep that sometimes I can't get down there and figure out what they are, but I try. I never would have done that before. If I don't understand it, I read it again, because I have thirst for what suffering people think, how they do it, how they survive, how they go on. Maybe when I am done reading all the books, I will have a better understanding. Maybe I won't until I see you again. Maybe at that time I will know everything I need to know.

Downstairs in another little cabinet are all the books I have read; I keep adding to that pile regularly, and I even decided that sometime this winter I will have some bookshelves built in order to house all these books. I imagine someone might come by one day and look at my books, look at the titles, and think to themselves, *This poor woman, look at all these sad, sad books. Look at all these books she had to read to survive her daughter's death.* Maybe another person will think, *Wow, look at all these books; maybe she learned something really important.* That is what I would say. I don't think it's pathetic that I keep reading about mourning, suffering and grief, but I will read books about hope as well, because any book on grief usually always ends with hope. They never leave you hanging, never leave you without something. So I am going to keep on reading, Jenny Bug; and while I am reading, I will keep on talking to you.

Another unusual thing about this weekend…there was a Stephen Ministry meeting last night. I was asked to join many years ago when they first started it and I didn't want to. I was afraid. I didn't know if I had anything to share with anyone, if there was any way I could help someone. Sure, I had a soft heart, I could listen, but what could I listen with, with just my ears? I needed to learn to listen truly and deeply with my heart, and I think I can do that. I think I can have total empathy and compassion, and I can help someone. At Stephen Ministry we also learned about hospice care.

A woman came from the Lapeer area with her daughter who had many physical similarities to you…long blonde hair pulled back, taller than me, like you were. She had a look in her eyes that reminded me of you. I thought, "Oh, dear God, don't let me cry. I don't want to bring attention to myself by having to leave the room." I knew that everybody would know why I left when this woman came in with her daughter. So, I got myself under control without anyone noticing and the lady started talking. She did not get very far into the discussion before she looked up and said, "A year ago, I lost a daughter in a car accident." For a second I couldn't breathe.

I hear too much about death. I have run into all kinds of people who have lost children, but an oldest daughter…it was almost more than I could bear. So, she talked and laughed and spread her joy among all of us. She was really sweet, not an intellectual, not a comic, just somebody who loved God so much and brought joy into someone else's life. We really enjoyed our time with her. She is coming back next month, and I am going again.

Her daughter was behind me, and I turned around and talked to her a little bit afterwards. I asked her, "How old was your sister?" and she replied, "Almost twenty-one." Her sister had been married a short time and was about to celebrate her second anniversary the day after her death. We talked about how it felt, and someone else asked her a question, and she looked up and said, "You know, I just decided it is what God wanted, and I don't ask why anymore; there must have been a reason."

I was thinking that this young girl is wiser than me. She made that decision just a year after her sister's death. I don't think I did until about two years after you died.

Well, we've talked about how good I am at talking to myself. Don't you think it's an excellent way to write you? I know that I'd sit down in front of the computer and go totally blank. But give me a picture of you and tell me that I can go ahead and talk out loud to myself, and I could write for the rest of my life. I love you, Jenny Bug. Bye for now.

November 11

Hello, Jenny. Yesterday was a very odd day. It was a heartbreaking, heart-wrenching day for some reason. I was supposed to go somewhere with Jackie in the afternoon, and she had canceled the day before and then rescheduled then canceled again all within twenty-four hours. Maybe I was just totally, totally depressed yesterday. I missed you so much. I miss you all the time, but some days it is deeper than others. Some days I can feel the emptiness like it is crawling all over me, and I long so much to be back to normal, but I don't know if I ever will be. I wonder if my equilibrium will ever return to normal. I hope that it will come. But this disequilibrium is something that is very hard to live with.

I know that a lot of people deal with it every day. It almost feels like a mental illness of some sort, but I have always been a person who likes to live a peaceful, balanced life; now I am like a teeter-totter. Anyway, I got through the day. I talked to your dad about you a little bit, and he always tries to ask me what's the matter, and I am not even sure what to tell him. I just finally said, "I miss my daughter," and then I cried.

Later I felt better and went up to Stephen Ministry meeting. I talked to a trainer afterwards and told her sometimes I am not even sure if I am doing the right thing by being there. How can I help someone, how can I listen to someone's pain when I still can't learn to deal with my own? She finally said, "Maybe it will help you to learn to help the other person." And I know she's right. That would help me. But even when you know what would be good for you, you just can't immerse yourself in the situation. The ambition and motivation are not there.

I wanted to tell you about when Joanne and I took Sharon, the woman whose son took his life, out to The Cooker, where you used to work. After I met her, I asked her if she had seen the beautiful plaque the restaurant made for you soon after you died. Another plaque beside it says, "*Friends Don't Let Friends Drive Drunk*" because you had helped someone the night you were killed, and *Jenny Bug Smith* and the date you died are one it. It has your poem, *Summer*. I like to read it and touch it every time I go in there, even though I haven't been there many times since you died. They really liked you, Jenny. You were a good waitress. I used to love to come in there when you were working.

Anyway, Joanne and I took Sharon to see it, and we had a nice talk. We laughed. We cried. She is in so much pain, incredible pain, and her pain is so fresh. I thought her pain would remind me of when my pain was that fresh, but I can't remember that time. I was telling Joanne that I know it existed, I remember, but I don't remember how I felt because I think I felt almost nothing at the time. I was so numb. Even a few weeks after, I was a zombie. Anyway, I hope I was able to help Sharon.

I am almost done with *In the Wake of Death*, and I can identify with this man because what he has been struggling with all along is the fact that he is responsible somehow for his daughter's murder because he was not there. I struggle with that feeling still sometimes, but I am much better than I was. I keep thinking if I had done things differently in my life, you wouldn't have been in that car. Remember how your dad and I used to get in the car on Sunday afternoons and ride around after church, hoping to find a house that wasn't in a subdivision that we could really fix up. After a while, we gave up and decided to stay where we were, make some improvements, and let you kids stay in the same house you basically grew up in. But, oh, if we had done one thing differently, what might things be like now, Jen? Would you have had the same boyfriend? Been at the same party? I don't know…possibly.

You wonder if past actions had spiritual consequences, and this man wondered if God was punishing him by letting his daughter die. Parents wrestle with guilt and we go over and over it in our minds. Was it this, was it that? Then you tell yourself God would never do that. God couldn't do that. That is not the kind of God we have. He does not take one life to try to save another.

Your father said something to me the first summer after you died when we were up north. I told him I sometimes feel that you died because I was imperfect, because I made mistakes and that God felt I didn't deserve you. He said, "What makes you think that it was you, that you're the reason she died? What if it was something I did?" We all deal with our own demons. I never thought about it from his perspective.

One counselor I saw for a while said, "Do you think you are so important to God that he would take a young girl's life to change you, to punish you?" That idea relieved me of my guilt, but I don't know if it's about guilt. I was just trying to pinpoint some reason, trying to understand your death in some way. I think a parent would feel guilt no matter what.

I don't think you can overrate the guilt when a child dies before a parent. So, I just have to accept the fact that there will always be some kind of guilt, but it has nothing to do with any decisions we made. Someday, I won't have to ask God why He took you because I will just know.

Hi Jenny. It's November 14 [1996]. I just got back from MOPs. I don't know why I volunteer there; your Aunt Carol asked me to help watch the babies first, then last year someone asked me to teach, and now I'm the moppets chairperson for the little ones. It gives me something to do, somewhere to be needed.

Today we had a Thanksgiving party, and then I went and got your truck washed, Jenny. It is still good. Not a scratch on it. You loved that truck—your very first brand new car, though you didn't get to have it very long…maybe six months. I am trying to be proficient at driving a stick.

I know that you used to tease me sometimes about that, but I am taking good care of it for you.

I finished *In the Wake of Death* last night. The father overcame two obstacles in the death of his daughter. One was guilt, and the other was fear. The first was superstition, and I had my own feelings about that. Do you remember the day I came home for lunch from work, and you were getting ready to go to work? You stood in the doorway between the family room and kitchen and said to me, "You know, Mom, Tara's got this friend, this man who is a psychic, a friend of the family. Her mom had a party, a psychic party, and this man told Tara that she was going to lose a friend…a friend of hers was going to die. And he predicted this old man with gray hair would die, and that Tara would lose a friend who rode a motorcycle, and that happened." I was trying to convince you that it was nothing to worry about and that I didn't believe in those kinds of things when you said to me, "With my luck, Mom, it will probably be me."

I forgot all about it until after you died, and then it totally shook me up when I remembered. I was terrified. I was mad. Someone knew, and they didn't stop it. And I started wondering whether he knew it was going to be a girl, and why he didn't do something. It bothered me for a long, long time. I finally talked to Tara about it, and she talked to him later on; he said he didn't know it was going to be you.

I started thinking of superstitious reasons why you could have died. One night I couldn't sleep and was sitting on the couch in the living room waiting for you to come home. This was perhaps a week before your death. Suddenly a black cat jumped up onto our porch. I remember wondering if it was an omen. I remembered being called up for jury duty on a case of a young man arrested for selling cocaine. We decided, after a great deal of deliberation, that he was guilty. Afterwards, the prosecutor told us he had been supporting his family in South America by selling cocaine, and that made me think. Since we put him in jail for life, did his mother or father or family curse all of us on the jury?

It's silly, isn't it, Jenny? Stupid things go through your mind when fear invades, and they become a part of you. You become obsessed with negative thoughts. It is all in your quest to find out *why* that this fear and guilt develop. So those are my superstition stories.

I have a couple of books to read by psychics and life after death, but I don't think that is the direction God wants me to take. If God wants me to talk to you, if God wants me to see you, He will take care of it. I don't have to go to someone.

I have had a cold now for over two weeks. I never had trouble getting rid of a cold before, but they say things change when you lose a child. Sometimes you are not as healthy as you used to be. You have more stupid little accidents, bumping into things, knocking things over because your mind is preoccupied a lot of the time. I have done some really silly things in the last couple of days, like let the soup boil over because I was thinking about you. I fell down the stairs on the first anniversary of your death. I have missed exits on the expressway and missed my turns because I am deep in thought. I probably should be more careful, because I don't want to hurt someone else.

Something else I wanted to talk to you about Jenny, since I have lost you, is that I feel so alone; I feel like no one understands my pain. I feel like I'm the only person who has ever felt such pain and this loss. I know that's not true, but I still have these feelings. Sometimes when I think that way, I have way of talking myself out of it. You want to know what it is? I thank God when I feel sorry for myself; I guess that's the best way to put it. I thank God that you didn't suffer. You were killed instantly on impact. If I thought you even felt pain for a second, I don't know if I could stand it. You lived more than twenty years in perfect health. I think of all the children that are born unhealthy, crippled, deformed, blind, or deaf. Not only do some of them die young, but they never even get to enjoy the time they lived.

I'm thankful, Jenny, that you didn't suffer like some children. God blessed me with a beautiful, healthy child that I cherished.

I try not to compare you to the ones who live because, even though there are always worse scenarios, there are better ones too. I look at women with their daughters and am reminded of how I used to look at women with their mothers. What was it like to have a mother? I had one for fifteen years. I remember my mother, but I remember her as a child. I never got to know her when I was an adult, never got to share with her, ask her silly questions about motherhood and marriage. I always thought that couldn't possibly happen to you, not the way it happened to me. When you teased me about being a health nut, all the while I was thinking that I must stay alive for my children and stay healthy so I can be here, because Jenny is going to need me like I needed my mom. You didn't have sisters like I did, so I felt you would need me even more, but then Jenny it turned around the other way, didn't it? You left me.

I think it would be easier to be the one who leaves than the one who is left.

One of the things I remember asking God when you first died was why He let my mother go and then my daughter too. Why did I have to miss those two adult female relationships? I love my sisters dearly, I love my aunt, and I have a wonderful stepmother; but I still feel slighted for not having my mother and you. Once again, there are worse scenarios, and I am thankful for the years that I had you both.

When someone I love dies, I can't remember one negative thing about them. I try, but I can't. All I can think of is how wonderful they were, but that is good. Good memories are the best, so those are the ones I will keep. Unconditional love, I think they call it. That is what I have for you, my mom, my dad and others in Heaven.

I wanted to talk to you about Jesse. The year before you died, you were so in love and happy; and you became more beautiful than I ever thought possible. Jesse won your heart with his big, brown sleepy eyes and his beautiful smile, but boy did he love you. He was with you that night. He was driving behind you. I am sure you looked in your rearview mirror and saw Jesse driving behind you. He wanted to just have you come with him in his truck, his little matching truck. You had the white one and he had the black one. But you wanted to drive your friend's car back home for her. You didn't want her to drive, and I commend you for that. But Jesse was the last one you saw. He tried to save you. I can't imagine how hard it must have been for him to see that car coming at your car and not be able stop it, not be able to have you hear him as he called out to you to look out, but he held you. He stayed with you. He ran and got help, but that is another story.

I will talk to you about your accident some time, but now I think I will just tell you about Jesse. I am sure you know all of this, but I like talking to you. Jesse had such a difficult time for a long time continuing with his job. I think he went fishing a lot with your friend Jeremy. And then he came to visit us one day and told us he was going to join the Marines. Remember when he wanted to join the Marines, Jenny, when you were dating and you said no way, if he joined the Marines you weren't waiting four years. So, he didn't go, but then he saw no reason not to after your death. He is a good Marine. We went to his party when he graduated from boot camp. He came to see us a few times before he left. It was nice to talk to him. I could see the pain in his eyes. I could see how hard it was for him to be at our house. Now I haven't heard from him in a long time. He got married and, guess what? He has a little boy.

Remember when you used to tell me you were never having babies? You just couldn't bear the thought of giving birth. You thought it would hurt too much. But then when you fell in love, you said, "I want to have two little boys that look just like Jesse when he was little." I was excited. I thought, *Great! Jenny finally wants to have babies!* Then I would yell at you when you didn't drink your milk. "You need your milk, Jen. You're going to have babies someday; drink your milk!" And you would just laugh at me.

We will never forget Jesse. I have a beautiful picture of you and Jesse sitting here next to me. You have never seen it. Jackie took it in January on New Year's Eve, and then you didn't see her until February. You both look so happy and content. I love to look at it and remember. I think it may have been the last picture taken of you.

November 23

Jennifer, I have six pictures of you in the family room; some of them were my favorites. One time I got you father's magnifying glass and held it above your picture, and it felt like you were right there, looking at me. I could see the twinkle in your eye and the tiny pores in your skin. It was awesome, but I only did it once. You were so real and alive. It hurt afterward and I was afraid to do it again. Your graduation photo is on the mantel. You are smiling and wearing a necklace that I tried so hard to find. I did find it, but that is another story.

I have three other pictures in my lap. The first one is when you are about ten in front of Lake Huron. You're wearing a hooded sweatshirt, and those famous bangs are blowing in the wind—your hair was so blonde it looked white. I always used to cut your bangs for you just to the eyebrows. You look at me out of those little blue eyes, and I long for those days when I was so important in your life before friends replaced me. I was your mommy then. You needed me. You were precious.

I have the last photo taken of you and our family. It was your last birthday with Jackie as she turned twenty-one eight months before you. Erin is sitting on your lap and Jesse is next to you. Erin remembers you, but not in the way I wish she could. She is almost seven years old now. She was four when you passed. When she came over to our house, she would make you get a hairbrush and have you sit on the floor so she could brush your long hair. You both loved it. That is what she remembers about you.

Another picture is from your senior trip. Boy, you were miss popularity your senior year, you and Jenny Z and JoJo. The three of you are looking ever so glamorous. I suppose getting ready to go out somewhere in Cancun. Tan, slender, happy, so young. I bet you girls just felt you had the world in your hands that night. Your hair is pulled back off your face. It is one of the few times you did not have bangs. It is long. Where did you get those long, beautiful arms, so slender. You are all hugging each other. I am so glad you were so happy.

And the last picture, Jen, this one had to be in Myrtle Beach with another one of your very best friends, Jenny C. You're in a condo. You got around, didn't you, kid? You went down there a couple of times, but this was the time I let you take our new car. It was never the same when we got it back. And even while you were down there, I remember you found a note on it where a delivery truck had hit it in a parking lot. You were so scared to tell us about that incident.

You were independent. The one thing you always longed for, and you had a little taste of it before you had to leave this earth. I think you were striving for it from the day you were born. You are on your own. Nobody is telling you what to do.

What would I do without pictures, Jenny? Many times, I have heard people say that when a loved one dies, they have a hard time picturing their face later on. It's sad they forget features unless they are looking at a photo. I do not think I could ever forget anything about you. I can go from the top of your head to the tips of your toes and see every bit of you as if you were standing in front of me. I can hear your voice as clear as a bell. I can smell your perfume. The essence of you is in my mind. It can never leave, because you are my daughter. You are my child. You are my baby.

I have a lot of things I want to talk to you about, Jen. I know that eventually I am going to have to get down to the business of talking to you about your accident. I have not really relived a whole lot of that. I have relived little bits and pieces, but to talk about the whole thing at once is probably going to be hard, but I want to do it.

I also want to talk about change. Losing a child changes you, and you are never, ever the same. Most of the books I read say that you become better in some ways. You become stronger. I guess I keep waiting for that, keep waiting until the day when I think I am better.

Well I guess I better get on with my day. Sometimes I feel like I am here and going through the motions, but I am not really living. I am doing what needs to be done day after day because I am in a body that has to be taken care of, living in a home that has to be taken care of, living with people I love that I want to take care of, but I am not really alive. I still feel that way sometimes and that everything I do is just mechanical. Don't get me wrong, Jen. I do have moments where I feel genuinely happy because I forget for a little bit. I have even felt joy for a few minutes. I think that I died when you died, and the struggle now is to learn to be alive again. I have to be reborn as a different person. When that happens, with God's help, maybe I will survive this.

November 27

It is the day before Thanksgiving [1996], Jenny, and I had another extremely short dream about you. I can recall having only four dreams about you in the two-and-a-half years since you died. For some reason, there was a motorcycle contest of some sort between a guy and girl, and you were chosen out of many girls. You were to go up a ramp, pick up speed, come around and do a jump. You did it the first time, and I was in some sort of a little trailer watching you. As you came around and went up the ramp to jump again, I kept saying, "Be careful, Jenny, be careful, be careful." When you came down off the ramp and jumped, you fell, and the bike dragged you. It kept going and going and going and people were yelling, "Stop her, stop her!" I was screaming, "Jenny, stop, Jenny stop!"

The motorcycle skidded across a parking lot real fast, dragging your body. I saw that your knuckles were being dragged on the asphalt, and I thought, *that isn't too bad, just her knuckles. We can fix that.* Then you kept going and going and going. People were chasing after you when, suddenly, you were coming back towards the trailer I was in. You were very close to it and I was screaming when I woke up. Those dreams are traumatizing.

The very first dream I ever had about you after you passed was when we still lived on Regency. In the dream, I was lying on your bed when I realized someone was lying next to me with their head on my stomach, and I was caressing this head over and over. I looked down and realized it was a blonde head. I just said "Jenny," and you looked at me. We got up, and you were in a long, white robe, almost like a choir robe and your hair was completely straight and so pretty. I remember hugging you, and you hugged me and said something so typical of you: "I have to go, I can't stay here all day," and then you left.

The next dream was after we moved to the house on Twin Lakes. I dreamt that I found out you were in a hospital all along, and you really didn't die, and that you had been somewhere with people taking care of you, and I didn't know. When I found out where you were, I rushed over to the hospital. I remember not knowing where to go, how to find you in that big hospital, so I just started screaming, "Where is Jenny Smith? Where is Jenny Smith?" and someone took me to you. When I reached the ward, you were totally under the covers except for your head. We were crying and so happy to see each other. I can't remember the conversation, but I was there for a while, and before I left, you were dancing on your bed and you were fine. I think I was afraid you would never dance again.

I had another one not very long ago. I dreamt we were living in different house. You and I were the only ones there, getting ready to move into a new strange house. Someone knocked at the door, and I let them in. I called for you, and you came walking out of your room with a basket full of things you didn't want anymore…which was so typical because you were always cleaning out your room and leaving a bag or pile of things out in the hallway because you didn't want them. Sometimes it would be a little pile of clothes, sometimes it would be just a garbage bag. I always went through it to make sure there wasn't anything of real importance in there.

I will never forget the day I came home from work and went up the stairs to find your white wicker headboard in the hallway. You just didn't want it anymore. I remember finding the frame when you wanted your mattress on the floor. That is just the way you did things. I remember the day you told me you didn't want your dresser anymore. It was big with a large mirror, and I thought it was a girl's dream to have a dresser like that. In the hallway it went, and we had to go to K-Mart and buy you plastic cubes, and we piled up six of them for you to put your clothes in. I wonder why you were always getting rid of things. I think about that often. Your wicker headboard is now on my bed at the cabin.

I don't know why I've only had a sprinkling of dreams since you died. I long for you to come to me in my dreams so I can see you, so we can have experiences together, but it just doesn't happen often. Perhaps my own subconscious mind is trying to protect me from the pain of waking up from them, because it is hard to wake up and find out you weren't really there. Sometimes I felt rather happy, but with the motorcycle dream I had last night, I woke up feeling just totally sick inside. It is such a horrible feeling, and you just lie there with your eyes wide open for a while trying to figure out what that was all about. Someday I really hope that I have a wonderful dream that you come back to visit me and we get to spend some time together. I think it would make me happy, but then again in my dream you would have to leave me again, and maybe that is what I am trying to protect myself from.

After you died, other than these few dreams, I did not dream at all for two years. Someone told me you don't dream when you are very depressed. Maybe that's it. But I guess the fact that I do have dreams now means that maybe, just maybe, I am getting better.

Next Monday [December 2] there is an Advent by candlelight at church. I have attended the last two years. The ladies have speakers, stories and music. I remember the first Christmas after you died, they asked me to sing "O Holy Night," and I barely got through it. My voice shook, my hands shook. I just couldn't get that music out of my soul; my heart wasn't in it. Then Judy, Pastor's wife, came up and gave me a nice book by Joni Eareckson Tada about Christmas and spoke a little bit about you. The second year, I just enjoyed the whole program, and it was quite nice.

This year, Aunt Carol and I are hosting a table. We are going to make our food, and then I am going to get up and sing one song, I think *Christmas in Heaven*. I am going to sing it for you. I will let you know how it all goes.

I forgot to mention I am hosting Thanksgiving dinner tomorrow. Your dad and Jamin both brought home a turkey. Everybody is coming to our house, Jen, and we will give thanks that we are all together. Everybody has been safe so far since you died.

For the first time in two-and-a-half years, I will have company. Every time you are able to do something you couldn't do before, that is a sign of improvement. It is a sign of growing, recovering, learning to adjust, to live with the loss.

Morning, Jenny. It is December 4, 1996 and getting a little closer to Christmas here. Thanksgiving is over, and I did it. I actually had company. I don't know, it's funny how sometimes you just don't know what to talk about with your own family. I talked very little and was kind of sorry I did. After the kids left the room, I talked about Jamin going to college. Someone always has something to say about something that isn't their concern. I know he's not in the mood right now, but I hope he will someday. The end of the day was hard because the house was full of people and then everyone suddenly went home. Everyone left, and your dad went to sleep. It was so lonely. It's more than just being alone. It's more like feeling as if you're the only person on earth.

I watched Jackie mope around without you all day. It made me so depressed. She looks like she's lost in the jungle. She has always had her holidays with you. It was that way for 20 years. The boys had the boys and you two had each other. You were her best friend, born eight months apart. She has friends from college, but nobody that is really close. She did get her own little apartment. You would love it . . . you'd probably live there with her if you weren't married.

Jamin doesn't go out much Jen, not like you. He has friends, a few friends, but mostly he hangs out with David just like when you were here.

The night you died David came to pick him up. He was not driving yet. He is still doing the same thing except that now he drives himself. He goes to David's or David comes over here to practice music. Sometimes he sees Brian and Jeff.

Anyway, I cried myself to sleep Thanksgiving night because of feeling bad for Jackie, feeling like a failure as a mother, feeling like a failure as a wife—it's funny how things just come pouring down on you all at once. It is not just one little concern or one little bit of guilt. It is tons of guilt, all at once, and I felt like I had failed you because I couldn't keep you alive in this world. I tried so hard, so very hard. I nagged you every time you left the house to "watch out for other people, drive defensively, be careful, I trust you, but you can't always trust everybody else on the road." It's funny how I knew I would lose you that way, isn't it, Jenny? I didn't know when, and I really didn't know for sure in my conscious mind, but in my subconscious mind I knew. I started worrying about it when you were little. It is also funny how I knew it would be one man, I was always afraid one man would hurt you. I don't know why that stuck in my mind either, but that is what happened. Odd, isn't it? I think mothers just know things.

I never once thought about ending it all like I did that Thanksgiving night. I guess I am not selfish enough to do that. My pain hasn't reached the point where I lose all touch with reality and all concern for others. I hope it never gets so severe, that I totally lose myself in this world. I really don't understand suicide except that somebody's pain must be so great that it clouds all rational thought, all concept of right and wrong, all concerns about what will happen after your body's found. So instead I prayed, and I cried myself to sleep. The next day I was determined to punish myself somehow, I guess, because I went Christmas shopping with Joanne on the busiest day of the year—but I actually enjoyed it. So that was our Thanksgiving. Did you have a feast in Heaven, Jenny, a big feast? I hope so. Instead of a football game, you had angel choirs singing. That's the way I picture it.

December 9

It must be the holidays, Jenny, because I keep saying to God and myself, "I can't do this. I can't do this." That's how I feel. I don't want to do this. I think the pain is just too great.

I don't know why this Christmas seems worse than the other two, but all I can think of is that I was in shock for the first one. Plus, we were getting ready to move, and I really could just about ignore Christmas if I wanted to. I did a few things the first year like buy you a memory candle. We put up a Christmas tree in the family room, and I lit the candle along with buying you a dozen yellow roses. I remember Jamin saying, "Aren't you going to decorate? Are you going to put up more decorations than this?" But I didn't want to. I think he probably needed it so badly, but I didn't see that. I just did what I was comfortable doing.

Then our next Christmas was in this house, and I put up a Christmas tree and a little teddy bear tree in the front hall because there was room. I might have put a few scattered things out and about, but not many like I usually do.

Aunt Carol told me you used to say, "I love the way my mom decorates at Christmas." So maybe it's that…I don't know, but I seem to be trying to decorate this year. I am going through all the boxes and finding little homemade ornaments you made. I am just trying so hard after almost three years to get back to normal, but it doesn't feel normal, Jenny. It does not feel normal at all. I pull out all the boxes, and then have absolutely no desire to put the stuff anywhere…so I have a mess everywhere. Now that I have all the stuff out, my heart's not in it.

I know that if I just keep trying, I can do a little at a time until it is done. I just need to remind myself that I can decorate a little more than I did last year, but I don't have to decorate a lot. I am actually having some people over at Christmas time—maybe that is why I am decorating. I have not had anyone the last couple of years, so there was no real need to do anything. All of the Smith family will be here on Christmas Day, which reminds me that the last time they all came was our last Christmas with you. And I can see you so clearly on that day watching Mara's baby, sitting there with Jesse, all of us crammed into the living room. You received your leather jacket from Jesse that you wore the last time you saw Jackie. It was actually your first Christmas with Jesse…and your last.

I also agreed to host part of a MOPS progressive dinner this Friday. Sometimes you volunteer because you are trying so hard, but then you realize that you have to do work…and you have to follow through on your promise. I just don't know why this Christmas hurts so badly.

Maybe I just don't remember how much the other ones hurt, but I can't seem to stop crying. I cry about every half hour for a couple of minutes. People don't even know I am doing it. I've gotten very good at trying to keep my face normal looking when my body just trembles inside with tears. I can cry without making a sound, like I do when I am watching TV. Your dad's in the room, and he never notices. I think it all started Thanksgiving night…just must be a holiday thing. I just keep getting grief spasms over and over again. It's like you are right there, but I can't touch you and I can't see you. I swear I'm feeling every human emotion possible: anger, frustration, guilt, loneliness. I get angry at absolutely anything and everybody for no good reason at all. I guess it's all just part of whatever is going on in my mind.

I sit here looking at the ribbon on the Christmas tree, a ribbon I have because you said I should try putting ribbon around the tree because somebody's tree you saw had ribbon and it was so pretty. You loved beautifully wrapped packages. I remember how you used to come home with all these neat ideas and share them with me. This year, I will try even harder to make the ribbon on the tree and the presents as pretty as possible, Jenny, as if you were watching over my shoulder saying, "Yep, that's good, Mom." I tried so hard to do the ribbon just right, but as I sit here talking to you, I see it is not right at all. It is twisted and uneven and I will have to do it over. You are not here, but I'm trying to please you. Life seems twisted and uneven.

You know, Jenny, I had a dream about you again. I don't know what number this one is. You were younger. I think that might be because I just keep longing for the time when you kids were little. Aside from Jesus' birth, Christmas is joyous because of children…the decorating and Santa Claus are magic because of children. I can no longer find the magic. A couple of years ago, Jamin asked, "Why aren't you decorating?" Now, at nineteen, he says, "Don't just do it for me." He is no longer interested.

Then I think, *Who am I doing it for then?* But I was talking about the dream, wasn't I?

You were about ten. I just remember that you had changed your clothes a couple of times and looked so nice. The rest is so foggy, but we were in the bathroom in the house on Regency, and I remember feeling that I had just one more chance to tell you how very much I loved you—I was holding you and hugging you so hard and I was trembling inside. I remember hearing you say in your little voice, "I love you, too, Mom."

Remember I colored your hair in that bathroom? I remember not really wanting to do it, but I am so glad I did.

Last night, in the paper, there was an article about death and the holidays. It was the first time I ever felt what was written was truly honest—he didn't act like recovery from grief within a certain timeframe was a given. He wrote from a place of pain. He said getting over the death of a parent usually happens with time because you expect parents to die before you. And though it takes time to get over the death of a spouse, that also heals in time for most people. But the work of dealing with the death of a child usually takes a lifetime. That's what has been so frustrating for me is that I keep thinking *I have got to get better.* But I've reached a place where I think *This is as good as it is going to get, and I just need to adjust to the person I am right now.*

I don't foresee any time in the future Jenny that I will ever think of you any less than I do now, and I think of you almost constantly. I am so engrossed in you to the depths of my soul, and I cannot seem to get out. Though it's probably temporary because of the holidays, it is not fair to Jim, Jamin or even me to be this way. I see them, I talk to them, I listen to them, but I am not giving them what I should, because I am just lost in a cocoon of pain. I get off track often, don't I?

What I started to say is that I am ashamed of how I am seen in God's eyes, terribly ashamed. I have blessings all around me. I don't feel like I need to apologize to anyone for my actions or my grief, except God. Overall, I have a husband who is a good provider, an honest man, and he tries. I have a boy who doesn't cause me problems. I have my family, and so far, my health. We can see, we can walk, we can hear, we have all our limbs, we have cars, clothes, food, all the material blessings anyone would need to live—so I am ashamed of being so miserable when I have so many blessings; but God understands. I am sure He does. But still, I cannot seem to stop feeling this pain. I ask God often, "What should I do?"

In church yesterday, we prayed for a little seven-year-old girl with terminal lung cancer. Why should I feel sorry for myself? What right do I have to feel so sad? My child didn't suffer; you died instantly. The Lord was gracious to you even in death. I am sure you are in Heaven, Jenny. That is one of my big problems right now; what right do I have to be sad?

In Grand Rapids, Michigan, a mother was driving down the road on Thanksgiving Day and lost control of her car. She lived, but her three little girls died. You would think that hearing something like that would snap you out of your agony, but it doesn't. I guess there isn't anything that can lessen my pain, even hearing how bad other people's tragedies are.

What makes God decide who will suffer and who won't? When you hear that God doesn't give you what you can't handle, you think *What makes Him think I can handle this any better than anybody else?* I pray someday I will find out when I pass on. I want to know it all. I will be a very demanding spirit. I want to know why. We accept with faith, but, oh, we long to understand.

I was telling you earlier about singing at the Advent service. It wasn't an easy evening. I did sing *Christmas in Heaven*, but it wasn't what I had hoped. We had a special guest that was supposed to speak about angels. But instead she started speaking about accidents and worrying about your children. She said she would go to the ends of the earth to protect her child from an accident. Then she started to talk about an accident in a very descriptive, very real, very similar way, but with one difference. Her daughter lived. I got so caught up in the story that I started to cry. I tried not to make a sound as my body was wracked with sobs.

Shortly after the speaker finished, I had to get up to sing. I couldn't back out. I started to talk, stopped, waited, cried, and started to talk again. I told the audience I had PMS. They laughed and it helped. Singing that song, choking it out, was one of the hardest things I have ever done. Everyone was already sad, and I think I made them cry more. When I was done the speaker grabbed my hand. She didn't know. To her, her story was the nightmare, and it was. But our nightmares had different endings.

After I sang, three very important things occurred: Cathie said I was her hero, Laurie said I was a blessing to our family, and Jackie said I was her idol. It meant the world to me. When I am feeling like I will never really be anybody again, I can remember those three things. The second night Pastor's wife spoke and afterwards I talked without crying, and I sang effortlessly. I received so many compliments. But not like the first night when I was a hero, when I squeaked out the song and I was a blessing, or when I got up to sing though my body was shaking with tears and I was an idol. I learned it's not perfection that touches hearts. It's being real.

It's December 19 [1996]. Good morning, Jennifer. I was hoping to feel your presence somehow last night. I really needed you. I was having the most terrible grief spasms. It always hurts, but sometimes the pain gets so physical, you just feel it throughout your whole body. Sometimes it feels like your body is full of disease and you are dying. You feel it in every muscle, starting with your heart, and tears well up. Usually it is at times when you are not alone, and you have to hope nobody sees the pain on your face. It happens at the store. I had to leave church the other day. It happens a lot when I am watching TV. It's Christmas commercials, or coffee commercials, or Hallmark cards. I love to see people happy. I don't know why it makes me cry.

The progressive dinner for MOPS went well. It was our first real social gathering other than family. It was fun to pretend that for a little while everything was okay. I think your dad enjoyed it, though I don't think he really enjoys much of anything. I don't know how to help your dad; he just seems so miserable. We don't know how to help each other. I don't like to talk too much about him. I came home from cleaning Aunt Jackie's house for Christmas, and we had a terrible fight, Jen. He was in a bad mood and said it was his job. I don't know what's going to happen to us. I have read that fifty to seventy-five percent of couples that lose a child end up divorced. Maybe that is where we are headed. We never really grieved together. I don't see him grieve. I don't see Jamin grieve. I have really just grieved by myself. But I know they feel the same way I do. I hide it as well. Once in a while they will say something about you, but most of the time it is just business as usual.

I have been meaning to talk about the spiritual and the magical times that I've had since your death. I think the first one was about a week after we had gone to Florida after your funeral. When we came home, your dad and I slept upstairs in our bedroom (which ended up being the only night that we slept upstairs until we moved almost a year later). I remember waking about six in the morning. Your dad was still asleep. I had a beautiful feeling of euphoria, like love, happiness, joy—all the good feelings all rolled into one. I enjoyed it for a minute, but I also thought, *Jenny is here with me now, and I feel this because this is what she feels; this is what it feels like to pass to the other side.* I would love to have that feeling again.

I woke your dad and asked, "Do you feel it?" He said he didn't, then the feeling slowly faded away, but I know it was you. I know you were there, and you brought that with you. It was a strange peace. But it didn't last for very long, and nothing happened for a long time…not until August. I have these little experiences organized in my mind and I will share them with you as I talk.

I was supposed to go up north with your dad this weekend before Christmas, but I don't think I am going to go. I am not sure it's good for us to be together right now. I believe he is in so much pain that he just does not know how to deal with it, and it's hard for me to be around him because I feel like I get the brunt of his misdirected anger. So, I am going to stay home and make some more Jenny Bug Bears.

1997

It is January 6 [1997]. Christmas is draining. I'm relieved it's over. It started out fine, but it became hard toward the end. I couldn't get anything accomplished. We were all up wrapping presents on Christmas Eve. I used to be one of those people that had everything ready two weeks ahead. For some reason, this Christmas was harder than the last two without you. I felt your absence so strongly. This one seemed more real. I also tried to make a Christmas this year because the Smith side of the family was coming, where I just let the other two come and go and did as little as possible.

Your dad and I actually went out on New Year's Eve. We went out to dinner with your Aunt Cathie and Uncle Chuck, and to see the movie *Michael* with John Travolta. It was about the Archangel. I cried. I love angels. They give us hope. I invited my family over on New Year's Day for a feast of leftovers. Fortunate, aren't we? Sometimes I have to stop and think about how grateful I am for the things that we do have. I am working very hard on that, Jen.

I bought a book called *Simple Abundance* by Sarah Ban Breathnach, one for myself and one for Joanne. It is just a daily book on how to appreciate your life and how to see blessings that you overlook every day and how to be grateful. I am looking for growth with all of this, and I feel stronger already.

I am buried in books, Jenny. I can't tell you how many piles there are everywhere. It is embarrassing. I told Jamin last night if someone had asked me what got me through your death, I would say, God and books. I don't think reading can ever, ever be a waste of time.

Another thing helping me right now is Jamin bought me this tape called *Peaceful Pachelbel*—an orchestral version of Canon in D Major by Johann Pachelbel. It is so soothing to the soul. I guess right now I feel hopeful, Jen, real hopeful.

Last night I was reading a little section of *Simple Abundance* and it talks about how to find the authentic person inside. I thought my authentic person would be a person who uses all her God-given talents. So, maybe that is another goal. One day I think about you and feel that all is lost, life is over, hope is gone, and I might as well give up and throw in the towel. Then there are days like today where I feel like, *Darn it, I am going to do this. I am going to fight; I don't care what it takes. I am going to do it for Jen because Jen would do it.* I kept living on when my mother died. If I have to be here without you, then I am going to darn well try to enjoy myself.

I also wanted to tell you I picked up Grandma Ginny and went to Aunt Jackie's house where she once again had this fabulous dream Christmas Eve with all the decorations and wonderful food and presents everywhere. I tried to get into the spirit by just enjoying Erin and remembering what it was like to be here for Christmas Eve when I was six years old. She opened all of her American Girl doll gifts, and I swear I was as excited as she was. I think I tried to live through her that night.

Aunt Jackie says she is not coming back next year, or if she does come back she won't have it at her house. We tell her we'll do it, she can just come visit. So next year should be my turn, Jen, and I am going to do my darnedest. I have already gone to all the after Christmas sales where everything is 50% off and bought what I thought I needed to make a real Christmas next year—but I am talking about the Christmas you see, not the Christmas you feel. That is another thing. It takes Jesus to pull that off; to have that kind of Christmas; so I like to combine them both.

Anyway, we made it through. Your dad was generous as he always is at Christmastime, and he and Jamin and I had our little present-opening session in the morning. We do it, but every one of us is keenly aware that you are not sitting here with us. I try to remind myself that you would probably be married by now. You probably wouldn't be sitting here opening gifts with us, but maybe you would have been. Maybe you would have spent the night here, like Dave and Jackie did with their mom and then open presents with us Christmas morning. I don't know. It is fun to dream and think about what it might be like, where you might be, what you might be doing. Actually, it is making up a fictional story in your own mind. I can do that with your life. I can pretend you are married with two beautiful children, or that you are in Europe traveling before you settle down. I can make up anything I want. But what I want most is just to be able to talk to you once in a while, see you once in a while and just know that you are okay.

Your dad gave me something for Christmas that Aunt Cathie helped him pick out and it was a little gold bracelet. Nothing fancy, nothing expensive, but it was beautiful. I had it on two days and was cleaning the sanctuary at church. Something made me pull up my sleeve to make sure my bracelet was safe, but it was gone. My heart sank, not because it was a valuable piece of jewelry, and not because it had tons of sentimental value; I had only had it two days, but there was something symbolic of my marriage and how things have been going since you have been gone. I just felt that my marriage has been lost and now this little present your dad gave me was lost, and I just felt like everything was lost.

I finished up what I was doing at church and went home, deciding to come back the next day to finish cleaning. I tore the house apart looking for it, but it wasn't to be found. Your dad told me not to look through the garbage, that he would replace it. I told Judy about it, the pastor's wife, and she told me about something she lost once and how important it was to her and how she prayed and how that night she found it in her shoe. So we prayed. I got up Monday, and in a place I had already looked quite a few times, I saw something sparkling. It was the bracelet. I was numb. I showed your dad, and I think we were both just relieved. A found marriage? I don't know. Who knows? Is it symbolic of something? But every little bit of hope helps. Then I took it back to the store to get it mended, and they gave me a brand new one just like it instead; so it is symbolic of a brand new start, I guess you could say, or hope.

Another good thing yesterday, Jamin and I had a wonderful talk. I miss the talks you and I used to have. Even when they sometimes got heated, they were stimulating. They were real. Jamin and I don't have stimulating talks. We don't argue much, but we had a wonderful talk last night about girls and love.

So that was our Christmas. I wanted to explain about my hope for the future. Hope's good, even if you only feel it for half an hour out of a day. The one gift that God gives us that most of us don't even realize is that every morning when we wake up, we have a choice about how we are going to live that day.

January 13

Well, I just got through reading my *Simple Abundance: A Daybook of Comfort and Joy*, and my *Daily Word* about God. I am proud of myself as these are the things I promised I would do, starting January 1, and I have done them faithfully for thirteen days. I also purchased Sarah Ban Breathnach's *Journal of Gratitude* and every night before I go to bed, Jenny, I write down five things that I am grateful for. When I do that it helps me concentrate more on the positive things in life before I fall asleep, rather than just thinking about a lack of you. I know there are still other blessings, ones I was overlooking and taking for granted. Even the memory of you is a blessing. The fact that I had you at all, that God blessed me with this adorable baby girl is a blessing. Now I am counting them all and thanking God for them. Not that I haven't thanked Him all along, I am just concentrating daily on my blessings. The more you fill yourself with your blessings, the less you fill yourself with your grief.

The more you fill yourself with gratitude, the less you fill yourself with emptiness and loneliness.

I want to tell you more about the miracles or the spiritual things that have happened, Jenny. First, you had a necklace that you wore in high school that I had given you, a gold necklace that said, *I love you* all over it, and it had a little charm that said *I love you*. I gave them to you before your graduation and had forgotten all about them. I had forgotten about it to the point that I didn't recognize it in your senior picture. When I looked at the picture after you died, I'd often ask, "Jenny, where is this charm? What is it you're wearing here?" I looked through your jewelry for it, but I only found your class ring, which I put on and have never taken off. I couldn't find anything that even resembled what you wore in that picture.

You also always used to wear a little necklace that Jesse bought you in Myrtle Beach. You wore it all the time. I remember seeing it on you every day for about a year. On the night of the accident, no one could remember if you had that necklace on. Jesse wanted it. He wanted it very badly to remember you by. It wasn't in your belongings. We all looked. They searched the house you were in the night you passed. Jesse looked in his truck, but no one could find that necklace. We looked through all your jewelry in your room. I don't know how much time went by, it could have been months.

I remember talking to Jesse's mom on the phone, then wandering around the kitchen. I remember saying aloud to you, "Jenny, where is that necklace?" I walked over near the basket where we all just threw stuff, and I don't remember what possessed me—there was nothing I wanted in that basket—but I stuck my hand in it and pulled out the necklace Jesse had given you. It was unbelievable. I was stunned. It had been by the kitchen sink all along, but that would have been an odd place for you to leave it. Maybe you left it on the counter, and I threw it in there—I don't know. I did often find your dental retainer on the kitchen sink—it was one of the things I used to get so angry about that I can laugh about now.

Anyway, I called Jesse, but he wasn't home. All of a sudden he was at the front door. Why did he show up at that moment Jenny? I just remember him coming to our door and I said, "Jesse, you will never ever guess what I found," and I gave it to him.

But Jenny, the biggest thing, the most anointing, religious, awesome thing was the other necklace. I continued to search and ask you, "Where is this necklace, where is this charm?" It happened on August 15, 1994. I couldn't talk about it then.

A few months after you died, I woke up on the couch, sighed like always, and said to myself, "I will never be happy again." I looked at the curtains, thinking, *I've got to get up and face another day, move this body, make it walk, make it talk.* Then as I started to move, I saw something so bright that I had to close my eyes against the intense light. The room was so full of energy that it caused an intense ringing in my ears. I couldn't move. I felt electricity throughout my body. I lay there, knowing that something miraculous was going on, and all I could think is that you were there, and I wanted to see you.

Though I couldn't move, hear, or see, I could think. I knew somebody was there, so I spoke and someone answered, but I couldn't really discern what was said. I murmured, "I am not afraid, I am not afraid." I don't know how long I stayed like that, then it slowly faded away. As soon as I realized I could move, I popped up so fast and called out, "Jenny, Jenny?" I felt maybe I could catch you before you left. Suddenly I was just filled with this overwhelming excitement. That was the day that I was supposed to pack up my bedroom for the move to Twin Lakes. I remember going upstairs finding a pair of folded pajamas on my bed. I didn't remember putting them there. I went to put them in my summer pajama drawer, and it was a mess. I saw a bowl of costume jewelry that I must have shoved in there at some point, but I hadn't seen that bowl in probably over a year. I wondered where the bowl and the messy drawer came from, because I put pajamas away all the time.

Grandma Ginny had given me the small, milky white antique bowl; it was very intricate and beautiful. I picked up a wad of necklaces and chains that I used to wear to work, and there was one item left in the bottom of that bowl. Immediately I knew what it was. It was your charm with the words *I love you*. I put it around my neck, and it is still there where I can touch it, and I often do. That day, I ran downstairs and called your Aunt Cathie because I knew that she was the only one that would believe my story. I told your dad; I don't know if he believed me. It wasn't until a long time afterwards that I told my best friend, and she admitted that earlier she'd thought I was losing my marbles; I had to convince her all over again that I wasn't.

You have to be careful when you are telling people things like this, so I haven't told many people. They have a tendency to think you are a little off your rocker or your grief made you dream or whatever; and how do you convince people it wasn't a dream? I mean, I am forty-six years old. I know what dreams are. I know what's real and what's not real. I was awake. I didn't fall back to sleep. I didn't have a dream. The charm around my neck is real. That isn't the only miraculous thing that happened to me, Jenny. But today I'm going to get going and do what I need to do. I will tell you about the other little miracles later . . . but I shouldn't call them little. I don't think any miracle is little.

January 27

Good morning, JenBug. It has been a few days since I talked to you last but I have been at the cabin with Lynn, Cathie and Tracy for four days. Aunt Lynn is an excellent cook. She did all the cooking, and Tracy made the breakfast and it was enjoyable and relaxing.

I am so used to spending so much time alone that I found I was looking forward to drinking my coffee alone and staring out the window thinking of you, because it seems like I have a thirst for that every day. It's just something I have to do before I get started with my day.

I wanted to tell you more about what I feel to be miracles. They happened in our old house on Regency. I don't remember exactly when, but probably about a month or so after the first one. I was lying on the couch in the dark with my back to the room. Your dad had just gone upstairs to get ready for work, and I always felt lonely when I was left alone with my early morning thoughts, which weren't very positive.

As I began to think, I felt a tingling again, and I felt something move into my body. I didn't lose my hearing or sight or ability to move. I just felt something slowly and peacefully move in and fill me with love, beauty, calmness, and euphoria. I smiled, and after a bit, I felt it go out of me the same way it came in, slowly and gently. That is difficult to describe. Again, I can't say it was you...I can't say it was anything. Maybe it was something my mind imagined, or something my mind created in order to help me get through that most horrible moment when I first wake up.

Another time, I woke up with something swimming through me. I can't describe it other than a swimming feeling. I remember thinking *That was wonderful*. Jesse said he had a similar experience. The following October, I woke up on the couch with that same feeling, but this time I said, "Jenny." I thought surely it was you.

The final time in that house, I woke up to that feeling again. Jackie, had spent the night, and she was sleeping in the Lazy Boy chair. I am surprised I didn't wake her up because I said out loud, "Jenny, don't leave me." Then I thought, *It's not going to happen again.* And it didn't. I feel you were telling me you were leaving. You had somewhere you had to go. You couldn't be with me anymore. I was sad.

Then, two years later, I had an argument with your father and was very upset. Neither of us is very good at handling our emotions these days, and I wonder if we ever will be. I came upstairs and cried and cried. I laid on my back in bed, sobbing, with the lights out, and suddenly, something came over me again…a presence, an energy. All of a sudden, my tears stopped. I felt a soothing, a release. It was as if someone just put their hand on me and said, "Stop your tears; it's okay." When it ended, I wasn't crying anymore; in fact, I smiled to myself and rolled over and went to sleep.

Now it's 1997, and nothing else unusual has occurred, but I wonder, Jenny…all those times, was it you? Or was it my imagination, my mind conjuring up something I thought I needed?

Every death, every tragedy takes something away from you, something you can't get back, so you have to let go of that part of you, that part of you that died with that person; then you have to re-build that part, that section that's gone, you have to develop it into something different. You can't leave it empty. That is one thing I have discovered. You fill it up with God, knowledge, hope…and if you don't, you will surely die. So that's what I am doing every day, Jenny, trying to fill up that large part of me. I always say I lost a quarter of myself when my mother died and another quarter of myself when my father died and half of me when you died. I basically need to rebuild my entire self.

I also wonder what is in the future. How does your death work into God's plan? In Romans they say all things work together for the good of those who love God and whom God loves. I really didn't like hearing that when you first died, because my first thought was, *how can anything good come out of the death of such a beautiful, young, vibrant life?* How can anything good come to your father or Jamin or me or Jackie from this? How can anything possibly be positive? I still have a hard time with that, though I know God must have a reason, so I wait patiently, but what is it?

I can't worry about what good comes for Jamin or your father. That is something they have to work on. They have to dig deep and find whatever strength this tragedy has given to them. All I can do is work on what I feel God wants me to do with this tragedy. Does He want me to help others? Does He want me to write a book, though I'm not a writer? Does He want me to make Jenny Bug Bears and start a business that way? Does He want me to copyright my songs that I wrote for you? Does He want me to continue in the Stephen Ministry and help others?

If one person out there in this world benefits from something I say through all of this, and if it's just that one person that I touch, I guess that's pretty important, pretty awesome.

I guess I have some other things I need to talk to you about, like your accident. I must do it for me, because everything that I get out of me is less to eat away at me and destroy me on the inside. I don't think anybody else could listen to me the way you and God do. I can talk and talk and talk. Your death has become my life. You can't get up and walk away. You can't say, "Alright, Mom, that's enough." I love you, Jenny, precious girl, hero of my heart.

Journaling

JANUARY 29

I am sitting in my warm comfortable bed in my cozy log cabin. I am alone. I left for a few days (all I could afford) because I was hurt. My marriage hurts. I've never left before because of pain. I would never leave my children. Jenny is gone to heaven and Jamin is grown. No one needs me home anymore. I am fine. I'm quite well actually. It's so peaceful with the snow falling gently all day. I hear people go by but see no one. I'm keeping a small journal to unload my brain when it gets so full that I'm stressed and overwhelmed. I must learn to love life again as it is a must for survival. God will know that I didn't give up even in the worst of moments. I will go home tomorrow but will have to be cautious about the snow.

JANUARY 30

I did it. Aunt Cathie's friend Rita, who reads auras, called me back. Earlier in the month I decided to go and visit her even though I promised myself I would not go this route. I will see her on February 8. Will she know? Will she see Jenny? God, I hope so. How will I react? I must make a list and buy some extra tapes. I'll have so many questions. Was Jen's death a punishment for me or someone else (stupid)? Does she know how much we all love her? What does she want done with her ashes? Did she meet my mom?

FEBRUARY 1

My home life is so lonely and my marriage so empty and angry. 1. What if married couples gave a fourth of their time and attention to their marriage? There could be a big improvement. 2. What if spouses were treated with the same respect as a friend or co-worker? 3. What if spouses didn't dump all their emotional garbage on their partners? 4. What if spouses took their spouse's greatest flaw and tried to help with it instead of resenting them for it?

What will happen to us? I am scared. Please, no more traumas, no more pain. My heart can't take it. However, I have to try and be a whole person instead of an empty vessel. God, help me.

February 2

I don't have to write every day, but it was a good one. Jim and I must be so weary because we seemed to work on our marriage. I saw effort and it was wonderful. The trick is, can it happen again? I remember reading about deposits and withdrawals in relationships. Jim and I make too many withdrawals and our account is empty. I must talk to him about this concept.

February 3

I don't want to write this, but I can't just pick and choose what to write about. I have to be honest. Joanne is extremely down. I will try and do one thing a day to cheer her. I'm going to make a list. Joanne and I seem to be drifting. We can't seem to cheer each other anymore. We are two broken souls trying to support the other when we cannot even keep ourselves upright. She needs someone who will let her be the only miserable person. We are better when one of us is up and the other down. When we are both down, our misery is doubled. Somehow, I feel guilty that Jenny died. Would she rather have Brad in a box in the spare room?

This situation brings a painful memory to my mind. My stepmother Ginny, at Jenny's funeral, talking to Joanne. Ginny knew about Brad's accident and she told Joanne, as Jenny lay in her casket, that her situation was worse than mine. Brad was in a wheelchair, but he was still Brad. He had a future. Was Ginny saying to Joanne that her son would be better off dead? Joanne came up to me and told me what Ginny had said. I was too numb at the time to let it hurt me. But I will never forget it. I'm sure Joanne won't either.

I didn't see Joanne at all after I decided to cheer her up. I did get some cards to send her. I'm sure we care, but maybe we're getting weary of each other's heartache. She is good at giving advice but will never listen to mine. I want to help. It's possible that we have days when we don't want to be cheered up. I give up. No, I don't. I don't give up. But for now, I will give her some space.

I awoke to Jenny's music box playing all by itself. I love things like that.

Voice Recordings

FEBRUARY 5

Good morning, Jennifer, my hero. I have had a lot of interesting things happening. I am going to have to tell you about them if I can remember them all.

First of all, yesterday I was lying in bed awake, and I started thinking about the time that girl bit your finger when you tried to keep her from hitting your friend. I relived that whole incident in my mind. They had to operate on your finger; she bit right through your nail. For the longest time you had a little Band-Aid on the end of your finger, but the nail grew back in time for you to die. You did your nails that day, and you had that pretty long nail on your baby finger. I often think of the irony, like the dress you picked out for Christmas that looked so nice on you, that you ended up wearing in your casket. But that is not what I was going to talk about.

I wanted to tell you that while I was lying there thinking about this incident with your finger, your little music box started playing, *It's a Small World After All*. Before we moved, I always used to try to get that music box to play, but it was broken. If I set it down hard enough, it would play two or three notes. For some reason, yesterday morning it decided to play the entire song, and I just sat up in bed listening to it. I had the biggest smile on my face and I just said, "Hello, Jennifer." There are people who would think of a logical reason for it to play, and maybe there is one. I wouldn't doubt it, but maybe there isn't. That's what I have come to really learn since you died. I was always such a skeptic, but since you died, I have no doubt in my mind of what exists. I am not saying I don't believe in heaven, but I have realized that spirits can be everywhere. When I was a child and afraid, my mother said that it's not ghosts you should fear, but people that are living. I didn't understand it very well then, but I do now.

So many odd things that happen that I wonder about. Sometimes songs you loved play at the most unusual moments, as if prompted by something or someone. You knew your dad collected pigs up north at the old cabin, and you guys had just been playing Pass the Pig up there, you and Dad and Jamin and Jesse. One day, soon after your death, your dad was walking to his car after work and he looked down and saw a little pink pig from Pass the Pig on the ground next to his car. It still sits in your truck. Yellow roses show up, or people bring them to me. So many things, Jenny. I find neat things with yellow roses on them in unusual places, like a beat-up box with a yellow rose and a poem to *My Mother* that a lady said I could have for two dollars. I wish I could remember all of them. Little moments when I just felt that you were there or that something happened for a reason. Cathie called me this morning and said she was going through the mail and found a stamp with a yellow rose. Then she was at her favorite cross-stitch store in Davisburg and found a beautiful picture of yellow roses with a ladybug on the stem. I put a ladybug on Cathie's Jenny Bug Bear.

Sometimes ladybugs will just show up at my house for no reason at all, especially in the wintertime. Just the other day Jamin called out, "Ma, come here, in the bathroom, there's a ladybug," and I said, "Don't kill it; just let it live in here for a while."

It has been almost three years since you died, and so many things are happening—gifts from God, visits from you, I don't know. Jackie called me last night, excited about a job interview with a Christian Counseling Center. She has had three very vivid dreams about you lately. Aunt Carol sent her a box of cassette tapes that Jackie had been looking for. They were tapes you and she had recorded when you were kids, just acting goofy and talking about school, church, and Pastor's sons, Mike and Mark, when you guys were all in love. I haven't heard them, but she said she listened to them over and over and cried so hard and so deep that she thought she should call someone to come help her, but then she realized that she needed to do that, she needed to get that out and sometimes we just do.

I have grief spasms more than crying. The pain will come into my head so quick and hard that my eyes slam shut, and my face scrunches up and my muscles hurt. It's like this massive flood wants to come out, and I stop it. Then, I can't describe the pain that just floods over me, but it goes away as fast as it comes. It is usually triggered by something I see on television…a girl with long blonde hair and blue eyes, a morgue, a show with autopsies. I just have to look away. Last night I was watching a movie where they were getting a man ready for a funeral and sewing his lips shut. I couldn't handle it, Jenny. I totally freaked. Not out loud, because dad was here, but in my mind. I couldn't stand the thought that they might have done that to you. My heart and mind can't handle it. Other times, it's just an unbearable aching in my heart, an empty spot. I try to tell myself that emptiness can be filled with good. God promises us that those who mount up with wings as eagles shall renew their strength, and if we try, He will be there to help us. (Isaiah 43).

I am nervous today, Jenny, nervous and excited, because I am going tomorrow to see Rita to have my aura read. I'm nervous, because I am afraid no one will come. She sees our loved ones around us, and I'm afraid nobody will appear. I have a lot of faith in myself, don't I? You know who I want to come. You know who I grieve for the most, who anyone would grieve for the most, their child. I don't really have too much to say about it except that I'm going.

FEBRUARY 8 (JOURNAL)

Jim is mentioning a possible move to Chicago. My self-esteem is zero. I just prayed that the Lord would sort it out. I think, I read, I hope, and I pray. I feel I will never come to terms with Jenny's passing. I will spend the rest of my time here trying. I feel there won't be room for accomplishments because survival will be my only goal. Again, Jenny's death has become my life.

FEBRUARY 11 (JOURNAL)

I haven't been writing. I think of February 6 and Rita much too often. What a strange change in such a short time. I think I may have thought the meeting was authentic for about five hours. Feelings of doubt crept up on me. I will discuss it on my recorded tapes. Should I talk to Pastor about seeing Rita? For the time being the marriage is stable. We are not moving to Chicago.

February 12

Well, Jen, I have a lot of things to talk to you about. I have been doing a lot of thinking, a lot of pondering, a lot of soul searching, and I can't say that I have come up with anything at this point except confusion, but I'll tell you the story. I thought I would be really nervous or excited to have my aura read, but it turns out that I was totally calm the morning of February 6. I had a meeting at church, though I have to say that I wasn't really at the meeting in my mind. I prayed hard to God before I went. I said, "God, please, if you don't want me to do this, if this isn't right somehow, let me know; if it's not right, I don't want to go."

I arrived at Rita's house, and we went upstairs to this little bedroom that she turned into a sitting room so she could talk to her clients. She lit a white candle. She said it was the light of God and she was keeping this light around her because delving into the spirit world might stir up something evil. Believe it or not, she told me a lot by looking at my hand. She told me I had two children, a boy and a girl, and then said, "Your daughter has passed on." I started to get choked up, when she put down my hand and she told me that suddenly a spirit was very quickly and strongly coming into the room. I was excited and thought, *Jenny's here, she came, she came.* The two things I recall are that you were sorry for the pain that everyone went through and that you were worried about your dad that he wasn't dealing with your loss. She said Jamin would someday have a little girl and that you would be coming back to us in this little girl. I did not want to hear anything about reincarnation because I want to meet you in Heaven when I die? She went on to describe your accident and she revealed more, and quite a few things were totally wrong, but I give people the benefit of the doubt. We finished the session, and I left there feeling rather numb and uncertain. I played the tape for your dad, and he didn't act skeptical. He just listened. I think he enjoyed listening. He didn't do or say anything to make me feel stupid for going or anything that would hurt my feelings.

Jamin, who had seemed so excited before I went, called and asked what had happened. I told him a few things, and all of a sudden, he began to explain it away. I guess he's not as excited about this as I thought. He never listened to the tape. But that night, Jenny, something began to happen to me. I got horribly sad. And it wasn't until later that I began to find out what was bothering me. I didn't listen to the tape again. I thought I would listen to it over and over and over again, which is why I wanted it, but I didn't.

Then Sunday night, when I went to my Stephen Ministry class, we got on the subject of spirits and someone asked Pastor, "What do you think of spirits?" and he replied that he thinks that spirits that exist on earth, since believers are supposed to be in heaven with God, are not from God. I immediately began defending my actions to myself. I thought, *He's wrong. There are good spirits on earth too, not just bad spirits, but good spirits from God.*

Well, I went home and felt more uneasy, thinking, *Okay, fine, then what Pastor is saying is that if somebody came to me, it wasn't you, it was something evil, it was something sent to seem like you, to fool me, to take my thoughts away from God, to make me go back to this lady again and again, to pull me away from religion and into this.*

I thought deeply about that. I started to be a little less harsh with my thoughts about Pastor and one day I talked to my sister, Carol, who knows absolutely nothing about the psychic. I was talking to her about what Pastor said and she asked, "Do you ever read the Bible? Do you ever see what the Bible says?" I decided to get my Bible right while I had her on the phone. I looked up a few things and saw, *Mediums*. Where it said *Spirits*, it said *See demons*. So I'm shook up, of course. Then I discovered a section that said *Spiritual gifts* and I thought I'd research that. My Bible is still open to that. I know I need to read it because I will have proof that you weren't there at all. I'm afraid to read it. Of course, I would like to think you were there. So, at that point I was still totally confused, but then I remembered how I prayed. I remembered how I felt the evening of the day I went. I had prayed to God to not let me go if He didn't want me to go. I started to think, *Alright, you asked Him to do this for you, but you had to make that choice. He was not going to keep you from going. He wanted you to go, He wanted you to learn something, He wanted you to see something, to understand.* The two things that had bothered me so much popped up in my head again and again. One, I asked her what you looked like, and she said you had dark hair. I said, "No." You were as blonde as blonde could be. She said you were thin. She said you were pretty. Okay, I can agree with that. But she said you were so surrounded by light that it was hard for her to see what color your hair was. Okay, I understand that, but in the beginning when we were talking about the accident, she said, "He is still alive," and I didn't know who she meant. She said, "He's alive, isn't he?" and then it hit me that she was talking about the man who killed you. I said, "No, he's not alive."

Were those God's answers to me? Did God say, *You go, you will learn, you will discover for yourself that this is not from Me, this is not of Me?* He gave me those ideas, those thoughts. Also, in the Bible, it says that one of our spiritual gifts is the gift of discernment. I will have to look into that, because I am not sure if that applies to this, but the reason I was so uneasy that night was probably not because I had felt close to you and then you were gone from me again; it was probably because part of me knew this wasn't real or right. God allowed me to see that for myself. He answered my prayer by letting me learn, letting me grow from this experience, letting me see for myself and I did.

I have to admit, Jen, I am still fascinated by George Anderson and Rosemary Altea, because they write about their experiences and I read George Anderson's book, *We Don't Die*. I have read Rosemary Altea's book, *The Eagle and The Rose*, which of course would draw me in like a magnet just by the title [because of] a poem you wrote in school, *The Eagle*, where you end it by saying, *I'm Free*, and you will always be yellow roses to me. So, I read that book too. She is so full of love and talks about being so connected to God and what she does is a gift from God, and she helps people. How could it be wrong? How can it be evil when she is talking about being kind and loving and gentle to other human beings? And so, I guess I will continue to have this confusion, this tug of war in my mind; but I did decide to pray about it and maybe talk to Pastor. I know what he will say, but maybe he can ease my mind about this. So, Jenny, if it wasn't you, that is fine because I want you to be happy and peaceful. I do not want to disturb you. I still truly and deeply believe the experiences I had earlier when I knew you were there with me. You see, that is the difference. That is discernment. When you feel peace, love, goodness, and joy, you know that is from God.

I am working on my inside, reading, growing, and I must start working on my outside. If I'm not comfortable with myself this way, then I've got the ability to change that. There are not a lot of things we can change in life, Jenny. I cannot bring you back. I can become a stronger person than I was before. I can look at your death and think, *You can go backward, you can stay the same, or you can make Jenny proud of you. And you can become even better because you knew her. You can become even stronger because you had her for 20 years.* I can do that. And I will, because it is one thing I do have control over.

FEBRUARY 15 (JOURNAL)

Buried Dreams

The other day I came home from a redeeming Ash Wednesday service to Jamin telling me he hated college. He's not sure what he wants to do in life. God, I felt like a failure. Dreams of a future with Jenny are gone. Dreams that Jamin would go to college may be gone. But it's my dream, not Jamin's. I feel he would have a better life. Sometimes losses hit hard. The happy marriage, Jenny's wedding and grandchildren, and a secure future for Jamin were my dreams, not God's plan. But after the pouting and disappointment, I decided again to live my own life. I cannot keep living for and through others. I will be stronger if I let go of dreams. I can still move forward with me. I love Jamin no matter what he chooses for his life.

FEBRUARY 21 (JOURNAL)

Lynn and Tracy arrived at 7 p.m. tonight. They brought some pictures of Jenny from Saugatuck. She looks so sweet. God, I miss her. Tomorrow they are going to see Rita. We will see how that goes. I weigh more than when Jen died. However, I am only half of what I was. I have only half a soul, half a spirit, and half a heart. Perhaps I am half dead. I am fighting for my whole.

FEBRUARY 24

It's Monday morning. Jenny, yesterday I was commissioned as a Stephen Minister. I have completed my 50 hours of training. Now I will see if I can apply what I have learned. I have already been given my first care receiver. I can only say it's an older woman in a nursing home, and

I hope in some way I can bless her life. I know that when that happens, in return I will be blessed as well.

Your cousin, Tracy, and Aunt Lynn came for the weekend and we really had a good time. We got comfortable, drank tea, and talked about books we were reading. We behave like much older women. It's crazy how Tracy just fits right in with that being that she is in her mid-20s, but she is so close to her mom and they have a wonderful relationship. She is an only daughter like you were. I understand how important that relationship is.

We went and met your Aunt Cathie for breakfast and the four of us took off to go visit Rita as I mentioned earlier. The lady was gracious enough to let us all in. She was sweet and kind. I sat and I listened, and things happened. It's private for them, so I won't discuss it here, but things occurred that made them cry and made them laugh. In some ways Rita was very right on, and other times she was way off. Rita kept asking if there were questions. And they had a hard time coming up with some at the time. She said you were standing behind me. I didn't feel you. It was a very emotional couple of hours, but they may go back. I probably will not go back again. It's not that I don't want to believe in this, it's that I want to follow God's Word.

Again, I will speak of irony. After the session we went to the bookstore at Somerset Mall. You would love this mall Jenny. I had asked Rita how she equates what she does, and her gift, with what the bible says. She told me to look up an author. I wrote down his name. These particular books weren't available, so I scanned the religious section. It's strange how you can look at hundreds of books, but there will be one book that will pop out at you. That night, when Lynn and Tracy and I were all cozy in our pajamas and drinking our tea, we listened to the tape of my visit with Rita, and toward the end of the tape, I started to peek through the book I bought. I felt that you wanted me to find this. Every time I feel your presence it is a gift, a gift from God, and I thank Him. Well, in the beginning of this book *Still by Your Side* by Marjorie Holmes , the first line is, *It began with the music box; the faint, sweet tinkling sounds that woke me one night after my husband's death.* I thought of your music box playing for me. She heard hers many times just as I did. Then I went on to the next page and will read you what she wrote, because I had to read it to Tracy and Aunt Lynn. I felt bad. I don't want to burst their bubble. I have to feel the way I feel, and they have to feel the way they feel. I don't try to make them Christians. Perhaps that's bad in God's eyes. Maybe I should try, but I don't. I basically just tell people what I believe. I don't try to change their life or tell them that they're wrong or that they're not going to heaven. So, I can't say I read this to them because I was trying to change their mind; I read this to them because I thought this was God trying to talk to me.

I had gone that afternoon. I had sat and I had listened, and I hadn't said a word. He knew that He was first and foremost on my mind. I wasn't going to let Him go and go over into the psychic world, so I just felt this was something I had to read to them; and they could take from it what they wished. Marjorie says on page 12 of her book, *To me this is so significant that I want to share these experiences as I describe my life without my husband and what I have learned from grief. Actually, such things are not uncommon.* And she is talking, Jenny, mostly about little gifts that she has been given since her husband died, gifts like I feel I have received from you and from God. She goes on to say, *Such things are not uncommon and can be beautiful if received as a gift from the God who created us and Jesus who promised us eternal life.* Then she says, *But they must not be sought or contrived. I can't warn you too strongly, beware of anyone who would claim to induce them, hear them for you or interpret their meaning. Such people are not God's messengers. At best, they are fallible human beings who may mean well, but are woefully misguided. At worst, false prophets, as condemned in the Bible who could lead you astray. I know because once long ago when I was young and vulnerable, I briefly followed that precarious path, but within a year I was seriously disillusioned and learned a bitter lesson, which I think God must have meant me to have in order to warn others.*

Well, needless to say, how would anybody take this? Here I am sitting in there in Rita's reading room, with my relatives and then a short time later out of rows and rows of books I pick out this tiny little yellow book, when I was looking for something completely different. Wouldn't you think that reading first about the music box and then what she says about seeking that other path, wouldn't you think God was talking to you?

February 26

Jenny, I think that today I have something more like a prayer I need to pray to God. So, I will talk to Him for a bit. God, I have heard so many times and read so many times since Jenny's death, from Romans, that all things work to the good of those who love You and whom You love, and I have been so patient. Next month it will be three years and even though I know that I am climbing the steps one at a time, I continue to have periods where I feel that someone is pushing me or blocking my way up the stairs or someone is behind me pulling me back to keep me from going forward. Just when I feel that it is true, that adversity does make you strong and that soon I will be able to handle anything and be a better person, I fall again. I keep expecting all these improvements, like being better instead of bitter and so many other clichés about not giving up. I have read that over and over again in other people's stories and in books of faith and the Bible. But why is it I have days when I sit down on the couch after a busy day and cry and think, *I don't want this. I can't do this. I can't live like this. If she's not here, nothing means anything to me.*

A couple of nights ago, after a busy day, I went up to bed and didn't want to read or write anything. I just wanted to lie down and go to sleep. I prayed, *Dear God, just let me go to sleep and sleep and sleep and sleep, and I don't care if I wake up.*

Then I will get up the next morning with a new hope and a new strength and the desire to keep fighting. God's power to survive is planted in my soul. I believe it is a gift because He knows that living in this world can destroy us emotionally. Without his protection planted deeply within us, our first encounter with adversity might end us. I think I've got it mixed up now, Jenny. I started out talking to God and now I think I'm talking to you both again. Anyway, all of the sudden the urge to fight this battle comes upon me once again, and again I start climbing the steps. Then I have a time like yesterday afternoon when I did my work for the day and I was tired and I came home. I sat down on the couch with the sun in my eyes as it filtered through the trees in the back yard and I just started to cry. I cried out to God, "I miss her so bad." Suddenly my head starts to hurt and I feel like I cannot bear it another moment.

Then I realize, as I start wiping away the tears and notice the clock, that there is somewhere else I have to be, that no matter how I feel, no matter how often this feeling comes, I have to keep climbing those stairs, and boy are they steep. Some days I can manage only one. Some days I feel light as a feather and I can run up as many as I want and never get short of breath. Then there are going to be days when I fall down a few. The fall is going to hurt. But if I don't keep trying to get up every day and climb those stairs, I know I will die. It is a choice that I made right after you died. I didn't have a choice because I had people who I felt needed me—people I would never have hurt by taking my own life. I couldn't cause any more pain than what's already been caused. So, I made a vow that I would not let myself go under.

I sure wish I knew what Jamin and your dad think. They don't talk but I see what they feel. I read it in their faces. What thoughts are in their minds about you? But once again, Jenny, I have major steps to climb today because yesterday I fell down too many. And I imagine this is what I will have to expect for many years to come, if not the rest of my life. I don't think I will ever get to the top of the stairs until the day I see you again.

When your Aunt Lynn and your cousin Tracy were here last weekend, they brought me a beautiful gift—a little pack of photos of our trip to Saugatuck with your cousins, Nicki and Tracy and your aunts, Cathie and Lynn. It was just us girls. I had forgotten about that trip, but when they brought those pictures, every memory came back to me.

When I showed them to your father, I could see the pain in his eyes. Everything that I talk about on these tapes, everything that I pray about, all of those same emotions are in his eyes. I know he is feeling exactly the same things I am, all the time, but he gets up and goes to work because he has no choice. He is the main support of our family. But it helps him survive and for a time he can bury his thoughts. I had the choice to stay home and grieve. He gave me that. I admire him, but I also think everyone's different. He needs his work. If I had gone back to work and buried this, I don't know if I'd be here right now.

So, this was my talk. My talk that started out to be to God. I think He understands I am just so used to talking to you on the tapes that I automatically just started talking to you in what started out to be a prayer. A prayer asking God to please help me when I feel that I cannot climb another step, where I ask Him to please stay behind me, keep pushing me and pushing me, because it's the only way I'm going to make it.

But I do have a new adventure today, Jenny. As a Stephen Minister I will go and see my first care receiver, and boy am I nervous. How will I feel walking in and talking to a 90-year-old woman, looking at someone who has been on the earth so many years when some of the people I have loved the most were here such a short time, but I'm sure she will have so much to tell. And you know what, Jenny? I stop and think how you will never, ever grow old, never have a wrinkle on your face, and you lived such a short, sweet, beautiful life. You won't feel the pain of losing others, as this woman probably has lost so many before her. I hope I will bless her life and I know she will surely bless mine. So, wish me luck, Jen. Be with me God, guide me. Let me listen with a very caring heart and I pray that she feels comfortable enough that she will want me to come back and see her again.

March 3

It's a Monday morning. Well Jenny, we are entering the month that will make it three years that you've been gone, and I'm not sure how I feel. Sometimes I think, okay, it's been three years, I do feel better, and other times I think, three years, and nothing's changed. I really believe that's the way it is going to be for the rest of my life. I decided I will give it another maybe four or five years before I make that statement.

I am at the point where I come out [of my tunnel of grief] for periods of time. I feel like I went back in the other night though. Basically, your dad and I, before you died, were starting to realize that it wouldn't be long before you moved out permanently and Jamin was taking driver's training and a lot of changes were happening. I was working full time. You were working a lot of hours. Jamin, of course, was still in high school. We were all kind of going our separate ways, but your dad and I realized we had to start concentrating on time just for ourselves and learning how to be together with just each other. So, every Friday night we would go out to dinner. It was a given. We would talk about the future and what we wanted to do. We found out we had a lot of things in common when it came to our future, just about everything actually. So, we were going to travel around during the summer, and we were going to stop in at your house and stop in at Jamin's house. We talked about how we would take the kids off your hands so you and your husband could take a little trip or go do things you wanted to do. Maybe we would pick up our grandchildren in a motorhome and take them somewhere fun for a few days and make memories. But when you died, all of that shattered like somebody took a rock and threw it at a huge reflection of our dreams. They shattered, and the pieces scattered everywhere across our lives.

We didn't go out on Friday night anymore, because it was a Friday night that we were out dreaming when you died. We even bought a video camera that fateful evening. One that would never capture your reflection or your voice. When we did finally decide to go out after you were gone, it was always a Wednesday or Thursday. We just recently started attempting Friday nights again. One evening started out badly. I was anxious to go out, and your dad was frustrated by the time we left because he had received an email from someone at work and he was perturbed. I had to try and draw that out of him and get him to cheer up. I succeeded, but due to other experiences at the restaurant, and thinking about our last time there with you and Jesse, I was in a low mood, so he was trying to cheer me up. He gave me some compliments and said some sweet things, then we got up to leave. I was getting my coat on and I turned around and he was gone, as usual. I've asked him before, please do not leave me in the restaurant and take off. I was a little upset and when I walked by him at the door, I said, "I thought I'd asked you, Jim, please wait for me."

Well, he got defensive and then angry out in the parking lot, and he screamed at the top of his lungs. There were people behind us, and I felt humiliated. I got in the car. Since I lost you, I have always been afraid of losing it because I always thought I would go crazy, so you really try hard to hold on to your sanity. You try so hard not to freak out, but I had a feeling I was going to freak out and I did. I had one margarita in the restaurant, and I guess that was enough to give me the courage to lose control and let go of my sanity. I started yelling at your dad, and I started yelling about everything in my life. I don't think it was just directed toward your dad. It was anger that had built up in me because I am always one of those people who try to keep the peace and harmony, and I don't like to rile things up. So, I guess I just let everything out. I think I wasn't just mad at your dad, I was mad at God, I was mad at fate, I was mad at everything. I screamed all the way home about certain things being unfair in the world and injustice and bad luck and everything else. I even told him, "Well, if you get transferred for your job, maybe that would be a good time for you to go your way and I will go mine. You go there, I'll stay here." I said some awful things.

At home, I went upstairs and picked up my current book about the death of a child and read until I went to sleep. The next morning, I thought, *I can't live like this, I can't be mad, I can't stay mad. I just can't survive and stay angry. I can't live with anger and I can't hate.* Some people thrive on anger. Some people can go for weeks and not speak to their spouse or perhaps they even leave. Well, I can't function that way. So, I called your dad and told him, "I found out this morning the reason for my outburst, and I guess it was PMS. Perhaps that, combined with having one drink, I guess I just have to blame it on PMS." And you know what he said to me, Jenny? He said, "Well, I have PMS too." And I knew at that moment that everything was okay. I laughed and he laughed. That's all we had to say. We didn't have to go over it. He took me seriously, but in a way, I guess he just knew that once in a while I have to let go of it too. I have to let go of the pain, and I think I cleansed myself a little bit that night.

I wanted to talk to you about your dad and how his sense of humor does save us sometimes. Even though we don't really connect these days, I don't really want to be alone either. I feel so sorry for couples, the strain on their lives and on their relationships that they experience after the loss of a child. And what surprises me is how your dad and I are still holding on when sometimes it was a struggle to hold on before you were gone. We had to work at it. We have two entirely different personalities, and I think one of the things that held us together was our love for our children and our hope for the future. Maybe it's our shared pain that holds us together. No other person on the face of the earth shares our intimate struggle. Only the mother and father that created the child can understand the other's agony. I feel that some days we hold on by a thread, just a thread. Will it keep holding us? Or will it break someday? Only God knows, Jen.

March 5 (Journal)

How can things change in such a short amount of time? All of a sudden, nothing matters. Is it March? Oh yes, the dreaded month. I feel like I'm losing my mind. I can't concentrate on anything important. I am so tired of this roller coaster ride. How long can this go on? No matter how hard I try it won't work. Everything is falling apart. My marriage, my body, my health, my mind, my energy, and my motivation are things of the past. They have left me in the dust.

March 7 (Journal)

I am sitting on my bed, looking outside into the woods. We were gifted with an unexpected snowfall, so the branches are coated in silver, the sun is shining, and the sky is postcard blue. This seems unusual since we have had so many gray days lately. The last few days I have been so down and depressed...because it's March, and I am probably going to struggle with that this whole month, just as I have in the past. It just hit me the night before last like a big gray cloud that moved in and settled over the top of me, and I get so bad that I can hardly move. It presses down on me, and I can't breathe. I can't concentrate.

I went to see my care receiver and missed my turn twice and went way out of my way. In trying to correct my mistake, and return to the right direction, I went right past the nursing home. It's enough to shake you up, especially when you think, *Okay, where was my mind when I went by it? Was I even conscious? Did I lose time? Was my depression so bad that I slipped out for a few moments?*

We have so much grief, so much loneliness and just when we think we can't stand it anymore, God sends us a ray of hope or a friend. Through all that suffering, we are gathering strength and courage. I'm beginning to think life is just one big lesson from beginning to end. When I grieve my daughter, I often go back to the Holocaust and think of families who lost families. Mothers who lost all of their children, not just one. I think I have talked about this before. I think of parents who watch their children suffer before they die. And I think of my beautiful, shining daughter and how fortunate she was to have twenty wonderful years instead of a few years of suffering, pain, and then death. God, how blessed I am. How very, very blessed I am. If there is ever any time that depression weighs down on you, don't let it last more than a day or two, just start thinking. That's why I read, because when you read you find out about other people's lives. Don't close your mind to all the adversity and all the pain that goes on in the world ... Don't run from it. Read about it. Research it. It can only strengthen you, and it can take you away from yourself, away from self-pity. It can help you to reach into the hearts and thoughts of others.

You are not alone. In fact, in most cases, you are a lot more fortunate than a lot of people. Be grateful if your loved one had no pain. Be grateful if they were healthy up until they died, because so many aren't. So, I must remember this during the month of March. This painful month when that dark oppressive cloud keeps pushing down on my head. I am going to fight this. I am not going to give into it. I gave into it for a day and thought I would lose my mind, but then yesterday there was actually blue in the sky and God has repeated that gift today.

March 23

JenBug, I am sitting here on Palm Sunday. I fixed a cup of tea and decided to talk to you. You died on a Saturday at 2:15 a.m. Palm Sunday was your first Sunday in heaven. I think the beginning of this nightmarish week actually started with March 17. Remember the fight we had on St. Patrick's Day? You and your friends had gone to Canada because you knew that's where your boyfriends were headed. Perhaps you girls were going to get even, I don't know. You were really upset about some bar Jesse had gone to. I remember asking Jamin that night where you had gone, and he said you went somewhere with your girlfriends, but he didn't know where. I don't remember why he didn't know or if he did and didn't tell. But I remember thinking you were okay, you just went out with your friends. But when two o'clock rolled around and you weren't home and I hadn't heard from you, I knew something was up, so I got up and started pacing, waiting, and praying. I finally woke your dad up and told him that you weren't home yet and I was worried, so we both worried.

Finally, I think it was about three o'clock when you finally arrived home. You hadn't been driving, and you were on your way home from Canada, so you didn't call; but oh you were in such a bad mood. We started telling you how worried we were and yelling at you for not calling and not leaving a note and all kinds of other things that parents do, and you fought back. That's when you told us about Jesse going to that bar, and I could tell that was bothering you the most. You just were upset about where he had gone. The thing that sticks in my mind is when you threw your alarm clock at me and told me to get out. I just went to bed. I was just relieved you were home. Then you came in my room asking me for an alarm clock because you had to get up in the morning and yours was in pieces on the floor. I wouldn't give you my alarm clock. I guess it was just a bad night.

So that began the last week of your life. The next morning, I got up and was too sad to even get ready for work. I called and told them I was going to be late. You and I talked for a while. It was strained. There was tension, and we both felt horrible; but I went to work. I remember telling some of my friends about this terrible fight we had. It upset me for quite a few days. I remember asking you the Wednesday before you died if you wanted to go to the mall after dinner. I had decided to cheer myself up and go get shoes I'd been looking at. I thought if you went with me, we could spend some time together and talk. When I asked you, you thought about it in your unique way and then you said *Nah, I am going to Melanie's*. So, I went alone. I wore the shoes to work the next day, Thursday, and came home for lunch. You and I talked about how we were going to settle things if you were going to come and go as you please. You were almost twenty-one. We talked about the possibility of you paying room and board, and you said you would clean the house for your room and board, and I said, "Okay, we will give it a try."

Then you had talked to your dad that week as well, and you told him you were going to go back to college and you said, "If Jackie can do it, I can do it." Your dad was proud of you. By Friday, we were all pretty perky. I remember you had called me that day at work because you had driven your dad to take his car in for repairs in the morning, and he needed to be picked up from work. You asked me if I would do it because you were getting ready for a 21st birthday party, Melanie's and Heather's who were two of your good friends.

I said, "Jenny, remember I have a tanning appointment, but I'll go get him after I am done." But you told me to go tanning because your dad and I were going to go to Florida to see Grandpa Smith. We were going to leave you and Jamin home for the first time. I didn't like tanning, but you did. When I got home, your dad was already home because somebody had given him a ride. So, it worked out. But I hear that telephone call, I hear it so clearly, Jen, my last telephone call I would ever get from you. It was just, "Hi, Mom, whatcha doing?" I said, "Working." You said, "Will you pick Dad up for me from work?" I remember when I got home, there you were doing your nails while sitting on the side of the couch where you and I always sat. We always sat the same way with our feet curled up underneath us. I remember coming home, and I had my new green raincoat on that I had just purchased. I still have it. I was all dressed up like I was every day when I went to work. I remember the muscles in my face were sore, like they were every Friday from a whole week's worth of tension at work. But I plopped down on the couch where you had been sitting doing your nails, and you got all excited and got up to show us the outfit you got out of layaway that day. I am glad you did, because they would have called us and asked for you and told us you had a layaway to pick up…and it would have crushed my heart. Thank goodness you picked it up. So, I watched as you went to pick up the outfit that you would die in. I was worried you were going to wreck your nails, so I only saw a piece and told you I would see it later. I would never see the rest, but your friends described it to me.

I was so tired my head was spinning, and I was so glad it was Friday. So, there you were, right in front of me. I remember exactly how you looked. You had been shopping that day and took your friends to lunch, your last full fun day. Thank God, it was your day off, and you got to enjoy it. You got to sleep in your last day, put your make up on for the last time, take a shower for the last time, make yourself beautiful for the last time. The next person making you up would be someone in a funeral home, that didn't even know you, didn't even know how you wore your hair or how you did your makeup, what color lipstick you wore—somebody who knew nothing about you. I didn't see you when you left, but your friends told me you were so beautiful that night, so radiant. I started up the stairs to say goodbye to you but your dad honked the horn. Your dad and I went out to dinner and bought that video camera, then I came home and went down to my friend Barb's to play cards, came home, watched a little TV and went to bed.

I guess this is as good a time as any to talk about your accident. I don't know if I will be able to remember it all, and I didn't see it afterward because they, your friends, didn't call me. I never saw the car. I never saw you until that person who didn't know you fixed you up. I will tell you what I remember.

I was in bed, and sirens woke me up. I was drifting in and out of sleep because I had a couple of drinks at Barb's; I hadn't had a drink in a long time, and it was making me sleepy and awake at the same time. I heard the sirens and knew it was about the time you would be coming home or calling if you were going somewhere else. You were either home by two or you called at two; it never failed. You had left a note that read, *At Mel's*. I think you were planning on staying the night. That is why we were so worried on St. Patrick's Day.

When I heard those sirens, Jenny, my first thought, as always if you weren't home, was you. So, I lifted a prayer up to heaven and asked, *Dear God, please don't let it be Jenny*. I thought that's it, it's okay now. I fell back to sleep. I don't know how much time passed. I think it was about three o'clock or so when the phone rang. Still in that half-awake, half-asleep state, I jumped out of bed and said "Jenny, it's Jenny." I picked up the phone, but your dad had already hung up from downstairs where he'd fallen asleep on the couch.

I ran downstairs and asked if it was you. But your dad was pacing the floor and said, "That was the police station telling us that policemen are coming to our door." It was only a few seconds, and they were there. Your dad stood by the steps when he opened the door, and I sat down on the steps in my pajamas. Two policemen stepped in, and I hoped and prayed so bad that they would tell us you got arrested, you were in fight, or you were in the hospital…anything, but don't tell me she is dead. But they did, Jenny, they did tell us you were dead. And then I just sat there, and they stood there, and I just stared at them.

First, they said you were in a head-on collision on Joslyn Road. That is why I heard the sirens. They added that a man had crossed over the line and hit you head on. Then I think your dad asked, "Is she dead?" And the policemen said, "I am sorry, she is." I thought about this man who they said hit your car and asked, "How is the other person?" He was dead, too. I don't know why I asked that; maybe I needed to hear that he was. I think I was worried about him as well. I just know I sat there, and my heart stopped, and I thought about your dad, *how is he still standing up?* He adored you and loved you. You were so special to him. How could he ever live without you? How could he ever live knowing someone hurt you, his little girl? But he stayed standing and neither of us screamed, neither of us cried and the policeman said that he would be in touch.

"Do you have somebody to call?" he asked. Then he told us they were taking your body to the morgue. He asked me if I had any clothes to put on, which I thought was a really strange question. The policeman gave Dad a card and said to call him or he would call. Now, as I talk to you, I wonder how policemen handle having to tell a family that their child is dead. It must be so difficult. Your dad went into the family room and sat on the couch, and I went upstairs because I thought maybe we were supposed to go somewhere. I didn't know. Were we supposed to go to you? What were we supposed to do? I went upstairs and put on a pair of jeans. I remember mumbling to myself in the closet, but I don't remember what I said. I reached for a sweater with shaky hands and put it on, then I brushed my teeth. Heaven knows why I did that. I had just brushed them a little while before, but I brushed my teeth.

I went downstairs, and your dad was sitting on the couch. He started to cry, and I sat down next to him and tried to comfort him. He said, "She is never coming home again." Then I thought *I have to tell someone. I have to call somebody*. I can't remember, Jenny, if I cried yet, I just can't remember. I think that I thought I was dreaming or something, so I called your Aunt Carol and I told her that you were dead, and she came over and then Pastor came over and Pastor sat with me and sat with me and sat with me. Oh, I forgot, I called your Aunt Cathie too, and she came over. And she and Dad went to Dave's where Jamin was spending the night to pick him up. They went to the door, and they had to tell them that you died.

All I can really remember after that is Pastor being there, just sitting on the couch with him, and people moving and walking all around. I remember when Jamin came in and he sat down on the end of the treadmill. I know there were people around, but really don't remember who was there, but I remember Jamin saying, "Now what am I going to do, what am I going to do? She was going to help me. She was going to help me get through twelfth grade."

I should ask him to clarify if this is what he really said, but that is what sticks in my mind. I remember Barb and Paul and Jeremy coming because Jeremy had been with you that night and had left in the car right before you. He had been waiting for you at Jesse's house. You and Jesse never showed up, and then they got the phone call from Jesse. They all got back in the car and came flying back, so they were at your accident. They saw you. Jesse saw you, Toni, Jeremy, Jesse's mom and her boyfriend. I don't know a whole lot about what went on there, other than Jesse had stayed with you. He had torn the steering wheel off of your chest and the door off of its hinges, and after he had run to find a phone, he sat with you and buried his face in your neck and kept telling you how much he loved you. That is what he told us. And when the EMS got there, he wanted them to revive you, wanted them to help you, but they told him that he wouldn't want them to revive you. They knew you had a broken neck. They knew that it wouldn't do any good, and they also didn't know how long exactly since your heart stopped.

I wish you could have lived long enough, Jenny, not for my sake, but for your sake, to donate some of your organs, because you had that on your driver's license, and I was proud of you because I was always chicken to put that on my driver's license, but it is on there now, Bugs. It is. Because you make me stronger. I think of you, and I am not chicken about anything anymore. I am not even afraid to die. Not the least little bit. Because if my daughter, my little girl can do it, so can I. If she can be brave and die, I can be brave and die. It is one bit of relief you have in your life to not be afraid of death. Some people are so afraid of death that they can hardly handle living, but I will never be afraid again.

Well, as I mentioned, I remember Barb, Paul and Jeremy coming in. I was standing in the kitchen, and they were wailing. I don't know any other word to describe it other than wailing, screaming and crying. I was watching them as if I were watching a movie. I was detached from reality. Poor Jeremy. Poor, poor Jeremy. He adored you. So did his brother Zachary. And you adored them. You were such great friends. Barb and I met when you and Zach were in our wombs. But, that is why you were alone in the car that night. You told your girlfriend, you told Toni, "Go with Jeremy, he likes you, you like him, go with Jeremy." You were trying to play matchmaker, weren't you, Jen? Always trying to help your friends, always trying to help out. So I remember them crying, and I remember people on the telephone calling other people.

I remember Pastor asking us about a funeral home. I didn't want the one in Lake Orion, and I am glad because the man who killed you was at that one. It would have been horrible to have you both there. That wouldn't have worked out at all. So, I am glad I picked the one in Rochester because it was an old house; it was real pretty, and they were really nice. I remember such a nice, young, handsome man taking care of you. He said not to worry, that he would take care of you; and I believed him. I showed him your pictures that we brought, and he said you were beautiful, and I knew he would take care of you.

I remember that same morning that you died, later on about 11 o'clock, your dad and I were upstairs when we got a phone call from the coroner. He said if we wanted an autopsy done he would have to know by 12 o'clock that day. I didn't know what to say. I think we told him we had to think about it, but he said it was usually required in accident cases for insurance reasons or whatnot, but I think he was lying. I don't believe him. I don't think it had to be done, but he led us to believe that it did, and I will never forgive him for that. But he led me to believe it was necessary, and then I said, "Well, what are you going to do? She has already been hurt enough. I don't want her to be cut anymore." And he said, "Oh we are only going to do this, and we are only going to do that." I won't even say it Jenny, because I read it in another book when somebody described it, and it just grabbed at my heart. It made me so sick. It is horrendous what they do to a human body, a sacred human body. He promised me he would do very little, and I believed him. They lied, Jen, because when we got the autopsy report months later, it was awful, just inhumane. So now I tell people don't ever [give permission for that], unless autopsy is 100% necessary.

I used to wonder why my dad didn't have an autopsy done on Mom so we could see exactly what it was that killed her. She had cancer in so many different places we didn't know which one actually took her life. I didn't know about autopsies then. I thought they just looked inside your stomach and that was it, but I was a kid. I can't stand it when I think about what they did to you. You were my baby. I hate myself for allowing them to, but it is over, and you didn't know it, and it didn't hurt. Once you are in heaven your earthly body is of no importance to you anymore. My only solace is that the autopsy said you died instantly.

I don't think I can continue talking about this, but you did have such a beautiful funeral, and someone even called me after and told me it was the most beautiful funeral they had ever been to. And I am glad because I don't know how people can throw something together so fast and have it come out so perfectly, but it was. So next I will talk to you about that. But I can't right now.

March 26

JenBug, made it through most of this day so far. I think yesterday was worse in some ways. This year was worse in some ways. The first year, I think I was still in shock. The second year, I was on medication. For some reason, this year really hit home. All day yesterday I kept thinking this was your last day of your life. You didn't know. Nobody knew. I kept thinking about what you were doing at this time and what you were doing at that time and last night when I went to bed, I was afraid to go to sleep because I would wake up and you would be gone. It was as if I was back in 1994. It is so much more real on days like today. I think of the days ahead, not just yesterday being the last day of your life or today being the day you died, but the days that went on between the funeral, all the people, and then the 30th being the day of your funeral, the last day we would ever see your earthly body. I want to talk about your funeral. I need to do this, but I can't on a day like today. Maybe tomorrow, maybe Good Friday, but I think today I am too sad to even talk, and I don't know what to say. So I am going to try to busy myself with some things that need to be done and put on one of your favorite CDs and just let myself cry. I will talk to you later, Bugs.

April 2

Boy, Jenny, never have I felt such an urge to be with you than I have this last week. I tried to enjoy Easter and think of its true meaning, and that is probably what kept me going, but I had to think also on that March 30th that we were having your wake in that very same room where I was eating Easter breakfast. On that very same day and at that time, you were being taken to a crematory. Not pleasant thoughts to have on Easter, is it?

The next day I dove headfirst into what you would call, Jenny, deep depression, anxiety, anger, bitterness—all of them rolled up into one. I really thought if ever there was a day I was going to lose it, it was March 31 this year. I lost my ability to think rationally, called your father up at work and told him that I was dead inside, that I was just dead and that when he retired from his job, which he was planning on doing in five to seven years, that there wouldn't be anything left of me for him. I am still in that mindset.

I was alive yesterday because Erin spent the night, and we ran errands and talked and laughed. Her dad came over for dinner because her mom was not home. She didn't want to leave again. So I am at least human enough to entertain a child and the child have a good enough time that they don't want to go home, but then today I was supposed to visit my care receiver—but it is awkward, and I don't enjoy it because I have to make conversation. I thought that being a Stephen Minister, I was being trained to be a caring listener. So, sometimes you are not always listening, and I am not good at trying to think of things to talk about.

How do three years go by, Jenny, and then I watch my progress slip, fall overboard, and sink to the bottom of the ocean. It is gone, you feel like it was never there, and you are just sick inside. I feel like I can't move again, and I am just numb with pain. I guess I thought, *Okay, it has been three years, so this must be how it is going to feel for the rest of your life now.* And sure, I can pull myself up and dust myself off and keep moving and maybe even improve a little bit each day, but then your birthday arrives in July, and you would be 24, and it will hit me again.

I used to love holidays. Every holiday is like someone smacking you in the face with a big wet rag, knocking you down. But you get up and you trudge forward. I was reading another book about the death of a child. A daughter describes her mother after the death of her brother, and the thing that I completely understood is that she said her mother died at the earliest opportunity. That is how I feel right now. I have been telling God for three days now that I am ready. I don't know how I have not become physically ill yet, but I take my vitamins and, believe it or not, I got up this morning and put on my exercise clothes because I still have this determination. If I have to be here, I have to at least try to feel good, because as far as I am concerned right now today, I really am dead. My marriage is dead, my life is dead, and I don't have the ambition to try and make something out of it.

I know that I am not always going to feel this way, Jenny. I know it is a setback, but it doesn't matter. Why should I work so hard to recover if I'm just going to become ill again? Maybe I will even need help. I will have to see how long it lasts. Your dad has a new position at his job again. Whenever that happens, which seems to be quite a lot, we lose him even more. He just lives for that. He trudges on; maybe it is his way of coping.

But it just adds more to my dying. Jamin, he is in and out. I see him here and there, but he doesn't talk. He is in his own cocoon of pain, though I try to talk to him.

He is great, though, at calling and letting us know where he is. Last night as we sat at the kitchen table, even though I knew Jamin was working late, he was later than usual. I had prepared a big dinner, and the anxiety and panic started. My mind started popping out all those possibilities—where could he be, what was wrong, hijacking, accident. Then stupid me, after worrying for 45 minutes, I walked in to call someone and saw that the light was flashing on the answering machine. What an idiot I am. I had Erin with me when I came home, and we had packages and we had cookies to make and dinner to make and I never went and checked the messages, and evidently your father didn't either. So, I listened to Jamin's voice saying that he was going to David's after work because yesterday had been David's birthday. So, all that worrying for nothing. We probably spend three quarters of our lives worrying for nothing, but then there will be that one night when we don't worry and that is the night we should have.

Well, Jen, I don't mean to sound so negative, but this is me right now; it is who I am. It will change. It was a beautiful day yesterday. It is going to be a beautiful day today. Spring is supposed to be the beginning, a new start, a cleansing, a renewal, but I am still living in the dead of winter.

April 8

Jen, I wanted to talk to you about something. I had a daydream. Last Saturday night, I decided to go soak in the tub to try to forget for a little bit, but I didn't forget. I lit a candle and turned out all the lights and immersed myself in the steaming water and then started having a daydream. It would be so easy to sink down into that water and not come up. I could be with you. Maybe I could be with you in a very short amount of time, maybe less than an hour. Maybe just minutes. But what about the mess I would leave behind. How much more could Jamin and your dad handle? What right do I have to disrupt other people's lives? Your Aunt Cathie and Uncle Chuck were heading off to Las Vegas. That would be nice of me, wouldn't it? And Jamin would never have the least bit of a normal life with a dead sister and a mother who killed herself.

Your dad would be the one who found me. I kind of went through the whole thing in my mind, Jim finding me, the police coming, members of my family being called, their reactions and then I thought how utterly selfish of me to even think about it. I can't do it. I know, I understand the despair and the pain that would allow someone to, and I would never say they were selfish. I would say they were in unbearable pain that clouded their judgement.

But there is that tiny spark in me, that spark that has been there since the day I was born, a little spark that turns into a fire and says fight, keep going, keep trying, don't give up. That has been the word that has been on my mind the last two days. Fight, fight, fight! Every negative feeling, every bit of depression, every bit of loneliness, every worry about my marriage, fight it, do not let this world take you away. I will not go through what I did this March. I will make sure I plan something for next March. I am going to be gone. I will spend a week or two planning that week, and then maybe it will not hit me like a three-ton boulder falling on my head. I don't know how your dad and Jamin dealt with the anniversary because neither of them even talked to me. Jamin did bring home three yellow roses that day, so I know he was thinking about you. Jackie went to the tree. I wanted to go and get your ashes and hold them, but I didn't have the courage. I shake when I hold them. I tremble. So why would I do that to myself? I know they are there. When I try and talk to your dad about you and how he's dealing, which is difficult, because a woman can talk about her feelings for hours and sometimes she cannot draw one feeling out of a man, we argue; and then we always end up the same way: *Okay, fine, we can't get anywhere, we can't communicate, let's separate.* But it seems that both of us have these unspoken words that we have the hardest time getting out, but eventually it's *let's try*. I don't know if either of us has the energy for that much work. It is all we can do now. I have read varying statistics and every number appears to be different. 50%, 65%, 75%, 80% of couples who lose a child divorce. We don't have to be in that percentage. We could be in the other.

I have been fighting getting going the last few days, the last week, getting up, doing what I have to do. It is amazing how when you are doing something normal, you feel more normal. I am not successful every day, but I have been trying to do aerobics and walk at night, even in the cold, just walking and trying not to think. I push myself hard to get all of this out of me. All this tension starts building and building when I know the month of March is approaching, and then I spend the whole month of April trying to recover from the pain of that month. I learned something, and I won't let March do this to me again. I look at your picture and I think of how physically fit you were and how much you exercised and all those salads you ate. So sometimes when I am hopping across the floor to Richard Simmons, I look at your picture; and it makes me say, *don't quit. Do it for her. She would have done it. When she had a body, she took care of it.* Dieting has not helped. So, my only other choice is to start moving my body.

APRIL 18

You would be so proud of your brother, Jenny. He was on the Oakland University radio station with David and Jackie. They played their music and the DJ interviewed them; your father and I were so proud. We both cried. I think it was first time we felt real joy together in three years. It was rather scary; the feeling was foreign, and it threw me. I didn't know quite how to handle that emotion because I thought I would never have it again. I have short fleeting moments. But for a moment there, just a moment, I felt happiness. But you would have loved it. Jackie sang a song she wrote, and Dave put the music to, live on the air. It was about you and for you, called *Drooze*.

Drooze

Race the ocean, skim the waves
Wear your beads you rolled with Dave
Absorb the sun into your soul
Then use the rays to make us whole

Kiss a star for us Jenny
Wear its warmth and glow for free
Never leave that pinecone day
You live and breathe in songs we play

Send us tasty times of you
Dance and groove among the drooze
Vibes of you will fall in rain
Blood and soul ties never change

Now, it's the middle of April, and I feel that God has once again poured grace upon me and given me hope. It has been a long haul Bugs.

Perhaps I'll take a class and try to do more to get back into the land of the living. I listened to a marriage tape this morning about understanding men, and it is complicated. Actually, laughing here. I think I learned from it, because I turned into a big nothing in the last three years—helpless, a person who is lucky she got the house cleaned up and cooked a meal and did the dishes. That is the way I feel sometimes, Jen. I feel like a person who has just barely survived and whose self-esteem has plummeted to the depths of the earth. How can I expect your dad and Jamin to respect me when I have turned into this big, grieving blob.

Then other times, I look at the three years and think *Look how far you have come.* Sometimes people at church will say that to me. Sometimes, I don't see what other people see. But I am a different person out of the house than I am in the house, so what they see and what your dad and brother see are two different people. I am more confident outside of the house, like during my Stephen Ministry classes, and I am more cheerful when I am around people. We are so good at hiding our true selves in public. But that is how your dad and Jamin can know how much I love them and how comfortable I am with them, because I feel like I can just be myself. I can break down and sit and stare out the window. Sometimes I feel your father gets impatient with me. I felt that this time, especially as I was trying so hard to improve, and then just plummeted again. I noticed him losing more respect and interest in our relationship and throwing himself even more into his job. I really didn't think it would be that bad, and now it almost makes me fear next year even more. But like I mentioned, I will do things differently.

Every once in a while, I think about your 24th birthday coming up in July, and it is like you just get over one difficult anniversary and another one arrives. Perhaps each one makes you stronger. If any anniversary made me stronger, it is this one. Hitting rock bottom again just makes you fight all that much harder to get out. You can climb up slowly, but when you keep falling down, you're like *Dang, I am not going to let this get me.* And you climb even harder with more determination than ever before.

Your daddy, bless his heart, always seems to find ways to try to cheer me up. We ended up having a nice talk about how we need to put effort into our relationship instead of just letting it float on by. We have to either let it go or make it a challenge that we have to face. And after a lengthy discussion, we decided we would try to conquer it. I don't think either of us, even with the statistics stacked against us, wants to let go of 27 years. Since we had that conversation, it has been better. We decided to start compromising. I know your dad really wanted a pontoon boat at the cabin, so he just decided to sell some things he didn't need and get one. I am happy for him, and I am sure that will be a nice change of pace up north. And he knew that I was looking to try to start fresh and feeling even more determined to start letting go of bits and pieces of the past. I haven't been feeling very well, so I am trying hard to take care of myself again.

Your dad called me from work a couple of weeks ago to talk. I think this is just because he knows I need motivation. I also felt I was being treated like one of his kids, which is something I worry about, because with you gone and me acting so helpless, it is easy for us to assume those roles of him as the father and me as the child. Not good for a marriage. But he said, "If you can get that basement organized (which we had never done since moving in this house two years ago) and that laundry area organized, we will go shopping for a new bedroom set." We have had our mismatched furniture and mattress for 27 years, and I responded just like a child, "Oh, goody, okay, I can do that, no problem." So, we went out looking and since I always wanted to do the bedroom in antiques, I decided to go that direction. We looked at so many I was dizzy but ended up with a lovely set that I'm sure I loved much more than your father.

I made a vow, Jenny, to not blow away my mornings anymore like I have been doing. You know I got into a terrible habit of getting up late if I could, if I didn't have to be somewhere, making coffee and just sitting and staring or reading a little bit and thinking, thinking too much. I'm what you might call an abstract thinker. I think beyond basic ideas. I'm always trying to solve a problem. It would be easier if my thoughts didn't float outside the book. I read a paragraph and then ponder it for ten minutes. I think of possibilities. It is probably why I feel like I am going crazy sometimes. I give myself too much time to think.

Today I got up early, made my coffee, had my time to sit and read, and then I did my aerobics for an hour and a couple of things around the house. Then I took off for the day and realized as I was coming home that I had accomplished so many things before one o'clock in the afternoon, whereas before I was just getting out of the house at one o'clock in the afternoon. I can change things, Jenny. I do have control. I do have choices. I think just the thought of going back to work and then taking a class motivates me and makes me feel stronger and more in control.

That's it, the word *control*. I have been so out of control, and that is what I think we so eagerly try to regain after going through such a tragedy. Men start controlling from the first moment of tragedy, because that's the way they were raised. Men are supposed to take charge and be strong. They are having all the same feelings women are. They hurt just as badly, but where we can choose to sit back and faint and cry and stay in bed all day because we are depressed, most men, when grieving, will pick themselves up, get themselves off to work, take charge, thinking, *I have other people in my family I have to take care of, or my poor wife, she is going to fall apart; I have to be strong for her.*

I have to be strong for him too. I will be. I am basically just beginning to see the horizon now. I know I still have a long way to go, but I am shooting for it. I like to think that you are with me, that you are right there with God and you two pick me up off the floor and dust me off and point me in the right direction one more time. So today I will go up and clean the church.

July 20

I haven't talked on this tape recorder in quite some time. I painted my bedroom for the new furniture and poured everything into my closet, and the tape recorder went in there. It is your birthday today, Jenny. You would be 24 years old, and I can't remember how I felt the other birthdays, the other three that you have missed. I know the first one well and the other two I know I was away from home and busy, but I thought it would get easier, but like March 26, it doesn't get easier. I was up north at the log cabin. I planned all day to talk on the recorder after Aunt Lynn, Tracy and Aunt Cathie left after a visit, but I haven't been in the mood. I haven't done any of the things that I hoped I would do last time I talked…like get up early, lose weight, get a job, start school. I haven't done any of it. I stayed up north because I just wanted to be alone. I will head home in the morning, back to cleaning. I have tendonitis in my right hand. It keeps me up nights from using it too much. Your dad said I will have to stop cleaning, but I don't know when I will do that. I don't know when I will do anything.

I have been on Prozac once more since March. I am finishing what I have now, and then I am not going to take it anymore. I just happened to have some left, enough for the summer. I will definitely be on my own, so who knows what will happen. I have little Hannah here with me to keep me company. I have a good book. I go back and listen to all my tapes, and each new one sounds as silly as the last one, and I don't know what I will do with them. I am a fighter one moment, and a quitter the next. I think I am okay and then I listen to myself and think I am not okay at all. I am a silly woman who doesn't have anything better to talk about than buying bedroom furniture, but so much has happened since last time I talked. But it is late. I am not in a good mood today. I miss you something fierce. I hurt. I am angry. I am going to go get my book and escape for a little while. I will be back to talk when I feel like I have something intelligent to say. Good night Bug.

July 25

It's Friday at 12:45 p.m. I am lying in my bed with a towel on my head. At least I took a shower. That is the only thing I have done today. They are working outside next door and I can hear the trucks going back and forth down the driveway and the clanging and clunking noises of machinery. I don't know exactly what they are doing. I talked to your dad about doing something to this house, but I am not even sure we are going to be living here that much longer. He said something about moving up north and having a condo down here for him to go to work which would separate us even more. Why would he want that? Does he have something to hide? A person? a bottle? I wish I had just a clue, an inkling of what our future held. I keep thinking I am going to get better, but I am doing the same thing I did after the March 26th 3rd anniversary of your death. Now just days after your birthday, I feel like I am plummeting again. I am trying to take the Prozac every couple of days because I only have a little bit left, so I don't know if that has anything to do with it.

I actually pulled out the scale this morning and got on it and found out that I have gained six more pounds. I thought I felt heavier ... I don't know what to do about the weight, but I have a feeling that unless I do something about that first, make that my number one priority, that none of the other things like a job, energy, or school, are going to happen. It's a good thing I was thin before. I notice the difference more than others. I think that self-esteem has a lot to do with those things and since I've never been very heavy in my life, I think that emotionally and physically I can't deal with that either. So, I suppose I should make that my number one priority. I've not eaten anything yet today, but that doesn't mean anything. What I should do is try to go back on Weight Watchers. I look at my yellow bedroom that I tried to fix up so I could stand being up here alone. I have sunny yellow walls and a pretty rose border and the TV with your nickname blocks BUG on top of it, your prom picture over on my dresser in a frame, surrounded by little yellow sunflowers, a picture of you and Jackie on the nightstand—she is very well defined with her dark hair and dark eyes and you, with your pale hair and blue eyes, look as if you are already fading away from us two months before your death.

Maybe that's why you looked so beautiful and translucent. I thought you never looked more radiant, more angelic, more surreal with a kind of beauty that's hard to describe than during the last few months of your life. Were you already starting to leave us? Were you already starting to belong to God at that point? The month before you died when Grandma Ginny looked at you at the restaurant and said how beautiful your complexion was...we were already starting to lose you, weren't we? You didn't know, and we didn't know; only God knew that little by little you were leaving this world. You were transforming.

Oh, if only I were not so afraid to pray. Why am I so afraid? I don't know what to say to God except four little letters. *Help*, just help. I got a letter from MADD yesterday explaining when their next meeting was going to be. If I wasn't going to be up north, I'd attend because the subject was feeling alienated, feeling alone, shut out from the world and other people. I do hide in my house. I only go out long enough to water my flowers and take out the dogs. I haven't spoken with one neighbor this whole year. They're in their world, and I'm in mine. There's no connection. It's as if I'm looking out of a big glass bubble at the world moving around me. I hear children. I hear their laughter. I see them toddling down their driveway, but I have nothing in common, nothing at all.

I wonder if I adopted a small child would I feel alive once more? Would I live for that child? Would I feel I had a purpose in life? Your dad has his job. It's number one in his life and, if he has time for me, then maybe we'll talk or see a movie. Jamin is in his own little world, his musical dream, but I know he is just as confused. He doesn't know where he is going or what he wants to do. He kind of *hangs out* in life. I saw Grandma Ginny yesterday, and we had a nice visit. She bought a new puppy because Aggie died. I fell in love with it because it came to me, enjoyed me, needed me, touched me. Grandma Ginny was talking about how she really didn't have anyone she hung out with anymore. She had friends that she had appointments with, lunch dates, visits, but nobody just to hang out, and I said, "I'll hang out." She said, "I don't have anybody like Joanne," and it made me realize how lucky I am to have this friend. Ginny and I went to lunch, we hung around a Hallmark Store and stopped at a garage sale. All I felt was this longing to come home. I always have this longing to come home, no matter where I'm at or what I'm doing.

It's like there is somebody there that needs me, but who? My puppy? My dogs are glad to see me when I come home. I always think I should be busy instead of sitting down and letting my puppies lie on my lap.

I feel like I'm falling asleep and drifting, but it's one in the afternoon and I really, really have things I have to do. I have to clean the church. I have to go grocery shopping, and I have to straighten my own house. I have plants that need watering, floors that need sweeping. If only someone would make me do it. If only there was a reason to do it. If only I wanted to do it. If possible, I could just lie here all day; it wouldn't make any difference in anyone's life, or mine.

Maybe I'll try to go to the next MADD meeting. Maybe there will be some people there that I've read about in the paper who've lost their children to drunk drivers. Maybe I would scare them at the thought of being still so unhappy after three years, like I was at my first meeting when I saw someone that was still so unhappy after one year. It scared me to death to think that I would still have that pain, but now I know I'll always have it. It's not going to go away, not after five years, not after ten years. Then someday, on July 20th, I will be saying, "This is Jenny's

30th birthday, this is Jenny's 35th birthday," and if I'm still around or alive, "This is Jenny's 40th birthday." Maybe when I am in my 80s, it won't hurt so bad to think, "This is Jenny's 60th birthday." I love you, Jenny. I ache for you and I pray *God, help me, make this pain go away. Make this longing for my daughter lessen so that I can at least function, at least look forward to something.*

I still have so much to tell you, Jenny. I missed the whole spring, I have to tell you everything that's been going on, but it seems so long ago, spring. I was actually living then. Doing things, going places. Well, I guess I have a choice now; go to sleep, into oblivion, letting the sound of the machinery next door lull me to sleep, or I can get up and force myself, push myself to move to the bathroom, take this towel off my head, put clothes on my body, maybe even pick up a load of laundry. Who knows? Only God knows what I will do in the next five minutes, because I don't.

August 14

It's a beautiful summer day, Jenny. My heart aches for you in the summer. You loved it so much. You thrived this time of year. I'm not thriving. My hands hurt so much from cleaning. My right hand falls asleep all the time and aches up to my elbow. It wakes me up many times during the night. It was suggested I may have carpal tunnel. I'll have to look it up.

Tomorrow is the third anniversary of the day that I felt you came to me to give me back the necklace I had been searching for. I had been writing in a journal at that time and I told you just a bit about it and that I would talk about it later. I think I was afraid to talk about it. I had that same journal up north with me recently. I found that two weeks before that spiritual experience, or on August 1st, 1994, I wrote to you. *Come Jenny, swim through my soul, dance through my being as you have done before. Let me breathe in some of your strength, your courage, your energy, and your love. Let me absorb your peace and your joy. Please daughter, swim through my soul.* I like to believe that my experience on August 15, 1994 was your response.

Jenny, Jackie just went out west with two of your friends. When your friends are close to Jackie it's like holding on to a part of you. I don't really have a part of you in that way anymore. Your friends have quit coming over. I did run into them at the café one day, and it was a blessing. Jesse is married; I don't even know how he is doing these days, but I know your friends had to let go. They had to let go of us in order to let go of you. I understand that. Zach, Jeremy, all your friends and our friends. We were too much. It was too real for them.

I remember a friend telling me that one of her relatives had lost a son and she still saw the pain in her eyes after ten years. I pray to reach the point where I have decided that I can live without you even though I love you. But everybody's different and I am not to that point yet.

I understand why we don't see your friends, and I understand completely why we don't even see our old friends. Maybe it's our fault. Maybe we are the ones that ran away from them. I was in the mall not too long ago and ran into two of my old neighborhood friends, Debbie and Jill. They were so kind to me. I was the one who was uncomfortable. I was embarrassed, with my extra pounds, looking a lot more unkempt than I used to. I saw them and wanted to run. I didn't want them to see me because I wasn't the same as them anymore. My life wasn't the same. It was different. I was marked.

I was the one that finally said hello to them because they didn't see me, just like I had hoped they didn't. But they were right in front of me. I couldn't walk away. I just couldn't. Maybe they saw me and weren't sure they wanted to say anything, but when I did speak, they were so kind. They invited me to have dinner with them, and I went.

I remember when my mother died and I was fifteen, I felt I was starting to move forward after a few years. When you're young you can learn to put things behind you. But when you lose a child, there are no rules, no set time, no boundaries, and no end. It goes on and on until the day you die, and you join them. But I'm waiting for a time when I can put my pain into perspective, and I can hold onto you and still grab ahold of life. That's going to come for me; I know it is. I just feel as if I stepped out of life. Your father couldn't. He had a job. He had a family to support, a mortgage payment. He couldn't step out of life. I feel badly that he couldn't. Yet I also envy him for the fact that he was able to go on, that he had to go on. It was too easy for me to step out of life, being a woman with a second income in the family. So, I did. And I haven't really stepped back in yet.

Sometimes tragedy has a way of making us really look at ourselves and our lives. I've been traveling that road for a while now. I must find a way to turn my grief into giving. I just hope I'm not too old by the time I do.

August 27

The summer is almost gone Jenny, but September and October are usually my favorite months anyway. Your birthday is not in them, nor the anniversary. They aren't close to holidays. They are simply months. I like them for the coolness, the crispness, and the turning leaves. September is Jamin's birthday month and October is mine. Perhaps it's a lingering or leftover childhood excitement about the birthday month even though they are nothing special anymore. I just perk up in those months. I always have. I'm getting older. I'm going to be 47 years old. I lived two years past my mother now. I hope that this means that this terrible bout I had with depression is coming to an end once more. I'm reminded of a song from my youth. I believe it's Cat Steven's *Trouble*. *Trouble, trouble set me free; you're eating my heart away, there's really nothing left of me.*

I did something this week, Jenny. I got on the scale and I hit 149. It scared the heck out of me. And I thought, *I am just going to keep going up and up and if I don't do something, if I don't start caring, then my health is going to go down,*—my health that I have always taken such good care of until you died. I'm not going to be here for Jamin. I'm not going to be here long enough to try to live with my pain and live a normal life again if I don't start doing something. Aunt Carol said that she lost some weight taking supplements. She gave me a flyer to look at and I got fascinated with it and thought that it would be fun to sell. I hadn't even tried any of the products yet, but I signed up. I am going over the training materials. Right now, it's just the beginning and even that feels good…a beginning of doing something again.

I went to a MADD meeting last night for the first time in quite a while. I recognized one person, but everybody else was new. I asked about victim impact panels. I thought about them before but just never had the guts to do anything. They suggested I come and observe a few of them. They did say they are very emotional and hard to get through. I wondered whether I could speak before 100 people who were first-and second-time offenders for drunk driving and tell them what happened to our lives and hope that they might not do it to someone else someday. I decided I will go watch one.

And then, what usually happens to me when I am around any people from MADD, I went to ask about victim advocates—a person who is a support person for a family who has just gone through a tragedy. I found out that I could not say the word *victim*. I tried to say it, but it came out strange every time. It was as if I was trying to say a foreign word. My mouth and my tongue would not work. Finally, the nice woman said she knew what I was trying to say and smiled. I found out that you take classes to be an advocate. Maybe I could help a family who is going through what we went through. That sounds strange too. I think I may have found the key to the locked door. I'd rather spend my time helping. Maybe it's time, Jenny, maybe it's time to start living again, time to start trying again. It's nothing I can make myself do. It's something that's going to have to come naturally by itself.

I'm dreaming again; I wonder if that's a sign. I haven't had many dreams the last three years. I'm dreaming profusely, but still no dreams about you. I'm waiting for you to come to me in a dream, Jenny. I had a dream about a house…and there was a window I loved. It was mesmerizing, and I couldn't stop obsessing over it. I wanted to buy the house just for that window. I feared someone else would purchase it and I would lose it forever. I thought that was strange until I woke up and figured out that it was the window that led me to you.

September 8

Hi Jenny. I must tell you some news. Heaven had the arrival of a princess and also the arrival of a saint. Diana, Princess of Wales was involved in a car accident just over a week ago. I went to bed thinking she would survive. That was not the case. Her death broke my heart. I'm not a follower of the Royal Family but I was surprised at how much I was affected by the loss. She was so young and left two young sons. The world mourns her. Even a princess who was protected and watched over can die in a car accident. I stayed up all night watching the funeral and cried the entire time. I knew my tears weren't just for her, but for all young people who die tragically in the prime of their lives. And Mother Teresa, who devoted her life to attending to the poor and sick, is now enjoying her heavenly rewards. She will be missed on earth.

I'm going through a season of hope and renewal and feel as if I'm working on myself. My next little mini goal will be that I've got to try to fall asleep sooner and wake up earlier. I'm feeling a little cheer in my heart, Jen, no matter how slight; I'm thankful to God for it. *Those that mount up with wings as eagles shall renew their strength* (Isaiah). That's my goal. I'll keep trying.

In eight days Jamin will turn twenty. I'm nervous. Who wouldn't be? I'm sure it's on his mind. Will he make it to twenty-one? You didn't. There is a certain anxiety that comes with turning the same age as a loved one when they died. I remember when I turned 40, the age of my mother when she got cancer. It was normal to fear the same disease. When I turned 45, the age of her death, it felt strange and I wondered if I would make it through the year. Of course, I did, and Jamin will as well. I love you Bug. You may be unable to enjoy the joyful times here, but you are able to escape the tragedies. Please say hello to the princess and the saint.

September 17

Hi Bugs. We missed you last night. It was Jamin's birthday. Jackie, David, Brian, and Jeff were here. Now your brother is the same age as you. I think he was apprehensive because he didn't even want anything for his birthday. I bought him a gift and gave him some money and though none of us have mentioned it, this birthday is affecting all of us.

We had a nice time, and I tried to celebrate Jamin's birthday as much as he allowed me to. I picked a yellow rose and put it on the counter for him from you. He used to be so excited about his birthdays, but it's like he wasn't sure whether he wanted this one to come. He had no interest, and I can't blame him. I remember your 20th like it was yesterday. We went to your favorite restaurant. Jamin picked the same one for his.

Your father is drinking more. I have to take my blinders off and see the truth I've been trying to avoid. I think I finally came to the conclusion last weekend that he's gone from drinking a little in the evenings (what I told myself) to deal with his grief, to possibly being an alcoholic. So, we will have to deal with that one day at a time as well. Since we discussed it a few days ago, things are much better, but we'll see.

As for me, I've been reacting to life with insomnia lately. I am perfectly fine until I go to bed and then when I turn out the light my skin comes alive and just won't rest. My mind is tired, my brain is tired, but my body does not want to lie still. I called my doctor to get a prescription, but he wouldn't call it in; so they left a message, and I have to call him back. I don't take medications anymore, but this has been two weeks now; I'm starting to suffer from sleep deprivation. I didn't get up until eleven today, and I hate that. I absolutely hate that, but when you don't fall asleep until almost morning, it's hard to get up.

It's almost the first day of fall. And, this is the first year since you died that I've actually looked outside at the autumn and felt that same sense of joy and peace that I used to feel and I'm so grateful for that, Jen. A familiar old feeling. So, sometimes they do come back, those old feelings. It lets you know that things you think you'll never enjoy again, if you're patient and you wait, they'll come back. Fall is like a promise from God. Everything gets ready to go to sleep—the leaves, the grass, the flowers—they all leave you and rest, but they don't rest forever. God promises us that they'll be back. I love that promise because people don't come back; once they fade away, they don't return.

OCTOBER 8

I think insomniacs could possibly be dangerous. I probably shouldn't even be on the road. I still have a weird type of insomnia that has lasted for over a month now. My legs want to get up and run a marathon. My eyes burn because they're tired, and my mind is so foggy; but my legs keep me awake. They move, twitch, and stretch out; and I roll over and twist and turn. I think I keep Hannah up all night. This new symptom scares me, and I fear something is coming.

Your dad and I haven't been getting along very well. I have been trying to avoid the statistics of divorce caused by losing a child, but I think the courage I've gotten from you—or I should say the courage I've gotten from God and from you since you died—has changed me. I'm not scared of divorce anymore. I think I'm more scared of staying married. Your Dad was talking again, like he always does, about taking a job in another city or another state. This time it's California. Jamin was all excited. I told him he could go, and I would stay in Michigan. That I thought that would be a good time to part, and Jamin could go to California with his dad if he wanted. He will always be my boy, but I have to let go sometime. But then the day before we went to close on Hooterville (our old cabin), your father came and said that he loved me and wanted to make it work.

So, why is it that just when I get up the courage to be strong and start thinking how I'm going to handle things and making plans, like keeping your little white truck, trying to get a condo, and getting a job, he decides to say that. Does he sense me trying to distance myself from him and then tries to pull me back in? I don't know now. I never wanted to lose what was left of my family. It doesn't take much to sway me, does it? I've lost ten pounds. Most likely it's from moving around all night.

Jamin and I are on St. John's Wort, a new herb. It's supposed to be the new natural antidepressant for mild depression, and I've only heard good things about it, so Jamin and I are giving it a try. He wants help, but he still won't talk about it. When he comes home, he gets a nervous stomach and can hardly eat dinner. I don't know if it's because he knows his dad and I are having problems, if he knows his dad is drinking, or if he's just not sure what he wants to do with his future. I look at him. He reminds me of your father at his age. He's so utterly handsome and yet so shy. He's playing music again. He and his cousins played at a club recently. The owner liked them and invited them back. I'm so happy he has his music. I know it saved me when I was young. It still does.

I'm going to spend some time with Joanne today. We don't get to see each other much anymore. We talk often. I talk about being lonely. She talks about not being able to come and go as she pleases. I am free and I don't really want to be. I like hibernating in my little house. She would like to be able to leave hers. She likes my freedom. I like the fact that she still has a young family that needs her. I think we always want what we don't have.

I will be having carpal tunnel surgery soon. As I sit here holding my little recorder, my right hand is fully asleep. I have thoughts of what I want to say to you, but insomnia takes the words away as fast as they come. As I talk, I am watching the leaves fall in the woods. Never is any other time of year as beautiful as this. I think of how you looked right before you left us. The earth looks this way because it's dying. It's saying goodbye. To me it says, *I'll give you one last beautiful look at me. I'll change my colors and I'll paint the landscape. I'll give you cool breezes and autumn blue skies. I'll give you all this beauty and then I will leave you.*

OCTOBER 22

My birthday came on October 12th. There was a new yellow rose from you. You've sent one every year since your death. I cut it and took it to Mary, my care receiver, at the nursing home. I told her it was a very special rose from heaven and that it would bloom beautifully. I thought since it already blessed me, I'd take it and let it bless her too.

I continue to live in my beautiful fall mode. Jamin asked, "What's with all the little pumpkins and stuff all around?" I answered, "It's autumn. It's harvest time. I felt like decorating this year and I'm glad." But I was so sad on my birthday. It has nothing to do with turning 47. I don't worry about age. The other day my dental hygienist said three times that she couldn't believe I was in my forties. I hate my birthdays because you're not here. I pulled out the last cards you gave me and put them by your picture. My favorite is the one where you just wrote *Happy B-Day Mom* with a big smiley face and *Love, Bugs*. Then the Ziggy card where you wrote, *I'll bake you a cake and I'll get you a gift as soon as I get to the store*, and I laughed because you always had such a good heart. Even if you never got around to doing either of those things, you never failed to say Happy Birthday to me at the beginning of that day.

I missed you Jenny. Jamin spent the night at his cousin's house so he wasn't home all day, and Dad tried. I was in such a bad mood he didn't want to give me the birthday card he got me. He said it didn't go with my mood. When I got in the car to go to church, his card was still in the visor. I decided to open it. There was a big hairy guy on the front with a big belly sticking out, and it said inside, *Happy Freaking Birthday*. I thought no wonder he didn't want to give it to me. He usually buys me pretty romantic cards, but I don't think he was feeling romantic this year.

That night, Jamin came home and gave me a little box and a card. I think it was the first time Jamin ever gave me a gift on my birthday. It was a statue of a Chihuahua. I was so happy. It really touched my heart.

November 11

Hi, Jen. Things are starting to change again. It seems like everything stayed the same for so long.

I had my carpal tunnel surgery on October 23rd. It was a painful thing for about a day. The doctor said I'll have to have the other one done in a couple years, but if that's the worst thing that ever happens to me, I'll be pretty lucky.

One thing, having this surgery done has helped me make a decision: I'm not going back to cleaning. I did clean the church last weekend with someone's help because I had to do it with my left hand and I couldn't vacuum, but I'm not going to keep cleaning. Today I'm running over to the mall to try to get a job at one of my favorite stores. I'm also going to try part time, but your dad and I think it's a good thing because it's a start back out into the land of the living.

Your brother had a date! Her name is Maria. I keep wanting to sing the song from a musical I heard so many times when I was young. I walk around singing it to Jamin. He said they had a great time. She comes from a large family. I don't know what will happen, but he seems happy for now and that makes me happy. I think your brother has more integrity than any person I know. He doesn't want to date just to date. When he does, it's because he really cares for someone and something might come of it. He doesn't want to take advantage, and I hope no one breaks his heart. When he finds a wife, he will be as loyal as they come. I hope that whomever he chooses will know that.

I think my major goal right now is just to survive and get by each day and hope to get a little better. I never pay much attention to the house until something comes up. It's nice, but the walls aren't painted and special things like stenciling and wallpapering are absent—all the things I used to love to do. Boy, I wish I could be that happy person again with bright and shining eyes. How do you cover up the pain? You can smile and even laugh, but it's always there. Does the lightness ever come back?

I really have to get into prayer, which I feel I'm not good at, and the Bible. It's the only way to truly, truly recover, if that's possible. Just by reaching out to God, my best friend, the first One I think of when I get up and the last One I think of when I go to bed. Asking Him to fill me up so there is no room for pain. And what should I do with all these journals I write in and tapes I record? This is my therapy. Should I try and put them in a book? Where would I find the motivation? It would need revisions and editing. How do I get there? The only way is to talk to God.

I told you about Jamin, but Jackie met a guy in Wyoming while she was out west. He came to visit and is thinking of moving here. It's good to see her happy. Love is around us. Your dad and I went to a Gary Smalley marriage seminar. It was excellent. We had to find out what animal we are like. We learned your dad is a Beaver so I call him *The Beav*. Of course, I am the mushy Golden Retriever who loves too easily and is sometimes taken advantage of. But I do love people and I miss them. Maybe someday I will find them again.

I miss you, Jenny, so much. Do I need to go back to therapy? Or will I get over this hurdle? I had more information come in the mail for MADD…a candlelight vigil. We have been to two of them since you died. I think about the pain of that very first one, and the big slideshow with your picture being last. They left it up there for the longest time. God, it was hard. And you know I remember that pain and as much as I want to do this, the thought of it just scares me because I don't want to feel that again; and yet I want to be involved. How do you stay involved in something like that and ever be able to let go? The question was solved for me when I looked at the paperwork, because the deadline was November 1st, and this is the 11th. What a relief.

NOVEMBER 17

Hi, Bugs. I just wrote a note for your dad and Jamin to make a list for Christmas. We used to have three lists. It's funny how when I used to look for your gifts, I was not quite sure what to buy. Now, everywhere I look, I see things you would love. You wouldn't be the person you were then. I'm getting over this last stage I've gone through or a repeat stage and accepting the fact that God did what was best for you. He wasn't thinking about Dad and Jamin and me. He loved you. Again, I tell myself

All things work for the good of those who love God and whom God loves. I wonder how long I will accept it this time before I go back to asking why?

I knew I was different after you died, Jenny, but never realized I have one huge burden that every human being carries around with them that's gone now. It's not that I don't worry about you anymore. That's not the burden I carried. I still worry about you. I know you're safe, but you're out of my sight, you're not with me. When a child is out of its parent's sight, the parent will worry and wonder. But the burden I no longer carry is *fear*. No one can hurt you again.

Aunt Jackie, Aunt Carol, and Aunt Laurie and I went up to our cabin just for one night. On the way home from this sweet little trip, the weather grew treacherous. Aunt Jackie was terrified because the car was sliding on the overpass. But I trusted her, and I told her that I did. Never once on this dangerous ride home was I afraid. I just had no fear. When I really stopped to think about it, during the last four years, I really haven't had much fear of anything, Jen. When I told my Steven Ministry group about this ride home and how scared everybody was and how totally calm I felt, someone said, "Well, yeah, you don't have any fear because you've already had the worst thing that can happen to you happen."

What is there to be afraid of? Most people fear illness and death. I'm not afraid of death. I know I am forgiven for my sins. I know where I'm going, and I know you're going to be there. God has promised me that already. All I can do is wait. It wasn't until this weekend that I realized I wasn't fearful—not afraid of being alone, not afraid of the night or the dark. I sleep calmly when I'm in the house by myself. That could change with time. It could be temporary. For now, I will feel the peace.

December 25

I've been really busy, probably a blessing. I went back to a regular job I like, but I've been working so many hours. I managed to have all of our family over for Christmas Eve last night, and I managed to get to church for the eleven o'clock candlelight service and sing all the music with my friend, Joel. Once again, I sang *Christmas in Heaven*. I managed to include you in the ways that I've included you for every Christmas since you've been gone. I took the wreath that Jackie and I made that first Christmas.

We decorated it, and I took it to your memory tree in the park on the 23rd. The tree has grown so much since we planted it. And then I bought you beautiful yellow roses with pink tips, and I brought out your Christmas candle I bought that first Christmas without you. I lit it and burned it all Christmas Eve and into Christmas Day, because I stayed up until 2:30 in the morning. I bought you your Cherished Teddy for Christmas. It was rather plain, but if you bought that particular bear, a foster child got one as well. It gave your gift even more meaning.

On the way to your tree, I said a prayer. I asked God if it was possible that while I was there, as the sky was getting dark and I knew I would be all alone in the park, if he would just let me, just for a moment, feel your presence like I've done before. I haven't felt it in so long. But I didn't feel it, and that's okay because God lets things happen in His own time. I just went home.

Some days I feel totally useless. I told someone the other day that there's only one thing I want on my tombstone when I die, if I'm buried: *She Tried.* That would be good enough because I do try. I try every day to live without you, and I try to live even though I'm lonely. Your brother, Jamin, has turned out to be a wonderful young man. He's kind and thoughtful. But your dad and I exist in our own little worlds. I don't know what will happen to us, only time will tell. Sometimes I feel we're close, and other times I feel that we couldn't be further apart.

Jenny, years ago I bought Christmas stockings for you and Jamin that had a special place to embroider your names. I hung them for years without your names. When I went to hang them after you passed, I saw your absent names and felt horrible and lazy. I decided to put your names on them. It took time, but they ended up being beautiful. I'm so sorry I didn't do it before you died. It's there now with your name on it, and it hangs with your dad's and mine and Jamin's and the dogs', because I will not leave you out. It's my choice, and if that's what I have to do to survive, then that's what I have to do. In your stocking are notes I've written to you. Your absence hangs in the air like the scent of your Christmas candle.

Often, I think back to some of our beautiful times and some of our stormy times, of which there were many, because the majority of the last few years of your life you were a teenager and it wasn't easy. Then you turned 20, and I could see you changing and developing into the person you were going to be. I could see your strengths and your weaknesses. I would be in awe at times of how strong you were and how unafraid and how fearless.

Only God knows what's in my future. If there is a job He wants me to do, I surely will try. I've been waiting for four years for Him to put me where He wants me. So, I'll continue to try, but I'll continue to miss you and love you and survive for three reasons: one is for God because He put me here for a purpose; one is for you, because you certainly wouldn't be a wimp and you wouldn't want me to be one either; the last is to be here for your brother so I can see him settled and happy. Your father doesn't seem to need me as much as his job or his medicine of choice. So I'll take the strength that you left behind, Jenny, and I'll use it to grow. Someday maybe I can look up at the sky and just smile because I'll know that I'm where I'm supposed to be. I won't be talking to you on this recorder next year but I'll talk to you from my heart. I love you, Bug. It is heaven's kind of love that I feel, just a pure spiritual, wonderful love that will always be with me.

I sure wish that there was some way I could help your dad. Especially at Christmas. I'm so busy preparing and busy with all the Christmas business that goes on and I have my faith, but sometimes he looks so lost. He needs some help, and I pray that God will help him. I have been dealing with my grief, but I wonder if he is avoiding his by focusing on his work. Your brother has the outlet I had when I was young and my mother died—his music. That helps so much because he can pour his pain out into that. But your dad, he just looks so sad. I'll pray for him, Jenny. I'll pray that he can come to terms with his grief. He once told me that he fights it. He seems especially lonely when all of the family is gathered and I think it's because when everyone is gathered, you're supposed to be there too, but you're not.

Guess what? I've stopped buying books, for now. That's a miracle in and of itself. I think I've collected enough grief books, enough stories, enough nonfiction to last me for the next ten years. I'll never be without something good to read. But I no longer have the urge to go in and search the shelves for something that is going to cure me, because I've learned that the answer isn't in a book. I can read them for knowledge, but I'll never find what I'm looking for, so I accept that. There will always be memories, special little things like my Christmas stocking filled with tea lights in the shape of little ladybugs, or yellow gold roses filled with perfume that your Aunt Cathie picked out for your dad. People know I love these little tokens of remembrances of you, and I will cherish them always. Maybe I'll talk to you again at the New Year, Jenny. I always thought we'd ring in the year 2000 together.

I'll let you know how everyone's doing before I finish. I've filled up so many tapes. I have so many things to include if I type this up. So many poems people wrote you, and so many letters. I will include some of them because this will be a story for you, a story of a mother's love for her daughter. It's a story for the hero of my heart.

I have some room left on this tape, and I wanted to share some thoughts with you. I remember telling you and your brother to always be careful because if anything happened to one of you, I couldn't go on living. Sometimes other mothers will share their feelings about my loss. Very often I hear comments that I'm not sure how to answer. *If I lost my daughter, I would never be able to handle it. I don't know how you get up in the morning. I could never go on living if I lost a child. You must be very strong because I could never get through what you went through.*

When people say those things, what I hear is, *You must not have loved your child the way I love mine.* If I could have given it some thought while they were still standing there I could have responded in many ways. I would say, yes, you would live. You would live because your heart is still beating, or your heart is too young to betray you just yet. You would live because you have one or more children you love, and they need you. I had just as much reason to live as I did to die. You would live because you love your children equally. You would live because you are not a victim, but a fighter. You may be miserable, but you would get up every morning. If I had been old, my suffering would have been shorter. You would live because you have no choice.

I've also had people say *Are you over it yet?* or *Has it gotten easier?* or *You should be over it by now…it's been…years.* Again, if I had the ability to think clearly in those moments, I would tell them that you learn to merge the loss into your life. The pain never leaves because you can be called back into it at any moment. It never gets *better*. It becomes manageable.

1998

January 2 (Journal Entry)

Dearest JenBug, I am up north at the log cabin. I left my recorder at home. I'm so fortunate and blessed to have this get-a-way. I finally got some time off of work. I should have a much lighter workload as the Christmas season is over. Aunt Lynn is visiting me. We are playing old ladies and drinking tea from old china cups we discovered in a shop today. We are listening to music as we nibble on ginger cookies Lynn made last night. Moments of pure relaxation are possible if you create them. Lynn lost her mother nine days before Christmas. My heart aches for her and your cousins. Lynn and I are on the same time schedule. Either that, or we just adjust easily. As I told you, I've developed a habit of getting up in the morning and sitting and drinking coffee. I don't like wasting time, but I forgive myself. We agree that as long as we can be somewhere if we need to, it doesn't pose a problem.

January 3 (Journal entry)

Hi. I came back home to reality once more. I'm in bed listening to a Christmas CD I purchased up north. I have to hear it once before I put it away for a year. Tomorrow I plan on putting all the Christmas decorations away. I used to want to hold on to the holidays. Taking it all down made everything seem so empty and lonely. I really don't mind anymore. I'm looking forward to cleaning it all up and getting back to normal. Perhaps I'm changing in that I'm more anxious to get through life and get to you. Jamin is just as important to me. I think I'm still confused about that. I probably will always be torn between heaven and earth. I accept that.

On my way back from the cabin I was listening to an audio recording of *Molecules of Emotion* by Candace Pert, Ph.D. It explained why we feel the way we feel and how our emotions affect our health. I learned about neuropeptides and opiate receptors. It was very technical and full of scientific data. I started to giggle as I thought my neuropeptides were out of sync. I started to think about how I've never been good at standing up for myself. It always seems to backfire somehow. I realized I had been more assertive lately. I recounted some of the times in my mind. I started to feel good, and it felt as though my brain started to produce its own opiate. Have I changed because of you, Jenny? Am I stronger or more resilient? I always hoped that some good would come from your death. If the world can become a better place because someone lives in it, can't it be a better place because someone was once here? History teaches us that.

I must look outside of my world. I know I'm not fulfilling my purpose on this earth. Jamin is still lonely, and my marriage is still teetering. Perhaps the good is somewhere outside of my current life, or somewhere I've yet to discover. I remember the scholarship your dad's workplace gave to Oakland University in your name. Perhaps it went to someone who will make a difference in our world.

January 4 (Journal Entry)

I am trying to end this writing because I know I must move forward. I feel awful today. I attended church but couldn't get myself to go out again to my Stephen's Ministry meeting in the evening. I'm 47 years old now. I'm beginning to fear menopause, even though it is years away. I never did before, and I didn't care. Now when I think of its approach, I wonder how I will manage it along with my grief. I'm too sad to even write.

January 5 (Journal Entry)

Dear Jenny, Now that I'm writing instead of talking, I find it so easy to just pick up this notebook. Maybe it's because I can write even when Jamin and dad are at home. Talking into the recorder was never private. Jamin told me that your friend Jenny C. is getting married on March 24th. That would be so hard to attend just four days before the fourth anniversary of your death. Then he told me that Jesse would be their best man. I felt it would be sheer torture. There is no way I could see Jesse's wife and attend a wedding on that date. Then Jamin said that the wedding was in Las Vegas. Relief flooded my body. I would have made myself go. I would have hidden my pain. I am happy for Jenny C. It's just hard.

January 14 (Journal Entry)

Bugs, gosh, I wish I knew how much or if you are really around us. Aunt Cathie went to see Rita again. Now Aunt Lynn is coming to see her as well. I'm going to the cabin with your dad. I'm confused. I'm torn between wanting to know and believe and remembering what the Bible says about fortune tellers and conjuring. Of course, I'm desperate to hear from you. I want to do what's right, Jen. Aunt Cathie told me once more that, according to Rita, a book must be written. She told her that it would help me and others.

Today I read that a 16-year-old girl died because her car slid on the ice. I read these things in the newspaper all the time. I always wish I could call these people and tell them that I know and that I want to help. I don't know what to do. They don't know me, but I feel their pain. I hurt for how they are hurting right now. The shock, the disbelief, and the fear that you will survive and be forced to go on. I feel it afresh every time I read the news. I'm so glad that I'm a Stephen's Minister. I do believe one can help people in pain when you know what they really feel like. I've been told I have empathy. It's supposed to be a gift. It doesn't feel like one.

I began talking and writing to you to help myself deal with grief and because I promised you and myself that people would know you were here and that you mattered and were loved—that you left something special with everyone you knew. Maybe it could be more. Aunt Cathie also shared that you have come to me and I had accepted you. I asked your dad once if he ever felt your presence, because I had felt you. Once more he told me that he fights the feeling. I don't what he really means by that. I never will. Like I said, "I am not afraid, I am not afraid."

February 7 (Journal Entry)

Jennifer Marie Smith. I just needed to write that today. I am away again. This time I called Aunt Lynn and invited myself to Grand Rapids. It had been a strange week. I was backwards and out of sorts. I was even writing letters and numbers backwards. I was slipping, so I called Lynn. I had to go somewhere different. I told her not to go to any trouble, but that I just needed a place to lay my head. But here I sit in a tiny room she prepared and told me she had fun fixing up. A comforter on the roll-a-way, doilies, candles, and potpourri welcomed me. We talked and we walked. We spent time with Tracy. Tracy finds things. I told her I loved Ernest Hemingways's book *In Love and War* and wanted to read *A Farewell to Arms*. She found it in a used bookstore today. I mentioned trying to find a 1995 copy of Life Magazine's tribute to The Beatles for Jamin. She found it in an antique store. She listens, she remembers, and cares for the needs of others.

February 9 (Journal Entry)

I forgot to tell you, Jen. I went to get your Christmas wreath from your memory tree in the park. Jackie and I have put it there every Christmas since your death. It was gone. I called the township park and they said they would look into it. Jackie said she cried herself to sleep after she heard the news in a message I left. I left the wreath too long. I should have picked it up after the New Year. They finally did call me back. The groundskeeper threw it away. He thought some kids put it there. I don't understand. It was clearly a memory wreath with your name on it like the plaque at the base of the tree. It was tied on so tightly so the wind couldn't take it. It had a cross on it, along with an Angel and a Lady Bug. It didn't look like a toy. It withstood wind, rain, and snow for three years. I haven't told Jackie it was thrown away yet.

February 16. (Recorded)

It's your father's birthday tonight, Jenny. Your dad and Jamin and I went out to dinner, like we usually do on each other's birthdays. Your absence will always be there surrounding us. Another Valentine's Day came and once again I brought you your Cherished Teddy. It was the last Valentine's Day gift you received from me. I don't know how many more there will be, but there is one for you today. I sent a card tonight to Pastor and Judy because this Wednesday, in a couple days, will be Mike's birthday. I explained to them that I realize that even though they have great knowledge of the Bible, and of all God's comfort and words of strength, that it doesn't change their grief. It doesn't change what a difficult time you have on your child's birthday. Faith helps. Faith strengthens, but nothing cures grief. Grief is something you learn to live with, not something you get rid of. My pain is no less, my longing is no less, my need of you is no less, but my strength gets stronger. I believe my self-esteem did plummet, but in my quest to revive some sort of life, it has gone higher than it was before. I respect myself. I understand myself. My naiveté is going away. I really do believe I was one of the most naïve people on this earth. Seeing only the good in everyone, most of the time, believing most everything everyone told me. Nothing wrong with seeing the good. It's a wonderful trait to be forgiving and empathic, but I believe I've become more of a realist. I no longer look at people and close my mind to negative vibes or negative things; I seem to be able to separate the good and the bad in people and accept them anyway.

Having an enhanced knowledge of other people, a better understanding, helps me also to protect myself. When people face loss, I don't think they become hard or embittered. I think they become wiser, more aware, and certainly more aware of what can happen in this world. In some ways, I appreciate certain things much more, but I also see things much clearer. I find myself suddenly being irritated by certain things people say or certain ways they act that I would have never even noticed before. I imagine that just comes from not being so naïve, but when you've been through a tragedy like this, you really cannot be naïve anymore. You're shocked right out of that mindset.

I'm no longer the dreamer. I'm no longer the one who says, "Tomorrow will be a better day, and things can only get better." I know better now, but that's not a bad thing; that's a good thing. I expected too much sometimes, and when you expect too much, you get disappointed too much. I have sitting next to my bed a favorite poem of yours; now I know why you liked it so much, because it actually says everything that I have learned since you died.

After A While

After a while you learn the subtle difference
Between holding a hand and chaining a soul,
And you learn that love doesn't mean leaning
And company doesn't mean security.
And you begin to learn that kisses aren't contracts
And presents aren't promises,
And you begin to accept your defeats
With your head up and your eyes open
With the grace of a woman, not the grief of a child,
And you learn to build all your roads on today
Because tomorrow's ground is too uncertain for plans
And futures have a way of falling down in mid-flight.
After a while you learn…
That even sunshine burns if you get too much.
So you plant your garden and decorate your own soul,
Instead of waiting for someone to bring you flowers.
And you learn that you really can endure…
That you really are strong
And you really do have worth…
And you learn and learn…
With every good-bye you learn.

—Veronica A. Shoffstall

I have had a lot of goodbyes in my life, Jenny, but none has taught me as much as my goodbye to you.

FEBRUARY 26

Jenny, it's one more month to the fourth anniversary. I feel the tension starting. Your father and I can hardly talk. The thing is, Jen, that I don't know if it is that or if it's because there is a lot going on at his work, and I'm getting over a bad flu so I'm pretty weak. I could blame everything on grief. That would be simple. Sometimes, it is just life.

I watched an odd movie tonight called *The Crossing Guard*. It was about a father who wanted to kill the drunk driver who killed his little girl. What was made clear to me is something I've thought about but never really felt; the view of the drunk driver. He wanted to die. His guilt was as severe as the father's grief. I cried along with him and I cried for him. Then I thought about the man who killed you. Oh, how I hated him even though he died as well. But, what if he had lived? Could he have lived with his guilt? I don't think I could. Maybe God let him die too because He knew he wouldn't be able to live with it. I can see why the two men held each other's hands at the end of the movie. They both lived with unbearable pain.

February 28

I had such dreams the day you arrived.
Do you remember the love in my eyes?
I knew you were coming, and I was prepared.
I learned and I practiced, but still I was scared.
I had so much time to learn what to do,
And I patiently waited for you.

Little girl giggles and platinum pigtails,
Tantrums and tears in those childhood years,
We made happy memories and weathered some storms,
The sounds and the sights of our lives being formed.
Sunshine and clouds swimming over our heads,
And I patiently waited for you.

Grown up ideas, a mind of your own
Earned independence; autonomy grows.
Stubborn and strong, a fight for yourself.
I let go of your hand and asked God for His help.
Did I ask Him too often until He complied?
You are His now, and I patiently wait for you.

Mom

March 1

Dear Jenny, this was the strangest day. Most of my days are filled with thoughts of you. However, this entire day seemed to be built around you. First, Joanne woke me, and we talked for 1½ hours about how we feel physically, how we relate to other people's problems, and how we feel shut off from the world and "normal" life. Something I said made her cry. I'm not sure what. We both said so much. Then I decided I wouldn't do anything today until I finished a grief book I was reading. So, I read about grief all day.

Then your Aunt Laurie called me, and we started talking. She was telling me about a skit she saw once at a Christian concert. It was God and the devil conversing. The devil wanted a certain man because of his multiple sins. There were pages and pages of sin. God said he couldn't have the man because his name was in the book of life. The devil said, "Let me see! Don't you see all his sins written down?" God said, "There are no sins next to his name. It's blank. His sins have been washed away." The crowd at the concert roared. I love talking to your Aunt Laurie. She comforts me and makes me feel loved by God more than anyone I know. I told her that whenever I start to feel sorry for myself, I think of little children I see in television commercials with staring blank eyes, swollen bellies, and flies landing on their tiny faces.

Once in a while, I get locked into a negative thought process where I convince myself that God is angry with me, or He favors parents who don't have to know this pain. Then I picture that poor, tiny child and a happy, healthy child sitting at a table. Does God love that sick child any less than the healthy one? Why is the sick child's life so painful? Of course, He doesn't love him less. Laurie reminds me that Mary was highly favored among women to be the mother of Jesus. However, she wasn't spared having to watch His death on the cross. Guilt and pity are detrimental to the mind. I'm learning to fight it every day.

March 11

Hey JB, that's what your dad used to call you. JB is short for Jenny Bug. Your dad, like your grandfather, has a nickname for everyone. I am still Toots or Froggy. It's a beautiful day today. It's cold, clear, and crisp. So was yesterday, but March 9th was horrid in more ways than one. I had to run errands that day, though I really didn't want to go out. It was dull grey, sleety, and windy. The snow pelted me in the face like tiny knives and stung my cheeks. I had already run a couple of errands when I passed the Cooker restaurant where you worked when you passed. I thought about your poem *Summer* engraved on the plaque hanging just inside the entrance. Another plaque next to it says, *Friends don't let friends drive drunk*. I then thought about your friend who was drunk the night you passed and you feeling you had to drive her car. My thoughts ricocheted back and forth until I snapped out of it when I got to the bank. All of a sudden, I wanted out or away. I wanted to go anywhere but here in this state on these roads. I wanted to be somewhere else and be someone else.

I wanted to escape to a place where no one knew me and I could pretend to have a different life. By the time I left the bank, I was feeling quite ill. I barely made it to a gas station before I could run inside and vomit.

That same evening, I was to meet your Aunt Laurie at a shopping center. The wind was still treacherous, but I didn't realize how bad the roads were. I got about two miles from home when I came upon an accident. So many flashing red lights and flares spouting fire. So many cars pulled over to help. I immediately began to pray for the poor people involved. I do that every time I hear sirens. I just stop what I'm doing and pray. Traffic was stopped and right ahead of me EMTs were working on a poor soul on the road. My thoughts went to the family of this injured person, thinking they were probably unaware that something had happened. Soon they would get a call or a knock on the door. Soon they would know, and their lives would be forever changed. I couldn't breathe. I froze. How could I move my car and continue driving when the backed-up traffic was allowed to continue? Would everyone drive forward and be thankful it wasn't their body on the road? I was dizzy and tears ran down my cheeks. I remembered to breathe slowly and evenly. I had no paper bag to put over my mouth. We do finally move on past the horror of what we have seen, some of us in shock and disbelief, and some of us praying for the victim. I hope the injured soul made it. It's all I can do, just hope.

I look out at this calm sunny day and wonder how just a short time ago it was a different world. Like a hurricane that turns the sea into a murderer one day and a place of serenity the next. Mother nature is another killer. She can do what she wants and people lose their lives. I think of you and your love of life and your sweet face and wonder how you ever could have lost yours.

March 25

Jenny, the countdown starts on March 1st. Twenty-five days left, then two weeks, then one week, then one day, and now three hours. Not knowing we are going to die is a blessing, but it also seems so unfair. What happened to you was so unfair. I say that to God. One thing about grief is that I probably sounded more healed and positive six months ago. Today I am bitter. Today I am angry. I will allow myself that luxury of feeling whatever I want to with no apology. I worked today. I grabbed it when someone asked me to fill in. I worked hard, staying focused all day. It's a survival thing. I wonder how Jamin and your dad feel. They don't talk about it. I don't bring up the anniversary because I don't want to start a fire when there may only be a spark. We went out to eat together because I wanted to be with them. It was just my family, my little family. We made small talk. Just don't think to hard or too deep. Stay lightly afloat all day. Don't sink.

I will work tomorrow as well. I will mourn you all day. I looked for you in the mall when I went on break. It's where you were your last day on earth. I looked longingly at places they said you had been. It seemed that all I saw were young blonde girls with your hairstyle, young pregnant women and young mothers with children. I want to scream at God. I went to the coffee shop and got your favorite sweet Café Carmel. Your cousin Jackie will come and meet me for lunch tomorrow. Your aunts called me tonight. I don't even know what to say. I talk about everything else going on. How do I tell them how I really feel? They are most likely tired of my grief. I always say, "I'm okay. We are all okay."

I finally, after a few years, had a dream about you. I wrote it down, though I know I'll never forget. It was short and sweet. Again, I was speaking to you. This time we spoke over a radio in your car. You were telling me that you would come over and bring donuts and the dogs wouldn't go outside for you because they would smell the donuts. It sounded as if you were telling me that you do come to visit us. Perhaps when I'm not home and your dad and Jamin are alone. You were always good at that. Then on the radio I responded, "You know, Jenny, I would give anything in the world to have you here, but I'm glad you are safe with God." Then there was silence just like the last dream I had when I was talking to you on the phone. It was like you weren't allowed to say anything about heaven. So, I asked,

"Are you happy, Jenny?" "Oh, yeah," you answered. "Are you having fun?" I asked. With a giggle, you answered, "Uh huh!" That was it. You were gone. I wonder how long it will be before the next dream.

Grandma Ginny sent a card today. It simply says:

> In our sleep,
> pain that cannot forget,
> falls drop by drop upon the heart,
> and in our own despair,
> against our will, comes wisdom
> through the awful grace of God.
>
> —Aeschylus

It's beautiful, and I'm being so extremely patient waiting for that wisdom. I've taken some safe herbs to help sleep. My little Hannah is asleep next to me. Pets can be so healing and loving to the broken heart. I'll try to sleep, Jenny, and I will relive the inevitable. I feel that if I fall asleep, I'll wake up and you'll be gone again. It's like that every year. I love you.

MARCH 26

Hello in heaven. Every time I wrote this date at work, I hated it. Even numbers are triggers. You died today. Every March 26, you will die again. As I write this, I wonder if that will change over time. It will have to. That's what we are taught. Next week I will put this anniversary behind me and move on.

I saw Jackie today. At first, I just told her how mad and bitter I was this year. She talked about her boyfriend's mom and how her only daughter was murdered ten years ago. I knew her boyfriend had a sister that passed away, but it seemed to be private, so I never asked. Today she decided to share the how and why. She hesitated because she thought it would be difficult to talk about and even harder to hear. She began to talk about the young woman's life, and I thought it sounded like a terrifying movie. Her boyfriend's sister was raped and killed by a serial killer.

Once again, I was yanked from the depths of my pity pit. How awful for the woman and for her family. I couldn't stand it if you suffered. Someone did write a book about it and all the other murders. It came out today. Jackie and I walked to a bookstore. I bought it. That night I read one chapter. I couldn't go further. I never got to the young woman's story. I thanked God once more that you died happy and didn't suffer. God bless the victims and their families. Please, God, forgive my self-pity.

April 7

Hi, Jenny! Guess what? I saw Jesse's mom today. She was coming out of the drug store as I was going in. I thought she saw me, but she kept on. I stopped and turned around and watched her for a moment. I froze. I couldn't think of her first name. I knew it a few minutes later. Maybe she didn't recognize me, as I'm twenty pounds heavier than I was at your funeral. Maybe she wouldn't have talked to me anyway.

I've felt like I'm losing myself again. When is this pain going to let up? This past Saturday, I felt almost catatonic. I went up north alone for two days last week. It rained constantly. I went to The Lamb Shop and found one copy of a book called *Margaret's Peace* by Linda Hall. The jacket of the book said it was about a woman who lost her daughter and her marriage. She was going to run away to the house she grew up in and just inherited. It was a fictional mystery.

I bought it because she lost her only daughter and she was moving to the ocean. I long to run away to the ocean. I just want to sit and stare at it and listen to the waves. I have already talked to your dad about the possibility of traveling to Cape Cod alone. He said he wouldn't mind. I think it would be a healing sabbatical. I'm not afraid to be alone, but only to travel alone. I read the book in two days. I could identify with this Margaret. In one passage she is talking to her aunt. "And I suppose you, like everyone else, are going to talk to me about the sovereignty of God, whatever that word means, as if saying that word exonerates Him for all the evil in the world, and how her death was all for the best and how everything works together for good." In another passage Margaret says, "My struggles make me learn something so I can help other people who are going through the same thing. My question is, why do all those other people have to go through it in the first place?"

God, I have felt that so often. Margaret's aunt goes on to answer that God is not the author of death and that the reality of God shines through the reality of death and darkness. Jenny...I know that, so why doesn't it make this easier?

Margaret explains to her aunt that she came to the ocean to escape confusion and she was hoping the sea would give her peace. Again, her wise aunt answers, "The sea won't give you peace. No outside thing can give you peace. Not pills, not sitting by the sea. Peace has to come from someplace inside of you, a place that has accepted all of the ghosts and made peace with God."

Jenny, perhaps someday I will make that peace with God. I thought I had, but I want to run away too.

April 20

Bug, I returned from Florida yesterday. I went with your aunts to visit Aunt Jackie for her 75th birthday. She flew us down for her 70th five years ago. During that time, I called home to talk to you. I remember the conversation and the sound of your voice. This time you weren't there. Remember when we went down a week after you passed? I can't think of that when I'm there. It would make everything less enjoyable.

I think of you when the sun shines. It made you come alive with energy and happiness. We took a very bumpy boat ride to Key West. People were taking turns using the trashcan. Fortunately, we did not get sick. I thought of how much you would have loved a place like Key West. Maybe that's what heaven is like for you. Maybe it's one long sunny beach. When I returned home to Michigan, I had received a card from your cousin Tracy. Within the card she wrote down two poems.

Turn Again to Life

If I should die and leave you here awhile,
be not like others, sore undone, who keep
long vigil by the silent dust and weep.
For my sake turn again to life and smile,
nerving thy heart and trembling hand to do
that which will comfort other souls than thine;
complete these dear unfinished tasks of mine,

and I, perchance, may therein comfort you.

—Mary Lee Hall

I do keep long vigil by your side, don't I, Jen? Could I turn again to life if I do it for your sake? The other poem simply said very sweetly:

Jenny Kissed Me

Jenny kiss'd me when we met,
Jumping from the chair she sat in;
Time, you thief, who love to get
Sweets into your list, put that in!
Say I'm weary, say I'm sad,
Say that health and wealth have missed me,
Say I'm growing old, but add
Jenny kiss'd me.

—Leigh Hunt

April 27

Jenny, oh, how I wish you were sitting here. I want to talk to you, not the paper. I could get you a cup of coffee. I could listen to how your life is going and then I could tell you what a hard week I've had. If it's true that you must hit rock bottom in order to climb back up, then I'm on my way to the bottom. Did my spirit die when your body did, or has it slowly been dying for four years?

I found some old rolls of black and white film your dad took in 1981. I took them in for developing, and your dad could hardly wait to get them back. We knew you would be in those old photos. I sent out pictures to family members if they were in them. It's strange how I don't really connect the child you were with the woman we lost. It's like you were separate. Perhaps I knew the child would be temporary. It's the woman that was always supposed to be here.

We have an invitation to a wedding. We've had others but they were out of state. This is your friend Jeremy's wedding. He was with you and your friends the night you died. This wedding is just a few miles away. Will we chicken out or face it with our heads held high? Will Jesse be there? Your old friends, our old friends. Do we just go and let the pain wash over us all at once? Do we jump from the safe shore into the deep ocean? Do we shake hands, smile, and talk, while all along your absence and our pain are eating at us from the inside out? We haven't seen any of these people in three years.

April 30

Dear Jenny, a week or so ago, Aunt Lynn sent me a letter. In it she explained how she would be going down to North Carolina to scatter her mother's ashes on her grandparent's graves. She and some relatives would remember her mother with stories. I envied the closure she would have. I cannot let go of your ashes.

A week ago, I ran across a plaque put out for Mother's Day in a gift shop. It said simply: *A mother is someone who dreams great dreams for you, yet accepts the dreams that you decide to follow, and will always love you just the way you are.* I bought the plaque yesterday. I want Jamin to know that.

This morning your father called to tell me we would be celebrating a substantial raise tonight. He sounded happier than I have heard in a very long time. I was very happy for him. He has buried himself in his job as a way of coping, and it's great to see something good come from that. I'm not as happy about the money as I am at the joy of his being appreciated by his employer.

I came upstairs to shower and decided to get on my knees and thank God for bringing some joy into his life. I also prayed for my care receivers. I did finally get around to that but not until after I broke down and talked to you. I've been so troubled since the fourth anniversary. I'm not bouncing back.

You never got to experience the freedom and independence you earned by turning twenty-one. And what was I doing holding on to your ashes as if I kept them close, they would spontaneously turn back into you? Am I holding on to them for fear of losing you? Am I keeping you safe just as I tried so hard to do while you were here? I'm just keeping you home with me. I keep your spirit tied to me like a mother carries her baby in a snugly close to her body. Even a two year old starts to separate from the mother and walk around on his own. I am keeping you captive. If you were alive, you would be on your own. You would be free. I held you too close in life, and I hold you too close in death. I cried and vowed to give you a place of your own. I set you free.

After prayers, I left to get a congratulations card for your dad. I went down Orion Road past the little cemetery where one of our good friends is buried. It was so sunny there. Something made me pull in and drive around. So many young people buried there. You don't realize until you look at dates. I liked the place, Jenny. Not too many trees and no locked gates or mammoth cement sanctuaries. It was just simple enough. I wrote down the name and number to contact.

I went to pick up a card and I saw a Boyd's Bearstone I had admired in the past. It was so charming and comforting to look at. I picked it up, as there are always quotes on the bottom. It read *Life is no brief candle to me. It is sort of a splendid torch that I have got hold of for the moment.* —George Bernard Shaw. This figurine was large, so another quote was added. *Life was meant to be lived, and curiosity must be kept alive. One must never, for whatever reason, turn his back on life.* —Eleanor Roosevelt. The piece is a little bear sitting on her memories in the attic staring into a beautiful antique beveled mirror. They called the piece *We Are Always the Same Age Inside*. I bought the Bearstone.

On the way home, I stopped at a garden center where I picked up some flowers for your dad and some African Violets for you. They bloom profusely. All my flowering plants keep blooming since you passed. I bought Jamin a new planter for a Jade tree he keeps in his room. It was a small plant from your grandpa's funeral. Jamin keeps telling me that it's outgrowing the pot. While on my way home, I got stuck in traffic. I was on Flint Street and stopped in front of an attractive building on my right. It read Village Hall. It was the contact for the cemetery. Right in front of me was a parking space. I pulled in and asked for information.

After I gave your dad his card and flowers, I showed him my Bearstone and why I bought it. However, I'm struggling to remove it from the box. There are sweet sayings all over it, but the one that caught my eye said, "Mom . . . how far can you dream?" (Jamie Smith)

May 11

I had a Mother's Day gift in the form of a dream. I couldn't find you. I hadn't seen you in a long time. I think the last time was Easter. I knew you were living with your good friend, Jenny Z. (Your cousin Jackie actually lives with her now.) I couldn't find the phone number. I had to see you to see if you were safe. I called people, trying to get the number. I left messages. Once I called your phone number and got an answering music box. Though in my dream I didn't know where home was, I left a message for you to call. One person I got ahold of told me you were going to school in the morning and working at a restaurant as a waitress in the evening. I thought I could just go there and find you. But then you showed up when I was with my friend Joanne. We gave you something to eat. You looked adorable. Your long blonde hair was cut short and had a slight wave. It fit your little face perfectly. I felt so relieved to find out that you were doing okay. What is odd, Jenny, is that I don't remember you saying anything. You were just there.

Remember Jeremy's wedding invitation? I decided to face the fear of weddings head on. I couldn't avoid them all. I called his mother, Barb. I hadn't talked to her in three years. I told her I was nervous but really wanted to come. I guess Jesse won't be there. Barb and I talked like old times. Your dad and I met her and Paul for dinner. We laughed like old times and talked about growing old. They mentioned you with ease and comfort. I even felt a little like myself because we had known them for 23 years.

This Mother's Day weekend your dad and I went up to the cabin. Barb and Paul happened to be going to the Leelanau area for their anniversary. They asked if we would drive to Sutton's Bay to meet them. We decided to rent a little cottage on Little Traverse Bay and met them for dinner. The weather was beautiful, and the scenery was breathtaking. Again, we enjoyed ourselves and reminisced. It felt good to feel normal.

Your dad and I, or maybe just me, thought our friends didn't want to be around us. Relationships were awkward and distant now. Your dad and I felt *marked*, even though I can't explain it. I really don't want to believe that or feel like that. They were just nervous like us, and perhaps still heartbroken as well. One of the first couples we had dinner with after you passed blurted out, "So, what did you do with Jenny's ashes?" They were nice people and had made a genuine effort to keep in touch. It was all just too new at the time, and the question too simply stated. It shook your father to the core. At that same dinner, he also asked if we got your truck fixed. They thought you died in your own car. Why would anyone keep the car their child died in, if in fact you had? I told myself that at least he wasn't afraid to talk about you. Perhaps they were just curious.

May 17

Bugs, yesterday your dad and I celebrated our 28th wedding anniversary. I remember trying to celebrate our 25th less than two months after you passed. It was uncomfortable to say the least. We just sat and stared at the table. I took crayons they left on the table and drew your name and hearts all over the white paper tablecloth. However, I guess we are beating some statistics for staying together after a tragedy. I think our love for you and our need to be there for your brother keeps us going. Jamin was very down today. He's not sleeping well and has dark circles under his beautiful eyes. I made him promise he would go to the doctor if he didn't perk up soon. He's so lonely, Jenny, and I don't know what to do. I'm almost afraid to pray for him. I always prayed for you.

Our church had confirmation today. All those young teens in their white robes. I don't remember you wearing a robe because we argued when we were shopping for your confirmation dress. I still have it. I remember exactly how you looked, and I still have your banner and your speech. I fought back tears, but I had an overwhelming feeling of gratitude to God. Your confirmation brought you closer to Him and gave you faith. It took you to Heaven when you died. Pure and simple, I was thankful for your life. I wanted a baby. God gave me one. I wanted a girl. He gave me that also. So many blessings came to mind. It seems to happen that way. I feel bitterness creeping into my soul, and He comes and chases it clean away.

May 22

On the way home from work I remembered, Jenny. Jamin is exactly, to the day, the same age as you when you passed. Twenty years, eight months, and six days. He was here when I got home at 10:00 pm, but he and your cousin Jeff had to leave to turn off the sprinklers at Jeff's house. They will stay there for the night. I had to call to make sure they got there.

I also thought about you on the way home. I usually do at night. I started thinking about your hair. I remembered helping you put some color on it, even though I loved it the way it was. It gave a golden glow to your light blonde hair. A sorrow so great came over me as I recalled sitting in the tub with you so we wouldn't get any on the tile. A deep, sickly, empty, longing feeling engulfed me. (As I edit this, a statue I saw comes to mind. A grieving parent with arms and legs and no torso. Just an empty hole. A perfect depiction.) I didn't cry because, when I feel that way, I can't. The way I get past it now, as opposed to before, is that I know it will pass. It does for the time being. After I found out Jamin and Jeff made it okay, I sat on my bed and told God once more, "I can't do this, please don't make me do this." But, as always, I don't have a choice. So, I do it.

June 7

Your dad and I ran into your friend Kim and her mom at a restaurant. I hadn't seen her mom since your funeral. I think she was a bit surprised. I was. Kimmy is visiting from Tennessee. She is married now. She called me a few years back when she was in town, and I took her to lunch. We came back and looked through old photos. I love to see your friends because I see a part of you. At the same time, it hurts because I don't understand why you can't be living your life like they are. Why? God, I can't wait to understand it all. You and Kim were so close. Almost too close as young teens. The two of you were inseparable. Then one summer she went to Tennessee. When she came home, you had met some new friends that moved into the neighborhood. Things were never the same. I wonder if things would have been different if she hadn't gone. I wish you had stayed best friends. She said she would call me before she went home.

Jeremy's wedding happened. Your dad, Jamin, Jackie and I attended. It's confusing to be so happy for people and yet so sad at the same time. I tried to act like and be my old self. We all did. Jeremy was the lifelong friend you were trying to *fix up* the night you died. That's what I had heard. I started to cry at the beginning of the ceremony, so your dad went into the bathroom and grabbed me a handful of toilet paper. Once I had my means of mopping tears, I was able to control them. I kept looking for you. You should have been there. Your friend Toni was. She was the other end of the hookup. There were things that were arranged last minute that fateful night. It would be so easy to be bitter about her, but when I see her, I must be like you. You forgave her for many nasty acts against you before you became friends. I wish good things for her because you died helping her by driving her car. I don't want her to waste that. She hugs me, and I just say, "Take care of yourself." I stop and think about what Jeremy, Jesse, and Toni saw the night you died. They all have their own crosses to bear. I have a hard time looking them in the eyes. I see the pain in their eyes when they look at me. Zack, like the rest of us, doesn't have that picture in his mind. You two knew each other in your mother's wombs. He spoke freely about you. We danced. He talked of dreams of you, your hair, and how he still has the picture of the two of you on his dresser. He said he saw so much of you in me. At one point he squeezed me so hard I almost said, "I'm not Jenny, Zack." He said, "She didn't know it, but I was going to marry that girl."

I don't know if Zack really thought that the two of you would have ended up together or if he was telling me what he knew I always hoped for when you were little. We loved that kid. It's so easy to say what might have been. Nonetheless, he made me feel good talking about you. Jeremy and Zack loved you. You loved them.

Poor Jamin was so shy at the wedding. Girls asked about him. Grown women mentioned how adorable he was. He wasn't sixteen anymore. Toni flipped when she saw him and, later in the evening, gave him a hug he will probably never forget. I wonder how different things might be in his life if his social butterfly sister were here. When we got home from the wedding, he had a letter from his friend, Bill, saying he is engaged! Can you believe it, Jen? Little Billy is now 6'7" tall. Life is going on without you, Bugs, and I can't make it stop. I don't like you being left out of things. Not one bit!

June 8 – The Necklace

Dear Jenny, when I knew for sure that I would go to the wedding, I remembered a simple navy shift I had seen in a catalog. I decided to order it. When I did, I knew it would be a dress that could be worn with pearls. I had been given a gift of pearls some time ago and never had a chance to wear them. But I had a problem, Jenny. How would I wear the pearls along with the I LOVE YOU necklace of yours that I had worn since August 15, 1994? I thought about it and decided I would be brave and take it off for only one evening. A few hours before the wedding,

I removed my pearls from a drawer. I went to try them on and noticed that the clasp was broken. My heart started pounding, and I remembered. There are always things to remember. You wore them to senior prom and told me they broke. I never got them repaired. I searched through my jewelry box and found another string of pearls I received from your Grandma Smith. However, I couldn't figure out the clasp. I could only get the safety clasp to work. Your dad, Jamin, and even Jackie tried. I just put them on over your necklace and figured I would work on it in the car. I forgot. I wore the broken pearls over your necklace all night. I guess I shouldn't take your necklace off for any reason. I won't.

My heart is heavy today Jen. I know, when isn't it? I recognized the name of a 27 year old (one of two) that was killed by a drunk driver. I remembered him from your high school. I remember his mother jogging in our neighborhood and as a patient at the doctor's office I used to work at. The boy who hit them lived. Things have changed since you were killed. The drunk driver was convicted of two counts of 2nd degree murder. They can do that now in fatal drunk driving cases. It's a giant step. I think of the families of the boys who died. The nightmare is just beginning. God be with them all.

July 15

Bugs, your 25th birthday is five days away. I have your angel, but I will still get you a card. Last night, we had a couple of visitors. Your friend Heather (whose birthday you were celebrating the night you passed) and her son Cody knocked on our door. Boy, how you loved Cody. You talked about him constantly. Heather asked if I still had your memory chest with your "stuff." She asked to see it. I told her your ashes were in there so she wouldn't be upset. She wanted to see them. While Cody stayed and watched television with us, she looked at everything. There was a large framed picture of Cody, a framed picture of Heather and Cody, and Jesse's pictures. She remembered the clothes I had kept. She remembered how they envied your small bottom, tiny waist, and generous chest. She told me all the guys liked you in high school. It was so nice of her to come over. She said she needed a "Jenny fix," and so did I. I hadn't looked in your chest in quite some time. It's funny how I had just been feeling sad the other day thinking about your friends. I was wishing one of them had stuck around, knowing we missed having a girl in our lives. Then one came knocking at our door.

Barb and Paul came up to the cabin for the fourth of July. I mentioned to Barb my dream of going to Cape Cod by myself. I told her I had planned on going this September but was nervous. We talked about it, and now she is going with me. She is so excited that she's making me realize that it's really going to happen. I'm going to drive out East. I may have chickened out if I hadn't told her about it. I need the healing ocean. I told her it would have to be after Jamin turns twenty-one. I can't go until then. He has to make it to that birthday. I told them at work I would be gone in late September.

July 16

Jenny, it's 4:30 a.m. I'm awake from anxiety. My legs are itching. They have been itching since July 4th. They are getting worse every day. I'm just lying here crying because I suddenly remembered why. It's amazing what you can remember about your past in the middle of the night. July 4, 1973 your father took me to a doctor. You were due July 8. My legs were inflamed with hives from the waist down. The doctor called it pre-birth anxiety. By the time you were born on the 20th they had started to clear up. My legs were purple, and I remember explaining that during labor and delivery. A few days after we came home, they flared up again. The relapse was even more severe. I'll never forget the terrible itching. I would scratch in my sleep until I bled. Now I understand it will subside and it's not an allergy. I love you so much.

> *Life can be crazy and uncomfortable.*
> *But right in the middle of all the pain and chaos,*
> *I can still find a moment that seems just right.*
> *I deposit these moments in my memory because they are*
> *the bank of my happiness.*

July 25

I started a new notebook today. It's fresh and it's blue. I'm sure that someday the pages will yellow and the cover will be tattered and torn. But today it is brand new and ready for my words to heaven. Your dad and I are spending the last day of our week vacation at the cottage on the water. The weather is cool and calm compared to the humid scorchers at the beginning of the week. I actually got into the water. I was punishing myself by not swimming until I could fit into my old bathing suit. I broke down and bought a new one a size larger. Good for me.

Aunt Lynn came up for a few days at the beginning of the week. She was here on your birthday. We kept pretty busy all day. I sang Happy Birthday to you over and over until I fell asleep. Did you hear? I can't believe you are 25 years old. I tried to get your brother to come up. I think he enjoys his alone time at home.

We will leave tomorrow early so we can go to Billy's wedding reception. Remember Jen? Billy wrote a paper about you for school just after you passed. I have it somewhere. I must be brave and pull out the letters and cards from everyone.

I don't want to go home. I wish I could stay here the rest of the summer. Though I enjoy it and it's a change of pace, I can't say it's a cure all. My legs continue to itch and at times it's torture. There is no sign of a rash. I pray it stops soon. Time and only time can heal this wound inside of me. It will heal partially for a while and then some important thing or some simple thing can re-open it and make it fester all over again. I wonder if I'll ever be able to take the bandage off.

July 26

We came home today to attend Billy's reception. He was married earlier in the Upper Peninsula. It was good to see him and his family. His bride is lovely. Jenny, and you wouldn't recognize him. He's so tall but still the same sweet Bill. He had a troubled time in his teens and I'm proud he's overcome and moved on. When he thanked everyone for coming, he said a special thanks to us. I don't know why. He said he thinks of us every day. Jamin is spending the evening with him and some friends. It's good they can talk. On the back of their announcement bulletin there were names of those who were with them in spirit. You were one of those names. It read, Jennifer Smith (1973-1994).

Aunt Carol called this evening. Pastor's and Jerry's sweet mother passed away today. Now she is in heaven with her son and grandson.

July 27

Jamin and I spent the day together. That doesn't happen often. We talked about so many things. I am sure his life would be different and better if you were here. I could never influence him or bolster his self-confidence the way you could. When I say something uplifting or complimentary, I sense that he just sees me as a mom who is trying to help her child. I pray something positive comes his way very soon.

August 12

Well, Jenny, I'm going to actually do something I've dreamed of. I'm definitely going to Cape Cod in September after Jamin turns twenty-one. Barb has put a fire under me. We will drive to Wellfleet, Massachusetts, and rent a house. I don't feel any real excitement yet. Barb can't wait to go. I wish I could feel that happy and enthusiastic about it. After all, it was my dream and my idea. Maybe I'll feel it later. My legs have finally calmed down and stopped itching. Thank God!

David and Jackie came over tonight. I haven't seen them in so long. Dave has a girlfriend and Jackie has two jobs and a boyfriend. Even your cousin Jeff isn't over as much as he has a girlfriend. There were always extra kids over here. Poor Jamin. Life is moving forward for his cousins, and his stays the same. I think we haven't really wanted to move on in our hearts. He's thinking of going away to school just to "get a life." It's a phrase you used to say often. I think your dad, Jamin, and I all think along those lines. Wish us luck, Bug. We need it badly.

I am worried about your dad's health and his drinking (because he doesn't), and Jamin's happiness. I fear menopause will sneak up on me, as I will be 48 in October. No signs of it yet, but I am sure it's lurking around somewhere. I may crack. No wonder I itch.

August 18

Hi, Jenny. Aunt Cathie and Uncle Chuck had a Smith family get together today. I missed you. I remembered you standing on their deck in another time. With your long hair and faded jeans. You were polite to all as you said your goodbyes and went to join your boyfriend or friends. It's not fair. I try so hard to be normal. I know I'm not. Your dad, Jamin, and I are not the same as any of them. We never will be. They don't know. They don't understand. I see them as whole and unbroken. We have been smashed to smithereens and haphazardly glued back together. Our cracks show and there are pieces missing.

August 19

Once again, your brother and I spent the day together. We ate lunch, ran errands, and saw a movie in the middle of the day. I love spending time with him, but his loneliness breaks my heart even more so than my own. My prayer is to see him happy. Perhaps then I will be able to deal with my own loneliness. What I see in us is a desperate need for someone or something but at the same time wanting to be away from crowds and confusion. Sometimes being around people makes me feel even lonelier. Jamin may feel the same. I have a Stephen Ministry picnic with another church tomorrow. I sent my regrets. I am sorry, but I don't want to go. I pray that this too will end. Just when I think it's improving it sneaks up on me again.

August 25

One month from today, Barb and I drive to Cape Cod. I keep wondering if it will really happen. I must look into renting a car as our cars have too many miles on them. I tell your dad that if I find a little bookshop for sale in some quaint New England town near the ocean, I may not be back. He simply says, "Okay." Now I'm worried about him. I go back and forth between your dad and Jamin. Jamin seems good for a few days at a time. I think he's getting used to his new hours at work. He told me about a dream he had about you last night. He and Jackie were at our old house on Regency. They went up the steps leading to the front and looked through the screen door. You were sitting on the steps that go up to the bedrooms. They asked you to open the door. Instead you ran upstairs as they pleaded with you. You didn't come back down. He told me that his dreams of you are never really happy. Give him a sweet dream, Jenny. He needs it.

Of course, again, his dream makes me wonder if we did the right thing by moving. I hope you don't feel that we left you there alone. Remember when I was still there sleeping on the couch and I felt you near me and spoke right out loud, "Jenny, don't leave me." When I woke up, I felt as if you were saying goodbye. I felt you were going into the light (I watch movies) and you wouldn't be back. I was so utterly sad at that moment. I sound so crazy. I'll have no true answers about anything until I see you again. We sure could use some happy dreams.

I signed up for a computer class in October. I want to get all the tapes, poems, letters, songs, and diaries down in one memory book of you. I may never do much with it, but at least it will be in one place.

August 28

Hi Bugs. I've been writing to you a lot lately. Jackie came over when I got home from work yesterday. She brought her laundry and her guitar. She wants to learn *Oh Holy Night*. She would like to learn my version. I've sung it for so many years that I have many versions. We sang and played all evening. She's already a great musician so she'll pick up guitar quickly. It made me play again. I haven't had much of a desire to pick up my guitar. Maybe I just needed a reason.

I told her about the dream Jamin had about you sitting on the steps leading upstairs. As I was telling her we both had the same thought. I now view the dream differently. We thought maybe the door was locked and you ran upstairs and wouldn't come back down because they had to be kept out. They couldn't be where you were. It wasn't their time to be with you. In my dreams you always leave whenever I ask you a question. You are not allowed to tell us anything about where you are.

I took the dogs out last night and decided to stay out awhile as the sky was profuse with stars. I thought about the time I was pregnant with you. You were as close to me as anyone could be. Like now, I couldn't see you or touch you. I could only feel your presence inside of me. You were with me 24 hours per day. It's not much different now Jenny. You are inside of me spiritually instead of physically. This time you won't be born. I'll carry you until the day I die.

August 30

I had a dream, Jenny. We found you. You weren't dead at all, just lost. You were around ten years old. We had you back! But something wasn't right. Someone was missing. I remember feeling uneasy. I don't know why. I wanted my whole family together in the same house. I do remember the most important aspect of the dream. I wish I could get that feeling back again. I only had it for a few moments. It was a feeling of pure and utter joy at holding you. It was a feeling of pure, unspoiled love.

I did some organizing today. I went to a small drawer in a desk. In that drawer was a stack of memorandums from funerals, starting with my mother in 1965. I was adding a recent one for my mother's cousin, Donald. A crisp, new white one lay on top. I picked it up and when I opened it, all I saw was JENNIFER MARIE SMITH (JENNY-BUG). I dropped it. My heart stopped. My breath stopped. I couldn't move. It scared me to death that a quick dose of reality could hit me so hard. Could it be that I still don't believe you are gone? Maybe that's how we survive.

SEPTEMBER 10

Jenny, I cried all the way home from work. I ached for you. I guess I needed to do that. You have to let the pain out once in a while. I wonder if your dad and Jamin do that. I don't ask.

When I'm driving my mind travels to a place I'd rather not go. I play the game of what ifs. What if the traffic light at Joslyn Road had been a different color? What if the man that hit you didn't miss his exit (something your dad figured out)? What if the man hadn't been subbing for a bowler that had a wedding to attend? What if the couple getting married had picked a different date other than March 26th? If I let them, the what ifs can drive me crazy.

Jamin turns twenty-one in six days. You would have been so excited for your twenty-first. I wish you could have had the party you were planning. Jamin doesn't want one. I don't blame him.

Barb and I are all set to leave for Cape Cod on the 25th. I just need to pack. I'm not feeling excited yet and it puzzles me. I've always wanted to go there. What's the matter with me? Barb can't wait.

SEPTEMBER 17

Jamin turned twenty-one. He wasn't excited. He didn't want a party. He didn't go to a bar. We were going to go out to dinner, but he said he wanted to have dinner at home. On his birthday, we ran around getting our drivers licenses renewed and food shopping. Then I rushed home to clean up. Brian, Jeff, John, and Jackie came over. We had a quiet dinner of your and Jamin's favorite, turkey chili macaroni and shrimp kabobs. Aunt Laurie, Uncle Tim, Aunt Carol, Uncle Jerry, and Erin came over later for ice cream and cake. I forgot to get film for the camera. I can't believe it. I'm not good at taking pictures. I will buy some today and take some pictures of Jamin.

We found out this week that David is moving to California with his girlfriend and Jackie is moving to Seattle with her boyfriend. In addition, Jamin and Brian are looking for an apartment to share. Aunt Carol must be so upset. Jackie just told her last night. I'll miss them but they are alive, and we can get on an airplane to see them. Kids leave.

September 24

Dear Bugs, Barb and I leave for Cape Cod tomorrow at 7:30 a.m. I guess I am excited. I'm happy and fortunate to be going. I'm not sure I remember how to feel excited. I'll let you know. By the way, thank you for all the yellow roses. There are so many that I picked them to take on the trip because they would go to waste here. I don't think your dad or Jamin pay much attention to them, and Jamin says there are too many bushes and flowers. Your dad hates gardening. Every yellow rose that blooms is special to me. They are miracles from God. I'll let you know how the trip goes. I'm going to keep a journal. Pray we will be safe and watch over your dad and brother for me. I love you. Mom

October 16

Jenny, I have so much to tell you about my trip, my birthday, and Jamin leaving home. I've felt you so close lately. I felt you with me by the ocean. Maybe I feel you already know everything that's been happening. I'll write to you soon. I'm so very tired.

October 20

I've been working so much since I returned home. I just worked seven days in a row on my feet. It probably won't improve until I quit. I've hardly had time to think about how wonderful the trip was. The weather was perfect. I'm also thinking about Jamin leaving. It's Tuesday night, and he moves this Friday. I'm happy for him, but I've been taking care of a family since 1973 when you were born. I'm trying not to think of how it will feel.

When you moved out, you were only gone for three months. You returned home, and I was glad. You were only 19. Sometimes I think you came back home because you wanted to spend time with us before you passed on. That, or you were just tired of being an adult. If I can survive this long after losing you, I'll be okay after Jamin leaves. I have no choice, do I? My eyelids are drooping. When can I tell you all the things I need to?

October 21

Jennifer, when Jamin woke up to go to his afternoon job, I made him a nice dinner. We had stuffed orange roughy and shrimp with cocktail sauce. This was our last dinner together while he still lives here. He liked it so much, he said he would make it for his girlfriend someday. Tomorrow night I work late, and I'll miss his last night at home. I will be with him during the day.

I'm taking Jackie up north before she moves away. She has never been to the new cabin. I made these plans before I knew Jamin was moving out this weekend. Maybe it's better that I won't be here. I want to do things for him like buy sheets and food. He doesn't want me to. I did get a few things to get him and Brian started. I found a book I bought a long time ago about giving your child wings. I pulled it out. I need it.

I said I would write about the trip out east. If I didn't come home to all the changes, I would have done it sooner. Of course, it was like a dream. Barb and I loved Wellfleet and visited all the towns up and down Cape Cod. I enjoyed her company. We had wonderful conversations. We went to Nantucket (my favorite) and Martha's Vineyard. I can still see the climbing roses of Siasconset, and the blue hydrangeas spread throughout the cape. Someday I will plant them.

I kept a journal of the entire trip, but I will add only one entry here. One day I asked Barb if she would mind if I took the car and went alone to a beach we had seen. She didn't mind and this is my entry for that time.

October 2 – South Wellfleet Beach, Wellfleet/Eastham, Cool 65 degrees, clear and sunny.

I've dreamed of this my whole life. I was really all alone, the Atlantic and me. I walked, I explored, collected shells, and sat in the warm sand staring at the enormous waves. The only thing that could have made it better was to have Jenny with me. Going down the cliff to the water was easy. Coming back up was near to impossible. I kept trying to climb up where I came down. Five steps up, three sliding back down. I thought of how that climb matched my grief over the last four years. The sand had me at its mercy. I was trapped. I looked for another way up. I didn't see one. I could walk until I saw steps, but where would I end up? So I climbed. Ten steps up, five sliding down. My heart was pounding from the effort. Though it was cold, I was sweating. I started to crawl on all fours. Up a little, down a little. When I finally made it to the top and could see my car, I couldn't breathe. I regretted all those hours sitting and staring and reading. I opened the car door and hurried inside, blasting the air conditioner. If someone had seen me trying to breathe, they would have called for assistance. I tore off my jacket, stripped off my sweatshirt, and sat there in my tee. It was some time before I could breathe evenly. I started back to the cottage. I would never pick a random spot on the Atlantic again. I had thought it was a beach, but it was more of a lookout on the beach.

It was our last day on the Cape. Barb and I sat outside on the deck and had a drink. We laughed and laughed. Life was good.

November 4

Dear Jenny, I'm feeling sorry for myself today. Yesterday I was cheerful and energetic. Today I'm bitter and ache all over. But I'm not too bitter to be thankful for the good days. I think I'm working too many hours. David is on his way to who knows where in California. Jackie leaves this weekend for Seattle. I wonder if everything would be different if you were here. Remember the movie, *It's a Wonderful Life*? One person's absence from this world can change everything. Who knows, maybe you would be going with them. Jackie went on a trip out west with your friends and met her boyfriend who lives in Seattle. If you were here, she may not have gone on that trip, or maybe you would have gone with them and you would have met someone from a different state as well. Your dad always says, "Should of and could of don't count."

Jamin moved out, and though I miss him, I can deal with his absence because he is alive and healthy. I know your Aunt Carol must feel horrible about both her older children leaving the state, but we do have phones and airplanes and constant contact can be maintained. In your case, I must wait until God gives me a ticket to you.

I keep thinking about Cape Cod. I loved it so much that I'm thinking of going back next year. I'll wait until after Jamin's birthday when all the crowds are gone. All I have to do is make a phone call and reserve a cabin on the ocean. I must do that soon.

I spent the last two weekends up north. The first was with Jackie, your aunts, and Erin. We all attended church Sunday. After stopping to shop, I locked my keys in the car. We called a locksmith and went to wait in a tavern for him to arrive. After waiting a few hours, a man overheard us talking and offered to go and get his lock kit. He returned fifteen minutes later and was in the car in five. We tried to pay him, but he wouldn't accept it. I called the tavern, but no one knew more than his first name. I say he was an angel. Your dad said he was a professional car thief. Glass half full vs. glass half empty.

The second weekend up north was with your dad. He fixed the fireplace and got it ready for the winter. I cleaned and then we had 38 trick or treaters for Halloween. We raked the leaves and left everything in order. The only thing that didn't work out was the supposed installation of Satellite television. The tech didn't show. I can do without your dad flipping through 220 channels. Could you imagine?

Your dad just called. It was about another possible job relocation. The last time, I got all excited about moving to Boston and it fell through. I won't think about it this time. Well, Jenny, my job has called me in again today. I try to keep this job part-time, but it never fails that someone quits or doesn't show up. After the holidays, I will put my foot down. Love, Mom

November 5

I'm reading a book in my bed. It's midnight. I don't know when I've felt this sad. I always say that, but I know I have been much sadder. I don't know if I've ever felt so empty and alone as I do at this moment. I hear your father snoring downstairs. He sleeps there most nights, as he did even before you died. We disturb each other too much. I stay up and read and he snores. I wonder if he waits for me to go to bed so he can drink. He keeps it in the garage. A minute ago, I felt such despair that I said aloud, "I'm ready for my heart to stop now." It's been broken for too long. This sure isn't what I thought my life would be like five years ago. I always looked for brighter days and would daydream about the future. Right now, I don't see one at all. But, tomorrow I will wake up and go about whatever it is I'm supposed to do, and take care of what is expected of me, just as I have always done. Where has it left me? God in heaven, I miss you. Love, your mom forever.

November 10

Jen-Bug, Jackie left yesterday. A few days before, we celebrated her 26th birthday. We saw photos of her 21st birthday when we were all together around the same table. You were there and happy as could be, not knowing you would be gone four months later. She called me just before she left. Your brother helped her pack. She told me I was very special to her. The two of you loved each other so much. I wish her much happiness in her new life. It's probably not much fun for her being around all the painful memories of you. Often, I would remember going to see her at Michigan State not long after you passed. Her sweet roommate let me have her bed and stayed elsewhere. Jackie showed me a letter and a poem that same girl wrote for her while Jackie was home for your funeral. Jackie made me a copy because it was so heartwarming and so full of love.

Jackie, I can't imagine what you are going through, but I want to help however I can. I know you would give anything to have her back—but I hope the things we do can help ease the pain. Remember, however [awful] it sounds, God only gives you as much as he thinks you can handle. He must think you are superwoman. But He has to be right, He's God. You need to pull every one of your strengths in—Jenny's, your family's, your friends', and your own, and you will carry on. You were left here because your work is not done yet. Don't question it. I'm so glad you're here. And know that even if there is not a person around you, you will never be alone again. Jenny is with you. Feel strong in that and know that we are here for you too. I love you. You are so very special. —Teri Anne (3-30-94)

Jackie and Jamin

Jamin

November 15

My sweet Bug, my stomach hurts from crying. I watched the television show *Touched by an Angel,* and it got me started. I'm missing you so much. I am over tired from working too much and too hard. I don't know what happened to this part time job. I was so tired and upset about something at work (my boss is a nasty woman) the other night that your dad sent me roses at the store. I cried and so did my customer. I think the deliveryman almost cried as well. Or, maybe I was supposed to tip him. They are beautiful. It made me remember when you were just a small child and your dad bought you roses on your birthday. I have a picture of you so small with a big grin and bobbed blonde hair holding this huge bouquet of roses. Another reason my stomach hurts is worry over your brother. He came to the store today before we opened. He didn't know the mall opened at noon on Sunday. He has a lump in his groin. I hope it is just a hernia. I pray it is. He called for the doctor's number. He said he slept all day yesterday. I hope it's just his odd work hours. I hope he's all right. I pray he is. Help! Love, Mom

November 19

Hi Sweetie. We have a new Mega Mall about ten minutes south of us. Your dad and I went to see it as we have been watching the construction for some time now. We ran into your Aunt Cathie and Uncle Chuck. We had a nice dinner together and walked around for a while checking out all the outlets. Your dad seemed to get very sad all of a sudden. I can always see it in his face when he misses you. He may have had the same thoughts as I did. You would have really enjoyed this place. I was offered a job managing one of the stores when a headhunter came in while I was working. He made it sound very appealing, but being the loyal employee that I am, and knowing it would be stressful, I turned it down.

December 7

Hi Bugsy. Your dad used to call you that. Jamin is ok. He went to the doctor and found out he had a benign cyst that the doctor took care of. Unfortunately, it was in a rather private area. Jamin referred to his usual luck when he told me the doctor was a female substitute who brought in a female student, as well as a female medical assistant who went to his high school. What are the chances? But I am so very thankful.

I bought your teddy bear for this year. It's a bear holding a puppy. This will be your fifth one. Perhaps I will donate them someday. You see, Jen, I still get to buy you a Christmas present. I hung your stocking today. I thought twice about it, thinking I was quite crazy, but hung it anyway. I'll put in a Christmas card and a yellow rose.

I've been working over forty hours a week. It is hard on my feet and the nerves. Jamin came for dinner. He's so quiet. He seems so down that I don't know what to do other than pray and hope. He needs a positive experience in his life. I almost fear that he is afraid to live. It scares me. He was one of two kids and now he is alone. Your dad is moody and often angry. He misses you.

I decorated very little this year. There is no real need. No party, no company, and Jamin thinks I decorate too much anyway. He's right. I must keep it simple. Simple is good. You were my Christmas girl. Love you, Bug. Mom

December 17

Jen, your dad has taken to sleeping a lot. I worry about his drinking but I'm not going to spy on him. I wonder if he dislikes your stocking hanging up and your ornaments on the tree. Perhaps what helps me is painful for him. I wish he would tell me. See you soon, Bug, because where you are, time passes in the blink of an eye.

I gave notice at my job today. I work eight days in a row with little help. I am exhausted. I tried to be nice and help out but now it's becoming a regular occurrence. People start working and they don't stay long. I feel I'm being taken advantage of and I need to stop being people food. It sounds strange but that's how I feel sometimes.

December 25

My mind is a blank Jen. I bought one of Joanne's little Yorkie puppies last Tuesday and haven't been able to sleep well. Did I even tell you I was thinking of getting him? Aunt Carol bought his brother and Joanne kept the female. Their names are Buddy, Barkley, and Buffy. Hannah is mad at me. Am I trying to fill a void with three dogs? But Buddy is a sweetheart. Jennifer, the day started off badly, which none of us can afford. I was overtired and stressed. I worked Christmas Eve until 6:30 pm and went directly to your Aunt Laurie's from work. Everyone was already there. It was our first Christmas without you, Jackie, or David. Laurie did such a beautiful job preparing and decorating and it still didn't feel like Christmas. There was neither peace nor joy. I think Christmas includes giving, donating food, and gifts for needy families through church. Giving brought me joy and I didn't have the time for that this year.

For the first time ever, I drove myself home alone on Christmas Eve. Your dad, Jamin, and I drove separately. Jamin was coming to spend the night. I made myself think of all the lonely people out there, and those who always drive home alone and walk into an empty house. I was fine. I had nothing to complain about. It was just different.

On the way home I prayed that no one would kill anyone else that night by being irresponsible. Please God, send people home safely.

I finally brought Buddy downstairs after he woke me for the third time. Hannah's nails are so long that, while I was taking Pokey out, one got crossed over the other and she couldn't walk. I hadn't had time to get her to the vet. Pokey was barking, and Hannah wouldn't let me help her. She kept biting my hand because she was scared. Your dad was asleep on the couch and Jamin up in his room. I finally yelled for help. I was so tired and weary. Needless to say, it was quite a while before we opened gifts. It feels like we are living in a vortex of madness.

We had the usual family Christmas at your Aunt Cathie's. All the cousins are beginning to be friends again. You would have liked that.

1999

January 6

Jenny we are approaching the year 2000. Remember when we talked about how old we would all be? It seems so long ago. We talked about a big celebration. Now I think it will be rather quiet. I've heard many predictions. Christians think Jesus is coming (I'm ready), some think the end of the world, and still others think all technology will crash. I'll take whatever comes. We will have no choice.

January 10

I've been off work for three days now. The first day I dove into cleaning house. I started in the bathroom. I dropped the toothbrush holder and in trying to catch it, I cut my wrist quite deeply. I spent most of the day at the doctors getting stitches and driving in a blinding Michigan snowstorm.

Jen, your dad and I went up north with Jamin and Jeff. They all snowmobiled, but I stayed back. Zack was up there with his cousin, and it was good to see him. Seeing your friends and hearing about their lives makes me think of how much you are missing.

January 27

Jenny you won't believe this. I went to church Sunday and in the bulletin was a paragraph about European adoptions. They would be holding a meeting tonight. I showed it to your dad not expecting a response. To my surprise he said, "Let's do it." For two more days I brought it up giving him a chance to back out. Tonight, we listened to the presentation. As we talked about it afterwards, he became very negative and didn't think it was a good idea. Before the meeting he had been so kind and loving in his remarks. For two days I thought we might be able to give a child a home. I felt hope.

I had prayed about this before. I thought God wanted it. Jamin thought it was cool. I thought the notice in the bulletin was His answer. I was wrong and I must accept it.

February 7

Dear Jenny, today I was browsing in a large bookstore with your dad. It was his idea, which threw me. I've been trying to stay away from my book addiction. In looking at books, I started to think of what I would call these letters if I ever put all the scraps and notebooks together. I thought *Longing for Jennifer*. How do you like it? It's basically what all these letters are about. Longing is what I do. Even the adoption idea was a longing. A few days after my ranting to you, your dad said it could still happen. I'm alright now. I realize it was just a dream. I can't replace you. I thought I could make a little girl happy as well as make us happy again. But it's so complicated. You don't choose. You accept or decline. An older child would have a difficult time adjusting to a new life. Your dad thought of all the realities while I was thinking of possibilities. It would require a great deal of effort put forth by the family or it wouldn't work. We are already fragile. It wouldn't be fair to a child.

February 16

Bugs, you'd think that after almost five years, we would be getting used to you not being here. We missed you so badly today, though neither of us talked about it. Your dad turned 50 today. It was just the two of us. Your brother works Tuesday nights. I made his favorite meat pie, salad, and wine. That's all we did. You would have done something special, and we both know that. We just don't say it. Your dad still wears the shirts you gave him a month before your death. We should have had a party. You would have been there with Jesse. That's what I like to dream about. Instead I went and rented a movie after dinner. We sat and laughed together instead of doing what we should have been doing. We should have been celebrating with our children. Happy Birthday, Jimbo. Thursday Jamin and I will take him out to dinner and to a play downtown.

I haven't felt well lately. I'm having strange symptoms of pain, sleeplessness, and restlessness. I have started working on this house that I have let go since we moved in. I have this strange compulsion to get stuff done. Is it your five-year anniversary approaching? I've got the first room almost done in my quest to accomplish major tasks. The kitchen is painted, and I'm working on the stenciling. Is this moving on, or surviving? I'm working so hard my body hurts. Something is wrong. I am not myself in a different way than before.

February 21

Jenny, I forgot your valentine teddy bear. It's the first time. I was in a shop and saw them and a sinking feeling came over me. I've bought you one every Valentine's Day, just as I had the last month you were here.

I couldn't believe I had forgotten. I picked one out. I usually had them way in advance. Does this mean I'm not thinking of you every minute of every day? Is this recovery? If it's a good thing, why do I feel so horrible? I don't ever want to get used to your not being here.

March 1

Jen, it's the beginning of the horrid month of March. Your dad and I are not getting along. He sleeps almost the entire time he is home. When he does wake up, he is disoriented. He's had a cold for over a month. I want him to see a doctor. He doesn't seem to be concerned. Frankly, I'm tired of it. Maybe it's depression and sleep is his escape. We had an argument about it today. He can't handle being home and I can't handle being away. We live so close to where you died. Maybe it's me. I'm trying so hard to fix things around here. Perhaps I should be done. We grieve so differently. I just have to let him be. It's his health I worry about. Maybe March does this to us. We get through any way we can.

March 8

Jenny, boy was I bitter on the first of March. It was just PMS. I found out your dad is just upset about work. He wants off the account he's on. He has worked with them since Jamin was a baby. He received a call from a friend in California. Remember the last time it was Boston. That didn't work out. He can't let his boss know that someone from the same company wants him for another account. They said they couldn't let him go. Well, this time, it's England for two years. After much deliberation, they decided to let him interview for it in California next week. England would be fun. It would different. It's keeping him awake!

Aunt Laurie, the boys, and I are flying to Florida to see Aunt Jackie and Uncle George. We leave early the day after tomorrow. There is so much snow and we are expecting more tomorrow. I must admit that I'm afraid to go.

I finished another grief book. I wonder how many I've read. I know grief and I know the stages and I've read it all before, but I never fail to be comforted by the endings. They are always so full of hope. Sometimes I feel like writing to particular authors to tell them how much I agree with their writings or how correct they are in their observations. I'm five years into this grief and I know what comforts. This latest author said all the right things. He pushed all the right buttons. Some books I have put away because they injected guilt. But this time I was left renewed. I think I can bear this grief if I know that it will count for something. Something precious. Love, Mom

March 20

Hi Jenny, your dad and I are at the cabin. Florida was short and sweet like a sunny dream you wake from and wonder if you were really there. I never fail to remember your love of sunshine. I've been told there is a 75% chance we will go to England. The three of us all thought it grand until I discovered the six-month quarantine for animals. I find that ridiculously sad. I understand quarantine but the length of time seems so cruel. I have three choices. I can stay home alone with the dogs, find others to temporarily care for them, or put them in jail for no other crime than being a beloved pet. I can't worry about it right now.

I told myself I would never come up north in March to punish myself for not coming up the weekend of March 26, 1994. I have prayed so many times that God would let me go back exactly five-years. I would tell you that the house is yours for your friend's birthday party. I would let Jesse stay the night. I would go anywhere but stay home. Why did we stay home? You would have been safely tucked into the house. You wouldn't have been out on the road. You asked me if we were going. My heart rips into pieces at the thought. All we had to do was go and you would be here. I was too tired from work when you asked. We never went in March. We had to drive on miles of dirt roads full of ruts and mud. We told you no. You had the party elsewhere. It would have been such a simple solution to avoiding death. I could count a million occurrences that ultimately led to you being on that road at that moment. If only one of them had been different you might be alive. These thoughts haunt me.

I think of you all the time, but around this time of year I think of things I'd rather not. I think of the day you told me that Tara's clairvoyant family friend revealed that one of her friends was going to die in an accident. He had predicted earlier tragedies in her life. I see you standing in the entrance to the family room with your work clothes on saying, "With my luck, it will probably be me." I told you not to worry. I brushed it off. My religion had taught me to dismiss such foolishness. That conversation will be with me forever. I don't remember how many days between that talk and your death, but not many.

Another unpleasant memory came to mind today, triggered by something I read. I remembered walking into the room you lay in at the funeral home for the family viewing. Legs that moved mechanically took your father, Jamin, and me to you. As I stood in shock over you, my eyes started to burn along with my nostrils. What had they done to you? The chemical smell was overwhelming at first. That couldn't be. You were the girl whose perfume would weave it's way like a mist from room to room until you went out the door and then lingered like sweet flowers. I don't want to think of these things, my sweet girl. They just come. After these negative thoughts come to mind, I chase them out. I remind myself of all the people who attended and filled that room for three days. I remember the music being played, and my friend Stephanie singing, and how someone passed out yellow roses that were placed one by one upon you as your friends and loved ones passed by you one last time. I was the last one, and the only part of you not covered in roses was your sweet face. Love always, Mom

MARCH 25

Jennifer, I'm trying hard to have positive thoughts. When unpleasant memories invade, I try to override them. We are keeping Erin for two days. She will be a blessing. I am in bed and counting down the last hours of your life. There are about three left. I can't help it. I will always hate these two days. I remember everything leading up to that fateful moment, and then everything is vague for the next year.

Pastor's wife Judy asked if I would be interested in running a grief group at church. She gave me a training video to review. I don't think it would be difficult and maybe I could help people. I'll think about it.

MARCH 26

Five Years Ago

Five years ago you walked the earth,
Twenty years beyond your birth,
Setting sights for things unknown,
Never fearing where to go.

One moment stormy, anger soars,
Then reversing, loving yours.
Searching out the harmony,
Needing peace, you were like me.

I've prayed to God so many times,
Let me go back and claim her mine.
He will not let me see your face,
For I must wait for heaven's grace.

Your face, it sits before my eyes.
Pictures never ever lie.
I know it's true, I've proof you see;
Five years ago you were with me.

Face aglow with fiery youth,
Could it be you knew the truth?
Never waste a precious day;
Call all your friends, come out to play.

Running up to say goodbye,
Your precious beauty fills my eyes.
Could I have borne this creature so?
How I wish you wouldn't go.

Come and sit right next to me,
Please don't rush, oh, can't you see?
Your face, it takes my breath away.
Let it linger; daughter, stay.

Your face, it sits before my eyes.
Pictures never ever lie.
I know it's true, I've proof you see;
Five years ago you were with me.

(Mom)

March 28

Jennifer Marie Smith…Sometimes I just like to write your name. The day is over. I'm doing better. So many people remembered you on the 26th, too many to list here. Many kind words were spoken, memories shared, and flowers sent. Joanne, Brad, Erin, and I spent the afternoon at the new mall. It was such a beautiful day. Spring is in the air. You would be in high spirits, as you always were when the weather warmed.

Jamin is sick. He's coming directly from work tomorrow morning to get some medication and sleep. I'll baby him a little. We both need that.

Today your dad and I shopped for a new suit. He'll meet with some people in Dallas in April regarding the job in England. I wonder what will happen and what our future holds.

Your Uncle Nick called from North Carolina tonight. I haven't talked to my brother in two years. It's funny how with some people you just start talking like you spoke yesterday. It's also sad that one could let so much time pass without talking to a family member. He is in the middle of a new relationship, and his divorce is final. He sounded well. I guess I had just added him to the list of losses in my life. I have always adored him. When I spoke of England, he asked if I would miss my family. Does he miss his? I told him I was much tougher than I used to be. As long as someone you love is alive, all is well, no matter where you are. Any situation is adaptable if one knows it is only temporary. Good night, sweetie.

April 13

Jenny, a sunny day is sure easier to face than a dreary one. I think it basically depends on my state of mind. If things are going well, the weather means little. I am well, Bug. Am I surprised? I guess if I go by some of the books I've read then, yes, I am. I've learned so much about myself in the last five years. Mostly, I am a fighter. I am making it because I don't give up. I was telling someone the other day how I've had to re-learn joy and happiness the way a victim of a head injury may need to learn to speak or walk again. I've learned that I must appreciate every little blessing and every precious moment. I must file away each joy in my soul so whenever I need to feel happiness, I can pull it out of storage.

Joanne and I went up to the cabin for a few days. She feels trapped and unappreciated for her efforts. Her counselor was right. She told Joanne that my loss is different, and that I have options. I could leave my household at any time. I could, but I don't want to. On your five-year anniversary of your death, your father offered to send me anywhere I wanted to go for a week. I turned him down. I needed my family, and I needed him. So, we came up here, Joanne and I. Two days turned into four. We enjoyed the quiet time. I tried hard to keep her positive, and we counted blessings. One of hers is that her husband is a teacher, which frees her up in the summer. She gave me a mug that said I was a miracle. It reminds me of the refrigerator magnet that says, *May I Always be the Kind of Person my Dog Thinks I am.* I hope I can always be the kind of friend she needs. I think I am well enough now to try.

Your dad leaves for Dallas April 20. He has a meeting with the man who wants to hire him for the account in England. Perhaps we will finally find out what's going to happen. I'm not sure if I want this to happen. I'm afraid it will happen and I'm afraid it won't.

April 20

Jenny, I'm on pins and needles. Your dad is in his meeting. Last night he called and told me that the job would require a great deal of traveling in the Middle East. He is not sure about being gone all the time and may not take the job. Jamin and I are anxious. He has called twice today. He would like to go. I told him I would be a little disappointed because

I view this move as a midlife adventure. Our family may need this. He said that if we didn't go, there would be no bowling ball rolling down the center of the lane of his life.

April 25

Bugs, my life is like Michigan weather. If you don't like it, wait a minute and it will change. At the moment, I'm at the cabin with the dogs. The sun is filtering through the curtains giving the log room a warm glow. I'm listening to music and drinking tea. This is selfcare. I have a dog on each side of me and the outdoor temperature is 70 degrees. Your dad left Dallas for home a few hours ago. It has been a busy four days.

I went to Brad's high school graduation ceremony last Wednesday and out to dinner with his family. I'm so proud of what he has accomplished. It's not been easy for him or his family. When I got home, your dad was already there. He had taken an earlier flight. I asked him how it went. He said, "Good for me, bad for you." I calmly said, "We aren't going to England are we?" He answered, "No." "Okay, what then?" I asked. He explained that in England he would be traveling 50% of the time; Jamin and I would be alone. Again, I said, "Okay." I thought at least we'd be able to keep the dogs and not worry about our home.

Then he dropped what I felt was a bombshell. He said he wanted to go to Texas for a year and then on to California. I had already told him I wouldn't move to Texas some time ago. The weather report had stated 30 or more days of 114 degrees last summer. I am miserable in heat and would hate being indoors all the time. I told him he could go, and I'd stay here.

Jamin called, and I told him the news. He left work, came over, and in his gentle way played mediator between your dad and me. He was so good at it, Jen. I was fine about not going to England. I didn't want to move to Texas. An hour later, he left the house frustrated. He came back in from his car and went upstairs to the computer. I went up to see him, and your dad went to bed. Jamin cried. My heart tore in half. He said he was frustrated. I told him that this whole mess was not his problem, and it wasn't his responsibility to fix it. We had all been hopeful of a change, perhaps a positive move in our lives. It was something to remove us from this city and this pain.

I told Jamin I would go to Texas. I just needed to be able to have my feelings. My mother lived there during WWII and used to tell us stories about the heat and having to put my brother's crib in bottles of water for fear of scorpions. It wasn't a place I found appealing. Jamin and I said we loved each other, and he left for work in one piece. I can't imagine how painful it must be for your brother to see his parents struggle to move on and stay together in the middle of all this pain. He is the reason I keep fighting.

The next morning, I talked to your dad about why I reacted as I did, and I said I would go. Somehow, the argument got started again. A few minutes later, he stormed out. All of a sudden, I became this tower of strength. I would not let this news, or his actions, hurt me. I had worked too hard during the last five years to let anything take me backwards. I cleaned up the house, packed up the dogs, and left for the cabin up north. I stopped and got a coffee. It was all I needed. It poured rain all the way up. I decided I should let him know where I was headed. No need to play games. I called home, I called work, and he didn't answer. All of a sudden I had a lightbulb moment. I called the cabin. He answered. Darn! He asked if we were going to argue. I said it was up to him.

The rest of the way, I watched for his car heading south. I thought I saw it once. I had decided that if he traveled all the way back home to avoid me, then our marriage was probably over. If he stayed, perhaps there was hope. I held my breath the rest of the way. When I got to the cabin, his car was there. It continued to pour the rest of the day. We said only what was necessary but didn't fight. I'm going to stop now, Jenny. I must clean up here and head home. The traffic will be heavy. I was going to stay until tomorrow morning, but for some reason I feel very lonely. I'll finish later, sweetie. Mom

April 26

I wanted to tell you that our first morning at the cabin your dad and I actually just talked. I just needed time to adjust. He went off to visit a friend, and I drove up to Mackinaw City. The sky was cloudy and grey, but as I headed north it changed along with my spirits. I didn't see many people due to the time of year. I went to my favorite bakery and got a coffee to take over to a nearby park. I sat and enjoyed the pristine beauty of Lake Huron. The sun sparkled on the water and on my face. I felt renewed. I enjoy thinking of it even now. It's one of those mindful moments you save to ponder later. The next day I bought five new books. I can't stop. Tomorrow I start a computer class at a high school. I really know very little about word processors. I'll keep you posted.

May 1

Boy, Jen, I didn't think I'd be writing you again so soon. Life isn't going to change after all. Isn't the fact that it's not going to change just another change? Your dad's account can't or won't let him go just now. He thinks he's lost the Texas job because of that. I know he wants off this account. He's upset. I'm concerned about him.

I find myself obsessed with you the last few days. I feel as if I saw you yesterday. You seem that close. I realize you are a wound in my heart I will not let heal. Just when I felt good about making it five years, I feel myself falling again. Is it because life has returned to its pre-move days again? Were we all trying to run away? I have the five books I purchased sitting next to my bed. Three of them are about the death of a child. Perhaps I should put them away and escape into fiction for a while. It could be a bandage on this bleeding heart.

Today, your dad and I were working on the garage. We want to clean up every corner of this house. Even though we have moved, I knew what we would find. Every discovery is a smack of reality. First, we ran across your childhood bath towels in the rags. Then we found your large makeup box, empty, but still yours. There were three pairs of your shoes in a box, and your 1991 Lake Orion High School water bottle with the names of all the graduates. In every closet and every drawer, there will be proof that you were really here and ours for almost 21 years. XXOO Mom

May 5

I'm writing you again so soon. April 12th I went to the dermatologist for a small bump on my head. She did a thorough skin check. She found something suspicious under my left arm. I knew it was there. It was a cute little mole the size of a pinhead. Our family has a lot of small, dark moles.

I went back a week later for a punch biopsy. Today she called me and told me I have malignant melanoma. The bump on my head was nothing.

May 9

Hi, Bugs. It's Mother's Day. I've been keeping real busy. I cleaned out my closet and reorganized my drawers. Even there I find little pieces of your life. Dad has the garage looking great. I wish one could reorganize and straighten out a life as easily as a closet.

Your dad brought home a colorful teapot of flowers for me and Jamin gave me a beautiful basket. The three of us went out to lunch together. I later went to visit your Grandma Ginny and Aunt Carol. Jackie sent us mothers a CD she recorded. It was a song about mothers being the salt of the earth. It was beautiful and I'm so proud of her for taking guitar lessons. She will far surpass me in talent and musical ability.

I have an appointment at the University of Michigan Hospital on May 19th. I'll visit their cancer institute for a consult and another skin check. I know how serious this can be. I'm hopeful that all will be well. No one wants to hear the word cancer no matter how early or curable. I feel totally unafraid and almost peaceful about it. It's just another mountain to climb and my climbing skills are improving rapidly. Goodnight, sweets. Thank you for all the years I was blessed to be your mom.

May 24

Hi Jen, On 5/19 I felt joy. I didn't know when I would feel it again. I thought maybe when Jamin falls in love, or marries, or when a grandchild arrives. It came ahead of schedule when, after my consult and skin exam, I was told my cancer was a stage zero. Didn't know that existed. They had another very long name for it that I should have written down. They didn't think it was melanoma. Basically, it is *in situ* which is confined to the upper layer of the skin. I'm grateful for the doctor who found it because it looked like a tiny little mole to me. Tomorrow, your dad and I will return to the University of Michigan for some surgery under my arm just to make sure no cells remain. Piece of cake!

Our 29th wedding anniversary was on the 16th. Your dad surprised me with a getaway weekend at an inn on the St. Clair River. There were flowers in the room and a beautiful view. Remember how your dad and I would take turns finding a place to go and keeping it a secret until one of us guessed or we arrived at the mystery spot? We haven't done that since you died. I think your dad and I are trying hard right now. It's so easy to grieve apart, and I think people may be more comfortable handling pain in their own way. I dream of surprising your dad with a trip to Cape Cod and renting a little cottage on the ocean.

I'm overdoing flowers this year. I've been planting here and at the cabin. I'm cleaning out and organizing. It's amazing how a health scare can make you work like there's no tomorrow. You'd think your death alone would have done that. But, I wasn't a *work away the pain* griever. I was a *sit and let it do its job* griever. By the way, Jen, your little music box played all by itself the other day without winding. I always say, "Hi, Bugs."

June 17

I decided to run a grief group at our church. Pastor's wife asked me. I'm really nervous. I brought home tons of materials to study and have a seminar in Ann Arbor in July. Somehow, I feel as if I already know all there is to know from experience and books, but I'll learn how to mediate a group. Some days, I still feel lost and trapped in grief, but Joanne sees me differently. She says I'm blossoming. The two of us are going up to Mackinaw tomorrow with our puppies. I don't think your dad wants to be left with three dogs.

July 20

Jennifer, Happy 26th birthday, sweetie. You sure would be quite the young lady now. I'd be teasing you about approaching thirty. I can't believe it's been so long. I still think of you as a part of my everyday life. You are alive in my heart, and I want to please you. To celebrate your day, I drove 115 miles from the cabin to Mackinaw City. I then got on a ferry to Mackinaw Island and rented a bike. I peddled around the island. It was a glorious eight miles filled with sights of happy vacationers, crystal blue water, and the fragrance of wildflowers at every turn. You've given me the strength to venture out alone. Your father had chores to do at the cabin, and he's not into bikes or the Island. He doesn't mind me going. I'm grateful for my freedom. On the other hand, Jamin doesn't like his mother venturing out alone. I can understand. I just went around once, had lunch, and hopped a ferry back to the city.

Your dad and I saw Jesse for just a moment. I recognized him instantly. We were turning out onto a road, and he was turning onto ours. I waved. He looked confused, but at the last second, I saw a look of recognition on his face. When our eyes met, that was it. My heart started to pound. My face got hot. Seeing him was like seeing you. I expected you to be in the truck beside him. I wasn't the same the rest of the day.

Well Bugs, I made it through your birthday without physical symptoms. It was a first. I think the key is to pamper yourself in times of sadness. Don't sit home alone and feel sorry for yourself. Do something you really love or visit somewhere you really want to go. Maybe to some, like your dad, it would be to just have the day to yourself. I did invite him to go with me. I have chosen to not waste my pain. As well as leading the grief group, the church is sending me to Stephen Ministry Leadership Training. I will use my grief to learn, serve, and teach others what I can.

Ironically, I spent another trip to the cabin watching coverage of a tragedy as a search goes on for the missing plane of John F. Kennedy Jr. and his wife and sister-in-law. I also ache for his sister Caroline losing her only sibling and last close family member. And, his wife's family has lost two daughters at once. I say that I can't even imagine, but then I correct myself and say I can. But Jenny, how does anyone handle losing two children at once? The unfairness of death is what causes this ache in my heart. No one is immune to tragedy. We will go to our grave asking why. God bless all who mourn. They will go on because the living have no choice. Thank God that He gives us what we need to survive. Loving you always and deeply, birthday girl. Love, Mom

July 24

Hi Bugs. I volunteered for MADD (Mothers Against Drunk Driving) today for Kmart's Race Against Drugs. Children drove scaled down electric cars on a parking lot racetrack. The charity travels around the country and the winners compete in Florida in January. I timed a mini blue car with a stopwatch for three hours. It was 90 degrees and windy, but I'm glad I did it.

August 2

What a perfect day Jenny. I have Erin for three days and we are sitting on the sun porch. Though today seems good, last week was not. A little four-year-old boy in our congregation passed away from an illness. It seems that I just sang at his parent's wedding and now he was gone. I was asked to be his mother's ministry care giver. I was terrified but I agreed. Could I help her? The day of his funeral his mother called me. Pastor's wife had given her a song I wrote for you and sang at their son Mike's funeral. It was *My Promise*. It was last minute, but she said the words were exactly how they felt and asked if I would sing it. I did what I told her I would do. I would do my best. It's so hard to sing when your heart is breaking. I think I'm getting used to it.

Jen, did I forget to tell you that Jamin moved back home? It's temporary until he and Brian can find a house to rent. He's so confused. He wants a girlfriend, a house, a job he enjoys, to keep his new Mustang, and to go back to school. I told him to pick his priorities and work towards those. I adore having him here. But I guess I have a smidgen of superstition. You moved away for three months with your friends. You came home for one year and then you died while living at home. I want your brother to find a place to rent soon. He wants to visit Jackie in Seattle this month. I do hope he doesn't choose to move there. It's so far away. As I have a young guest to entertain; we should start our day. I called Erin Jenny twice. Never did that before.

August 20

JenBug, we are up at the cabin for a week vacation. It's your dad's first in a long time. All three dogs are barking. Some days I feel that God gave me these three animals to keep me on my toes. One must have the patience of Job. Your dad went out on the pontoon boat to clean it. He'll come and pick me up at the dock later.

Aunt Jackie took your aunts and me to Chicago overnight last weekend. It was quite a city. I'd never been there before. You always talked about living in New York. I think you would find the fast pace, the ambiance, and the nightlife addicting. You always thought rural life was rather humdrum. We had taken a train and it was a long trip. We didn't get back to the station in Michigan until quite late. Aunt Carol and I had driven together and were almost home when I got stopped by a policeman as I was getting off at the same exit onto the same road where the man who ended your life exited. The policeman made me get out of the car because I had taken the exit quickly (Carol and I were chatting). I had to get my purse out of the trunk and show him I wasn't drinking. I wish a policeman had stopped that man who killed you. The policeman apologized. I wanted so badly to just scream at him, *Why didn't someone stop that man?*

Getting up to the cabin was an adventure to say the least. I was so tired from our quick trip that your dad left early with two of the dogs. I was to bring Pokey and drive your truck up to the cabin so we could leave it there permanently. It's bitter/sweet looking at it parked in the driveway every day. I locked up the house and Jamin left for work. Then I locked my purse, house keys, truck keys, and poor Pokey in the truck. Luckily it wasn't hot outside. I fretted for twenty minutes before remembering that I meant to hide a car key somewhere. Did I, or was it just a thought? I had to stop and think about how I hide things. I did find it in a much too obvious hiding place. I thanked God, because He's the One that got me out of the mess.

Feeling so relieved, I started on my way only to have car trouble thirty minutes into my trip. Your truck just quit. At first, I thought it must be something mechanical. This is when I realized that being tired, stress, and grief do not mix well together. I thought I had a full tank but had read the gas gage backwards. How is that possible? What was wrong with me? Luckily your dad let me have the car phone. I got it out of the zipper bag and plugged it into the lighter. I called your brother at work and told him what I did. A short time later, he and a friend from work pulled up behind me on the expressway with a can of gas. They followed me to the next exit and into a gas station. Again, I was saved after being so utterly careless. I never loved your brother more

Jamin and Brian leave for Seattle the day before Jamin's 22nd birthday. I hope they enjoy themselves and have a great visit with Jackie. I'm so happy Jamin has such great cousins. You were always so close. I also hope they come back home. But Jen, I think this way now. Jamin is alive. I want him to be happy wherever he is. If he is happy in Timbuktu, I'm happy. If he is sad in our house, I'm sad.

September 6

Dearest Jenny, September 23 will be my first Grief Share meeting. I still have much to prepare. Your dad and I are up north for Labor Day weekend and a rest. I've been working hard at home painting and cleaning. I can't seem to stop trying to fix up the house. I had no interest in the last five years. Why now? What is different?

I forgot to tell you about the grief seminar I went to with Pastor's wife. It was informative even though I feel as if I know a great deal about grief. We talked about steps of recovery. Of course, there is the initial shock. I know that one well. It's how we all got through your funeral. When I was fifteen and my mother died, I remember looking at her in the casket thinking it wasn't really her. She was just fed up with all of us and went to live somewhere else. Then there is touching. We get so much of that during the first three days. There are so many hugs at the funeral. Afterwards it becomes less and less until it ends all together. Then you become isolated and touched by no one. Even your own family members feel awkward hugging you. Then we have psychological symptoms in which we link objects to the deceased…like the yellow roses, bears, and ladybugs I bought. The body has symptoms as well. Everyone's reactions are different. Jamin and I have stomach issues. Your dad doesn't talk about it or he self-medicates.

Sometimes we feel alienated and lonely. Your dad, Jamin, and I all live this. Self-worth is diminished and there are certainly thoughts of suicide. Some, like your dad, become friends with Jim Beam. Guilt is a big one. I thought for sure my life sins had caused God to let you die. I really thought I didn't deserve you. I know better now, and I no longer feel that way. We feel anger. I was there for a long time, but my faith rescued me. Your dad is still angry. I have always put loved ones who have passed on a pedestal. My parents were perfect, right? I know they weren't. But of course, you were the perfect daughter in every way. I've forgotten the difficult times like a mother forgets the pain of giving birth.

Eventually we make peace or redemption. This is where I'm trying to go. This is where we take our grief and absorb it into that which we are. We carry it around and become used to the extra weight. We remember the good times and attempt to find balance. The pain becomes a natural part of our being. We become used to it. It never goes away.

We begin to pick and choose what we will keep from your life. I still have everything but your clothes. I do have your memory chest, but it's full. We may feel like traveling, or redecorating, or buy a new car or a new house. We have done all of these. Then we must resurrect ourselves. I have to accept that you are in Heaven and not think of you being so near me all the time. Healing will go on forever, and there will be grief relapses. I have them often. We learned that we are alive and whole. I will not accept that statement. I am not whole. I will never be whole. The Grief Share will help because I must not waste my grief and what I have learned. The church bulletin had a wonderful ad about the 13 weeks of sessions. Pastor said some wonderful things. I hope I can live up to them.

Those who bear the mark of pain are never really free;
they owe a debt to the ones who still suffer.
(Anonymous)

SEPTEMBER 21

Dear Jenny, I'm writing this on a tiny piece of paper. I keep feeling like I should stop writing letters, but I don't. I am up north for two days. I came to concentrate on fully readying myself for Grief Share. I am all set. Even though we put an ad in the newspaper, I still have a fear that no one will show up. I know how grieving people are. By the time they have the courage, they think they don't need help anymore. It's in God's hands. These past few days have been fruitful. I've been working out regularly. Because I'm not near the gym, I walked four miles today.

Jamin and Brian come home from Seattle tomorrow. It sounds as if he loves it there. I attended a wedding with your dad last Saturday. The bride was getting married a 2nd time. Your dad and I attended her first wedding one month after you died. I didn't attend the first reception, but this time I decided to go. I left to cry in the bathroom three times. My heart hurts because you never got the wedding you used to talk about. We never got to be the parents of the beautiful bride. I imagine it sometimes. I picture your dress, your hair, and your smile. I will never stop dreaming of you.

2000

January 1

Okay, Jen, it feels strange to write 2000. I really pictured it much differently when I was young. As it was, your father worked all night watching computers at work, and Jamin and I celebrated with family at the Czech Cultural Center with Aunt Jackie and Uncle George. Jamin looked dashing in his new suit. It was quiet but thrilling when all was still well in the world at one minute after midnight. The news media really hyped things up, and the world wasn't sure what to expect. I wasn't too concerned.

Luckily for us Jamin was able to attend. He's been sick with the flu. Two days after becoming ill and spending a good deal of time in bed, he came downstairs to get a phone call. I was upstairs and heard a crash. I ran down and he was stumbling around the kitchen. "I just passed out, I'm hungry and need something to eat," he said softly. He looked as if he was going down again. I went to him and put my arms around his middle and yelled for your dad who was sleeping in his chair. He ran in just as Jamin went limp in my arms. Your dad laid him down gently on the floor. He didn't look well at all, and I thought I was watching my remaining child die. I know fainting. I've done it many times. This was not a normal faint. I heard the fear in your father's voice. "Call 911, call 911." Jamin dropped the phone when he went down and I couldn't find it. I ran upstairs to use the computer phone. I remember talking, but not what I said. I couldn't breathe. The dispatcher kept telling me to calm down. Just before EMS arrived Jamin woke up. They examined him and said he needed to go to the hospital. He refused to go in the ambulance, and I understood why. We took him to the ER, and it was a long night. After three IV bags, Xrays, and blood tests, we were able to take him home at 5:00 am. Following orders, we went to see our regular physician. Jamin had a double ear infection, more blood work, and was scheduled for an electroencephalogram (EEG). As I suspected, his faint was not normal. He had been deeply dehydrated and it affected his heart. I'm trying not to worry Jenny and I'm praying often. You see, I remember how your Uncle

Steve died when we were all on vacation. You were young and he was in his thirties. His ex-wife drove him to the police station, and he passed out, urinated and that was his end. His heart had stopped. I thought that was happening to Jamin.

This past month, we also learned that Jamin's friend and co-worker, John, has terminal melanoma. He's only 23 years old. They've been friends since they were small boys. He hasn't started treatment yet. We will be waiting to see how he does.

At the end of November, we had our regular Advent by Candlelight. Pastor's wife asked me to do the music. I sang *Christmas in Heaven* once more. Many asked for a recording, or the words. Many said the song touched them in a special way. I feel these comments are jewels and that because of you, people are being blessed. Also, in November, I was asked, along with others who have faced adversity to be on a grief panel at our Stephen's Ministry Retreat. We were asked questions and had to answer in front of a large group of people. Lucky for us we had the questions in advance. Pastor got up last and told his story about his son Mike and the other two boys who died in a car accident. Pastor's pain tears at my heart. There wasn't a dry eye in the crowd. I don't think some people realize the pain carried around in some hearts each and every day.

My grief group is coming along slowly. I'll have to get another announcement into the newspaper. Sometimes I have people, and sometimes I'm there alone. It's okay. I won't give up.

One day I was thinking of how different things are between your dad and I. He seems so angry at times that I don't know him. It prompted me to go to the computer and write *The Tunnel*. We have taken different paths in our grief. He is avoiding and self-medicating with alcohol. I am throwing myself into helping others. I thought I was dealing, but perhaps I am avoiding in my own way.

The Tunnel

She's not boasting, just being observant. She's not a better person or stronger. She just knows her weaknesses. She had a fear of losing her mind. When their daughter was killed, they were both thrown into the opening of a long dark tunnel. They had a choice. It's a place uninhabitable by parents. It's a place full of unspeakable torment and heart-wrenching pain. Don't go in. Turn back. We can't do this. We can't see. It's much too dark. We'll get lost. Don't leave me alone in here. Please hold my hand. Please come with me.

He couldn't go. He didn't stop her and even encouraged her. He told her to do whatever she needed to do. She went into the tunnel alone. He had things to take care of. These things were important. She knew they were. Maybe he would come later and catch up with her. Maybe he would avoid the tunnel all together.

She stumbled and fell many times in the dark. She veered too far right and then overcorrected too far left. She was often lost and stayed for long periods of time in one area, afraid to move forward. She looked back often to see if he was coming. Perhaps it was taking longer to finish the important tasks. Finally, she knew she must trudge on alone. He wasn't coming, and besides she had been alone so long, how could he possibly catch up.

Books were her path. God was her guiding light. Friends and family called to her from the other end of the tunnel. She knew if she was patient, if she could just hold on without giving up, if she could pick herself up when she fell, no matter how bad the injury, that she would someday make it to the end.

She thought about him often and wondered how he was doing. She knew he had chosen a different path. She knew he had avoided the tunnel and found a quicker escape from his pain. She wasn't angry. Wasn't he always afraid of heights and tunnels? He had said so himself, and she always helped him over and under. He was just trying another way. But if she went one way and he another, would they find each other in the end? She was grateful to him for telling her to go ahead. What if she had waited? Where would she be now? That horrible tunnel would still be ahead of her. Maybe she would have lost her mind after all.

She thought of him as the captain of their ship. The ship was sinking, and he threw a life ring around her and threw her overboard where she was found and saved. Being afraid of the water himself, he was going down with the ship. She had made her grief her career. He had given her that and expected nothing more. He wanted a career without grief. One that he could escape to whenever the fear of the tunnel came to mind. It was his path and his guiding light. He knew he was leaving her alone, but he knew no other way.

She wondered what it would be like when she got to the end. Would everything be back to normal? How could it be without her girl? Would she still feel the pain? Was his way better? She was almost afraid to come to the end for fear things would be too different. What would their relationship be like since she had chosen one path and he another? Maybe she would have learned so much about grief and he about life. Perhaps together they could combine their experiences and somehow become a stronger unit.

One day, she did make it to the end. The light was too bright, and the sounds were too loud. It wasn't that long ago. She did feel stronger and wiser. Sometimes she dreams of the tunnel and she wakes up full of fear and loneliness. But she remembers that she already went through it and God will not make her do it again. She calms down and is grateful to God and to the one who made her go alone.

For them the news is not promising. She found that their paths were too different. She learned things about survival that he doesn't know. She can't share what she has learned, just as he cannot share how he avoided the tunnel. They don't have much to say anymore. They don't have the same memories of that time apart, and they were distant too long. She didn't lose her mind, but she lost something else, her companion, her partner, and her lover.

She discovered after a time that the tunnel couldn't be avoided. It was put there for a reason. It is for all grieving persons. If avoided, grief turns slowly inward and, like seeds planted in fertile ground, begins to sprout and grow into bitterness and anger. If taken, the tunnel takes grief and mixes it with grace, mercy, and love. It becomes a permanent but manageable pain.

It's very sad. She was hopeful. She doesn't know what he thought she would learn. She's not sure if he urged her into the tunnel to save her because he thought he couldn't be saved, or if he wanted her out of the way. He wouldn't have to deal with her then. He wouldn't have to hold her up or try to fix it. Well, it broke anyway. She is tired from her long journey and needs peace and to be alone. That he gives her too.

When they are together the peace doesn't last very long. She sees them as different beings existing in two different worlds. She doesn't know this person who lives a separate life. He can't relate to the person he urged into the tunnel. She is afraid of becoming another statistic. She wonders if he cares. Maybe he wonders if she cares. They don't know. They can't talk about it. Maybe it's the beginning of another tunnel.

Well Jenny, that is what I wrote. I think it helps me understand our relationship. I feel badly for him. I need to feel things, and he hates feeling. Once I asked him if he ever felt your presence like I did when we first lost you. I felt you often. He didn't say no. He said, "I fight it."

I bought you a large picture of an eagle from the Christian store. It has the words from Isaiah 40:31. *They that wait upon the Lord shall renew their strength; they shall mount up with wings as eagles; they shall run and not be weary; and they shall walk and not faint.* I gave it to my church, and it was dedicated Christmas Eve. It's my favorite Bible verse because that's what grieving parents have to do. I love you, Jenny, and Happy New Year in Heaven. Love, Mom

January 6

Bugs, I just dressed your last Jenny-Bug Bear and put my tag on it. I made seven in all and gave them away. This one is for Joanne. She's been very patient. I thought about starting a business, but they are so difficult to make. I start the bear from scratch and then make the dress to fit. I add little items like the paw holding a teddy bear or a basket of flowers. They take too long to put together. The tips of my fingers ache. This was my last one. But I enjoyed making them, and it was good therapy.

I just had a gift. They just show up now and then. I opened a drawer and pulled out a cozy pair of flannels. They were yours, and I had saved them. I put them to my face and after almost six years I smelled your room. It was you. I would like to wear them, but I don't want to wash them. I'll enjoy them while I can. I keep sniffing the sleeves. It's heavenly. Love, Mom

January 8

Jennifer Marie, I got a phone call today. A co-worker of your dad, whom we know well, had a death in the family. His son died. I asked how. The caller said an accident. Later in the conversation I asked if it was a car accident. The caller paused for a minute. I knew. It was suicide. I asked his age since I hadn't seen him in years. Twenty-two, she said. My heart sank like a boulder in a deep lake. That's Jamin's age. We've been worried about Jamin's depression again. Thank God for good and joy in the world. How else would we live with tragedy and pain? Only God knows the heart and the pain it holds. His name is Kevin. I must pray now. Love, Mom

January 9

Kevin was beautiful Jenny. The small room was so full of sorrow and tears. Your dad had to go back outside after five minutes just to compose himself. How could such a peaceful face ever possess a soul that held so much pain? Perhaps it's because his soul is free.

When we greeted his parents, they immediately remembered we lost you. "How do you do this?" she asked. After all these years, I was tongue-tied. How could I answer her? I didn't know. I stumbled and said, "You will in time. We're still here." How do I know if they will? I remember many times thinking *I can't do this*. I hugged her and whispered, "I talk to her and write to her."

"You talk to her?" she asked. "Yes, every day. I told her he was coming and to meet him," I explained. She replied sadly, "Oh, good, I don't want him to be alone." "He's not," I whispered. Fear overcame me. Did I say the right thing? Did I make it worse for her? I'm a Stephen's Minister. I'm supposed to know what to say. I knew what to avoid. I would never say *He's in a better place*. That is a lie. I was not comforted by that phrase. Even though they are a gift, they belong with us. I told Kevin's mother that I would send her my phone number as she said she wanted to talk. I ache for them...the ache I remember about those first unreal, mind-numbing, surreal days.

David is visiting from California. He's down in the basement with Jamin playing guitars. The loud noise is a tonic for our souls. Jackie called from Seattle to chat. God sends yellow roses into the dead of winter. We need to notice them. Only heaven knows how much I love you Jen. Mom

P.S. Wouldn't it be awesome if when I picked up my notebook to write you, I found a letter you had written me? It's right by my bed. Be my guest.

March 1

Hi, Jen. Jackie sent me an email from the Denver airport. She went to visit your friend Jenny Z and found an email I sent to her and thought it was perfect timing. She was mourning the loss of her boyfriend. It was an email with no author about how God is handling all our problems today and that they would be answered in his time, not ours. One section stated, *Should you despair over a relationship gone bad, think of the person who has never known what it's like to love and be loved in return*. She added this P.S. in her response. *Jenny Z and I had a talk about Jenny this weekend and both shared that her death changed us more than anything, and made us want to live our life to the fullest. I miss her a lot lately as I am in grief mode. Her life still continues in the ways that it has changed those who really loved her. I know that I am a different and better person because of her. Just wanted you to know that you aren't alone in missing her.*

March 26

Jenny! You've been gone six years today. If someone had told me at five years that I would be worse at six years…well, you know. I'm not sure I'm worse, just different. I don't know where to start. First, I will update you. Jamin seems better both physically and mentally. He looks so handsome. There's no one special in his life, but he's getting braver each day. He does meet girls, thanks to friends and cousins.

Jackie is alone in Seattle since her break with her boyfriend. She is hurting, but being a counselor, she knew it wasn't working. We talk often on the phone. She talked me into going into therapy again, and I did just that. I'm having strange symptoms she feels may be related to Post Traumatic Stress Disorder (PTSD). I'm supposed to stay home and allow myself to feel today. I'm afraid.

Jenny, I have an update on Jamin's friend John who had melanoma. As it turns out, he doesn't have cancer. He never did. I agonized over his situation. He told me he was estranged from his parents so I told him we would care for him because he was terminal. Jamin is the only one who doubted his story. Your dad and I believed him, and his employer and colleagues believed him. His workplace was so kind and raised money for medical costs. He accepted that money. His girlfriend who had previously broken up with him came back into his life. It wasn't until his employers started to ask for medical documentation that his lies began to catch up with him and he began to contradict himself.

Your dad and I are both angry and heartbroken, but I understand there must have been a sense of desperation on his part. Your dad thought he was bright and ambitious and got him the job. I remember your dad asking John not to do anything that would cause him to regret helping him. Jamin's doubt came from the fact that he said John was prone to exaggeration. We've known him since he was a child. We knew that, but we thought he grew up.

John no longer works with Jamin, nor does he have that girlfriend. We haven't heard from him. I worried about suicide but Jamin said not to. My heart goes out to him for having so much pain and insecurity that he could carry on that lie for so long. Something tells me he will end up just fine.

It's a beautiful March 26th Jenny. It's the kind of day that would have made you put on shorts, wash your car, and wear a smile all day. I see the beautiful sky, but first I see the dirty winter windows. Spring reminds us to clean up.

Speaking of cleaning up, that's what I need to do with myself according to my new therapist. Today, the dreadful anniversary, I am not to hang out with friends or relatives, go shopping, and run off to another place or city. I am supposed to remember you. I am not to disassociate, cover up, or repress. I began to become ill at the end of January. That's why I've been talking to Jackie so often. She became a licensed counselor. I was having some personality changes that were foreign to me.

Once when Jamin and Brian were working on model cars in the dining room, I leaned over to look, and Jamin asked in a fearful voice, "What is that thing on your neck?" I had been so oblivious to anything outside of my own forced ambitions that I didn't notice a hideous sore on a place I wash daily. My emotions were coming out on my body. It began as restless legs and itching. I had no desire to sleep or eat. They were the last things on my mind. I thought I was so good at everything. I remember mentioning something to you in a previous letter. I had made it!

I had my Stephen's Ministry group and care receivers. I had my Grief Share that was doing better. My energy skyrocketed. In fact, I sit writing you in my freshly painted *Raven's Rage* living room. It's a warm red and looks better than it sounds. I'm opposite my newly wallpapered dining room, and across from my adorable *Greenfield* green hallway and laundry room. I decorated the guest room for a girl. All pink and cozy with quilts. I spent so much time sponge painting the walls in pink and cream. It's a room for Erin when she spends the night. I could have killed myself when I was putting up a wallpaper border and stepped off the ladder into the wallpaper tray full of water which spilled all over the cord for the electric fan. I was barefoot and not even thinking responsibly. Excessive energy and two to three hours of sleep a night can decorate an entire house. I hadn't done any decorating in five years. Why now?

And, of course, there are the bears, Boyd's Bears to be exact. For my birthday last October Joanne had given me a club membership that came with the most charming mother and daughter bear having tea. The daughter bear was holding her own tiny toy bear. It even had a tiny tea set. It came with a lovely poem called *Tea for Three*. This gift was just the membership in an envelope and the club gift would come in the mail at a later date. We both liked the bears and we both had just a few. My first one was purchased just before you died.

One night, about a month later, I came home to a box on the porch. I picked it up and was thrilled to see where it was from. My bears were here. I set it on the kitchen counter and let the dogs out. Jamin was at work and your dad wasn't home. I sat down on a stool and opened the box. I took the bears out, and they were even more adorable than I thought they would be. Every little detail was perfect. There was also a resin set of the bears drinking tea together. I took out the poem and began to read. The tears began to fall, and I cried as I read. The further I read, the harder I let the pain out. I decided I would get a frame for the poem and set it up with the bears. I would shop for a tiny table and chairs for them. I set the poem down and let myself sob uncontrollably. Something happened to me in those moments. These tiny bears would soon become a connection between you and me.

Tea for Three

Come and sit with me and we'll have tea
And talk of things that were and things that are to be,
Of places we will go and things that we will see,
Just the two of us,
My dear daughter...and me.

A little wooden table
With chairs for two, not three,
Yes, of course you may bring your bear
And place him on my knee.
No longer just the two of us,
It's tea for three, I see.
My dear daughter, the bedraggled bear...and me.

The years passed by and you grew up
Framed in memory I still see,
Cherub hands dimpled daintily,

Clutching ivory cup of tea,
Twinkle laughter owns the moment,
Baby faced and full of glee.
Starshine dusted by the angels,
Oh, God's precious gift to me!

If I live to be a hundred
I shall never richer be
Than when I shared your dazzling presence
And together we sipped tea.
My dear daughter, the bedraggled bear…and me.

—Lee Scott, 1998

Jenny, since this poem, the Boyd's Bears have become an obsession. Resin bears, plush bears, bears having tea, bears on chairs, and every bear accessory. Joanne also gave me an angel Boyd's Doll. Since then I have purchased many more dolls and they have joined the bears on display. I create bear families of four, or mother and daughter bears. They started to spread to the cabin. I've calmed down for now because I realize the source of my obsession.

I have gone into hysterics over a painting problem and gotten a rush about driving to another city (more than once) just to look at bears. I understand everything now. I developed PTSD. I thought I already had that a few years ago when I lost some hair, but it's a lot more complicated than that. My therapist explained, and from what I've learned it starts when the mind tries to get you to accept your losses or experiences and you say *no thanks* and you do everything to avoid it. Your mind is holding on to trauma that needs to be dealt with. I will never accept the loss of you.

If you refuse to accept the loss, the symptoms begin. No one can say exactly when it will start for a traumatized person. I think I've been holding my breath until Jamin turned twenty-one. He made it past your age. Perhaps my mind said it was time to breathe. But I fought the feelings and thoughts. I guess I've been doing this for some time now. It involves emotional symptoms, physical symptoms, and pain all over my body from exhaustion, obsessions, and addictions. Jackie describes it as being sick to your stomach and you need to vomit, but you can't.

I've been trying hard to be well for everyone, including myself. I've been repressing and disassociating. I think of you all the time. How can I be repressing? I've been told that I've been reading, writing, and volunteering but not really helping myself. I thought I was doing everything right. So, where do I stand now? I do know that when I go to bed, I think about the accident I didn't even see. I start to picture it in my head, though I refused to look at the photos. I now think, what if I had seen those photos? I would have a true picture. When I begin to do that, I tell myself *don't go there, don't go there*. I change my thoughts. It's why I read until I'm really tired. So, I guess I do run from thoughts.

I'm just starting. I'm supposed to allow thoughts and feelings I don't want. I've had two cathartic experiences in which I was screaming and crying hysterically. They have been healing. One evening I was getting ready for Grief Share. I was early and I plopped down in your dad's chair. I suddenly paid attention to my exhaustion. Every cell, every muscle, and every joint in my body was on fire. I was going to cancel going to church. I have never felt that much physical pain all at once. My hypervigilance was catching up with me. I took some Motrin and left for my group. My therapist says I have other losses, even before and since you, to deal with as well. I have a long road ahead of me, and I'll be honest. I'm terrified. I don't know what the outcome will be. Only God knows. I guess my mind is acting like our computer has been lately. It's over-loaded and shuts down. Must delete files to make room. Okay, mind, start deleting. Just hit the delete button and make it fast and painless. I always said I would go crazy if I lost one of my children. It just took six years. I'll make it, but I have to make it for me this time.

March 27

Jenny, I tried to let myself feel pain and not disassociate. Dad and I took a yellow rose to your tree. As we were walking back to the car, we were both thinking the same thing. We need a place to go to you and not just a tree. You need a grave. It took a year to pick up your ashes from the funeral home. I just couldn't do it. Can I part with your ashes now? I chickened out the last time I tried. Jamin thinks your ashes are fine in your memory chest. There are still two things my therapist wants me to do. First, look at your picture for longer than one second. That's about how long I glance before I start to panic. I'm supposed to really look and feel. Second, I'm supposed to hold your ashes.

July 4

Hi Jennifer, I haven't written to you in quite a while. I miss you. I know you are happy and safe where you are. At this writing, things are going pretty well. At least some things seem greatly improved. My PTSD is on the mend, thanks to therapy and time. I still buy bears, but I am grateful that I'm no longer addicted to them. I am also off the computer, which is a great relief to me as my housekeeping suffered along with our bank account. My therapist is a very personal, remarkable man. I have learned a great deal about taking care of my needs and myself.

He told a little story last week about a tablecloth. It is made from a beautiful white fabric except for a single gold thread that runs down the middle of the cloth. It is so unusual and different that one tends to start decorating the table to enhance the gold thread. The table is set with gold place settings to accentuate the beauty. Then he told me he saw you as the gold thread and me as the decorator that is designing everything around the thread. In other words, as I live my day-to-day life, you are the main focus in the way I live. If I were to take a solid look at my surroundings and the choices I make, I would have to agree with him. Groups of bear families, lady bug items, and anything with yellow roses on it.

Your dad and I went to Maine for our 30th anniversary. It was a lovely trip for the most part. I really do try. Your dad, who enjoys his alcohol quite often, doesn't like it if I have a drink. He knows I get emotional on one cocktail. We were having dinner in Camden at a quaint place on the water. Having lost you, I often think of my father's first wife, Mary. They had a baby who was not well. He eventually passed away. According to the story my father told my sisters and me, Mary had a difficult grief, as all mothers would. It ended their marriage. My father went on to remarry my mother and adopt my brother and have three more children. Mary did not remarry or have another child. That breaks my heart. I was talking to your dad about that, and I got tearful. I wondered if Mary was still alive. It is likely as my dad would be in his seventies now.

I am assuming your dad wasn't pleased with my dinner conversation. He doesn't like talking about us. He usually loves talking about his job. When we paid the bill and left the restaurant, he bolted and left me behind. I didn't call after him, and I couldn't run to catch up. There were people around. I just stood there in shock. I couldn't go back to the hotel because I was sure that was where he went. I wandered around the streets at dusk. I found a bench and watched the tide come and rush in like a floodgate had been opened. The sun was setting over the water, and I wondered how such misery could stand to look at such beauty. I sat and thought about how I tried to be happy but was actually quite miserable.

A few hours later, I headed back to our room. He was lying on the bed with a six-pack next to him. We didn't speak. I went into the bathroom to take a bath. Soaking in the warm water, I thought of how easy it would be to just slowly slide down into oblivion. I thought about it seriously enough that I prayed. I couldn't leave Jamin. Everyone else would survive, but not him. It would be too much. I do understand suicide and the pain that steals away any sense of wanting to survive. I've felt it many times. Your dad and I never spoke of that night, and as usual just went forward as we always did. How dare I rock the boat? The PTSD was good for me in the sense that it forced me to deal with some issues that I had chosen not to. I grew from the knowledge.

We go to the gym together when we can. It seems to be beneficial for him, Jen. He seems to feel and look much better. I can look at my body and feel great instead of depressed.

Pokey, my little girl pup, became very ill in June. There was nothing the Vet could do. On Father's Day Jamin and I took her to the emergency Vet. We couldn't let her suffer any longer. She was over 17 years old. We handed her over to the Vet and said our goodbyes. We didn't want to watch. I will never forget the look in her brown eyes. Jamin and I went back to the car and cried. I will never let one of my dogs die alone again.

Joanne and I took our yearly trip to Mackinaw City and Mackinac Island. We took our two Yorkshire Terriers, and they attract quite a lot of attention. It's Joanne's only real vacation all year. Brad hasn't had one in almost seven years. It's hard to believe it has been that long since he had his diving accident. He is going to college and doing well. I'm so proud of him. Watching the change in him makes my heart happy.

This Saturday I leave for Seattle and Stephen Ministries Leadership training. I'll have one week of training at the University of Washington, and then I will spend three days with Jackie. I'm nervous about flying alone and the layover. I've never flown by myself. I'm also nervous about being with strangers all week. I keep telling myself that they are only strangers until we say hello. I'll have more responsibility in the ministry when I return. I've already taught the class on grief.

Jenny, I almost forgot to tell you. When I ran an ad for Grief Share in the local newspaper, I told the woman on the phone a little about it and why our church was going to host it. Pastor's wife, who does the Divorce Care, and I, will meet with her tomorrow. She wants to interview us.

I want to mention to you that your brother, though still lonely, is doing better. He bought a new dirt bike along with your cousin Brian and they have been spending time tinkering and riding trails. He is even thinking of going to a technical school in Florida for a year. This isn't something I would have been thrilled about in the past, but things are different now. He needs to experience life on his own terms and not worry about being here for Dad and me. I think he stays around more for us than for himself. I just want him to be happy. You would adore him, Jenny. You would tell him to "get a life," but you would be proud of the person he's become. Love, Mom

July 18

Jenbug, after I completed my leadership training, Jackie picked me up for a few days of relaxation and sightseeing in her old black, soft-top Jeep she bought soon after your death. I told her all about the old dorms and how lonely and isolated I felt until I met the other women on my floor. It was a given as we all shared one bathroom. We stuck together as a group during the training and got to know each other quite well. We vowed to stay in touch. I hope we do.

Jackie's and my visit to the Space Needle was unique because not too many visitors get to see the clear view we were blessed with that day. Our drive into northern Washington held views my eyes couldn't believe. I thanked God for sight. We played Beatles music and sang as loud as we could. We knew all the words. I pray that Heaven gives you the freedom to explore God's earth in ways we can only dream of.

Today is not a good Mt. Rainer day. For the last four days, Seattle has been clear and bright with breathtaking views of the snow-capped Olympia and Cascade mountains. Mt. Rainer has floated mysteriously above the city like a monument to the world. Today, clouds hide the beauty like it never existed. It makes me think of grief. Sometimes it's clearly obvious and other times it's invisible.

Today is my one solitary day in Seattle proper. Jackie is at work. I sit on Jackie's couch in her small Fremont apartment. She has a corner window with views of downtown Seattle, Lake Union, and Mt. Rainer. If I go up to her roof, the views only get better. Three extra-large sunflowers sit in a vase in the front window, our purchase from the Pike Street Market yesterday. We connect them to your love of the sun. We are both healing from our rough winter. She has met a young man named Jason. His initials are the same as yours, JMS. Jackie likes that. The three of us had dinner downtown last night. I hope things work out for both of them. Jackie left me her jewelry-making kit, some paints, and the movie *Singles* filmed in Seattle to keep me occupied. I'm not sure I will get to them because I'm in the mood to wander around Fremont and Wallingford.

Well, Jenny, while I've been away, the article that Pastor's wife and I were interviewed for came out in our local newspaper. Jason found it on his computer at work and brought Jackie and me a copy last night. The reporter did a wonderful job on the piece. She titled it *Parents Turn Tragic Loss into Help for Others*. Jamin told me there are some calls on the answering machine at home from grieving mothers. I will call them when I arrive home. The reporter quoted me as saying, "I knew that God was going to prove me wrong, that good would come out of this."

A lot of changes have occurred since last winter. I hope there are more positive ones that make a difference. I feel I have a mission ahead of me. Part of me fears what that may be. I'm not sure what it is or where it wants me to go. I guess I will go where God leads me.

I also fear being so far from home. I miss my family, my home, and my puppies. Fear is a part of PTSD. By tomorrow night I will be back in Michigan, and this will seem like a dream. I will have more responsibility at church and Grief Share will resume. The theme for our closing banquet in our leadership training was *So I Send You*. So, I go for God and for you Jenny. If not for you, I doubt God would be sending me at all. Love, Mom

July 26

Hello, Bugs, life is moving fast these days. In a few hours I will pick up Erin and have her for a few days. I always look forward to that. I am recovered from my Seattle trip.

Your dad saved the newspaper article for me. The photo shows me looking at your newborn baby picture in an album. It was so strange reading words I had spoken and knowing that people would know some of my private feelings. The article brought five new grieving people to Grief Share last night. I was so nervous because there were so many different kinds of losses and more than just a few people to try and make comfortable. I pray that God will bring them all back.

Jackie sent me an email yesterday. I had written a letter from the airport telling her that my flight had been delayed. It's a long story, but I arrived in Detroit at 1:30 am instead of 10:00 pm as previously planned. Your poor father waited for me all that time in Detroit even though he had to get up for work the next morning. He went above and beyond on that one. In the email Jackie sent, she said that she had never received a written letter from me and that I sounded just like you, and therefore must think just like you. What an honor to hear that. I'm flattered, Jenny.

Your July 20 birthday was quiet. I sang happy birthday to you a few times hoping you might hear. I thought of you now being 27 years old. I had both of my children by that age. Perhaps I would be a grandma.

Then the most amazing thing happened. Jamin told me that a big green van was in the driveway. I didn't hear anything. Later he went out on the porch and found a basket of beautiful flowers. I thought that perhaps your dad sent them. They were from all my Seattle friends from the conference. The ladies had remembered that I told them it would be your birthday when I arrived home. The card attached read, *The gift that your daughter was to the world is living in you.* I cried tears of grief and joy. I love you, Mom

August 10

Dear Sweet Jenny, I'm back up north with Erin for the second time this month. I feel so blessed to have her company. She's so good to me for a ten year old. I am watching her again for your Aunt Carol, and we decided to come up and go to Mackinaw City tomorrow. She'll stay the weekend, and then I'll meet Carol and Jerry half-way and they'll pick her up. Your dad is coming the day after tomorrow, and we will stay the week. Erin and I just finished watching a movie called *My Dog Skip*. I forgot how I get about dog movies and cried like a baby. We both did. It was partly because of the dog, and partly because I remembered how you and I could never watch a dog movie without crying. It made me miss you desperately.

I suppose you may know this, but Jamin is dating. He met a one of your cousin Nicki's friends. Her name is Ava. Her mother is in heaven as well. I had been praying. Jamin and I are not getting excited just yet. I haven't met her, but she sounds nice. She's already cooked him dinner. His eyes are shining. I haven't seen those beautiful eyes bright in a long time. Time will tell. I'll keep you up to date, Bugs. I love you, Mom

August 12

Jenny, you who used to tan so beautifully, how can I be on a boat for four hours and still have white legs? Your dad came up this morning. I resented the anxiety, impatience, and tension he brought with him. He enters a room as if he's carrying a bag of negativity on his back. He dumps it at my feet. The room changes and I feel my blood pressure rise. I'm back to reality. We took Erin out on the pontoon boat and cooked hot dogs. She loved it and wants to come up with a friend. I better take her up on that. We have such a great time together and she won't be ten forever.

Jamin and Ava made dinner at our house. We talked on the phone, as I wanted to hear her voice. She is real! I mentioned that I hoped she didn't think I was crazy because of all the teddy bears. She didn't think there were that many. I'm sure she was being kind, and I'm sure she didn't count them. Evidently Jamin told her the house was overflowing with them. I'm sure she understands the grieving heart. God bless hers.

August 27

Dear Jenny, I went to a wedding shower today. It's my first since your death. It was for the future wife of your buddy Zachary who said that you didn't know it, but that he was going to marry you someday. Your dad and I secretly hoped for that when you were kids. His fiancée is very sweet and cute. He chose well. I think I handled it quite nicely. I didn't cry until I watched a movie tonight with a leading man that reminded me of Jesse. I looked over at the picture of the two of you, which ended up being your last photo. When I turn north on our main road, I pass Jesse's house where he lives with his mom and stepdad. It's a different house than the one you remember. It's a different Jesse. I see his new black truck, as he no longer has the black one you knew, and I think *So close and yet so far.* He lives a mile from our house, and we may never meet again.

I met Ava. She is lovely and charming. I met her when I came home one day ahead of your father. She, Jamin, and I talked for three hours. I already knew from the newspaper, but poor Ava's mother was murdered less than a year ago. She died on the same road that you did. Ava has a great need and seems confused and searching for answers. I did pray some time ago that Jamin would find someone who needed him, and us, as much as she was needed here. Perhaps their lives connected for a reason. Time will tell.

P. S. I wonder at times. Do you know all this before I even tell you? Or when I tell you, do you hear it for the first time? My worst fear is that you are too far away to know anything at all. I wish I knew.

October 18

Jenny, I had quite a surprise tonight. I cleaned Aunt Jackie and Uncle George's house, and your dad came over after work. The four of us went to their club for dinner, and when I walked in, the entire family was there to celebrate my 50th birthday. I was in shock and hadn't a clue. The last time I had a surprise party, I was thirteen. A male admirer had planned it, and my jealous friend told me about it as we were walking down the street to the party. I guess this was my first real surprise. I think I was in shock the entire time, and it was great being with family.

I didn't like turning 50 years old. I've never been bothered by birthdays before. We all made it to the year 2000 but you. You were supposed to be here and be 27 years old. Another reason I'm not thrilled about it is that I spent most of my 40's in deep mourning. I just now feel as if part of me is returning to life. The man who killed you took away so much more than your future. He took away more than I could ever mention here.

Jamin and Ava are doing well. The trial for the first of the people involved in her mother's murder is over. It was so difficult for her family, and there was a lot of publicity. There will be more trials coming up. I'm glad Jamin was able to be with her. I met her family on my birthday. Jamin and Ava took me out to dinner, and her family came along. Your dad stayed home. Though her family was kind, her father was withdrawn as he had been at court all day.

Once again, your father has a job offer. This time it's in Denver, Colorado, for two years. At first, I avoided discussing it. When it finally came up, I told him I wouldn't go. Maybe a few years ago, I would have. I worked very hard to establish a new life here. Our relationship is strained. My son is here, my family is here, and my home is here. If he takes the job, we decided he would get an apartment in Denver. I would stay here with Jamin to care for the house and the cabin so he will have a home to return to. I will go back and forth to visit. It sounds like a plan. I wonder what you would think. Actually, I don't care what anyone thinks. I'm thinking of me this time.

November 3

Hey, Bug, what are you up to? Where is your spirit? Do you work in heaven? Can you watch over us or are you saved from viewing all the sadness and pain that exists on earth? Sometimes I think about these things until I feel like I'm going crazy. It's like staring at the sky and wondering if it ever ends or if there is a duplicate earth in a parallel universe.

Jamin and Ava are downstairs, so I came up to write you and go to sleep. Your dad is at the cabin. We seem to be better if we have time apart. He isn't going to Denver now. They lost the account. He may go somewhere else in the future. I've grown weary of the possible moves. I'm not going to think about it anymore.

Last weekend I sang a song I wrote for our new church school and family life center that will be added soon. By the time it was my time to sing, the anxiety was so great that I had a hard time playing the guitar. My hands were shaking, and I'm sure I missed strings. I barely remember singing. People said they enjoyed it, but I didn't. I'm sure they were being kind. I know how it sounded at home. Songs are always perfect in your bedroom. I decided to retire from my music due to my fear. This is something that developed since my PTSD diagnosis.

Sometimes God has other plans. Today, while cleaning house, I received a couple of uplifting calls. First Pastor called to ask if I would please sing my song for all three church services next week so the rest of the congregation could hear it. "It's just too beautiful a song to let fade into the woodwork," he remarked. What could I say? I told him I would sing in the back of the church as usual and not face people. Later that day, I received a call from our local cable station. They want to interview me about handling grief during the holidays. I agreed, but I will be terrified. I'd better get to sleep, Jen. Tomorrow is a Stephen's Ministry retreat on forgiveness. I'll be up very early and, if you remember, I am not a morning person. I pray you have sweet dreams of times with your family. Please never forget us. We love you. Do you sleep?

November 7

I realize you never got a chance to vote. I wonder whom you would have chosen for president today. Would you have voted per your husband if married? But then again, you always did have a mind of your own. I've never seen a race so close. I would love to stay up and root for my choice, but I must wait until morning to see who our president will be. I'm too tired.

December 13

Dear Jennifer, I often wonder if heaven prepares for Christmas or if it's Christmas every day. I just finished stenciling my bathroom. I always start a project right before Christmas. It seems to help me avoid preparing for the holidays. But Christmas is inevitable, and the chores and shopping must be done. Not for me, but for others. I can't just say I'm skipping out this year. Well I could, but you know how I hate to disappoint. Ironically, I spend time helping others in Grief Share try and get through the holidays as easily as possible. I just can't do it for myself. I believe it was easier in the beginning of my grief, when I was still numb. It is no longer the joyous activity it used to be. I just do what I have to and wait for it to be over. I know that someday I will feel the magic again and I must be patient. I did the interview for cable, but I haven't watched for it to come on. I'm not sure I'll see it.

This year should be much happier for Jamin. He and Ava are getting very close. She attends Oakland University, and Jamin just got accepted. Your dad and I are excited as my prayers have been answered in regard to his future.

My prayers for your father and I have not yet been answered. I fear for our future. I know I am no saint and my moods fluctuate as well. We don't really spend much time together with his job and my volunteer work. When we are together, his anger and impatience are beginning to exceed what I consider safe. I fear it may be alcohol related. I try not to write too much about that in case this journal gets read someday. I will say it's getting serious. Most of his time at home is spent sleeping in his chair. Maybe it's because Jamin works afternoons and I'm always busy. It's a situation he must try to remedy himself if he cares to.

Quite some time ago, just after I started to work at the retail store, I came home and couldn't find Jamin. I didn't know where he was, and I went into panic mode. I asked your dad and he said he had no idea. I finally located your brother, and he told me he had talked to your dad and told him where he was going. When I told your dad what Jamin had told me, I mentioned that he might want to seek help for his drinking. I actually had the nerve to mention the word *alcoholism*. He screamed at me and said, "If I think I have a problem, I'll take care of it." Once again, I will be patient. I could do the same thing my mother did before she died. I could start a fire in the backyard and burn these journals.

You know Jen, one of the things I miss the most since your death, other than you and normal life, is motivation. I had way too much energy with PTSD and now it seems to be waning, and I have no control. Physically I look much better than the past few years, but now that the house is finally painted and decorated with a zillion teddy bears, I'm starting to feel lost again. I have a big bear that plays music. I go into the living room, pick him up, wind him up, and just sit there and hug him. I will go now and try to accomplish some Christmas decorating. I pray for the desire and energy to get this done. As always, some days are better than others. For your brother, I now have hope. For your father and me, there is none. Because of a blizzard, I have been forced to stay inside and work. Thank you, Mother Nature. XXOO Mom

2001

January 5

Hi, Bugs, It's January already and still snowing. Christmas was pleasant at our house. Your cousins Jackie, Erin, Brian, and Jeff were all here, and the boys all had girlfriends, and one of them had a child who really enjoyed my teddy bear tree. All the commotion made the evening fly by. Your Uncle Nick came from North Carolina with his family of four and a dog. That's a crowd, but you lingered in my mind all night, and I felt you were just out of reach. Where was your laughter and your sweet face? I gave the little child one of your resin bears I bought for your last missed Christmas. It felt good to give one away. After all the preparing, all the celebrating, and all the cleaning up, I went to bed late and fell apart from the unfairness of your absence. I prayed for all the parents missing their children at Christmas.

Your father is at it again. Next week he is going to New York for an interview. If we haven't left Michigan in thirty years of marriage, I don't see how that would change now. I feel bad for him. I think he wants to leave this state so badly. I can understand wanting a new start. Going to interviews gives him something to think about. Perhaps someday we actually will live somewhere else. Happy New Year, Bug.

March 18

Jenny, I got through St. Patrick's Day without dwelling on the past. It's when I start reliving your last week of life. Today was Ava's birthday. We were both pretty sick but managed to have dinner out and cake and gifts at home. Her dad was gone today, so she was with us. She didn't have her mother or her father with her on her 21st birthday, and we didn't have you on yours. She fits right into the fold of our family. Jamin mentioned yesterday how it worked out that I got my wish. I said, "No, I got my prayer."

My mind is reeling. The closer it gets to the 26th of March the more frantic I get about getting things done. I have too many projects in my head. I still have rooms to paint, organizing, selling bears on eBay, exercising, and trying to read ten books at once. I'm trying to go to the gym with your dad. The computer has me hooked again. I have to pull myself away. I'm not as bad as last year, but I see similarities. I'm still buying bears but still selling too. I feel stressed and anxious. I want to do everything, and I want to do it now.

This week will be my last Grief Share for a few months after keeping it going for 18 months. I need a break. Stephen's Ministry will stay busy awhile longer because of retreats and then will quiet down for the summer. I now work at the new school at church. Once again, the job transfer to New York fell through. Your father was pretty sure about this one and even sold his truck. His company isn't taking the deal. This one wouldn't have been bad. Long Island, New York is about a 12-hour drive, and it would be easier to come home. I actually started to listen to your dad and get a little excited about a change. When will I learn?

I was talking to your dad about some things I wanted to take care of, and he stopped me and said, "Get a nice box for Jenny's ashes." He's right. They need to be protected. I haven't gone in your memory chest in a long time. It's in the guest room with Jamin's television on it. I'll look for a box, but not an urn. I don't like those.

I saw Jesse in his truck the other day. He was behind me, but he didn't know it. My heart stops when I see him. If I were to see him up close, I'm not sure I could handle my emotions. The past would slap me in the face. We live so close that it's bound to happen.

You're going to think your mother is crazy, Jen. Joanne's Yorkshire Terrier had a litter of seven puppies. The mother and pups were not expected to pull through as she had an emergency C-section. Yorkies don't usually have seven puppies. It's a miracle that they all lived, but the mother was very weak and couldn't feed them. I went over to Joanne's every day to help with the feedings. In order to keep track of who was who, they wore different color ribbons around their necks. Even though she was a female, Ross called the largest puppy Moose. I fell in love with Moose. I would feed her, and then she would crawl under my shirt and sleep on my shoulder. Joanne offered Moose to me at a savings, so I had been pondering the idea of buying her. The puppies are seven weeks old now. I decided to act as crazy as I feel and take her. Guess what day she comes to live with us? March 26th! Can't think of a better way to cheer me on that day. I'm not sure it will cheer your dad, because we will have three tiny yappy dogs. I am certifiably crazy. Good night, Bugs.

April 10

Moose fits in well. The first few days were stressful but she has become a good little pup. The day before March 26, I made a long list of chores and projects to keep me busy. I got up early and did aerobics, packed eBay boxes to mail, and started cleaning. All of a sudden, as I was scrubbing the tub, I realized I was completely overwhelmed and breathing very heavy and fast. I realized my arm was aching from scrubbing so furiously. I decided to take a shower and rinse the tub while I bathed. My heart wouldn't slow down, so I started taking deep breaths to calm myself. I thought I was doing so well and not dwelling on the significance of the day. Even staying busy and trying not to think didn't keep my body from reacting. Did I forget that my therapist said not to fight it? Out of nowhere, the tears flowed, and I cried so hard my head hurt. I wailed and moaned and then I screamed. I didn't scream because of the pain but because of anger. I yelled at the man who killed you. I always yell the same thing. "Do you know? Do you have any idea what you've taken from us? You took away who we were, who we are, and who we were meant to be." Afterwards, I am shaken but calmer. Months of anger and pain escaped from my body.

I'm still in project mode. I'm painting one room while starting on another. I'm doing anything to keep myself occupied so I won't think. I'm doing it again. I pondered your death for years before I went into hiding my thoughts. Your dad chose his job and alcohol, but that couldn't be my path. I chose projects and teddy bears. Sometimes I wonder if it's your dad's drinking that is causing this fear and panic. Aunt Carol and Aunt Laurie sent flowers on the 26th. A basket of eleven yellow roses arrived from your Smith cousins. There was one for each cousin including you. I was so touched by that. People still remember you were here. It made me think of your Grandma Smith's eleven little Christmas stockings hanging from her fireplace. Jackie is always there with a call and hurting as badly as we are.

I sat down with my guitar to ready myself for a Stephen's Ministry retreat on the 28th. I started to think of how my mother had passed on so much to us in her short time on this earth. There was music, religion, self-confidence, and strength. And her father before her had come over from Czechoslovakia as a young man and already a musician. I miss their music. I think of how pleased my mother would be about all the music that has flowed from her into our family. You should hear your brother, your cousins, and your Uncle Nick. I had a flashback of my mother playing the organ at her church one Sunday. I must have gone with her that day as we didn't go often even though she asked. I felt pent up grief and guilt well up inside of me for not going to church with her. It was such a simple request.

Who knows how to grieve at fifteen? By nineteen I was married and thinking of babies and a home. When did I grieve for her? Six months after her death, my dad was introducing us to women he met. I always missed her, but today I missed everything about her. How different would it have been to have at least one of my parents when we lost you? They would have understood. I cried for things lost and what never was. Grief never ends. It just settles like dust and the slightest movement can stir it up. It's 1:30 am and the time of year I don't sleep much. I'm buying bears again for comfort, and for some reason it works for me. Good night, my sweet daughter. I hear your voice and see your face like I was with you yesterday. You are right here in front of me all the time.

July 26

Jenny, your 28th birthday came and went on the 20th. Can you believe it? Twenty-eight years old. I had two babies by then. What I wouldn't give to go back to that time. I quietly sang to you on your birthday. Your dad and I were at the cabin, and Jamin was at home.

I am numb. Is there ever a happy ending? I really don't mean happy. I guess I mean will I ever feel like I have survived losing you. Over seven years, and I can't begin to even think of how many stages I've gone through.

When does it end? When does it smooth out, relax, or become acceptable? It probably won't be until the day you come and get me. I saw it in a movie. The dying woman's daughter came and took her into the light.

I am far from God. We were so close, and now I don't know where He is. I don't feel Him anymore. I don't feel your presence either. I am scared and apprehensive about starting up Grief Share once more. Do I want to continue to involve myself? Stephen's Ministry holds no charm for me, but I continue with it. A year ago, it fed me and drove me. I don't know if God is absent from me, or I'm absent from Him. Am I rebelling, or is my anger surfacing? I am nowhere. I'm trying to work on me as if I'm trying to make up for seven years of grief, and yet I still grieve. Maybe trying to take time for myself is just another PTSD addiction. I want to dream about you. I can't.

I'm not where I wanted to be. I wanted perfect progress. I was going to do this grief thing right and by the book. I was supposed to grow and be a better and wiser person. Right now, I don't want to be anything. I've been reading a book on miracles. It only makes me angry. Where was your miracle? Where are the miracles for little children who die from cancer and other illnesses? I am bitter, something I was never going to allow myself to be. I hide these feelings. No one sees this part of me, this misplaced person. On the outside I try to shine, but I feel the light dimming every day. I am in a tunnel of confusion. Though my belief in God is strong, my understanding of Him is becoming a fog. I miss you terribly. Don't leave me, Jenny.

August 18

Hi, daughter. Your father and I are at the cabin. It's 8:30 pm. We started to watch a movie at 7:30. Within minutes I couldn't keep my eyes open and I heard a soft snore from him. I fought it for a few minutes, but realized I didn't have to, turned off the television, and fell into a deep sleep. It seemed longer, but I only rested an hour. When I woke up, all three dogs were sleeping on me and the cabin was dark. Your father continued to snore. I looked outside and saw it was dusk. I felt a sensation of déjà vu. I knew the feeling, and it wasn't a good one. It usually happens after a nap, which is why I don't nap often. It's a feeling of complete and utter loneliness. In those few moments, despair floods my mind like a tidal wave over a seaside village. I realize what it is, and I know it will pass if I just wait it out. Naps are unnatural for me, as if I missed part of my life I wasn't supposed to. If I wasn't wise enough to realize it for what it is, I wouldn't be able to come out of it and forget it.

I have been up here for the whole week. Your father came yesterday. He had been in Dallas for five days in a training management class for employees who rank in the top 10% of the company. I'm proud of him. That is how he survives. Work saves him, and he's done well.

When I drove up last Sunday, I decided that Monday I would drive up to Mackinaw City, hop a ferry, and head for the Island. I rented a bike, had lunch on a terrace overlooking the sparkling Straights of Mackinaw, and took the ferry back to the city. I didn't get to ride the Island on your birthday this year, but I rode a month later. While I ride, I think of you and pretend you are with me in spirit. Maybe you are the warm breeze I suddenly feel on my cheek or perhaps you are the butterfly that lands on my handlebar; maybe you are the bird singing in a tree, or maybe you are the single cloud overhead. We don't know a single person among the tourists. It's just you and me. There is a feeling of peace and freedom. There is freedom from all negativity and heartache. I see, feel, and hear things that stay with me. I have moments of happiness that I tuck down into the deepest parts of my soul because I know I will need them. I realize what I seek. I am looking for peace.

I have a need to step away from all my obligations and become selfish for a while. I want to make a CD with your cousin Jeff who studies music engineering. I would like to record *Christmas in Heaven*. It's time to start getting all these journals typed up. I know it won't be easy, but it will be left here with my family. Perhaps someone would read my private letters to you someday. I'm not sure if I would have the energy or know how to put it into a book, but who knows, right? You would not be forgotten.

Two of your cousins on your dad's side are getting married next summer. You would be so excited and most likely thinking of what kind of dress you would wear. Good-bye for now, sweets. I'm not sure when or if I can ever stop writing you. How would I end this?

September 4

Jenny, guess who came into preschool today? It was your friend Tara. She brought her three-year-old little girl into my class. She is adorable. I lost it. It was too much. Tara looked the same as when she lived with us for six months, and when you two moved out and got an apartment for six more, and then when you moved back home for your last year of life. She told me she named her little girl Bailey Marie after your middle name, and they call her Bailey Bug. Tara showed me a tattoo on her ankle of a palm tree with a shining sun, and under it in blue ink is the name *Smith*. The name is in a script that looks like blue waves. Other friends have tattoos as well. You would not believe how much of you is still alive in others.

September 11

Jenny, I decided I cannot stop writing you. Not after today. This morning I went to work at the preschool. During the 3½ hours there, we heard disturbing news of terrorist attacks in New York and Washington D.C., but no real details. Of course, we were all concerned and nervous, but 20 three-year-old children had to be protected until parents arrived. No one had any idea what was really happening. The adults became extremely quiet so the children wouldn't sense our fear. Was this isolated or was there more to come?

I hurried home, and Jamin was watching the television. He told me to call your dad. Your dad told me to get to the grocery store and that this was serious. I still wasn't caught up on what was happening, and what I was hearing sounded like the news media wasn't sure either. I left for the grocery store and did what your dad asked. I never shopped so quickly or efficiently. When I returned, I couldn't wait to get in front of the television. I learned of the devastation of the World Trade Center and the Pentagon as a result of hijacked airplanes. This was, by far, the worst event I have witnessed in my 50 years on this earth. There was the Holocaust before I was born and the Vietnam War when I was a teen. Those were horrific, and we find a way to mourn them and remember; but this was today, and it was here. It was surreal to watch because what you see with your eyes and try to comprehend with your brain just doesn't register. How can this be real? The weather outside was pleasing, and the neighborhood was peaceful.

This attack is something you would read about in a novel or see at the movies, like aliens landing on earth or a giant earthquake destroying an entire city. This story has been written before, and now it is happening. I was supposed to meet with a woman tonight who found me from the Grief Share program and wanted to meet in private. She had lost her daughter and son-in-law to a drunk driver five months ago. I called to see if she still wanted to meet. She didn't want to change her plans. On the way, I feared that I wouldn't be able to focus on her story. We would talk about her daughter, and I would tell her a little about you and offer coping tools. And yes, my heart ached for her, but part of me wanted to say, *So many people lost daughters today. Four planes hijacked and full of people. Streets full of people. Thousands of mothers, fathers, sons, daughters, and grandparents gone.* That's where my mind was.

When I returned home, I planted myself in front of the television. I thought about how calm I was during my meeting. I had thought the worst that could happen to us already happened, but what if you had died in something as tragic as this? So many people were not coming home tonight. Tomorrow we will learn more, and I will be glued to the television again. We won't know if this is the end or just the beginning. Heaven is a busy place tonight. Pray for our world, Jenny.

September 13

Jenny, I can't describe it and I wonder if souls in heaven know what is happening down here. I watch the news constantly. I've only been doing what I have to. It was numbness and not calmness that I felt before. I only feel heartache for the grieving and a fear of the future. We are not going to fly to Seattle to see Jackie next month, nor am I going to plan an Alaskan cruise for your dad next year. Life as we know it is changing around the country. Those who perished have names and faces now—all those poor souls we couldn't see when the Towers fell, and the Pentagon burned. The shock has faded, and this is real. It will take a long time to figure it all out and to clean it all up. Some things I can't even think about.

September 17

Yesterday Jamin turned 24 years old. Your dad, Jamin, Ava, and I went to the Renaissance Festival. It was a refreshing break from the news. I tried to stay away from the television today, but it's very difficult. Your dad and I had decided against flying to Seattle, but Jackie called last night and tonight. She is lonely now that she and her boyfriend have parted. She wants me to come, and I told her I would. I will pick a few days and get a ticket. Your dad won't go. I can always cancel if things don't look good. She needs someone.

Letters on a Laptop

OCTOBER 23

Jenny, this is my first letter to you written on my new lap top computer. It's a tiny notebook. Your dad was generous and gave this to me for my birthday. He wants me to start writing a book about losing you and how I survived. I'm not sure I can open up my life to anyone who chooses to read it. But I can continue to write you without my hand getting tired.

Last night I returned from my visit with Jackie. I went to be a sounding board. The person Jackie really needed was you. She always trusted your opinion and, even after your death, you have had an influence on her. It should have been you chatting in her apartment and going out to eat. But I went for you.

Jackie and I had a bashing session about the man who killed you. I don't remember what prompted it. I don't usually feel anger on the surface. Perhaps it is a low simmer that can boil over at any time. Something has to turn it on.

I am currently talking to two women who lost older children like you. One lost a daughter and one a son. Their pain is fresh, but if I can give them just a spark of hope I can deal with bringing up my own past. You wouldn't have it any other way.

P.S. Jackie told me that I raised the perfect man. She thinks very highly of Jamin. I don't feel I can take credit when the past seven years have been filled with grief. He just did what I did, he chose a certain path and it was the right one. Love forever, Mom

October 28

Jenny Bug, your dad and I had a great weekend. We had Paul and Barb up to the cabin. We laughed and laughed just like we used to. I felt more like the old me again. Sometimes I look back at the last seven years and wonder who that person was in my body, and what they did to me while I was busy grieving. What did they do to my health, my body, and my home? First, I was a thinner quieter version of me who just read books whenever I didn't have a particular duty to attend to. Then I became someone who found protection in cleaning the church and other's homes just to keep busy and be alone. I was depressed and hated everything about my life except my son. When I think of those days, I practically shiver inside. Luckily, I was smart enough to get out of that rut and get my job that connected me with people again. That started me back on the road to me. It would be a long time though.

I think the breaking point was my PTSD and the teddy bears. I had to go through that to find the new person I would become. All the unpleasantness came knocking and tried to get to the surface. I remember living on Pepsi, and sometimes Joanne would call and ask if I had eaten, and of course, I hadn't. She would run out and bring me something to eat. It was such a bizarre time. Had I known what a breakthrough it would be, I wouldn't have fought it so hard. But, that is what PTSD is. You repress what your mind cannot deal with. But thank goodness for Jackie and her suggestion of therapy.

I had to realize that I would never find the old me and accept a different wounded version. It brought me to this point in my life. Thank God people say I look a lot younger than I am because I don't know who I was from 43 to 50. But like I tell Vivian and Kathleen, the two women I am talking to, it is possible to survive. When you lose a child, you have to be patient because it takes such a long time. I am still on the journey, Jen. I may always be on it. But if I can feel normal now and then, I can keep on walking down that road.

Your spirit keeps me going, too. You would have nagged me about my life and what I let happen to it. No, Bug, you wouldn't have been happy. But I hope you are now. Maybe when I get to those tapes and journals, I will just feel as if I am writing about someone else's life and not my own. That's the only way I will be able to tolerate hearing and reading about that person. Jenny, I love you for being so strong and giving me your strength to survive. I love you for helping me remember that I have to take care of my mind and my body. I also thank God for sending the books, people, music, and opportunities into my life that I needed to keep going. I still have a long trek ahead of me, but I have an idea of where the path will lead.

Love and kisses to Heaven,

Mom

NOVEMBER 11

Hey, Bugs, I wish I could ask you what's new and you could actually tell me. That would be too good to be true. Well, this day started out well but ended with frustration. My church had the dedication ceremony for our new school. I was asked to sing my song I wrote before they started building it. I was fine until I sat down to sing. The same thing happened that I went through the first time I sang it at a dedication gathering to earn money for the school. My hands started to shake. I am upset at the fact that I have been doing this for so long and can still be overwhelmed with stage fright. I get angry with myself for letting my nerves get the best of me. I am giving up public singing, at least for a while. I don't doubt my ability, just my fear of crowds. I will sing just for myself and perhaps I will record *Christmas in Heaven*.

We had a visit from Jamin's friend, Bill, our old neighbor. His life has been difficult lately. I'm not sure it's ever been easy. I wonder how you would react to him now. He mentioned the paper he wrote about your death for school and how he used to talk to you when he would come over to our house, upset. He used to love talking to you. He told us that he used to look at our family as the *Leave It to Beaver* family with everything running smoothly, etc. I had to laugh at that. It was nice to see him.

Well, that's about all that is new. Your dad is still on the same account and hating the drive, and Jamin and Ava are still together and working and going to OU. My life is pretty boring. Tomorrow I will see Kathleen, one of the ladies I am talking to about losing a child. We are going to a movie and out for dessert instead of just talking for a few hours. Time to sleep. I tried to dedicate my song to you today but still got nervous. It could be my PTSD. It changed me for the better but left some lasting damage. Perhaps this is my new normal. Nonetheless, I love you. Mom

November 14

Hi Bugs, I keep thinking about the future. I woke up Tuesday morning feeling angry and lost. I still had a feeling I wasn't where I was supposed to be or doing what God wants me to do. I was heading to work at the preschool for the morning. Absolutely everything irritated me. I was not nice to my dogs or myself. For some reason it was the last place I wanted to go. Once I got there, I completely cheered up and enjoyed the little children. Coworkers were kind and had their own problems to deal with. I envied them for knowing that they were where they belonged and comfortable. I'm not uncomfortable there, just not certain. Lately, I have not even been sure I feel comfortable at my church anymore. I feel like someone is knocking on my door, and I'm just not answering it.

I've been thinking about going to school again. I ask myself if I'm nuts for even considering it. I feel like I need to do something. I thought about it all day yesterday and tried to talk to your dad last night. We don't have the money to spend on an education for me. If I went, I would want to go full time and go for a BA in nursing or a counseling degree. I may be too old to start nursing. It takes a great deal of physical stamina. I need to be in a helping profession. I'm not happy doing all the things that used to fulfill me. I am a Stephen's Ministry Leader, help grieving mothers, do music for church, and work with children. Why is this nagging at me, and why would I need to do more?

I decided to talk to Grandma Ginny today. She started college in her forties and retired a teacher and counselor at a high school. She didn't think I was off my rocker. Then, because of our conversation last night (didn't think he really listened), your dad called today and said we were going to have our first family meeting. Finally, he is treating us like his co-workers. Jamin said he already knew his goals, but we wrote them down, nonetheless. Your dad's goals were, of course, work related. I wrote down all I wanted to do and my current responsibilities. My priorities were a possible book, recording one or two of my songs I wrote, and going to school. After talking to Ginny today, I decided I would go talk to an advisor at OU. Ginny thinks they will let me take one class if I want. I want to see what they suggest, and I can afford one class right now. All of our money is tied up in retirement accounts. If I do well enough, I will try to figure out a way. I told your dad that I wanted to pretend I was starting over again at 43, the age I was at your death. I still feel 43, as that is when time stopped. Your Aunt Carol thought it was a great idea. I love it when people support your goals. I will let you know what happens, Bug.

I heard from Vivian and a friend, Judy, from my days with Grief Share. Both were so kind and hurting. One said I was very perceptive and the other, a widow, said she was having a problem, and I was the first one she thought of to talk to. I really need to help people. I understand pain. I want to do this. Our lives would change tremendously around here. Jamin wants to go to school full-time. We are working on that as well. If I do decide to try to put the journals together and try and listen to and type up the tapes, I'm going to have to get started soon. I told Jamin and your dad that it's already written, it's just not organized. I would like to leave something about you and all of the dysfunction that occurs after the loss of a child. Say hello to all of your fellow saints, Jenny. Love, Mom

November 24

Well, Bugs, I filled out an application for Oakland University and I have an appointment with an advisor on Monday. I'm nervous, excited, scared, and afraid of disappointment. I'm going to go anyway. It would sure beat hanging around for the next six years just watching myself get older. I can learn instead. Sounds good to me.

December 9

Dear Bugs, I had to write to you. Last week I brought Bailey, Tara's little girl, home with me. We had a great afternoon. She looks just like Tara. You would love her. I may not have a grandchild any time soon, but I can borrow one once in a while. I haven't heard from the university yet. I'm still waiting and still wondering. It will determine my future.

I am not in a Christmas mood. My shopping is done, and some gifts are wrapped, but we have no other decorations up yet. We did get a tree, but it's still in the garage. That is another change I accept in myself. Sometimes I feel like enjoying a holiday, and sometimes I'm just not interested. I don't know why I feel so indifferent this year, but I don't question it anymore. I just accept how I feel.

I did something new today. Grandma Ginny took us to see the Nutcracker at the Detroit Opera House. Both were beautiful. But during all the dancing and the beautiful music, a severe sadness came over me. You never saw a ballet or any of the Historical buildings in Detroit that take your breath away. I do remember you went to the Detroit Institute of Arts with your dad for a school paper. I am grateful you did see that. The rest of my life I will be aware of all the things you will miss....like meeting Bailey Bug. The only peace for my aching heart is the fact that Heaven is more beautiful than any earthly music, breathtaking ballet, or detailed architecture.

2002

January 1

There will be a new beginning for a new year, Jenny. It could be a great one or not. Are saints in Heaven aware of a new year on earth? First Bug, I was accepted at the university. I have orientation on the 3rd and start on the 7th. I will take one class per semester until fall and then start full time. I had a conversation with Jackie during the holidays which prompted me to run to a bookstore and purchase many books on how to study, ace tests, improve memory etc. I even found a book on going back to college in your later years. Now, I just have to make the time to read them. I'm quite certain that I will skim through them, put them on my desk, and never look at them again.

I got a phone call the day after Christmas. It was the radiologist where I had a mammogram two weeks before. All I really know so far is that I have to return tomorrow for new photos and an ultrasound of my right breast. This is new to me, but I am not surprised. I am only a little nervous. I called my doctor, and he said not to lose sleep over it. I'm not.

Unfortunately, Jackie and Erin came to the front door as I was getting the news on the phone. I was shaken and told Jackie. I asked that she not tell anyone. I don't think I have cancer. Your dad said, "They cure this now." Maybe he thinks I do. I have already lived six more years than my mother. And, I have been without cancer eleven years beyond her onset. It's strange; I had a desire to pull out the three old family videos over the holidays. I watched the first tape. It looks as though I had the perfect childhood. But as it approaches 1960 when my mother got cancer, I notice her changing. Her looks and her spirit were fading. She hadn't had the operation yet, but her glow was gone. I'm afraid to watch the next tape.

I was worried about Jackie coming home. Flying is crazy right now, and just after she got home, a stewardess on a plane found a man with a bomb in his shoe. She diverted a disaster. Another terrorist. Things had been rather calm. But thankfully there were no incidents on New Year's Eve. The war is still on.

Jackie is happy. She is back with her boyfriend, and I am happy for her. She is much better than the last time I saw her. I hope all goes well. I would hate to see her in that pain once more. Aunt Jackie and Uncle George came home as well. We had a great Christmas Eve at Laurie's and a great Christmas Day at Cathie's. I always think life would be perfect if you were here. But, I'm smart enough to know that if you were here, I might pursue perfection from a different route. I drive myself crazy.

Last night we had a special New Year's Eve. Your dad, Jamin, Ava and I went out to dinner with Joanne, Ross and Brad. This was their first New Year's out since Brad's accident over eight years ago. I was worried Brad would be uncomfortable with Jamin and Ava, but everything went beautifully. We went back to their home afterwards and enjoyed more time together. They liked Ava. She enjoyed them. I hope we can do it again soon. People need to see what a delight it is to be with Brad. His spirit is nothing short of amazing. I'm so proud of him. I was telling Joanne that everyone in her home had been through adversity, and all had come out stronger and braver. We were all survivors, and I was very proud of us. I pray there are many blessings for my best friend's family this year.

I need to add that my repeat films and ultrasound of my breast were negative. It was just some fluid. Thank God.

I received a gift from Vivian from North Carolina; we exchange emails. She sent a beautiful angel for the Christmas tree. Both Vivian and Kathleen emailed, and both faced the first Christmas without their children. Both e-mails were a blessing to me. I'm thankful for every blessing I give and every blessing I receive. I cherish the kind thoughts and words I hear. I feel that every blessing I give and receive is a gift from God for enduring my grief.

Earlier in my writings I vowed not to waste my pain. I heard a line on television the other day: *It was four years ago, and it was yesterday.* Well, Bug, that sums it up for me. It was seven years, nine months, and six days ago, and it was yesterday. I love you. Mom

Never Waste Your Pain

Dear Lord…
Please grant that I shall
Never waste my pain, for…
To fail without learning,
To fall without getting up,
To sin without overcoming,
To be hurt without forgiving,
To be discontent without improving,
To be crushed without becoming more caring,
To suffer without growing more sensitive,
Makes of suffering a senseless, futile exercise,
A tragic loss, And of pain,
The greatest waste of all.
—Dick Innes (Used with permission.)

March 25

My beautiful Jennifer, I sit at my desk. On the corner is a picture of you in front of our Patricia Crab tree in stunningly full bloom. You are radiant, even with the sun in your face. Your blonde hair is curled, pulled back at the sides, and flowing over your shoulders. Your skin is flawless, and the coral dress compliments your golden skin tone. You stand ready for prom with a remarkably handsome Zack. I remind myself that you were real once. I tell myself that over and over. You weren't just a dream. Eight years ago, this was the last day of your life. I still remember everything you did and most things you said. I know it well.

No matter how unconventional, Jamin and I go to school together every Monday and Wednesday for Psychology 100. Of course, we don't sit together, and I don't embarrass him in class. We drive together, and then we walk in as if we don't know each other. It happened by accident. I picked a class at orientation, and he happened to already be enrolled in it. He wasn't thrilled, and that's when we made our pact. Jamin and I walk out and don't meet up until we are in the parking lot. One day I told the young man who sits beside me that my son was in the class. He kept trying to guess who it was, but he never did. I told him I would tell him the last day of class. He made a pouty face and said, "If you were my mom, I would sit next to you." I really enjoy the class, and I'm doing well. One more midterm and then the final on April 22nd. I will take Social Psychology in the spring. I'm still keeping busy with preschool and Stephen Ministry.

Within one week, at the end of February, your dad had a test done on his esophagus, and I had a second sinus surgery due to so many colds. I had the first when you were a child. I am recovering but we found out your dad has Barrett's esophagus. It's a disease that could turn into cancer. He has abnormal cells now. So, we just wait and take the appropriate steps when needed. We are okay with this for now. Jamin is having stomach problems, which we are still trying to figure out. He has had one visit to the doctor. We will watch him, and hopefully he'll feel better soon. He and Ava are still together and doing well. She just had her 22nd birthday.

April 1st, the day after Easter, your dad leaves for Los Angeles for three months and maybe three years. We won't know for a while what is going to happen, but here we go again. We have traveled this road before. This time, though, he is going. I do have to remember the time he was going to do this in Denver. He was at the airport when the deal fell through. Jamin and I will be alone for a while. I will just study and clean my own house. Not so bad. I think that is it. I think that is enough.

Eight years. I swear it was just recently that I saw you. I wanted to write to you on what I always call the fun, last day of your life. It was fun, wasn't it? I hope so. Until we meet again. Love, Mom

P.S. It has been six months since 9/11. The lots where the Twin Towers stood are nearly cleared. So many have their graves there.

May 23

Hey Jenny, I wish I could say what's up, and you could tell me. At least I can tell you. You'll never guess where I am at this moment. I'm on a plane somewhere between Detroit and Dallas. Your dad is still working in California, so I'm on my way to visit him for the Memorial Day weekend. Your dad will be there for another month. So far, we've been going to move and not move three times. I think he will be coming home. We went through all the same old stuff. Should we sell the house, the cabin, what will Jamin do? The stress has been overwhelming. Hopefully we'll have a few nice days to relax and see some of the sights. We may visit with your cousin Dave.

I ended my psychology class with a 4.0 GPA. Now I'm trying to do that again with Social Psychology. I hope this stressful situation does not hurt me. I love school. It's the one thing I'm actually on time for and sometimes actually early for. I suppose it could be another escape from having to think negative thoughts, but I can't think of a better deterrent, can you? I have a goal, but I take one day and one class at a time. I've signed up for fall and hopefully will still live in Michigan. I'm doing this for you and because of you. You are my motivation.

Jamin is good. Feeling better and doing well in school. I think his health problems were stress related. They started around the anniversary of your death. He would most likely say that the anniversary is not the problem. Sometimes we don't know. This is something that will affect us all for the rest of our lives.

I am finished working at the preschool and Stephen Ministry. I taught the grief module and suicide module to the new Stephen recruits. It was kind of fun, if that sort of thing can be. I still have a care receiver I see and continue to help Kathleen and Vivian. I will probably continue to be involved in helping others through grief. I learned in Psychology that sharing with others that have experienced the same losses or illnesses can actually boost your immune system. I can believe that. Love always, Mom

May 28

Bugs, I'm on my way home. I don't remember when your dad and I had such a nice time together. He still is uncertain about staying in California. I had lunch with a few of his coworkers. He is working with wonderful people. We went to some of the same locations we visited in 1971 and 1987. We went to Los Angeles, Hollywood, and Malibu. We called your cousin David and took him out for dinner. It was so good to see him.

My favorite areas were Pasadena and La Verne. We also drove down to San Diego. The ride was breathtaking. Of course, where we stayed in Pomona wasn't too shabby. The hotel was in the foothills of the San Gabriel Mountains. What a view. Even the weather was perfect. I have to really hold on to these precious moments.

On the flight to California, I was lucky as far as seat mates goes. On both flights I sat next to men who were helpful and talkative. On the second flight from Dallas to California, I met an especially wonderful man named Rick. We talked for three hours. Not too many men are comfortable with that. I did learn that he lost his first wife in a car accident ten years ago and was left with three small children. He is remarried now and happy, but I sensed a sadness in him that only people who understand loss can detect easily. He met your dad at baggage claim, and even they had a nice conversation. I told your dad how lucky I was to have such great traveling companions, as he is not always as lucky. He said that Rick was the lucky one because he got to sit next to me for three hours. Wasn't that nice thing to say? But then I think of all the time I spend with your dad when he is sleeping in his chair. I'm confused. I hope his kindness isn't a temporary ploy to make me want to move. He knows me well, and he knows exactly what to do.

Now back to reality and school. Your dad will be coming home for the weekend in two days. Sometime within the next month, we should know if he is staying in California or coming home to Michigan. Also, flying first class is quite nice, as I've never enjoyed that luxury before. I don't fly much, but when I do, I feel somehow closer to you when I'm above the clouds. Also, having a laptop computer is fun on a plane.

The newspaper left at the hotel door this morning had a frontpage story about three teenagers being killed on a highway near us in California. Whenever I hear or read about something like that, I have the urge to reach out. I feel their pain because I remember mine so vividly. God be with them. Love and kisses, Bug, Mom

August 10

Jenny, too tired to write and so much to say. I will say this for now. Your Smith cousin Reed got married on your birthday July 20th. He had a nice wedding. It was not an easy day for your dad and me. I did not handle it well at all. It's difficult to be so happy for people and carry such an ache in your heart at the same time. Today your Smith cousin Nicki got married on a beach on Lake Huron. It was a small ceremony with just her dad's family. I'm sure it was lovely. It's heartbreaking that you are not here to experience all these joys yourself. I am happy for them, sad for you. There will be many more weddings and births to face. Will it ever get easier without you? No, but like every other day, we will get by.

This has been a very hard time for me. It's not the weddings, but so many other things weighing heavy on me. I'm just too tired to even think right now, and I'm heading for bed. I talked to you today. I mean really talked out loud. I feel like you didn't hear me. No one would ever know, would they? Maybe you don't know us anymore. Maybe there is nothing.

September 11

Hi Jen, I said I would not watch anything about the 9/11 events from last year, but I found myself watching bits and pieces. It is just as upsetting as it was when it happened. They are showing us much more than last year. It is just heart wrenching. I remind myself that you died in much the same way as all those people, suddenly and tragically. Death is death. You will never be forgotten either, Jen…not by anyone who ever knew you or of you. I tell many people you existed. I don't just blurt it out to strangers, but if I'm asked, I say that I have one son and a daughter who lives in heaven.

I went to California again in July. The trip was great. We get along while I'm there because he has so much to show me and we stay busy. Plus, he's being nice for a reason. I can tell. He is moving out there and will continue to work on the account. He comes home every other week, but the longer he is gone, the harder it is for us to get along. The separation is putting a strain on our already delicate relationship. I was registered for my fall semester and so decided to just stay in Michigan, as he does not have a place to live. He has been in hotels for over five months. No wonder we have stress. Though I'm not certain I will go, I have applied to a school out there and hope to hear soon. I ended last semester with a 3.85 GPA. I had hoped to do better, but Research and Statistics was a bugger. I heard a rumor that they make you take it early in the program to rule out those who might not be serious about psychology. Pretty good for a middle-aged lady, huh, Jen?

Jamin and Ava are upstairs doing homework. The three of us are always doing homework. In fact, I should be doing it now. But I am happy. I absolutely love it. I'm not sure why and many reasons could apply. It keeps my mind occupied, gives me a sense of purpose, keeps me focused on the future, allows me to feel I'm doing something for you, and builds the self-esteem that is robbed from you when you lose a child or someone who is a part of your body. I have to fill the half of me that died with you. I will never be whole, but I can be 3/4 someday.

I don't want to move, and the thought terrifies me. I would be saying good-bye to Jamin, transporting animals, and leaving the house and cabin to be taken care of by others. I'm afraid I will depend too much on your father for companionship, and I'm not sure he'll have the time. We were out to lunch on one of his trips back home when he asked me to come. I was honest and told him I didn't think I should go. I told him our relationship was not strong enough to sustain me out there. I'll have no other soul near to me. I've never been away from home. He was begging me, so perhaps I could try. I also know why he's begging me. Why am I so weak? I'm afraid to rock that darn boat when I should be sinking it. I made it through the hardest thing in my life, and I can surely do this. I can try to think of it as an adventure, but I will only be disappointed if it is not. So, if I think the worst, maybe it won't be so bad. I'm pretty good at making the best of just about any situation, so maybe that innate gift will come into play. I know I don't feel you around so much anymore, but

I'm sure you will be with Jamin while he is alone, and your dad and me when we are homesick. If I can find a school, I can just keep on studying.

We had a Becker Family Reunion on August 18th. Becker is my mother's maiden name. Your Uncle Nick came from North Carolina with his wife, Pam, and Aunt Jackie flew Dave and Jackie in. It was small but turned out great. All the descendants of my grandpa's family were there. Most I will probably never see again except at a funeral. I saw people I haven't seen in many years, and we are all getting old. There was also a reception this month for your cousin Nicki and her new husband Tony. You would have loved these parties, Jenny. You were the party girl. I assure you that your presence was missed.

The president is talking about 9/11 on the television. He just said we are reminded that we are only here for a time. He is talking live from Ellis Island, New York. That's where your Great Grandpa Frank Becker landed when his family came over from Czechoslovakia. He carved his name in the hand of the Statue of Liberty. I wonder what he, or you for that matter, would think of this event. I was going to try to crack a book tonight but it's after nine p.m. Maybe it would be a good night to just go to bed early. My battery is running low, and it's time to go, Jen. Please visit once in a while when you can. I'll be waiting. Hugs, kisses, and lots of love, Mom

P.S. Your dad has his six-month checkup for his Barrett's esophagus on October 11th. I will keep you posted. Pray that nothing has changed. Also, a family on our street lost a young mother to breast cancer last week. She left three little girls. I had met them at MOPS. It brings back memories of when that happened to your aunts and me when our mother passed from the same disease and left the three of us. Sometimes you have to work at being happy or just numb yourself to certain things. The sadness is just too heavy.

December 27

My beautiful Jennifer, I am writing to you now so your dad can pack my laptop to take with him on the plane. He came home for Christmas on the 20th after being gone since my birthday on October 12th. It's the longest time we have been apart. His medical report came back from the

University of Michigan. His disease did not worsen, and there was a slight improvement in abnormal cells from a trial medication he's been on. We will check it again in six months. He is leaving to go back to California in two days. We are busy cleaning out drawers and closets. I've been putting away all my Boyd's bears, resin figurines, and dolls. My security blankets are gone. I finished my fall semester, and now it's time for me to go join your dad. It's something I need to do to save this marriage. Once again, I don't want to leave. I cannot even think about saying goodbye to Jamin. He will stay in our home and keep Hannah and Buddy. Moose can go with us, as we can have one pet in the townhouse where we will be living. She is the youngest. I will attend Mt. San Antonio College where I can take only general education classes, because any psychology and math classes will not transfer back to Oakland University. College is going to take longer than I thought. It will also cost much more until I live in California for one year.

Jamin and Ava are great. He just bought a new car. It's about the size of your friend's car that you were killed in. I'm a little nervous, but I am aware of the fact that I have to move on and let go of every little fear. I really have little control over everyday life. Jamin seems happy and content. He is still struggling with a decision about his college major and his future. Ava is talking about marriage. He does not want to get engaged until he is more certain about his future. I'm proud of him for having the insight and maturity to make that decision.

Christmas came and went so quickly this year. School kept me busy until the 14th, and I was forced to simplify the holidays. It actually worked out for the best. After writing a 20-page research paper on *Simplicity*, it was quite easy to do. There was very little stress involved and it made Christmas much more pleasant. Of course, there is always that Martha Stewart wannabe hiding inside me, but I've been there and done that and can let go of the perfect Christmas. We had Christmas day with the Smith family at our house. It went very well and very fast. We will come home for Christmas after we move. That is a must. It was also my first Christmas without my Aunt Jackie in my entire life. She and Uncle George decided to stay in Florida instead of coming home. We made it through our Christmas Eve without them.

Cathie mentioned quite a few times that she would like me to record the songs I've written since your death. I always found some reason to avoid it even though your cousin Jeff, who is becoming quite the expert after majoring in Music Technology, offered to record them for me. Cathie really wanted my *Christmas in Heaven* song. About a week before Christmas, I started thinking that maybe it was a possibility. Maybe I could do just one. Ironically, Jeff called me after his finals and told me he had some time if I wanted to do any recording. We decided on that one song. I went over, and we had it done in four hours. Christmas Eve, he presented me with eight beautiful CDs complete with my favorite picture of you on the cover. I was thrilled. I gave one to your Aunt Cathie as a surprise on Christmas day. I feel as if I now have some sort of a tribute to you that no one can take away.

Your dad and I are going over to Barb and Paul's home tonight for dinner. We will give them the keys to our cabin and your little truck. They are invited to use our cabin while we are gone. I know it will be in great hands, and I won't have to worry. Also, many people have offered to be here for Jamin if he needs them. We have a great family, Jenny. Like I said, I don't know how I'm going to leave, but I'm sure I will manage.

Your Uncle Chuck is going to drive me to the airport because I want to say goodbye to Jamin at home. I will write to you when I get to California and let you know how things are going. I will be honest. If I'm miserable, I will tell you. If you were here, I would not worry so much about Jamin being alone. I'm sure he will be fine and probably enjoy it, but I also think he will miss me. He has Ava, and she mothers him as I do. He'll be fine. I'm sure you'll be watching over him. We've just never been apart. But, it's also time. He's all grown up! Love you, Bugs, Mom

2003

January 6

Jenny, I'm sitting on the plane. I brought a journal to write in. This is all surreal, and I feel as if I'm out of my body watching everything around me. No, I haven't had a pill or a drink. Moose and I were supposed to take off fifteen minutes ago. She is sleeping in her carrier under the seat in front of me. Oh good, the plane is backing up. We are on our way to Dallas and then to the airport in Ontario, California.

I hugged and kissed Jamin this morning. I kissed Buddy and Hannah. I'm worried my pups will start looking for me in a few days. It's good that they are in their own home with someone they love, and with each other. I actually feel little emotion right now. I am numb to all of this. I don't believe the reality of what I may be getting myself into has sunk in.

I sit and wonder what life will be like in California. Most people seem to envy us, as if we are headed on a grand adventure. Your dad will be working, and I will be studying. Let the adventure begin. I am apprehensive and nervous. Will your dad be able to fulfill the role of companion, friend, and provider? I can't expect all of that from him. It's not fair. I'm more needy than he is. He works and sleeps. I must make my own way and my own happiness. I'm already used to being alone. We should be alright.

Does anything ever run smoothly? There goes my positive outlook. My flight to Ontario is cancelled due to high winds. I find this out at the Dallas airport after taking a train and walking a mile pulling Moose in one hand and a suitcase in the other. At the desk they tell me to walk all the way back to where I came from to catch a flight to Los Angeles. I took this layover to avoid that airport. I am now on the largest plane I have ever seen. It's as big as a house, and the seats are like Lazyboys. However, I hear Moose crying because they locked her in a compartment behind me and she is terrified. I am terrified.

The flight attendant is not in a good mood, and when I ask why Moose can't be on my lap, as I have seen other dogs out of carriers, she states that those people are celebrities. I am livid, and I want to go home. I pity the passengers near me as Moose cries, but it's not my fault. At first, they wanted to put her in the overhead compartment, but I protested. The only reason she is back there is because of my bulkhead seat. There is no seat in front of me. There is no seat partner and I have no one to talk to. Moose gets to come back to me after we are in the air, but she cannot be out of her carrier. Poor baby, she's scared, and it's dark in there. What am I doing leaving home?

Jenny, your poor dad gets to drive all the way to LAX instead of picking me up a couple of miles from our condo. Also, the poor man sitting in front of Moose's compartment must be going crazy. He paid for first class. I am so angry. Moose screamed for fifteen minutes. They won't let me hold her to calm her down. The flight attendant is treating me as if I brought a poisonous snake on board. This is Moose's first flight, and I fear she will be traumatized for all future flights because we will be flying often. If my head could boil, it would be spilling over.

January 27

JenBug, California is just what everyone says it is. At least, it is in Upland. I've been here three weeks today. It has been beautiful every day, and we are surrounded by mountains. I cannot really believe what I'm looking at sometimes. I wish I could enjoy it the way most people would. It took a while for me to even trust where I was. When your dad picked me up from the airport, the Santa Ana winds were in full force. We tried to get Moose to do her business, but the winds scared her. She fell over sideways. She weighs less than five pounds. She hadn't gone since morning.

We had to drive straight to Mt. San Antonio College where I had to register for classes. I stood in a long line at the college, and when I finally got to a person, they told me I would have to take placement tests before registering. I had my transcripts from OU and assured her that I didn't need them. We went back and forth until she finally gave me the number to register in the morning, and I agreed to take a math placement test as I had no math classes from OU. When I left my head was spinning from stress and hunger, but I had to get that done. Your dad patiently waited and tried to get Moose to go again. No luck. She was as stressed as me.

We finally started making our way to the condo. The car swayed back and forth in the wind, and I white-knuckled the seat and the door handle. By the time we got home, it was dark. Your dad pointed me to the area with grass, and I tried to get my poor puppy to relieve herself. Still she would not relax. Once again, the wind took her down. We went back in, and I carried her around while your dad showed me the condo. It was clean and neat. There was a coffee pot in the tiny kitchen and a chair and blow-up bed in the upstairs bedroom. That's all I needed. I put Moose down for one second, and she started to pee. No surprise. I tried to pick her up, but she ran the length of the room, emptying her bladder across the freshly cleaned carpet. I sat down on the steps and cried.

Your dad comforted me and told me to take my pajamas upstairs and get ready for bed. When I came down, he had a frozen pizza ready and a proper margarita in a wide rimmed glass complete with salt. We took our dinner upstairs and sat on the bed to watch his tiny television. I felt the stress start to leave my body. Moose was happier too after emptying her bladder on the carpet downstairs. I was so tired that I slept through the night and your dad getting ready for work.

I woke up to the sound of a boom box playing music in a car below my window. I looked out the blinds and saw nothing but garages, rows of garages. Where the heck was I? I took Moose out and saw the front of the condo and all the others that were exactly the same. I would not venture out past my little spot on the patio in this windy community. It was a few days later that your dad told me where to find our mailbox key and the mailbox. I finally walked off our patio. I turned a corner, and for a second I couldn't breathe. The San Antonio Mountains were right there in front of my face, all snowcapped and majestic. I stood there in awe of their beauty and felt that if I just reached out, I could touch them. I would never be afraid to leave my condo again.

The first week was difficult because your dad worked, I had nothing to unpack, and the car hadn't arrived. I could not even email because it was long distance. That has been rectified, and I can use my laptop for other things as well as writing to you. The movers arrived the second week, and school started. I didn't have time to think. But this third week has been hard. I talk to people at home where the weather is so cold, and I still envy them. Am I crazy? One day I called Aunt Laurie up north at her cabin, and she told me Brian and Jeff were on their way up, and they were all going snowmobiling. I was so envious. We had just started to get into that with you, Jesse, and Jamin when you died. Here I was, all alone 3,000 miles from my son, and a lifetime away from you. That night I felt that familiar aching pain inside. It was that empty hollow feeling that I know I just have to deal with. I have no choice. In time it fades.

There have been some good times too. Whenever your dad and I go somewhere, it feels good. It's all new and fresh, and there is so much to see. Every day I learn more about the area and how to get around. I found I just have to move out of my comfort zone and seek life here. The first day I ventured out to the grocery store, I was proud of myself. I'm surprised I went anywhere again after my first day of school at Mt. Sac. Your dad showed me how to get there, and I even did a practice run. I was all set. The first day of classes they closed my exit for road repairs. I was detoured to another freeway, where I quickly got off and realized I had no idea where I was or how to get to school. I wasn't going to cry. I made that decision because I had little control over anything else. I pulled into a state park office and two very nice men helped me. One of them had me follow him to the freeway. I must have looked terrified. I made it to class on time, but I'm sure my professor wondered why I was red faced and out of breath. But now I'm a pro, and I get braver every day.

Today I decided that I would not sit inside and study all day. I made my way to a picturesque little town called Claremont. I took Moose, and she and I walked around. I sat and had coffee outside and watched people.

So far school has been uplifting. It actually seems much stricter and a little tougher than OU. I'm going to have to work hard, not that I haven't always. But I'm glad I have that to keep me busy. I need friends here, Jen. That won't be easy. Good friendships take time and energy. I will be okay if I can just shake off the loneliness that plagues me at times. The worst was Saturday night when your dad was called into work and he and 25 others tried to fight a computer virus. We had one chair, one small table, and one lamp. I curled up in the chair. It was my first night alone, and I allowed myself to cry it out.

I seem to be okay with Jamin. If I talk to him every other day, I manage. I just need to hear his voice and know he is all right. I guess after having to live without you, I am content to just know he is alive and well. It's not much different than if he were to marry and move away, but instead of him moving, your dad and I did. I remind myself that, in what I call covered wagon days, when a child married and moved to another state, parents often never saw them again. Also, if the separation were to be too painful, I could always go home. If I were miserable, your dad would not insist that I stay. But I feel I belong here with him. Don't I, Jenny? I guess I just do what I feel I have to. That's my life. Come visit me here, okay? It's your kind of weather. I love you. Watch your brother for me, sweetie. Love, Mom

April 7

Hi, Bugs, I'm starting to feel more at home and know the roads pretty well. School is still much harder than OU, maybe because California schools are run by the state. I'm holding my own and doing pretty well.

I was supposed to study at my friend Martha's home a few weeks back. Instead, I ended up curled up in pain. I thought I had appendicitis. Your dad took me to the doctor, and he sent me to the hospital for tests and blood work. It was a very scary few days, and I thought that once again my life was going to change drastically. It turns out that the doctors were looking for ovarian cancer. Your dad and I thought I was done. Luckily, according to the lab tests and scans, I didn't have cancer, but the doctor still wanted to do a hysterectomy. We signed all the papers, and it was scheduled.

Two days before surgery, something woke me up at 2:00 am. I bolted out of bed feeling dizzy and disoriented. Your dad was sleeping in his chair downstairs. All of a sudden, I heard a voice say, *Don't do this.* I didn't know what to do or where to go. I just stood there wondering why I heard that. I went into my study to check the computer, but I saw a book I had brought from home. I hadn't read it, but it was about menopause. I wasn't in menopause. I looked up hysterectomy and sat in bed for hours reading about all the unnecessary surgeries performed on women and how it changes their lives. It scared me enough to wake up your dad. We sat and talked until it was time for him to get ready for work. He agreed with me and stood by my decision.

I called the doctor the next day and made an appointment for a consultation. Your dad and I argued with the surgeon because we didn't think such drastic measures were necessary. He was angry with me, telling me that if I were his family member, he would want me to have the surgery. We ended up faxing the test results to my doctor in Michigan, who said I didn't need surgery and should see him when I get back home. He actually called me and said, "Don't do it!" I felt such a sense of relief.

I do have a benign tumor on my right ovary that is twisting it and causing me pain. My doctor said he can remove it without major surgery. When it is not bothering me, I feel great. I'm just going to be careful until I get home.

I met a nice woman at the department store, and we started talking. She is from Ohio and missing her grown kids as well. We made arrangements to meet today, but she canceled. It's perfect out, and the birds are singing. I do feel very guilty as Michigan had one of the worst ice storms since the 70s. Jamin has been without power for four days now. He runs a generator to keep him and the dogs warm. We lost many of the trees on our property, and the neighbor says it looks like a war zone.

Jamin bought Ava a promise ring for her birthday in March. She will be graduating from OU soon. I'm so sorry we will miss her graduation. I feel like I'm missing so much. I wonder if I will ever stop feeling that I'm not at all where I'm supposed to be. I will tell you a secret. I'm not supposed to tell a soul. Jamin bought Ava an engagement ring. He is not sure when he will give it to her. Shhhhhh. They are visiting us in July but first I'm going home at the end of May for a month, and your dad will join me.

I'm excited because Cathie and Lynn are coming this Sunday for a week. I cannot wait. I'll be on break from school, so we should have a great time. Last week we got a beautiful climbing yellow rose bush for you. and your dad put it in a big pot. It sits on our tiny patio. The blooms are breathtaking, and it smells heavenly. Are you doing that, or is it just California?

Love you forever, Jen, and missing you like crazy. March 26th was nine years. It was a very quiet day. Your dad and I went out to eat. Aunt Carol sent flowers remembering you. I'm thankful. No one could ever forget. Your forever Mom

May 13

Hi Bugsy, Another Mother's Day came and went. I was completely childless on this one and missing both of my children. I often wonder how my life turned out this way. I don't understand any of it. Is it useless to dream or make plans for the future? I'm beginning to think so. Even school is one day at a time. Maybe I'll make it, maybe I won't. Jamin sent a dozen yellow roses on Mother's Day. I cried. They are beautiful, and I know he sent them because of you. Thank you, Jenny and Jamin.

Ava graduated this month and spoke at her graduation. She is extremely bright and ambitious and already has a job at General Motors. I hope things work out for her and Jamin, but I don't like to count on too much. Whatever happens will happen. They are both coming out here on July 16th and will be here for your 30th birthday. I cannot even think about how you would be turning 30 already when you were so young when you died.

Aunt Cathie and Aunt Lynn's visit was great. It didn't always run as smoothly as I had hoped, and some moments were stressful. I got lost on my way to Balboa Island and ended up in Malibu. Finding just the right restaurant was a challenge. I did feel badly for them as the weather was horrible compared to what it has been. We managed to have a good time, and I was sad to see them leave. I was so happy they made time to visit us.

This is my last week of school, and then I have finals. I'll be anxious to see how I did. On May 28, I'll be heading home, Jenny. Jamin went up north and got your truck so we'll have a vehicle to drive. I think of how your little truck was brand new and now it's almost ten years old. Can that be? It seems you left yesterday. I will be home one month and having surgery on June 11. I'm praying for Band-aid surgery. I don't have time for much else.

California is wonderful; there are always places to go and beautiful sights to see. At Easter, your dad and I went to Balboa Island since I missed it with your aunts. I was talking about you, and then I took a picture that came out with the most unusual shape and stream of colors. I say it was you. Even your dad said that it was unusual for a digital camera to pick up colors like that. I often feel I see you in different forms. I like thinking that you may be around. Why not? If it helps to feel that way, then what harm is in it?

Easter Sunday, I drove your dad 7,000 feet up into the mountains. He will not drive on narrow roads or venture up very high. It's like an entirely different world to me. It's hard to believe it is only minutes away. I want to go back and go even higher. I have no fear. The closer to you, the better. Soon I'll be seeing Jamin and my puppies, Hannah & Buddy. It will be great to see everyone. Just wish you were there waiting, too. Love, Mom

June 27

JenBug, I've been home almost a month. It seemed strange at first, but after a few days just felt like good old home again. Jamin and Ava picked me up from the airport. It was so great to see them. I was also very excited to see my puppies and they were so happy. Your dad came home a week later, and our medical escapades began. First, I went in for my surgery to have my right ovary removed because it was twisted. The doctor said I should be good for the rest of my life and that nothing would change. I was in the hospital for two days. The last time I was in the hospital overnight was when I had my babies. I'm doing well now and getting better every day. I even ended both my classes with a 4.0 GPA. I count my blessings. But, though my story ended happily, your father's didn't. His Barrett's...

October 13

Hey Jenny, this entry should be a novel in and of itself. I read my last entry and see that I stopped suddenly. I believe the phone rang, something else came up, and my letter to you had to be put on hold. I had no idea it would be this long.

I supposed I should stop the letters and put this journal into a book that I can always keep. I cannot seem to let it go, as if somehow I will lose you again if I do.

At this moment, I am sitting alone at a cozy table in the Mt. Baldy Lodge. It's a very old log structure that must be older than me. Far up in the log rafters I see cobwebs that can't be reached. There are few people here this time of day, but the walls are full of buck and moose heads staring down at me. I had a nice weekend, the weather is beautiful, and I just could not stay inside. I love riding up into the mountains, though this is my first time up here alone.

I guess I should start where I left off months ago. Three days after my surgery, while I was still very stiff and sore, Joanne and I drove up to Mackinaw for a few days so I could rest. Jamin was to take your dad for a colonoscopy, which turned out fine, but the doctor told him that his endoscope had shown that his esophagus had developed high-grade dysplasia, and he would need surgery as soon as possible. Your father called me on my way up north. We were both devastated, and Jamin was worried about your dad's state of mind. This is a very serious and life-altering surgery. I was in a daze my whole time in Mackinaw. How was your dad going to handle this additional change in his life?

Your dad flew back to California to organize things and tell his boss the news. He was planning on being off work for a long time. I wasn't sure what to do about school or if I would be going back at all. He came back to Michigan, and we went to see his doctor to talk. He said we needed to see a surgeon, but that he needed tests to rule out cancer anywhere else in the body. If that were the case, the surgery would not be performed. We both felt that was basically a death sentence. Earlier, we had thought my death was certain, and now we are dealing with this as well. Your father and I could hardly talk without arguing. His fear made him almost impossible to reason with. I understood. He had the body scans and other tests and fortunately they were clear.

Meanwhile, I was supposed to go back to California to register for classes. Jamin and Ava were supposed to come out on July 16. So we returned and waited for the test results and information to be reviewed by the surgeon at the University of Michigan Hospital. We figured we would go back when the time came. I looked into online classes at Mt. Sac and registered for two. I could complete those no matter where I was. My nerves were shattered, and I couldn't imagine your father's fears. My doctor had told me that my hormones would be out of sync for a few months due to my surgery. That did not help our situation.

Jamin and Ava arrived, and we had a wonderful week. It was a perfect distraction from our worries. On the 20th, your birthday, your dad and I woke up early and went to the open market in Claremont. We got you yellow roses. It was so hard to believe you were 30. My 30th seems like yesterday. Of course, I wondered how your life would have been. I cannot think too deeply about that without feeling sick with grief. I never go too deep.

The highlight of the week was our drive to Las Vegas. We stayed at a beautiful hotel on the strip and tried to enjoy ourselves—and Jamin proposed to Ava. We were all very happy and very proud. Among the pain spread out over our lives, we have scattered magical moments. We need to absorb all the happiness and euphoria of those moments and save them up in a tiny corner of our hearts. We said good-bye to Jamin and Ava and told them we would probably be back home soon.

A week later, your father got a call from the surgeon. He didn't want to do the surgery just yet. He wanted him to double up on the medication they gave him and have more tests in Michigan in six months. Dad is scheduled for tests around Christmas. I cannot tell you how pleased we were and what a sense of relief we experienced. I cancelled my online classes and registered for school.

I flew home to get Moose—I'd left her with Joanne when I thought we were coming back soon—then I came back to California expecting to move ahead and enjoy my thankfulness. That wasn't going to happen. I came down with such a state of depression that I couldn't eat and had no energy to even move my body. Your dad didn't like it or understand it. I didn't care. I went to the doctor, got my hormones checked, and everything was balanced and normal. He wanted to put me on antidepressants and send me to a therapist. I refused. I'm tough when it comes to taking charge of my own body. I assumed this would be temporary and that I just needed to adjust. The summer had been too much. I had not been so depressed since you died. But I soon recovered on my own. I went to a vitamin store and tried a supplement that called itself a bottle of sunshine, though that wasn't the name. I sit here today in a wonderful mood, thankful for every moment. I do have a gift for making the best of things. I consider myself to be an existentialist. I can choose to have an attitude that looks forward to a better future.

School is going great, and we have our tickets for Christmas. I'm not sure how things will go after your dad has his new set of tests, but we have six months before we have to worry about that. We have discovered Newport Beach and Santa Barbara. We've really been trying to make the best of life out here. The beauty of the state is indescribable. My 53rd birthday was yesterday. We spent the day in Santa Barbara, the American Riviera. It is properly named. The significance of this birthday is that I was 43 when you died. Almost ten years have passed. I don't have much to show for it except that I survived…and Jamin.

I raised a wonderful son, Jenny. He and his cousins played a gig at the Blue Note Cafe in Pontiac. Not a bad place to start. Jamin has started a website for their band, Out and Out Pleasure. You would be so proud. I wish I had been home to watch them play. I would have cried, I'm sure.

I forgot to tell you that Jackie visited in August and Aunt Jackie and Uncle George were visting his sister in Burbank. We all got together for dinner. Now I have a trip planned to Seattle in a few weeks. Love, Mom

2004

MARCH 26

Hey, Bug. Well, it's been ten years, Jen. You have been gone half as long as you were here on earth. Today was a special day. It was a day I feel God had planned for me. I have a 4.0 GPA at Mt. San Antonio. It's because of you. You motivate me. Your dad and I just got back from my National Honor Society induction.

Just this week, I was in the shower (which seems to be my place to cry for you) and I was thinking of the poem I used to say to you about an angel. I cannot remember if I am correct, but I think it went like this:

> An angel on her way to heaven
> One perfect, starlit night
> Remembered one she'd left behind
> And pausing in her flight
> Looked back to earth and shed a tear
> For love left so forlorn
> Whereon fell that pearly drop
> A pure white rose was born.

Did I remember it right Jen? On March 26th, your tenth anniversary of your death, I was given a certificate and one white rose. The president of the Honor Society said it stood for purity. Was it the pure white rose in the poem I have recited for almost ten years? Only you know.

I went to Seattle to see Jackie and had a wonderful time. I love Seattle, and I think you would as well. I can picture you there with Jackie living in her houseboat on Lake Union. I kept waiting for it to rock, but it felt like it was sitting on solid ground. Finally, one day it did move. It took me by surprise. I thought of how wonderful it would be to fall asleep with your house rocking. Her houseboat had a kitchen, living area, reading area (I sat there often), bath, and two bedrooms. She also took me to see the *Sleepless in Seattle* boat from the movie. You could see it from her floating house.

School is a lifeline for me, and I hold on tight. I love learning and putting my heart and soul into something worthwhile. It's stressful at times, but worth it. It is something I can put work into and actually get something out of. It's like a bank account. You put money in, you get interest. You invest, you get dividends. But, mostly it's for you. Your life will make a difference. I have to help people survive. I have to tell them they can continue on. I have to tell them they can gain strength from their pain.

I talked to Jackie today. We talked about your strength and power. We talked about how you weren't afraid of anything or anyone. We agreed that we both get our strength from you. You fuel us. She hurts so badly for you. She makes a special day of your birthday and the anniversary. She said something about trying to let you go. I said *NO, don't try.* Jenny never leaves us. I feel bad for saying that. She must do what helps her own heart.

The bond between a mother and daughter is so strong that even death cannot break it.

—Anita Hermalin

I will fill you in on your daddy. He loves his job. He hates his job. Like me, he takes one day at a time. The good news is that he went for his health tests at Christmas. The doctors at the University of Michigan called after the holidays and told us his dysplasia was practically gone. His double medication worked at clearing it up. It was a miracle, Jenny. That's the only way to figure it. He went from needing surgery right away to being cancer free. I thank God he is doing well.

We had a blowout about his drinking and, after dealing with it, he is doing much better. We fought because he picked me up at the airport messy and intoxicated. I had to put my foot down. It's not an innate trait of mine. I'm pretty sure I'm co-dependent. I know I should leave, and I've talked to him about moving back home by myself. However, the thought of leaving him here alone without anyone to make sure he's safe is scary. If something happened, he would have no family here. One night I came home from an evening class and couldn't wake him. There were no bottles around, so I went right for the garage and found two large bottles under some rags. I brought them into the house and put them on the table so he would see them in the morning. Then I watched some television. I finally went to bed, and he never even knew if I arrived home. He never mentioned finding the bottles. Nor did I ask. The situation is under control for now. I'm not sure how long it will last, but I'm happy for the break. I tell myself that he has worked hard and taken care of me and my children. I can't give up on him.

Me. How am I? My life is school, your Dad, and Moose. My health has been good since my surgery, but I'm going through menopause. Like some women I know, I thought I was pregnant. Your dad wanted me to take a test. He was actually excited. I knew in my heart I wasn't, but I took it for him. It's just nature taking it course. I feel great. So far, no big deal.

I call home often to talk to Jamin. We went home for Christmas and had a wonderful visit. I love being here for the weather and the ocean, but Michigan is my home. Jamin and Ava's wedding is coming along. It's not too far away. July 3, 2004. I can't think too hard about the fact that you will not be there. You can count on me filling you in, Bugs. Though I have a feeling you will be front and center, along with Ava's mom. Ava is quite the planner and has it all organized to take place in Corpus Christi, Texas. I'm sure it will be beautiful. Most of my family will be there. Jamin is still at Oakland University. He is a junior now, and I'm very proud. He takes care of our home and Hannah and Buddy. Just last week, your dad got the camera hooked up to the computer, and I could talk to Jamin and see his face. I saw Ava, and they held up Hanna and Buddy so I could see my sweet puppies.

I haven't tried making anymore friends. I meet people in class, maybe hang out at lunch, have some nice conversations, and then class is over, and we move on. I have to admit that I have lost my desire to make friends. Perhaps it's because I would rather do homework, or I know when I go back to Michigan, I will never see them again.

I finally found a way to lose the rest of the weight I gained since your death. I'm taking an intensive nine-week class in the Psychology of Reasoning and Problem Solving. We have to do a behavior modification project. Mine is to lose weight before Jamin's wedding. I'm changing my behavior, instead of dieting. It's working so far.

I sure wish you could write to me, Jenny. I need your strength and confidence. I need your guts. I need your nerve and your ability to say whatever you think. Why did you have to leave? I think back to when you were in preschool and I went to conferences. Your teacher told me you were so painfully shy that you would most likely have problems in your life. I'm not sure when you magically transformed or experienced metamorphosis to become the beautiful, brave creature that you were.

Ten years means nothing but ten years. I remember my last moments with you. I let my tears fall on your face so you could take them with you. I touched the yellow roses that covered your body so my touch would always be with you. I kissed your head for the last time so my love would go with you. The intensity with which I miss you is unchanged. The level of pain I carry is unchanged. I long for you every day. Your soul is who I am. Because you lived, because you died, I will keep on living until I get to you again. I have learned that some people are more powerful after death than in life. Spirits like you never die. Love, Mom

May 26

Hey, Bugsy, At the moment I am up in a plane on the second leg of my flight to Michigan. So far things are going well. Traveling with a dog is never easy, but I am flying first class to Detroit because of an airline error. No one even comments or notices the dog carrier in first class. It fits perfectly under the seat and Moose has become the perfect traveler. Too bad I can't do this every time. I finished my semester with a 4.0 GPA again. I don't know how I am doing this.

I will have a great deal of work to do at the house and the cabin, but I enjoy fixing it up and cleaning. Soon it will be Ava's home as well, and she can do what she likes until we move back. Jamin is picking us both up at the airport tonight. She has been in China and Korea for her job and just happens to be coming in tonight. It will be interesting to hear about her experiences. In a couple of days, I will be going to get a dress made for Jamin's wedding. I drew a picture of the design I would like and bought the materials. I have lost 12 pounds with my behavior modification class. I only have about five more to go to weigh what I did when you left us.

I have asked Erin to help me with cleaning and gardening when I get home. You wouldn't believe her, Jen. She was only 4 when you died, and she is now 14 and slightly taller than me. She has the same coloring as you, and I love being with her. We really have a good time, but I also know that becoming a teenager changes a relationship. I know it did for you. Well, I'd better sign off as they are bringing the lunches. Be back.

I'm a bit worried about leaving your dad for so long. He is used to me in California now, and I know he will be lonesome. He doesn't take care of himself when I'm not around. Watch over him for me, Jen?

Jamin's wedding is just about one month away. It seems like yesterday I was telling you how lonely and unhappy he was. I hope he will have enough happiness for the both of you. I will let you know how things progress. Love, as always, Mom

May 27

Dear Jenny, I am having coffee on the couch in the family room. It's just like the old days. You know, the days before moving to California. I still see you sitting at the other end doing your nails on the last day of your life. It will be hard to let this couch go, as it's getting old. When I took the dogs out this morning, I saw your white truck sitting in the driveway looking spent and speckled with bits of rust. I'm probably getting old and rusty too. I have finally reached the weight I was when you died. A short while after, I weighed too little. One day Jamin looked at me and said, "There is nothing to you."

I have so many tasks to accomplish before I return to California. I'm trying to get all the home maintenance repairs done and have finally taken to hiring most of them out. I'm not used to that but have no choice as I'm here without your father most of the time and I even have the cabin up north to take care of. By the time he arrives, most of the work will be done. Jamin and I are also trying to make room for Ava to move in after the wedding, and I'm not sure what to do with all my things. We are slowly making progress in that area. Ava, being the organized person, made me a spreadsheet of things she wants done before she moves in. I mean, I do love the girl, but a spreadsheet? I've told a few people, and they said I should throw it at her. It's not my style. I'm a peacemaker. But I don't think it's anything I would have done to my future mother-in-law, as I would have been grateful to have a rent-free home to live in. She is making your cousin Brian move out, but I can't say I blame her on that one. However, he is a gem to be around. He was such a great help when he was living here. Honeymooners should be alone.

Tomorrow is my first fitting for my dress. I had given the seamstress the picture I drew and the materials. She just whipped it up. The wedding is only two weeks away. Ava is busy at her GM job and planning the last-minute details, and Jamin seems to be in shock. We have handled some of the stress by being obsessed with the NBA playoffs, which the Detroit Pistons finally won last night. The last time they won, you were here. Now we have to concentrate along with Ava.

July 1

Dear Bugs, here I am on a plane. Big surprise. But for once I'm flying with your dad. I don't remember the last time we flew at the same time. It's so nice having someone along to help with luggage and tickets. I seem to always be the one they decide to check thoroughly at security. I guess a 53-year-old woman is more threatening than a 55-year-old man. This time they went through everything. Is it my name? Does it sound fake? It is very embarrassing. I am happy that the airports are careful these days. You may have guessed, but we are on our way to Jamin and Ava's wedding. Brian and his girlfriend are on the same flight somewhere behind us. We are supposed to fly to Dallas and then on to Corpus Christi. While we were waiting for our flight to board, we got a call and found out our flight to Corpus Christi was cancelled. We were put on a much later flight, and Brian and his girlfriend are on standby. This puts us in Corpus four hours later than expected.

I'm going to be writing to you throughout our time in Texas to keep you posted, though I have an idea you will be right there with us. You would not miss your brother's wedding.

We found a wonderful lady named Debbie to house sit and stay with Buddy and Hannah. Moose went to stay with Joanne. Joanne and I made it up to Mackinaw and the Island again this year. It's always such a treat . . . Your Aunt Laurie and I are going again on July 17th. I enjoy the Island once or twice a year, and she hasn't been there in years. Ava moved in, and we have boxes everywhere, but things will get organized and I hope they have a lovely year in our home. Carol and Laurie had a sweet wedding shower for Ava and everything was just perfect. I'm so thankful for all that they did. Aunt Carol always talked of having a shower for you one day. I'm glad she got to have that experience with Jamin.

I used to love listening to you talk about your future wedding. I remember all your dreams. Also, the day of the shower, June 19, Jesse got married for the second time. Barb told me she had seen him last October, and he told her he still cries over you. His new wife lets him talk about you and is understanding. I wish him great happiness.

July 3

Hello Jenny, are you coming to Jamin's wedding today? I've asked God for special permission. We had the rehearsal last night. It was very warm and humid, but no one fainted. I hope all goes well tonight. I have a feeling it will.

Yesterday was lady's luncheon and spa day. Aunt Jackie came with me and we had a wonderful time. Then it was off to the rehearsal. There are always problems, but they get solved one way or the other. There will be a yellow rose for you and Ava's mother at the altar. See you there.

July 5

My dear Jennifer, your baby brother is married. It was the sweetest ceremony and the most pleasant reception. The weather cooled just enough, and the winds off the Gulf of Mexico and the bay of Corpus Christi calmed to a gentle breeze; it couldn't have been nicer, considering the average type of weather this time of year. We were so blessed. I can't think of a single glitch. I couldn't see Jamin's face or hear all he said, but it wasn't necessary. Ava's grandmother and I lit candles and then gave them to the married couple to light the Unity Candle. Due to the fact that it was out of doors, it only stayed lit for a few moments, but it did light. Ava, in her embroidered dress, looked like a fairy princess from long ago. Jackie said, "Jamin is so cute it hurts." He was.

During the reception violin music was playing, just as it had been during the ceremony. Just that alone made me cry. I didn't feel as if I would cry unless I thought of you and Ava's mother. I can't even think about the sadness of your absence too deeply as it hurts my heart. When I entered the old Galvan Mansion after photos, I took my seat and faced a window. Being that it was so warm outdoors and cool inside, the windows fogged up. I looked in front of me and on the window were two handprints, forearms included. Between the handprints it looked as if someone had touched a face to the window. I stared at it for a long time, having my own personal feelings, but it wasn't long before Jackie and others noticed as well. Jackie and I smiled at each other. We had a common understanding.

I feel that I have never seen my family look so happy. After dinner a Mariachi Band slowly made its way into the old house playing softly, and then as they slowly entered, the music increased in volume. Oh, Jenny, what fun! Jamin had been unsure of having such a band, but I have to say it made the reception. It brought the perfect ending to a perfect day as everyone left joyful and uplifted even more than they had been. I never heard such beautiful harmonies and powerful tones. Ava's planning was perfect. It was a glorious blend of American and Hispanic culture. Whenever I think back on this wedding I will smile for the joy and happiness it seemed to bring to all who attended.

The next day, July 4, our family decided to go sight-seeing. Your dad didn't want to go, so I chose to stay with him. I wish I hadn't. We were heading for the escalator to go get something to eat. He was walking very fast, and I asked him to please wait for me. He used that as an opening to start an argument. I couldn't believe he would do this now. When I asked why, he walked faster and left me standing alone at the bottom of the escalator. He was gone. I was sick with heartache. I've always had to tolerate mood swings, but what was this? Though I was at my lightest weight in years, I felt as if my body weighed 500 pounds as I headed back to my room. I sat on the bed and cried. I knew he would take the rented car. Then I ordered room service and got whatever I wanted. I even had chocolate cake. I have no idea where he went, and I know better than to ask because I know what the answer will be. Perhaps he met a friend from Dallas. I decided to just assume he needed a bar day, where he is always at home. I know his alcoholism is getting worse. I know I should send him packing, but I can't ruin Jamin's happiness.

We spent that evening in Jamin and Ava's suite at the hotel watching fireworks. Downtown Corpus was alight with mixed colors and crackling pops. On the mantel of the old fireplace there were two yellow roses. I took them to my hotel room and then today I gave them to Ava's grandma to keep. Your dad and I are on our way back to Detroit. Jamin and Ava are headed for San Antonio for a short honeymoon. I still carry a heaviness in my mind and body. The only thing that could have made an improvement in this trip would have been to be with you as well. Then maybe your dad wouldn't act the way he does.

I have such a hole in my heart left by you and your dad, and nothing can ever fill it. I could go on and on about moments of sheer loneliness and emptiness. I learn to take the good with the bad and hold on to the precious moments. I will never understand why you cannot be here. Even now as I write, I cannot express this feeling. We are trying to carry on as best we can in this world. It is not always easy. The plane is descending, and I must pack up my computer. I will be home for three more weeks, and then I will really be alone, and this will seem like a pinprick of pain.

July 20

Happy birthday, JenBug. 31 years old. What would you be like? Where would you live? Would you be happy? Would I have grandchildren? How would you wear your long hair? What style of house would you live in? Would we have wonderful mother/daughter days? Would we go to our favorite places to eat and shop? How does one celebrate a birthday in Heaven? There are too many whats, wheres, and woulds.

I have only one week left in Michigan. Your dad went back to California after the wedding. I was glad to be on my own. Jamin and Ava are doing great and back to work. They are slowly merging their wedding gifts and her mother's things into the house. I have been up north a couple more times getting things repaired and to the Mackinaw area twice. I'm getting really worn out. All the repairs in this house are taken care of and today all the windows will be washed. In a few days Jamin, Ava, and I head back up north for the annual hot dog party in Evart. It's a tradition in your dad's family, and we take turns. We will celebrate your cousin Tracy having a baby, your Cousin Bob's wedding, and also Jamin and Ava's. It should be a busy weekend, and then I pack and leave. I have no idea how I will be when I return. Last year was not good, but I know in my heart I will be home for good in one year. Maybe that will help. I registered for classes, and I'm ready to dive into school.

Last weekend, I was in Mackinaw with your Aunt Laurie and on the way home I stopped at her and Tim's cabin. Brian and his girlfriend were there with her five-year-old daughter. We went for a boat ride, and I watched everyone. I just sat and observed. They were a family. They were doing what happens naturally in life. The progression of events was normal for them. As happens most of the time, I was by myself. Where was my family? One in heaven, one married, one in California, and one in Michigan. It's not quite how I pictured my life. However, I have a life, and I will not take it for granted. We are here for a reason. Have a wonderful birthday in Heaven. Maybe your grandparents will celebrate with you. I love you, Mom

2005

MARCH 26

Jennifer. How are you? Where are you? The time between letters is expanding. I guess that's a good thing. Am I busy, or am I healing? On a desk in front of me sits a single yellow rose for you on this day. I bought it in downtown San Francisco. I carried it all around town so you could be with us. We are on the 10th floor of the Hyatt on the Bay. What a spectacular view. Your dad and I are going home to Michigan in two months and wanted to make the drive up the coast from Los Angeles. Last night, we stayed at an adorable lodge in Cambria about halfway here.

As usual, we have had a hard week. It's the same week I relive over and over each year. This year the date hit on the exact day and Thursday night I thought about your last night sleeping in your own bed and what you did all day Friday. It's been eleven years now. My grief does not lessen. I am just getting used to living with the heartache. I still think about you and long for you just as much as ever. I'm very fragile this time of year. How fortunate for us to have this trip to take away some of the sting.

The drive down Big Sur was incredible. I did most of the driving on the edge of the Pacific, as you know your dad hates heights. I know the world has beautiful places, but this has to be one of the most breathtaking. I did have a special gift from you the other day. I had a beautiful dream. I don't often get to see you in dreams. I wrote it down.

I had the most wonderful dream of Jennifer this morning. It was a gift. She surrounded me in some kind of love that you could actually feel and see. It was similar to a cloudy mist that floated above me. Then I saw little footprints on my bed but nothing of physical substance. Then I felt someone lie down next to me. Then there was a little pair of socks. I said, "Jenny, is that you?" All of a sudden, I could see her, and she was a little girl. She thought it might be easier for me. We laughed and played. I can actually feel how it would be to see her again.

You stayed with me all day, Jenny. I still feel the joy of spending time with you. Tomorrow your dad and I are going to do some sightseeing. However, I need to fill you in on everyone and everything. I last wrote to you on your birthday.

I'm not sure I should even write about this, as it's painful to even remember. I've been so worried about your dad and his drinking. So far it hasn't seemed to affect his job. I'm sure you wonder why I'm still here. I just feel we must deal with each other's flaws. We still hang out on weekends and go to new places and different restaurants. Most nights he is passed out in his chair. I just do homework. On a Saturday in January we were getting ready to head out to Pasadena for the day. This particular Saturday he seemed very on edge. We drove out of our condo and into an area that has a breathtaking view of the mountains. Being January, they were dusted with a fresh layer of snow. How majestic they seemed up there against the bright blue sky. I asked your dad if he would mind if I took a picture so he pulled over. I got out and had my camera in my hand. I took the photo. I wanted to take another picture, but a car was in the way, so I waited for it to pass. It was only a couple of seconds. Your dad honked the horn the way he did when I was running up the stairs to say good-bye to you on the night you left us. I never did see you. Well, I jumped out of my skin and was shaking. I got in the car; I wasn't mad, I didn't yell, but I calmly said, "Please don't honk the horn at me. I really hate that." I thought he must really be hungry, or he needed a drink.

He quickly drove away, squealing the tires as he went. He was driving fast and went around a corner heading back home. He didn't say a word. He pulled in our driveway, opened the garage, pulled in, got out of the car, got in the other car, and drove away. I was left there wondering what the heck just happened. It reminded me of other times, one being in Camden Maine, another at your brother's wedding, and then this one. There were others before you died as well. I sat in the car. I called him on the cell phone and left a message asking him to please come back and tell me why he was so upset and how we could fix it. He didn't answer. I went in the house and sat on the couch with Moose. I called your dad numerous times. No answer. He didn't come home after a few hours, and I didn't want to look like the wounded wife if he did, so I ended up driving to Pasadena alone. I ate at a lovely lunch spot and walked all the way down to a mall at the other end of town. I walked around the mall, going into every store I liked, taking my time. I treated myself to a sundae outdoors. I didn't leave for home until it was dark. I purposely stayed away.

When I arrived home, your dad wasn't there. I just watched television and went to bed. I believe I'm starting to get numb to these situations. I didn't care anymore. Grandma Ginny used to say that it wasn't hate that's the enemy of love, but indifference. I did hear him come in and thought we would talk in the morning. When I woke up, he was gone again. Again, he stayed away for the entire day. I have no idea where he was, what he was doing, or how much he drank. I never saw him. I don't know if he was with people or just hanging out in bars. I didn't ask. I just knew that I was used to sweeping pain under the rug. Arguing or asking questions like why or where never did any good. Your dad is the king of happy times and the queen of misery. I remember how he wined and dined me to get me to agree to come to California with him. The king has a way of making me forget about the queen. So on to happier moments.

Jamin and Ava are still living in our house in Oxford. They will be there until their condo is finished. It should be ready around your birthday in July. Jamin is still in his band with his cousins. In fact, we talked to them tonight while Ava was getting ready for bed and Jamin was practicing in the basement. They do gigs now and then. Tomorrow will be the third Easter your dad and I have spent alone. Jamin and Ava will go to her father's house to celebrate. The kids are spreading out. Things sure would be different if you were here. If you still lived in Michigan and had children, I don't think I would be in California. I probably would never have returned to school. I would be busy helping out with my grandchildren. Anyway, Bug, everyone else is the same. Aunt Jackie and Uncle George are still wintering in Florida and Grandma Ginny is doing well. Oh yes, your cousin Jeffery is engaged. Val is a sweet and quiet girl. Jamin was the first of the cousins to marry. Who would have thought? Jackie is still in Seattle, and we keep in touch. In fact, she joined a band, along with doing her counseling, and will be playing in LA next weekend. Your dad and I are going to go see her. It should be exciting.

Remember how I have disliked St. Patrick's Day for ten years because you had such a hard day on your last one, a week before you died. Well, your dad and I went to check out one of the bars Jackie will be playing at called *Molly Malone's*. It was quiet and almost empty except for an old Irish gentleman named Eddie Madigan. All of a sudden, a large group of young adults came in bringing Irish music and wearing the green. They were being chauffeured by bus to all the Irish pubs in LA. They were having so much fun and were so alive. I watched and smiled and talked to a few. They danced the Irish Jig. For the first time in 11 years, St. Patrick's Day didn't seem so bad. In fact, your dad and I made Irish stew for his work potluck, and it was great. I made a vow to make it every year and drink a stout Irish beer. Maybe you didn't want me to hate it anymore.

Your dad and I are ready to go home. We went home for two weeks at Christmas, and it broke my heart to leave family, friends, and puppies again. I started my fifth semester at Mt. San Antonio. So far, I have carried a 4.0, but had such a panic attack during my last college algebra exam that I may have failed it. I don't know what is wrong. There are so many different variables that it's hard to put my finger on one. Stress, close to March 26, studying too hard, trying too hard, or being a dunce at math. I did great in the last two math classes. Oh, well, I'll just keep trying and hope it won't happen again. I'm researching math anxiety. I'll start back at Oakland University next fall. I don't know when I will be done, but I will finish. You are always in the back of my mind during all the reading and studying. Oh, my, Jenny, the biggest news of all. I almost forgot. In fact, I'm sure I forget a great deal because I don't write as often.

Your dad has had a huge mark on his head for years. His hair is so short, I can see it clearly. I have asked him many times to point it out to his doctor. He always says he forgot. I finally made an appointment for him out here in California because he had another problem that needed the attention of a dermatologist. I talked to the doctor beforehand and told her to look at it because he probably wouldn't tell her. She complied. A black mark on the head—not important to him, but a bleeding skin tag that gets his shirt collar dirty—important. When we got back from Christmas, there were frantic messages from the doctor on our machine. It turns out he has melanoma. The doctor sent him to a specialist in Pasadena. He had a serious surgery where part of his scalp was removed. Then he had to have a second surgery where they took out more. Finally, a third surgery closed it all up. He had large metal staples from the top of his head down to his ear. His cancer was in-situ, which means it was on the surface. That saved his life. It was a frightening situation that ended well as he looked like he had a face lift. When he returned to work, he wore a bandage that looked like a hat. One of his co-workers remarked that he had his own little built in pillow. Your dad thought that was hilarious.

Sometimes I'm not surprised at all when we feel extremely stressed and lost. There has been so much to handle lately. But we do what we have to do. To focus only on adversity destroys body and soul. I wouldn't be able to survive if that's where my thoughts lingered. It's not hard for me to focus on the good in life. It's a part of my personality. I just notice it, and I pay attention to what it has to say to me.

Well, Jenny, I will keep you posted. We are leaving Upland, California, on May 31. We are going to take our time and drive all the way to Michigan. I will write you before I go. Keep your energy strong, Jenny. Keep it flowing and moving. Go everywhere, see everything, and come spend the day with us tomorrow. Dad and I like to think that you would love it so much in California that you would have moved here. We can dream, can't we? Happy Easter, Jenny. You died the day before Palm Sunday. Love you always and forever, unending, unchanging. Mom

May 4

Hello, Jenny, I wanted to write to you before we left California. We will be leaving at the end of this month. A few times, we thought of staying. We would drive by a beautiful home, and your dad would tell me that we could have a home like that if we stayed. He knows I have a weakness for lovely old homes. One time his boss asked me why I was making your dad leave. I told him our families are in Michigan. When we moved here, your dad told me it would be around two years. That was the deal he made with the account. It's been two and a half. It was never supposed to be permanent. Your dad never begged me to stay and told me he was tired of the account anyway. No matter what account he's on, he is well liked and respected. You remember his work stories. He was always getting accolades.

I'm finishing up my last semester here and have started the ball rolling to return to Oakland University. I'm anxious to return home, but at the same time, I'll really miss certain things about California. The main thing is walking around campus in pleasant weather all year round. I seldom need a coat, and my hair never even gets messed in wind. It's almost like being indoors. However, walking around campus during a Michigan winter can be painful. I remember when Jamin and I had a class together, and we couldn't even talk to each other on the way to class because our faces were frozen. I'll think of Mt. Sac at times like that.

I never told you how Jackie's gigs went in LA. We went both nights to two different places. Both were super fun. You would love the music. Jackie did the backup singing and played the guitar. She was so cute and sang beautifully. I took tons of pictures. Needless to say, your dad and I were very proud of her. We had such a great time. We were invited to an after party. After we finally found the house, and after we finally found Jackie, and after we saw how much fun she was having with friends, and after we realized how old we felt, we said good-bye to Jackie and walked the mile to where we had parked. It was a party you would have loved. However, Jackie wouldn't even be in Seattle if you were still here. She wouldn't have left you. Who knows where anyone of us would be if you were still here. We would be different people altogether.

I ended up with a C on that math test I thought I failed. I'm having to humble myself with mathematics. Usually when I work hard, I can ace any class. Not so with math. I study so hard my brain hurts and then freeze up during the test. I did learn all about math anxiety, like I wrote you. It helped a great deal. During my test last week, I was totally calm and focused. However, I still didn't ace it. I received an 86. I'll take it.

I had two little blessings today. A pretty young Asian girl called my name. She was sitting beside me. She told me she had always sat behind me and thought that I had pretty hair. But today when she saw me talking in front of the class, she had to tell me she thought I was pretty. I almost cried. Everyone needs to hear kind words now and then. I found things I liked about her and gave her compliments as well. While she and I were talking, a young man I had coached before a quiz came up and told me I should be a teacher. He had aced that quiz. People can be so kind and loving. I won't forget those students and some of my teachers. There must have been a reason for my being here. I'm just not sure exactly what that is yet.

Today I took a walk and listened to music. I can walk forever when I listen. The second song that played was from Ace of Base, *The Sign*. You remember it, Jen. Your friends told me you loved it and danced to it on the last evening of your life. It played on your friend's Jeep radio as a crowd of us let go of balloons with messages to you on the day of your funeral. I heard it all the time after that. It was like a message from you. It was like seeing the numbers 333 all the time. But, later, when I started to really listen to the words and they blended with my grief, I started to see it as a message that you didn't want to live with us anymore. I know that is totally bogus, and I usually talk myself out of the feeling. Today, those same thoughts returned.

I remember mentioning to you that I connected you to my mother in so many ways. I often thought, in my grief, that you were my mother who returned to live with me. When I hear that song, it makes me think that you didn't want to stay. I feel I failed you and disappointed you. I hate when I feel that way. I give myself too much power. I take responsibility for your death. It's wrong. I kept talking to you and my mother as I walked.

I asked for some kind of sign that I was way off base. The next song that came on was an Amy Grant song. In it, she sang of God's plan. I forget sometimes that He is in charge. It was my answer, or so it seemed. He had a reason.

I just learned a psychological term called *positive religious coping*. It's much healthier to think in terms of God's plan for adversity rather than thinking of it as punishment. I have been very negative lately. I walked on and thought again about how I will not let your death stand for nothing. I won't let you down, Bug. I will get this degree and then my master's. I will help others learn to cope. However, if someone were to read this journal now, they might feel I need to seek help for myself. I wouldn't disagree. Grief does strange things to us. It's all okay. I'll write again before we leave, Bugs. You will be going home too. Your Jenny chest will go in the moving van. Your ashes will be with us. You'll drive across the country with dad, Moose, and me. Love, Mom

May 27

Hello Jennifer, I'm sitting on the floor in our little condo. It looks empty, like it did the night I arrived. The movers have been here for two days. Slowly everything is being removed. It has been a very stressful last month. I somehow managed to get my A in college algebra, so I ended my Mt. San Antonio College experience with a 4.0 GPA. How lucky is that? It felt good. But, it comes at a cost. That, along with getting ready to move, caused the top of my head to itch so badly. My nerves have always come out on my skin somehow. Hives, shingles, itchy spots etc. Oh well. I'm covering my head with Aloe Vera gel. After I rinse it out, the itch calms for a while.

Last night we stayed at the Shiloh Inn in Diamond Bar. I stayed there with your dad for a week before we moved out here. I enjoyed it, and it was so nice to relax. I felt the tension flowing out of me. For the next two days, we will stay at our favorite Marriot in Pasadena. I can't think of a better way to say goodbye to California. I'm appreciating the beauty of every palm tree and every mountain breeze. I'm imprinting the memory of every mountain, beautiful bed of flowers, and my favorite purple Jacaranda trees. I love them but they will never grow in Michigan. Your dad is on his way back from work, and the movers are finishing up.

We will start our cross-country drive on the 29th. I'll let you know how it goes. By the way, you are sitting right next to me on the floor. I found a beautiful little suitcase for your ashes. They fit perfectly, and you are encased in beautiful bouquets of violets. However, when I returned this morning, I noticed that the movers had emptied your Jenny chest. It has never been emptied in eleven years. My heart hurt. I'll deal with it. Have to run. Love you tons, Mom

2006

November 25

Hi Jenny, I guess it has been a very long time. I have wanted to write so many times. However, I didn't know what to say to you. I still don't. Things are not well here. They started falling apart when we got home. It was a little stressful here for a while and unpacking all the boxes and trying find a place to put everything was a challenge. Erin helped me a few times. Jamin and Ava moved on schedule. However, your dad started to drink more and more and finally hit what one would think of as rock bottom. It's a long story. I will explain.

One thing I must share because it's one of the times I've felt rescued. We were at the cabin and had gone over to your Aunt Laurie and Tim's cabin in West Branch. Your Aunt Carol and Jerry were visiting, and we thought it would be nice to spend the evening with them. Tim loves wine and is very knowledgeable about it. So of course, we all had wine. However, none of us got drunk, other than your dad. Wine got him through the drive home from California. Driving days were fine—nights were wine. I wasn't interested, so the bottle was his. I don't know how he managed to drink so much more than the rest of us at your aunt's cabin. He and Tim were having so much fun telling stories, as they always did. When it came time to leave, I could barely get him in the car. On the way home, he kept making noises as if he were going to vomit. I rolled down his window and asked him to lean out. This went on for the 30-minute drive. When we got home, I left him in the car and went into the cabin. I took the dogs out, and he managed to get himself to his chair and sat down and passed out.

I sat on the couch and sobbed. Would this ever end? I finally went to bed and decided to pray. I prayed and cried for the longest time. My entire body was shaking from my sobs. I asked God to please help your dad and take this debilitating stress away from us. All of a sudden, as in times past, I felt energy in the room. It lasted for a while, and I just froze. I felt my body begin to relax. Someone was there. I was afraid to look for fear they would leave. I felt the sudden *peace that passes all understanding* that I remember reading about in the Bible. I fell into a deep slumber and didn't wake until the next morning. It was the best sleep I ever had.

When I woke up, I thought about the experience, but it was quickly overshadowed by fear. I opened the door, and your dad was in his chair. He was wide awake. How does he do that? How is he not hung over? I sat on the couch. He was tying his tennis shoes. I asked if he was going out. He said he was going home. I asked him not to. I asked if we could talk. He ignored me and left. I felt so empty inside; it was as if he had grabbed my guts and took them with him. I had done nothing but ask him to hang out the window. I'm not sure he even remembered that. I sat on the couch and stared into space for a very long time. I stayed one more night and took your little white truck home.

Life can be so painful, Jen. I'm glad you don't feel this pain.

On October 30, Jamin came over and cried in my arms. Ava was leaving him. The only thing as heart-wrenching as having your child die is holding your child while they suffer in pain. The only thing going well is college. It has become my escape. I'm sorry, Jenny. I don't want to make you sad. Maybe you can't be sad in Heaven. I'm going to go to bed. Maybe you understand why I haven't written. I will explain it all. I promise. It's just too much. I love you. Mom

July 22

Now after all this time, Bug, where do I begin? You just had your 34th birthday. I have a card for you on the table.

I am up at our log cabin. I came up last week as well, and just went home to go to class. I graduate in a few weeks. In December, when they have their next formal ceremony, I will walk. I've worked hard. I hope Jamin will walk with me. He will be finished with his BA in December. I'm so utterly proud of him.

Should I tell you that your dad's alcoholism has taken over our lives? The long story I didn't tell you was that during a bad drinking day, he would get angry if I said anything to him about going out. He would get his keys, and I would tell him that if he drinks and drives, I will call the police and try and have him pulled over. I could not bear the idea of him becoming like the man who killed you. Yet that is exactly what he has become. Twice I called the police (I was never more scared in my life), and twice nothing happened. He would just arrive home sometime the next day.

After the third call, the police took me seriously. However, he wasn't arrested for drunk driving, but domestic violence. After he had left and I called, the police came to my door. My heart fell to my feet. The last time a policeman had come to the door was to tell me that you were dead. The policeman wanted to know why I had called. I told him. He asked if I was hurt. I said that your dad pushed me down when I tried to get to his keys before him, but I wasn't pressing charges. I didn't mention how hard he hit me and that I flew into the other room. I didn't tell him that after landing hard, I got right up and ran after your dad, begging him to please not drive as I chased him down the driveway like a mad person.

They sat me down at the dining room table and had a pack of papers. The policeman said he was pressing charges because of a new *no tolerance* law. Because of this incident, your dad went through a year of AA, probation, and other indignities. All in all, it did no good. I went to court with him. I supported him in hope that we might have a new beginning. I was asked to write a letter on his behalf, but he went up to the computer and changed or deleted many of my sentences. He is no longer your dad. He is a stranger, and I'm afraid. I know I'm being controlled. I know I'm being abused. I know I'm codependent. I'm aware my hope knows no bounds. He doesn't want to stop. I have called ambulances when he has fallen and hit the floor hard, or when I couldn't wake him. I have taken him to the hospital when he was so sick, he wanted to die. He would be well for a few weeks and then return to the bottle. I have suffered panic attacks that would last all night. Stress hormones made my brain burn so bad I thought my head was on fire. I would be driving to class and my face, neck, and arms would go numb, and I couldn't feel the steering wheel. I would blast one of Jamin's CDs as loud as I could while on my way home from class. I wanted it to drown out my terror. I was afraid to come home for fear of what I would find. I think I looked normal on the outside but inside, my body and mind were traumatized, and I felt near death. So, after all that time, I finally got to the point where I decided that I couldn't let his drinking affect my health and well-being. Jamin needs one healthy parent. I feel sorry for your dad because he is in such pain. However, I can do nothing more for him. It's his choice. I will not be co-dependent any longer.

Jamin is depressed but doing the best he can. After he left the condo he and Ava had, he lived with your cousin Jeff and his wife Val for a while. They couldn't have been kinder. They had a little baby boy named Jack. He is so sweet. I'm sure you are aware of that, and possibly everything else. Or are you? I never can decide what I think about that.

Once in a while, I have a massage and my masseuse is clairvoyant. I make myself get massages to relax my tense muscles. It helps temporarily. She says you come and visit me. Therefore, you would know. Even then, I'm not sure. Once she told me that as Jamin was being massaged, you stood next to him with your hand on his head. My common sense tells me it is not real. My heart wants it to be. Sometimes she says you, my mom, dad, and angels have appeared.

Jamin didn't want to be in the way after Jeff's new baby arrived, so he now lives with his cousin Brian who bought a house. They live well together, as this is the third time they have shared a home. Jamin still works for the same company as your dad, and he still has his band. A couple of weeks ago, Jackie was here from Seattle. All the cousins played a gig, and I went. It was such a healing time. You would love that whole scene, Jenny. Jackie sang a song she wrote for you called *Pink Plastic Shoes*. The kind of shoes the two of you had as little girls. I wish your dad could have watched the show. He never wanted to go.

Jamin is working on himself and his life. He joined a gym, is reading, and keeping his chin up. I'm proud of him. He is a wonderful son and is patient with your dad. He does, however, feel that I "live a miserable existence" and wants me to take care of myself. That is good to know. We don't hear from Ava. She had a yoga instructor she was interested in around the time she wanted the divorce. I remember when your cousin introduced Ava and Jamin. She had told Ava, "You better not hurt him." Perhaps she knew her better than we did. Jamin finally told me that she got caught up in a type of cult, after going to seminars, that led her to believe she was not of this world but from a star and was sent here to create positive change. Therefore, she needed to be with another star person. Evidently, that did not go the way she had hoped, and she ended up alone. Even knowing her state of mind, he offered to go to counseling to help save the marriage. I wish her well. She has been through adversity as well, and I understand her searching. I'm not good at cursing people or saying very harsh things. What good would that do? I wrote her an email and included photos. I told her what I thought clear and simple. I never sent it. I still giggle at my nephew saying, "Hit send, hit send." I'm grateful for the love she gave to Jamin for all those years and for what they taught each other. But I am thankful they are apart.

I am the same. I go to class, do homework, survive stressful situations, and move on. I start graduate school for counseling in September. The classes I have at the moment are motivating me to take extremely good care of myself (health and exercise science), so hopefully I will have the energy to attack grad school. I just can't be around your dad. So here I sit, lonely but at peace; sad, but content with my three little dogs. Hannah, who was born in your month and on Jamin's day, is now 12 years old. They keep me company. I am grateful for so many things that it is hard to be pulled into sadness or self-pity. Life is just life. We make the best of what we are given, what we choose, and hope to make correct choices. Unfortunately, we don't know that our choices might not be correct until after we have already lived them.

Happy birthday, sweet girl. Your card says, *Happy Birthday, Star Dancer*. How appropriate is that? Oh, yeah, we saw Zach and Jeremy a few weeks ago. They both have families and even some grey hair. Life goes on. In love with you always, Mom

2008

March 25, 2008

Hi Bug, it is now the eve of the night you died. March 26, 2008, 14 years ago, you left us. I thought I was handling things well this year, but dad's drinking got in the way again. The last time I wrote you from the cabin, I went home and found your dad extremely intoxicated and suicidal. I took him to the hospital where he went through detox, got on medications, and stayed in the psychiatric ward for two weeks. He then went into a six-week program to help him stop drinking. However, as soon as he was done and went back to work, they sent him to San Francisco. This time I stayed home. He fell right back into it. There was nothing anyone could do. He was in the perfect environment to relapse. He promised to get help and into a group as soon as he got there, but never did. He was there from September until just a few weeks ago. He was finally removed from the account and is waiting to get another. He has been trying to stay sober, but I came home from class and found him drunk last night. I try so hard not to get upset, but I get so hurt and feel so betrayed. For some reason, I believe him when he says he wants to stop. I feel so foolish. Jamin and I can't figure out why he can't stay sober for us. Are we not enough for him? We know he loved you and misses you like we do, but doesn't he love us as well? Even as I write this, I know it's not about love. It's about addiction. I called from class today, and he was drunk. I told him not to be home when I got home. He wasn't. I was relieved. However, I am so disappointed because he, Jamin, and I were supposed to go car shopping and out to lunch tomorrow. It would have been the first time in ages that we were all together on that fateful day. So, I'm not sure what will happen. I'm not sure where he is. I don't worry anymore. There is nothing I can do. If I ignore the drinking I feel like a fool, and if I don't, somehow, I pay.

So, again, I am alone by choice. I'm always in a good mood when things are going well. I guess I enjoy feeling normal once in a while. I am seeing my therapist again. This time I am trying to deal with thoughts of divorce. I'm still scared of the stress of going through a divorce at the same time I am living with the unbearable stress of being married. Either way, I can't escape. Right now, I am dealing with the acceptance of being undecided and in the middle. I am living in the grey area. I don't have a place to go while living with three dogs and working on graduate school.

On a good note, and a life event that makes my heart happy, Jamin and I walked together last December in Oakland University's graduation ceremony. He really didn't want to walk at all but gave in for my sake. I think he was glad he went through it. It is closure for a job well done. Aunt Carol had a little party for us, and Joanne, Ross, and Brad came. Your dad left early, and Jamin and I knew why. I am already half-way through grad school and hope to be finishing up my internship this time next year. I'm doing very well and enjoying it very much. Your dad helped me take out a student loan, because the cost is double what I paid for my bachelors. I'll let you know how things are going. I did graduate *magna cum laude,* which felt good. I felt like something went right.

Jamin is doing well. He isn't crazy about his job but is now thinking about getting a master's in counseling as well. I think he would make a wonderful counselor. I guess we wait and see. He is still working out and reading a great deal. Other than my complaining and seeing his dad intoxicated, he is quite happy just being single. I don't know what I would do without him. He is my heart.

We all got together for baby Jack's first birthday last Saturday and then got together for Easter Sunday. Dad was sober, or seemed so, and I got the dreaded "hope" again. Hope that maybe this time things would be different, and he would actually stop on his own. He made it four days. So, I may be alone tomorrow on March 26 again. I could call someone, but I usually don't feel like it. Maybe Jamin and I will have lunch. I will buy you a rose and go see your Grandma Ginny who is basically housebound after a stroke. Your Dad may be up north. It's hard to say. All his medications are here. Last week when I saw Grandma Ginny, she told me how lucky I was to have school because it's all I really have. I thought to myself, *Thank you, that's uplifting.* I guess she was right. However, I have a great son, my health, a roof over my head, and a safe place to live. I do count my blessings. I don't know how long dad will have a job. I hope I have one before he loses his. The economy is so bad in Michigan that houses aren't selling. I feel stuck, but my therapist says that is too strong a word. I'm just in between. He tells me that I carry around a huge ring of keys. I keep trying different keys in the lock. None of them fit. I need to put down the keys. Therapists will not tell you what you should do. They will, however, find a way to give you hints.

Fourteen years is unbelievable Jenny. I still feel you and hear you. Even your Aunt Laurie said I should be over it by now. She never lost a child. I can't expect them to understand. As I get closer to completing what I wanted to fulfill in your memory, my life is still falling apart bit by bit. I started writing this as a healing tool and then I thought it might give people hope. Hope that one can survive and make something good come from something bad. However, other than school, I am so terrible at handling my own life. I feel with my education I should be able to help your father somehow. I should know exactly what to do or what to say to end his substance abuse and his pain. However, deep inside, I know that it is totally up to him. All I can do is sit back, watch, try not to react, and wait. I wish to God it would not hurt. I wish to God I could just let him do what he has to do and walk away from it. Perhaps someday I will develop that skill. Perhaps it will kill me before it kills him. My strength is fading. Perhaps by July, I will have more positive news for you. Thinking of you always and forever. Mom

August 26

Hi, Bug, every time I sit down to write to you, which is becoming less often, I feel like the bearer of bad news. You had your 35th birthday July 20, and I usually write you then. However, it would be just about a copy of the one I wrote in March. Once again, your dad is doing poorly, and my heart is breaking. He did find another account for which he traveled from Michigan to Washington D. C. and loved it. He really wanted this one. I don't know how he managed to get by without drinking unless he drank just enough to avoid withdrawal. He will do just about anything for his job. This account required FBI clearance for him to stay long term. The morning the FBI came to visit, he was out working in the yard. I was surprised as he dislikes yard work. I had a particularly bad night with little sleep and was curled up on the couch in my robe with my head spinning and feeling like I wanted to die. I wanted him to get this account so I could be alone. I wanted him to go away. He came in the house and pulled me up off the couch. I froze up because I didn't know what he was going to do. He told me to relax. He hugged me and told me that he felt sorry for everything he had done, and he knew how much pain he caused, and he was never ever going to hurt me again. He was done drinking and our life was going to change. He promised. I cried because I needed to hear that so desperately.

After the FBI came and they talked to your dad, we went to dinner with Joanne and Ross. I felt my body relax. A blessed few hours of normal life, or what seemed normal. However, once the government did a check on his background and talked to the neighbors, he did not receive full clearance. Nor did he keep his promise. I didn't really believe him anyway. He blamed me for his losing the account. He had been truthful about his arrest on the forms. I reminded him that I had refused to press charges and that I just didn't want him to kill someone. His continuing to be employed is a miracle, and I am thankful that he is. I believe it's because he's so well liked and respected by his employees and co-workers. He had so much going for him. Also, I led them to believe he was struggling with depression. That, they would understand. And my telling his employers that instead of the truth is very co-dependent. I was helping him stay an alcoholic by lying for him. Maybe if I had been truthful when they called looking for him, they would have supported him and found him help. He may have changed for his job. If he were to be fired, he would lose his mind. His job and the respect of his employees mean so much to him. At this time, we are living apart as much as possible. He is at our cabin and working from there.

I often wonder if part of his pain and reason for numbing his feelings stem from the fact that Jamin and I remind him of you. Is that why he drinks when Jamin is around? Thinking back, just before I started my three spring classes (I had a two-week break), your dad was in a bad way. A couple of times I hid his keys as he slept, because I knew he would wake up and want to leave the house. Once I tossed them under our bed. Why was I living like this? Why was I hiding things from your dad? Why would anyone not want to get help when they are so addicted? Didn't he wonder where the hours and days went that he couldn't recall? It's not that he just enjoys it or wants to live his life passed out; it's because he's at a point where he can't live without it. He no longer has any control over his addiction. It controls him. He isn't your dad who would melt and do anything for you if you called him Daddy. He isn't the husband who would walk in the door and throw a compliment my way.

Hiding his keys did not go over well, and he reacted in such a way that I became very afraid of him. One time he was demanding them and started running after me. I told him I didn't want him to hurt someone. I grabbed my phone and ran outside, my heart pounding out of my chest. I called the police, and they came quickly. One officer talked to him, and one talked to me. He basically asked me why I was putting myself through this. He told me a story about his own mother and how his father's drinking nearly killed her.

Soon after, my PTSD symptoms returned as well as panic attacks and nightmares. I would dream that your dad was chasing me. I was afraid to go to sleep. My therapist told me I had been re-traumatized. This continued throughout the entire semester, and I do not know how I managed to get through it. I felt on the edge of a breakdown most of the time. Doesn't he realize he could kill someone just like a drunk driver killed you? That's where my fear comes from. If he kills himself, it's his doing. If he loses his job, it's his fault. If we lose our home, we would find a place to lay our heads. If he kills someone's child, mother, father, brother, sister, I could not live with that. I'm sure he couldn't either. He knows what a living hell it is. Again, I was attempting to appreciate every moment that seemed remotely normal. After the semester I had a bad week, but then started to meditate with some CD's my chiropractor suggested. They were making a difference and the panic and hyperarousal started to calm. I went off my sleep medication and was finally sleeping peacefully. It was wonderful! Dad and I tried not to be together.

Jamin requested a normal fourth of July weekend and drove to the cabin. Dad and I, wanting to please him, drove up together and for the first time in a while, he seemed good and life felt peaceful for a bit. We were both calm, and we talked. He mentioned that he had been drinking only wine in D.C. and that he hadn't had anything harder in a while. I wondered how he managed. I did remember your Aunt Cathie and I talking about the possibility that he may have been drinking at a family get together because he seemed so calm, and we were there for a long time. He never drank in front of people. I asked him if he had any alcohol at her house, because she and I wondered how he was doing so well. He calmly answered "No" and the subject was dropped. At least it was for me.

On the fourth he got very intoxicated on wine and started to talk about his family. I could tell he was angry that I asked him about the family party. I regretted it. You cannot talk to an alcoholic about drinking. You cannot even mention drinking. You must pretend that you have no idea what's going on so that the alcoholic can drink in peace. He stopped talking. We were sitting behind the cabin listening to the fireworks explode in the distance. It seemed like a normal evening. At times it was calm and relaxing. It was just the two of us as Jamin had gone to visit his cousin. I wanted it to stay this way forever.

The next morning when I woke up, he wasn't sleeping in his usual chair. I found him sitting in the backyard with a bottle sticking out of his pocket. He was barely conscious. I left him there. I let Jamin sleep, but when he woke up, I had to tell him. He was angry and hurt. He packed up his things and left. I sat down and cried. He had planned on spending the day with dad in the garage working on the snowmobiles, and he was disappointed. He just wanted some normal moments like me. He tried to create some. I realized I couldn't leave like Jamin did because your dad and I drove up together.

The next day dad decided to call his sister and complain about the two of us discussing his drinking. I don't know what he said to her as I wasn't close enough to hear. I just knew it wasn't good and I felt responsible. I grabbed my phone and got in the car. I started driving and called her. She was angry and asked that we never call her again. I didn't blame her and told her she wouldn't hear from us and hung up. I just drove around to clear my mind.

That evening, while he was passed out in the back yard, I did something I never thought I would do. I packed my bag, put the dogs in the car, and walked over to the neighbors. I told them where he was, that I couldn't wake him, and asked that they check on him in a few hours so he wouldn't get eaten by mosquitos. They were kind and agreed. I left him there without a car. I'm not sure how I even did that. He got a ride home the next day, took the other car, and went back up to the cabin.

So, Jenny, alcohol destroys all relationships and affects even those not living with the alcoholic. It's a shame, as everyone was so supportive and helpful in the beginning. After a time, one just gives up and waits. Your dad has lost 40 pounds and looks sickly. I spent the rest of the summer reading books on co-dependency and how to live with an alcoholic.

On August 16, he called from the cabin and was extremely depressed. I tried to explain once more that alcohol is a depressant. We talked for a while, and he seemed to feel better. I told him to call me if he needed something. He sounded as if even he was getting sick of the situation. Around midnight, I got another call. He wanted to tell Jamin and me that he loved us. We talked again for a while, and I made him promise to call 911 or me if he got too bad. He promised. He said he wasn't suicidal. My carefully bandaged heart started bleeding again. The next day he came home and said he never wanted to go back up to the cabin alone again. Of course, I said he wouldn't have to.

I was heading out to a seminar on trauma in Traverse City, so he stayed home with the dogs while I was gone for four days. I thought maybe, just maybe, he would try not to drink. As I sat in a Traverse City coffee shop feeling some peace, I called to see how he was doing. I started to regret going to the seminar just when he wanted to come home. I had already planned on it and paid for it. He sounded like he was drunk. That night I had panic attack after panic attack in my hotel room just from hearing his voice. Jenny, am I doing the right thing? Should I have stayed home with him watching his every move and falling right into co-dependency mode? When I got home, I asked him to go right back up north. No problem—he went.

I went to a clinic yesterday and talked to someone about getting on a medication that would control the panic. I started one last night and for some reason I was up all night and had a headache today. I went to breakfast with your Aunt Carol and Uncle Jerry and could hardly function. I'll try taking the pill in the morning instead of before bed. I just have to get through the next six months or so with school and who knows what else. I'm not depressed but can go right into panic and fear of what may lie ahead. I am reading books on mindfulness and living in the moment and hoping that my meditations will do as they say and raise my threshold that has been lowered by trauma. Where there is a will, there is a way.

On a lighter note, your brother has tried dating again, Erin went off to college, and Grandma Ginny is now in assisted living. Jackie is doing well, and not much else has changed. I still have three little puppies that keep me company. Also, I am thankful! I am thankful for the time I had you, your wonderful brother, my family, my faithful friends Joanne and Ross and their kids, my education, my health, my home, my woods, my peace and quiet, and for HOPE. I will write you again Jenny and keep you posted on the life and times of your crazy family. Love always, Mom.

2011

August 22

Dear Jenny, I've been waiting much too long to write you. So much has happened, and again, where do I even begin? If I wrote you more often, it would be so much easier. The fact that I'm writing less is a good thing. I think it's a sign of healing and of letting go, to a certain degree.

Why is it so hard to write something you may already know? Did you go and get him like I dream you will do for me someday? Or, were you just there waiting for him? Did you run to him with open arms? Was he ecstatic to see you again?

I received a phone call as I was exercising. I stopped the video and ran for the phone. The voice on the other end said, "He's gone." I wasn't sure who it was, but then she said her name. It was the woman your dad let live in the front of the cabin with her three children while he lived in the back office with the second bathroom. She had lost her home. Once he let them move in, which I understand, Jamin could no longer go up to visit your dad. I knew her and her children. Your dad and I both did. She was your age and we loved her little girl because she looked like you. They would come over and visit. It took me a few minutes to figure out what she meant. I had just talked to your dad a few weeks before, and he sounded fine. She was hysterical. As usual, as the reality of her words began to sink in, I found myself trying to calm her. At the same time, I started to feel my own emotions welling up inside of me. Did she say he was gone?

I started crying and talking at the same time. She explained that she hadn't really been there but staying at her boyfriend's house. Your dad had been drinking too much. She went to the cabin for something or other and found him. He died all alone. Even his friends left him. She called the police, and they took him to a funeral home. On August 15, 2011, on a Monday morning, your dad was finally with you again. I told her I would talk to her later. I broke down and sobbed.

When I pulled myself together, I called Jamin, Aunt Cathie, and then your Aunt Carol. Telling Jamin was one of the hardest things I've ever had to do.

He calmly said, "I'll be there in 40 minutes."

I responded, "Be careful."

Carol said she would be over soon as well. I made additional phone calls. When he arrived, your brother and I held each other. He was still calm. He said he had mentally prepared himself for this moment.

When I spoke to your Aunt Cathie earlier, we thought it might be a good idea to cremate his remains and then have a service near home. Jamin agreed. However, Aunt Carol, who always comes through in a crisis, asked if we didn't want to see him first. I didn't even think of that. Jamin said he would like to, and I agreed. We asked your Aunt Laurie and Uncle Tim if we could stay with them at their home in West Branch for the night so we could go to Houghton Lake to see your dad and make arrangements. Your cousin Brian came to support Jamin. Within 30 minutes, with two dogs in tow, we were on our way.

Jamin, Brian, and I went directly to Laurie and Tim's. We talked about your dad and tried to keep it light. We spent the night, and then Jamin, Brian, and I went to see your dad at the funeral home. Brian waited in the car, and your brother and I went in. My heart pounded and ached as we walked toward his body laid out for us. He lay as if he were sleeping. I can't describe how it felt to look at my husband of 39 years dead before me. Useless might be a word. It didn't have to happen. I loved him, and so did Jamin. We both spent time alone with him and said our goodbyes. My heart ached more for Jamin than for myself. We might feel we had been abandoned for alcohol, but we are smart enough to know that it wasn't your father that left us, but his addiction. It was never his plan to die this way.

2012

March 12

Jenny, I never did finish the last entry. At least it hasn't been a year. There was so much to tell you that I felt overwhelmed. The only comfort I had was that, most likely, you already knew about everything. I'll start where I left off. The day your dad passed, Jamin and I went to see him and say goodbye for the last time. He had himself under control for a while before he died. He had been having health problems and trying to stay away from alcohol. His doctor told him it was life or death. He even got a job at Wal-Mart in the produce section and loved it. He made friends. He sounded good on the phone. We talked often. He would text me as well. Once, while we were still married, he called and told me he drove himself to Urgent Care because he couldn't feel his legs and they were swollen. He had been sitting in his chair for days. They had rushed him to the hospital in West Branch. I grabbed my books and ran up there to be with him. When I got there, he was complaining about how they wouldn't let him eat because he had an inflamed pancreas. He was angry, impatient, and yelling out loud at the nurses. I felt bad for them. He was in withdrawal.

I must have already started to harden my heart. He yelled so loud that I picked up my things, went to the cabin, gathered up my dogs, and drove back home all in the same day. All the way home, he called me begging me to return and saying he was sorry. I couldn't do it. I couldn't answer the phone. It was killing me inside. I wanted to answer. He called and left so many messages. It was the beginning of regaining my self-respect. It was the end of codependency. I thought back. It reminded me of the weekend in California when he left me for two days and never answered my calls, though I begged him to come back.

I remember calling him and telling him I needed shoulder surgery in January of 2010. He was silent. He was shocked. I didn't blame him. I just said it was an old injury. I had damaged my shoulder when he threw me down while trying to get his keys. I knew something was wrong but thought it was my carpal tunnel returning. I had three screws put in my shoulder. I had been going through so much trauma that I didn't notice something was wrong.

Then he ended up in the hospital again due to heart issues. While he was there, he found out he had to wear a vest that would shock his heart into rhythm if it should stop. I don't know as many details as I would if we were still married. He needed to have some stents put in before he could discontinue the vest. Needless to say, he couldn't return to work. I believe he did get one stent put in and, though the next was scheduled, he never showed up for the procedure. Soon after, Jamin called and told me that your dad had received a DUI and was in jail. I wondered why he was in jail. Do people go to jail for their first DUI? Jamin told me the truth. I never knew about the first one as Jamin was instructed not to tell me. Your dad had given me some money because he left me the house payment. I unknowingly sent him the money to pay his fines for the first one. I thought I was helping him pay off a credit card debt. But after the second one, Jamin felt compelled to be honest with me. This one would be much more serious and the penalty much more severe.

After this second offense, having his license taken away, and a lock put on his car, he must have felt hopeless. He continued to drink until his heart stopped. As I write this, my heart aches. *This is just so sad* I say to myself as I type. Did it all happen because you died, or would it have happened anyway? Did I handle it all wrong? Was I missing something I should have seen?

Your father was cremated up north, and your Aunt Laurie and Uncle Tim brought him home. Laurie carried him on her lap and wept all the way home. Within a few days, Jamin and I planned a funeral. Jackie came home from Seattle and she, Jamin, and I went up to our church and talked with Pastor. We planned a ceremony. We wrote letters to your dad. I ordered food. People were called who then called others. Flowers were ordered. We had a beautiful memorial on August 20, 2011. People your father worked with, friends I hadn't seen in a long time, and relatives I had left behind when I moved on, attended. I think your dad would have been pleased. Jamin is keeping the ashes for now. I still have yours. Hopefully we will get a plot for the two of you and, though I said I would never let him have your ashes with him if he passed, I have since changed my mind. I was angry then. I will get a beautiful head stone that says you are together again and have you near my home.

Jamin's Letter

Let me tell you why my dad was a patient man. Many of you might be wondering if I'm talking about the same Jim Smith most of you knew, but I'll try to explain. One time my mom and I decided to go up north for the weekend. I had previously found some of my dad's old boots from when he was in the Air Force, and I insisted on wearing them. Combat boots were cool at the time. The fact that they didn't fit properly wasn't going to stop me from wearing them. I don't think I had my license yet, but when my mom and I got to the dirt road our cabin was on, she let me drive the rest of the way. When we arrived, I pulled up to the front of the cabin and had to hit the gas pedal to get up onto the driveway. Thanks to the ill-fitting boots I was wearing, I accidentally ran the car through the new front porch addition my dad had just finished building a few weeks earlier. My mom and I both looked at each other in disbelief, and the first thing we said was, "How are we going to tell dad!?"

After managing to squeeze through the mangled front door, we paced back and forth for a while trying to figure out how we would tell him what had happened. We had convinced ourselves he was going to be furious. After all, his hard work was just smashed to pieces. My mom eventually picked up the phone to call him and explain the situation. The first thing my dad said was, "Are you guys okay?" After my mom explained we were fine, he said, "Well, as long as you guys are okay, that's all I care about. It's just a porch, and it can be fixed." He never got mad at me...or my mom for letting me drive. He knew that disasters happen, and they can be fixed. However, I still blame the whole thing on those combat boots.

It was the little things that irritated him the most...Like dropping a screw while he was working on something or even worse...a screaming child. But when major life events came about, that's when my dad showed up for people.

Just as my dad might bore you with one of his work stories, I could also bore you with a million stories that would describe what a smart, incredible, funny and giving man he was. While I miss him terribly, it comforts me to know that he is finally at peace and with my sister. I was and always will be proud of him.

My Letter

Dear Jim,

Thirty-nine years is a long time. Like most married couples, we had our good times and our bad. We shared so much, we gained so much, and we lost so much. We made many good decisions, such as having two of the greatest children a couple could hope for, but some of our decisions could have been better.

When someone we love passes, we travel back in time and in our mind's eye we see all the positive experiences we shared as well as the negative. However, today I have made a choice. I choose to remember the great times, the times we made the right choices, the times we were courageous, the times we stood strong together, and the times we laughed so hard we couldn't breathe.

I remember how you were with our children and how you sometimes handled difficult discipline decisions so much better than I did. I would send Jenny to her room, and you would go up and talk to her calmly. Instead of getting angry with Jamin, you would tell him he "made an error in judgment." When our children made a mistake, you never shamed them.

I remember how the neighborhood kids would come over and ask if Jim was home. They liked to hang out with you. You made kids feel welcome and boosted their self-worth. You treated them with respect.

I remember your co-workers approaching me at work-related gatherings just to mention what a great boss you were or how you helped and supported them. I would say "My Jim?" However, I always felt proud of you.

I could go on and on if I had the time to remember all the good stuff. For today, and always, that is what I choose to remember. In my heart,

I had the best mother, a great father, and a daughter anyone would be proud of. I've been told I put people who have passed on a pedestal. I can't think of a better place for them to be.

I envy your blessed reunion with our daughter Jennifer. I know you feel joyous in seeing her face once more and that the two of you will soar through the heavens never to be parted again.

Emerson wrote:

To laugh often, to win the affection of children, to earn the appreciation of honest critics and endure the betrayal of false friends, to appreciate beauty, to find the best in others, to leave the world a bit better, whether by a healthy child, a garden patch...to know even one life has breathed easier because you have lived. This is to have succeeded!

Love,

Toots

Now I know why I have stayed away from writing you for such long periods of time. It was just too painful. Though I have written you all about your dad's last days and his death, I haven't told you how my life has changed. In order for me to tell you where I am at right now, I have to go back in time to where I left off in August of 2008. That was my last letter before your dad joined you. I remember telling you that I had to go on medication for panic attacks and that even though your dad said he never wanted to go up north alone again, he was only home four days. I don't mean to make this confusing and I will try and summarize as best I can. There were periods of calm, but they were short-lived. That seemed to be the pattern. As time went on, I thought surely your dad would die from falling, driving, or an alcohol reaction. The last time I called 911, a not-so-wonderful hospital told me to come and pick him up because it wasn't a place for drunks to dry out. I was exhausted and I took my time getting there. I didn't want to pick him up. I didn't get there until late morning. He was furious and he left for the cabin. That was our first missed Thanksgiving. He never called to come home.

Shortly before Christmas of that same year your dad did call. He said he had quit drinking on his own and hadn't had a drink for a while. That would be a first. He wanted to come home. I said yes. Why? Because he had never quit on his own before. I don't think he wanted to be alone on Christmas. But I realized something. I was the addict addicted to helping an alcoholic. I thought I was being strong by asking him to leave. And why wouldn't he? He could go up and hang with his friends and drink all he wanted. He could switch back and forth between his family and his drinking buddies. I have been blessed/cursed with an undying hope.

We had a great 2008 Christmas. We were all so happy. We were all so hopeful. I was on break from classes and had just finished my practicum. He did it on his own. I thought that was what it took. Every other time, he had been forced for some reason or other. This time, it was his decision. We knew he would do it this time. He needed us and loved us. We went out for dinner with Cathie and Chuck for New Years. We had a nice time. I told them about a grief group I was going to start at a church. I was excited to use my practicum proposal that was accepted by the university. Life felt normal. I suppose normal is different for everyone.

On January 3, 2009, Jamin was to come over for Irish stew and to set up a computer game I received for Christmas. Your dad seemed to sleep a lot that day while I busied myself with chores. One of his favorite things was napping in his chair. By the time Jamin got there, I couldn't wake your dad. We knew it. Why should it be any different? But Jamin said something again that reached down into the depths of my soul and crushed my heart.

"Why does Dad seem to get drunk whenever I come over?" he asked.

I had no answer for him. I simply said, "It doesn't have anything to do with you." But it reminded me of a remark Jamin had made that hit hard. He had once told me I lived a miserable existence. Jamin doesn't say much, but what he says comes from his heart and he gives it a lot of thought. Why was I allowing myself to be miserable most of the time? Why was I so forgiving? I think I know why. I didn't want to lose the little bit of family I had left.

Jamin and I played the computer game right in front of your dad. We golfed, and we bowled, making lots of noise. We had fun. Dad didn't stir. We had our stew. Jamin went home. It was as if we weren't affected. We were so used to being together with Jim passed out that we went on as usual. After Jamin left, I sat there alone with him. I watched your dad and my husband of many years. I watched his stomach going up and down. I stared at his face which was aged and tired, though still handsome. I listened to his snore that shot through my nervous system. I can't do this to myself anymore, and I can't do this to Jamin. This can no longer be my life. I went into the kitchen and wrote a note. I said, "When you wake up in the morning, please go back up north. And…this time do not come back home." When I woke up, he was gone.

A couple of weeks later, your dad called to let me know he had lost his job. He said he was retired. I knew better. I told him that I expected it, and that I had given up on our marriage. I had told him years ago that there were three things that would end "us" forever. One would be killing or hurting someone, the second would be a DUI, and the third would be losing his job because of his drinking. If he lost his job, it would mean that the one thing he truly loved doing, that gave him the most satisfaction, would no longer matter. He had given up everything to alcohol. He proceeded to tell me how our divorce would go. Again, he was controlling my life. I guess he had it all planned out. He knew I couldn't stay in the marriage. He knew his drinking was making me ill. I agreed to everything he said.

I didn't file right away. I was scared. Maybe I thought something would change. Finally, on February 9, 2009 I called a lawyer I had contacted two years earlier when I was terrified. The process began. I promised to tell you where I am in my story, and I am ready.

As I sit here writing to you, my husband Tom has just left for his Monday night bowling league. Before Christmas 2008, Tom, a man I had met through the University, had called and asked me to help him start a grief group at his church. We had said our goodbyes at the end of the semester before your dad came home for our last Christmas together.

When Tom first called, I didn't think I was qualified and not even sure if it was possible for me to help him. I remember talking to your dad about it. Your dad and I thought I should call my practicum professor and ask her advice. I finally decided to call her and tell her about the situation. She said it would be alright as long as I didn't "counsel" people, as I was not yet licensed. I thought about it for a few days. In fact, if that professor had told me it wasn't a good idea, I would have said no to Tom. I would have never talked to him or seen him again.

I called Tom back, and through emails, we set up subjects for group gatherings. He had lost his wife six months earlier, and many other church members had losses as well. He asked if I would attend the first meeting at his home with other church members. I found out he lived ten minutes down the road. He had lived there since he was in his twenties. In fact, before the first meeting, your dad and I had gone to the movies during his last Christmas home. Tom arrived at the theater to save places for his children. I introduced them, and your dad even saved the places while Tom went to look for his children and grandchildren. They couldn't get tickets. and Tom went home. So, your dad met him.

We had our first grief meeting December 29, and I met many people. There was a heavy, blinding snowstorm that night, and I almost cancelled. I remember how uncomfortable I was. One lady, Millie, came over to me and was so charming and friendly that I felt like I had known her forever. She and her husband had buried two sons. I went home and told your dad all about the meeting. It was just five days after that meeting that I asked your dad to leave and never return.

We had a second meeting on January 11 at the church. We had all brought letters written to our loved ones that had passed. This was my letter to you:

> Dear Jenny,
>
> Recently, I was asked to write a letter about what I miss about you. I find the question easy, as I miss everything. I miss the little infant I held in my arms that opened up a world of possibilities. I miss the shy little white-haired toddler whose inquisitiveness could destroy a room in five minutes. I miss reading to you and your brother and getting you both bathed and ready for bed so you could watch your favorite television show. I miss putting your hair into braids and pigtails as we readied you for school. I long for the days we went shopping for your Christmas and Easter dresses.
>
> As much as I disliked it at the time, I would live every teenage argument we had over again just to spend the time with you. If I had it to do over, I would worry less about

how you should behave and appreciate your quest for independence. I miss your bursting into the house with a quick "Hi, Mom," so you could run up to your room and call a friend. I miss the times I held you while you cried over a friend's insensitivity or a boyfriend's betrayal. There is a longing for the times you came close to my face and imitated, and highly exaggerated, my grin. I can see you standing in front of the refrigerator, searching, and saying, "Here we are in Ethiopia."

When I look at your photos, I miss your inner and outer beauty, and I am in awe of the fact that I even gave birth to such a lovely young woman. I still cannot stare at your picture longer than a few seconds at a time as I fear getting lost in your eyes and feeling that all-too-familiar pain of grief. There is no real need for a photo, as your entire being and the sound of your voice is forever imprinted on my heart and in my memory. Often, when I look at your brother, I see a glimpse of you, and I wonder how he ever went on without his sister who seemed his hero and protector.

Jenny, I miss the woman you could have become. Would your wedding have been exactly as you used to describe it? Would you have had that giant bowl of shrimp? You would have made a breathtaking bride. If you were here today, would you have those two little boys who looked like Jesse? You talked of having babies someday, but always spoke of boys.

I miss all the Jennys I raised, but I miss the woman you would have become, and realize that you would have continued to bring so much joy to our family and your friends. I try to imagine what you would be like now, how you would wear your hair, and if you would still be obsessed with exercise and keeping healthy. Would you be a stay-at-home mom, or a career woman? However, I realize that these things are not important, as you are exactly where you are supposed to be. You are with God and his angels. You walk with Jesus and sing with angels. Your spirit, along with the spirits of all loved ones, contributes to the glory of Heaven. You are exactly where God needs you to be. You are Home.

Love,

Mom

After that meeting, Tom came up to me and gave such a warm, comforting hug. It felt so safe. It felt honest and sincere. Tom went on to lead the adult group, while I worked with the children. Many grandchildren and cousins were mourning in that church. Tom became a friend and then one day called and asked me to breakfast to thank me for my help. We talked for a while and ended up going to a movie across from the restaurant. I told him I needed to leave and go to OU to buy my books for my last semester of grad school. He asked to go with me. We were both lonely. Even so, I was uncomfortable at times, and I told him so. I was still married. He has a kind disposition, a most gentle manner, and a compassionate heart. He is a retired schoolteacher who taught at the school you and Jamin attended, but we never met him.

Because of his religion, he has never taken a drink of alcohol. We found out that we had both said a prayer that brought us together. Most recently, he prayed for someone to help with his loneliness; years ago, I prayed because all I wanted was to love the person I was married to and feel loved in return. He feels we have answered each other's prayers, and that we were meant to meet and bring peace to each other's lives.

I tried more than once to warn him of my past traumas and how they affect me emotionally. I told him that we both needed time to heal and deal with our losses before dating. I thought it best that we wait and just be friends for a while. He agreed to give me time. One day he called, and I was feeling quite lost. Once again, I told him that I shouldn't be with anyone. I was a mess. I tried to talk him into letting me go. Finally, he said something that affected me deeply. He said, "But I love you." I put the phone down. I had to compose myself. Why? Because it sounded real. For the first time in ages, I believed a man. But I had concerns about my family and his children. My family thought the almost eight-year difference in our ages, with Tom being older, was too much. I worried about your dad, but your dad met Tom and liked him. In fact, your dad's common response to others was, "He's a much nicer guy than I am." Tom was a tax preparer, and your dad liked that he could do our taxes.

One day I agreed to go watch him bowl. I watched the way he interacted with others, and again I felt that feeling of contentment. He asked me to marry him and again I sat on his couch telling him all the reasons why we shouldn't. Though I and others thought everything happened a bit too fast, I have no regrets. Every day, I feel myself working through my pain and healing. Tom allows me to have my grief over you and your father. He understands and accepts me, no matter how flawed or damaged I may be. He has brought me back to life.

> *Happiness turned to me and said, "It is time. It is time to forgive yourself for all of the things you did not become. It is time to exonerate yourself for all the people you couldn't save, for all the fragile hearts you fumbled with in the dark of your confusion. It is time, child, to accept that you don't have to be who you were a year ago, that you don't have to want the same things. Above all else, it is time to believe, with reckless abandon, that you are worthy of me, for I have been waiting for years."*
> (Bianca Sparacino)
> *"Seeds Planted in Concrete,"* Thought Catalog Books

On October 11, 2009, we married under a gazebo at the golf course where Tom worked after retirement. Millie, the kindhearted person who approached me at the first grief meeting, married us. Jamin, who had been living in Arizona after following a girlfriend, came home and gave me away. Aunt Jackie was my maid of honor. Tom's son Brent was his best man. Erin was my flower girl, and Tom's grandson Ashton our ring bearer. Jackie sang the most beautiful song…about the God of second chances. Here we are.

Tom and Jamin also attended my graduation for my master's in counseling in April of 2009. I finally completed it, Jenny. I honored your memory. I was hired by the mental health clinic where I did my internship. I work there still. I started a private practice with the very name I used when writing a paper in California. I started Jennifer's Heart Counseling.

I didn't advertise and only had a few clients. However, I decided that it wouldn't be right to bring my pain into my practice. I recently changed the name to Hope House Counseling, and I have an office right here in Tom's home. Hope is what got me here. We put a big front porch on the front of the house with a swing and rocking chairs. We made his house our home. I am finally at peace.

We lost two of my puppies a year ago. Hannah was almost 16, and Moose died of heart failure at 10. They have little graves in the back yard. Buddy is still with us at 13. He was so lonely that Jamin went to Arizona to visit a friend and brought us back another Chihuahua we call Mesa.

Your parting has taught me so much; it has brought me such strength and courage. I read a million books because of you, I became a Stephen Minister because of you, I collected a million teddy bears because of you, I wrote music because of you, and I chose to live fully because of you. Today I posted something on Facebook along with your photo. This month, on March 26, you will have been gone for 18 years, the time it would take you to grow from infancy to adulthood. This is what I posted:

> Grief doesn't go away. We learn to adjust and cope. We find a way to work it into who we are. We are never the same. We are forced to find what works for us as individuals. Some try to run and hide from grief. Some absorb it into their souls and walk around with their broken hearts still beating. Their pain is only relieved by keeping their loved one alive through service to others. I mothered you for twenty years Jenny. Without you, I realized my entire identity changed. When you died, you gained a new identity and a new existence, and I have done the same. I'll love you forever Bug, Mom

2016

July 20

My dearest Jennifer, Happy birthday, 43 year old. I knew I would write you today. I was 43 when you transitioned (*transition* is my favorite word for death now). It's a surreal feeling. It's somewhat similar to how

I felt when I turned 45, knowing that my own mother transitioned at that age. Here I am, 65 years old, when the two of you passed away so young. As far as I know or can tell, I am in good health. Today, Tom and I drove home from Hillman, Michigan, where I have a little log home. I purchased it last January. It is my own. I live in Tom's house now, and Jamin, Devina, and Arjun live in the house I shared with your dad. So, I didn't really have a home of my own. Now I do, and I feel safe. Plus, I have my serenity place once more. We got home in time to pick Arjun up from his Montessori school at three p.m. We then went to buy yellow roses for you. We drove to the cemetery where you and your father are buried together. Arjun helped place the roses on your headstone. He is so precious, Jenny. But Arjun is another story.

I posted something special for your birthday on Facebook yesterday, because I knew I would be busy today. I enjoyed reading the earlier ones as well, as it's so nice to hear from all your friends and family members that still miss you.

July 19

Tomorrow, July 20, my daughter Jennifer turns 43. I was 43 the year we lost her. I could go on about her and how my heart aches every day, but I can also share my gratitude for those 20 years she gave me immense joy and filled my life with wonder. She wasn't perfect, and she gave me some major headaches. There were those worrisome evenings waiting for her to walk through the door so I could finally sleep, but that's parenthood. One day, I gave birth to a beautiful baby girl. She was the greatest gift, and I never felt such love. I kept her healthy and safe as long as I could. Even knowing what I know now, I would do it all again if only I could have those 20 years. The gap between our reunion in Heaven is narrowing. Those of you reading this post, please honor Jenny today by doing something special for someone else. Please remember that no matter what your trials or frustrations, you are here for a reason, and you have the gift of life.

Happy birthday, Jen-Bug.

Epilogue

2019

August

Dear Jenny,

It took so long to put all my journals, audio tapes, and computer letters together that I feel it's only fair to catch up with all those mentioned in your letters. Even if you already know what's happening down here (smile), others that read this may want to know where we all are now.

Jamin, Devina, and Arjun

Eight years ago, at your dad's memorial, a beautiful young woman walked in by herself. I noticed her right away when she was talking to Jamin. I walked over, and Jamin introduced us. She was lovely with long dark hair and the most beautiful eyes I have ever seen. She was also kind and personable. Jamin had mentioned Devina to me previously as a friend he had in his master's program at the university.

She hadn't been in the States for very long but spoke perfect English. She had come from India, after finishing her degree, to join her mother Anjali, and brother Kunal, who had already settled in Michigan. Her mother had married Deven, a man from India who had been in Michigan for quite some time.

I later learned that Devina had become infatuated with your brother while he was still nursing a broken heart from his long-distance Arizona relationship, and Jamin told me they had made plans to hang out together right before your dad's death. A month after the memorial, Jamin and

Devina began to date. Our family loved her immediately. Tom and I met her family, and they were kind and hospitable. Anjali and Deven prepared delicious Indian food, and we got together quite a few times.

We soon learned that Devina's mother was fighting brain cancer and we were all hopeful that Anjali would beat the disease. Deven had two children of his own but counted Devina and her brother Kunal as his. He would say he has four children. I loved him for that.

Jamin and Devina continued to date, and we all celebrated when we learned that they had eloped on May 3, 2013. Anjali called me to share the good news, and she expressed her happiness that her daughter was able to marry for love. They moved into the home your dad, Jamin and I shared before I married Tom. I still owned it since Jamin had moved in after he returned from Arizona.

We had a wonderful backyard reception with friends, family, and five dogs—and one of the five tried to snatch cake off of the tables and ripped the tablecloths in the process. It rained on and off, and at one point it poured. The paper tablecloths hung from the tables and littered the lawn. Thank God I had a tent. My well-organized party had an unexpected ending, and I totally lost control, but Anjali did an Indian marriage blessing and taught me to do it as well. The rain can't kill the mood when there is so much happiness and love. I only wish your dad could have met Devina.

In December of 2013, Jamin and Devina left for India and were given a beautiful Indian wedding complete with authentic clothes and all the ceremonial traditions. Devina's friends planned this ceremony and even had people stand in for her parents and Tom and me, as we couldn't be there. They had a wonderful time and Jamin met Devina's friends.

Jamin and Devina both started new jobs and continue to be employed in the same positions. Jamin didn't go the counseling route, but Devina did. She has a government job and is doing very well.

And now for the best news ever. In January of 2014, Devina and Jamin came over to see Tom and me. I knew something was up but had no idea what. They were both smiling.

"We wanted to tell you that we are expecting," said Devina shyly. Jamin sat on the floor. My mind was still trying to absorb what she just said.

"When is the baby due?" I asked cautiously, as if she was going to say she was just kidding.

"In August," said Jamin, who still had a huge grin on his face.

I jumped up and ran over to him with no idea of what to say or how to react, as I had never been in this situation before.

"Oh, my God, you made a baby," I shouted as I hugged him. I felt silly, as if I sounded like didn't think Jamin was capable of creating life. No matter how old he was, he was my little boy. I ran over and hugged Devina as well. And so, it all began.

Once again Anjali and I talked, congratulating each other on being first-time grandparents. We were both on cloud nine. We must hold on tight to those blessed feelings of joy for the times when life tries to steal them away. When Devina was only three months pregnant, she and I drove to her mother's home to say our good-byes. Devina went in with her mother and Anjali passed away quietly.

Grieving during pregnancy was difficult for Devina. She had trouble eating and was nauseous. It was so hard on Kunal who, at the time, had no partner to comfort him. How would Deven go on without the love of his life? Life was not fair for this beautiful, selfless woman who had already endured so much before finding Deven. It wasn't fair that Devina and Kunal would follow their mother to this country only to lose her.

If we are patient in our grief, joy finds us again. On August 27, 2014, little Arjun James came into this world at only four pounds and eleven ounces. He was almost full term yet so tiny, but he was also strong and ready to take on the world. Love swallowed me up as I saw him come into this world, and it still engulfs me today. Jenny, I can't even imagine how much you would love this little guy. He steals everyone's heart when he walks up and introduces himself. His eyes are magical, and his empathy is strong. I think of the time Jamin went to see your dad in the hospital up north. He was pleading for his dad's life in his own way. "What if I have kids one day, Dad?" I am sorry that your dad did not choose to stay around for the possibilities. It's the possibilities that fuel me.

"Hi, my name is Arjun," he says brightly. He then goes on to ask whoever he's talking to about themselves and tells them about something he has with him or at home…usually, a toy car.

I have been blessed to spend a great deal of time with Arjun. Though he has his moments, he steals my heart afresh every day. I am Nana, and Tom is Papa Tom. Deven is Abba. It breaks my heart to think of your father and Anjali missing this precious gift. Someone told us that your father and Anjali got to hold Arjun before he was born. I hope that is true. Arjun is a new story within this already long compilation of letters to you. But every book has to end somewhere and at some time.

On May 14, Devina became an American citizen at a ceremony in Detroit. I'm so proud of her for taking the journey. It was exciting to see so many individuals from many different countries go up to the judge and get their certificates. I had goosebumps from watching. Your Aunt Carol and Uncle Jerry attended also. Kunal came with his new bride Sruthi. They wanted to experience this moment with Devina.

Afterwards, when it was just a few of us, Devina told us she had taken a pregnancy test just that morning and it was positive. We were all congratulatory, but once again I thanked God, and once again, I was on cloud nine.

"Hi, my name is Arjun. My mama has a new baby in her tummy. It's a boy, like me," he now says to people we meet in the store or that stop by our home.

Arjun kisses his mama's tummy when he arrives home from school and before bed. He will be five this month, and our new little man is due in January of 2020.

Your Aunts, Uncles, and Cousins

As you remember, Jenny, we were always close to your dad's side of the family. We saw them at Christmas and at summer hot dog parties. As the cousins grew up, they tried to connect with Jamin more often and be there for him after you left us. He didn't feel like doing much of anything other than playing his music, but they tried, and I appreciate that. Since my marriage to Tom and your dad's death I only see Aunt Cathie. Most of the cousins are married and have children. I keep up with most on Facebook. (What is Facebook Mom?)

Since your dad died, we lost your Uncle Bill when he had a heart attack at Aunt Cathie's hot dog party. I wasn't there, but Jamin and Devina were. I went over after work to be with the family. Then your Aunt Lynn, Bill's wife, died suddenly. We went to the funerals and that's the last time I've seen the cousins except for Tracy, who is married with two boys. Cathie and I meet for lunch and, once in a while, Tracy is there as well. Lynn and Tracy wrote poems when you passed. I included them in this book because they loved you and their writings were beautiful. We have such excellent memories.

My sisters' children were like your brothers and sisters. We all lived close and, even after your death, we have stayed the same. So many changes have occurred since you left. We lost our dear Uncle George in November 2011. This loss was just a few months after your father. He and Aunt Jackie were the last family members left of our parents' generation. Uncle George was so good to us. He loved to start conversations just to see what our take was on things. Once when I was taking a break from cleaning for them, he sat me down and asked why I volunteered so much, why I was going back to college, and why I wasn't angry about your death. He expressed how angry he was when his own mother died and how he stayed angry. I didn't know how he could understand as he had no faith, but I explained my views to him. In summary, first, what good would it do for me, my family, and my health if I were to hold on to anger? Who should I be angry at? The person who killed you was dead. I couldn't be angry at God because he is my only hope that I will see you again. He didn't agree with me, but he complimented me on my strength. That meant a great deal to me.

Aunt Jackie didn't take her husband's death well at all. He was the love of her life. She slowed down tremendously. The life went out of her. When Tom and I went to Florida to visit her the January after Uncle George passed, she could hardly walk and had to keep sitting to rest. She was 88 years old, but it was hard to see her change so much. Somehow, your cousin Jackie pulled a trip together, and in August 2012 Aunt Jackie, now 89, took our family to the Czech Republic for ten days. She perked up a great deal. She wanted us to see our grandparents' homeland, or what my Grandfather Becker called the old country. It was the trip of a lifetime, but Aunt Jackie tired easily. She, my sisters and I, and our husbands would all go back to our rooms tired from exploring all day while our kids would go out and explore the nightlife and a good Czech beer. I remember hoping you were with them.

Somehow Aunt Jackie got the energy to fly back to Florida again that fall. We were worried about her being there alone, but she had great friends. Your cousins and my sisters would call her, and they wondered if she was drinking more than her usual evening Manhattan. Her voice was sometimes slurred. She also cried often, which was not normal for this strong woman. My sisters and I went down to see her for her 90th birthday, and Carol planned a small party. She was so quiet and spoke very little due to her voice. She was scared to turn 90, and when her cake arrived all fluffy and colorful, she put her hands over her face and cried.

We had a wonderful time with her in Florida, but when she came home in the spring her voice was getting worse. Your Aunt Carol took charge and got her in for some medical tests. She was getting harder to understand, and we got her a whiteboard to write on. She was finally diagnosed with ALS or Amyotrophic Lateral Sclerosis, also known as Lou Gehrig's disease. When she and your Aunt Carol got home from the doctor, again Aunt Jackie put her hands over her face and cried. Then she looked it up in a medical book. Then she asked if it was hereditary because even then she was concerned about us. From what we learned, 95% of cases are not hereditary. She also had Bulbar ALS, which means that muscles involved in speaking, swallowing, and breathing are the first to be affected. Hence, the slurred speech. We learned that Bulbar is more common in women and people over seventy.

Aunt Jackie has mothered us, you and your cousins included, ever since our mother passed and probably even before. She was at the hospital when our babies were born. She was the matriarch of our family. She took us everywhere, and we experienced so much more of life than we would have without her. She was our mom's best friend, and when she babysat for us, we cried when we had to go home. My mother wasn't jealous. Aunt Jackie couldn't have children of her own, so we were shared, and we loved it. When people would ask my mother about her children's attachment to their aunt, she would just tell them that we knew who our mother was.

Aunt Jackie took care of Uncle George, his children and grandchildren, my sisters and me, and our children.

When we received the diagnosis, we decided we would do what she had done for us—we would be there. I quit my job at the mental health clinic, Carol quit her job at a day care center, and Aunt Laurie was already retired. We took turns staying with her, determined that she was not going in a home. She was never alone. It's more of a story than I could possibly write to you, Jenny. She wasn't sure she wanted a feeding tube, and we all cried. She would die very soon if she didn't. We didn't want her to starve to death. She changed her mind. We had so much to learn about caring for her. It wasn't easy, and sometimes we had squabbles. We had schedules to keep, and things constantly changed. Because of past traumas, I became easily overwhelmed when we adjusted the schedule. People and helpers were in and out. Nighttime was the most difficult. It was so lonely because we couldn't talk or eat together. I didn't want to eat in front of her. She would point at my food and then at her mouth. She missed eating. Aunt Jackie sat in her chair watching television all night. I tried sleeping upstairs but woke up every 30 minutes to make sure she was okay. I finally started sleeping on the couch with the television on. We got very little sleep when we were there. Stressful situations occurred, and sometimes we had to call 911.

But, being the optimist and peacemaker that I am, I remember so much love and joyful moments. Sitting and feeding her, writing jokes on the whiteboard, watching fun movies and her giving a thumbs up or a thumbs down when it ended, folding laundry while she slept. She would smile at me while I was vacuuming because she was always used to me cleaning. We watched the deer feed on apples, brought by Tom from our backyard. Jamin, Devina, and your cousins came over to carve pumpkins on the floor as she watched. She wrote on the whiteboard and turned it to your cousin Jackie. It said, *Get married, have a baby!!* And my personal favorite…one afternoon when she picked up her whiteboard with tears in her eyes and wrote, *How can I ever thank you?* I ran to her and hugged her and cried, *No, how can we ever thank YOU!?* I proceeded to tell her how much she had meant to us and had done for us. We were the grateful ones.

We kept Aunt Jackie out of a hospital bed as long as possible. They scared her, as Uncle George died in one in that very same room. Only when it was an absolute necessity and she had trouble staying in her chair did we have a bed delivered. She wouldn't get in it. She refused. Your cousins would sit on it when they visited. Only when it was necessary for us to call in hospice did she get into the bed…and not without protest. The visiting nurse told us it wouldn't be too long, and we called all the kids. Jackie flew in from Seattle. We had given her the required medications, so we couldn't really say good-bye. As soon as she got in that bed, she knew it was time. We all sat with her…on the couches or sleeping as we leaned on her bed. I was on the couch and something woke me. I felt it was her. *Hey, wake up, I'm dying.* I ran over to her bed and sat beside her. I picked up her hand, so frail and delicate. I remembered holding my stepmother Ginny's hand. They were the same. I remarked that it wouldn't be long. Early in the morning on November 4, 2013, Aunt Jackie took her last few breaths. I put my head on her bed and sobbed.

Nothing tears people apart or brings them closer together than going through a situation like this. Your aunts and I have always been close, but we also get mad at each other. We aren't much different than we were as kids. But we made it. We all did.

Aunt Jackie had no idea how many children would be born after her death. Only two belonging to your cousin Jeff were born by the time she passed—Jack (named after her) and Audrey. She adored them. After she passed, Uncle George had his first great-grandchild, a little girl. Arjun was conceived shortly after her passing and was born in 2014. Your cousin Dave (my mom's first grandchild) married Shannon, who has a daughter named Kayla.

Jackie did exactly as she was told on the whiteboard and married her Jeff B. We all attended their wedding in Seattle, and the cousins played music while I sang. They soon had a baby boy named Wyatt. Jeff and Val had a third baby around the same time as Jackie. His name is Grant. Your cousin Brian married Amber and had a boy named Liam. They now have a brand-new girl named Mya, born on your birthday. Now your brother and Devina are having another little boy.

Little Erin, who was four when you passed, married Bill almost a year ago. They moved one street over from where your dad and I started our life together in 1970. We will all get together for their first anniversary and to see Jackie and Wyatt who will be coming home from Seattle.

Even though Aunt Jackie is gone, it's as if she is still our matriarch and running things from afar. So instead of just making suggestions to us or our kids and having us ignore them, it's like she's writing on her whiteboard somewhere and making things happen just the way she wants. Evidently, whiteboards work!

Jesse and Friends

In the beginning of my writings, I talk often of Barb and Paul and their sons, Zach and Jeremy. They are all doing well. Barb and Paul are retired, and the boys are married with children. I haven't seen them in a long time, but I mentioned going to lunch with Barb. I must text her.

Ha…text! That's something you missed that you would have loved. Cell phones and social media. You never even knew what a cell phone was. Perhaps that is for the best.

Jesse…I still hear your voice saying his name. I saw him with your friend, Jenny C, after I married Tom. We met at a local restaurant, and I loved looking into his eyes. I was originally scared to see him because of my reactions if I just saw his car go by. That's why Jenny came as well. We had a nice time, and they showed me photos of their children. Jesse had two little dark-haired girls. He looked well and happy, but I have learned from talking to people that he has struggled. He has had to live with such a traumatic vision in his mind, but I was told he had a good wife who understood him, which was reassuring.

At one point, when I knew I would possibly write this book, I found out how to text his wife and asked if Jesse could call me because I would need his permission to add his letters or use his name. He did text me and said I could use whatever I wanted. I pray that he and his family find peace and happiness. I will never forget him; he will always have a part of my heart. Watch over him, Bug.

Joanne

I need to tell you about a few more people. I need to talk about my favorite friend family, and yes, I called them my family—Joanne, Ross, Brad, Adam, and Kristin were such a blessed part of my life through most of these journals. Joanne and her family held me up through the worst of times, and I like to think I was there for them as well. I could write a book based on our years together. That friendship weathered so many storms on both sides. It was a given. It was something Joanne and I could both count on. Our friendship was written in cement, but cement can be worn down and cracked, even though you can still see a slight indentation of what was previously there.

Time was the culprit…or perhaps change or circumstances…though we still had the occasional dinner and get-together for birthdays. When we were together, things felt the same. I sang at Kristin's wedding and went to baby showers when Ross and Joanne found out two of their children were having babies at the same time. I still think of how we talked about wanting to have grandchildren and thinking we never would.

Sometimes I like to blame social media and cell phones. Joanne and I talked on the phone almost every day…until we learned to text. Texting saves time but separates the human emotional connection. I found out through a text that Ross and Joanne were having their third grandchild. When he was born recently, I texted her my congratulations. She sent back a text that said simply, *Thanks.*

Joanne's children have fared well. Adam and Kristin have significant others and beautiful children. One of the things Joanne and I talked about the most was our children and what was going on in their lives, and yes, our spouses. I always loved her kids, but Brad is special to me. Like me, it took him awhile, but he decided he would not be a victim of his circumstances. He finished at the university slightly ahead of me, went on to get his master's degree, and has since become a Certified Public Accountant. I always knew he would find love. I'm not sure others shared my optimism, but I knew there was someone special out in this universe. There always is, and he found her.

Not too long ago, Joanne and I had lunch together at one of our favorite restaurants. We had a pleasant time and talked about the same things we usually did. But somehow, when we left, I had a woeful feeling that the lunch was the conclusion of our story. I don't want to say the story has ended, because there may still be an occasional text; but the writer of our story has developed writer's block. I like to think that it's all part of God's plan. He put us there for each other so we could hold each other up when huge waves of pain and grief knocked us down. Joanne and I are swimming fine on our own now.

Your Daddy

I can't end this without writing about your dad. I know how much he loved you, because I know how much I do. I didn't plan on saying very much about how our lives disintegrated; he was alive when I was writing. But if I'm going to tell you anything, I need to tell the truth. The situations I wrote about were much worse than I expressed here...some I couldn't mention because they were much to personal and painful to explain.

I don't know why he chose alcohol. Perhaps it's just something people do when they can't express their pain. I don't know if he was an alcoholic before you passed. He was never easy to live with; our energies were just different. He needed quiet time, and I needed to be moving.

However, you are with him now. He isn't miserable anymore, and I thank God for that. I miss him. Sometimes my heart aches. I wonder if my grief contributed to his drinking, or if there is something else I could have done. If I could go back to when you and your brother were little, I would change so many things, and we would all end up happy and together. Like others say, *If I could go back, knowing what I know now, things would be different.*

I will end with these thoughts of him. He was so handsome. I will never forget running to the kitchen window when I was a teen just to get a small glimpse of him when he dropped off my boyfriend on his motorcycle. He had such a beautiful, bright smile; and when he was in a good mood, he made you come alive right along with him. His sense of humor was contagious, and he was always well liked. Like all of us, he had his dark side as well as his bright side. I wish I had learned to just stay away from his darkness and let him deal instead of trying to cheer him. That never went well.

Your dad was so giving of things, but selfish with himself. I always needed him more than he needed me, or so he let me think. But I realize now that he was afraid I would leave. It takes two to make a healthy relationship, and I hold myself accountable for my part and ask his forgiveness.

I didn't want to leave. I wanted him to get better. I waited so long and didn't go until I thought I would surely die if I didn't. I will always love your dad, Jenny. I know he loved me. He had so many different ways of showing it. If I close my eyes, I can see his smile and hear his laugh. May his soul find pure love and peace.

We've all heard *The Lord giveth and the Lord taketh away* (Job 1:21). That pretty much sums up life as far as I'm concerned. Anything we are given can be lost at any moment in time. A person, a love, a home, a car, physical health, mental health, or anything else we value. Every living adult knows this, and we go on our way hoping and praying we will not be the one who has something taken away. But what if we are the one? I have learned to count my blessings for what I am given and to accept with dignity what I lose.

I will always love you and miss you, Jenny, and I look forward to seeing you again, Lord willing. We are given the gift of what to do with what we have lost. I choose to be grateful. So, I leave you this most perfect gift. The gift that I had you…I loved you, I lost you, and I survived. I give these letters where I let my heart bleed and heal over and over so that because you lived, others may be healed as well.

At this moment, I'm watching a doe and her fawn out the window as I write. I'm in a very small loft in my little log cabin. It is here I have been typing up my journals and letters to you. Arjun loves coming to this place. This is where I continue to heal, as I feel my heart rate fall when I walk through the door.

I'm coming to a close Jenny. This has not been easy. It's taken a long time to find the courage to read over all my writings from the last 20 years.

I'm looking forward to meeting up with you and hanging out. You owe me that night out on the town we were supposed to have on your 21st birthday. Remember how you were going to tell me all the secrets you hid from us during your teen years? I'm sure we are going to need lots of time. Perhaps eternity.

Love, Mom

Jackie's Dream
March 26, 2019

Jenny pulled up on a motorcycle,
wearing a black leather jacket,
and told me to get on.
I was holding on to her,
and she was riding super-fast
through a rainbow tunnel.
I told her I missed her, and she said,
"I know."
I asked, "What do I do about that?"
She answered, "Just feel it while you are alive,
and when you die, like everyone, we'll be together."

▶ **Christmas in Heaven**
is on iTunes.

It's for both of them now.

www.ingramcontent.com/pod-product-compliance
Lightning Source LLC
Chambersburg PA
CBHW051416290426
44109CB00016B/1326